DATE DUE			
SEP 2 8 '76			
APR 2 1985			
NOV 1 5 1988			

THE HISTORY OF FOREIGN EXCHANGE

THE HISTORY
OF
FOREIGN EXCHANGE

PAUL EINZIG

SECOND EDITION

MACMILLAN
ST MARTIN'S PRESS

First Edition 1962
Reprinted with alterations 1964
Second Edition, revised and enlarged, 1970

Published by
MACMILLAN AND CO LTD
London and Basingstoke
Associated companies in New York Toronto
Dublin Melbourne Johannesburg & Madras

Library of Congress catalog card no. 74–124951

SBN (boards) 333 06492 5

Printed in Great Britain by
R. & R. CLARK LTD
Edinburgh

TO

THE LIBRARIANS AND STAFFS
OF
THE BRITISH MUSEUM READING ROOM,
THE LONDON LIBRARY,
THE BRITISH LIBRARY OF ECONOMICS AND
POLITICAL SCIENCE,
THE LIBRARY OF THE INSTITUTE OF BANKERS,
THE LIBRARY OF THE HOUSE OF COMMONS
AND
THE ECONOMIC HISTORY LIBRARY OF AMSTERDAM,

AS A TOKEN OF MY SINCERE GRATITUDE FOR
THEIR INVALUABLE ASSISTANCE IN MY TASK
OF COLLECTING THE MATERIAL CONTAINED
IN THIS BOOK

Preface to the Second Edition

ALTHOUGH barely ten years have passed since I wrote this book, important developments during that brief period have made it necessary to bring it up to date. The 'sixties witnessed a number of important institutional changes, the emergence of new practices, and a series of interesting Foreign Exchange crises. Literature on theoretical aspects of Foreign Exchange was far from inactive or unproductive, and there were some important innovations in the sphere of Foreign Exchange policy.

Even so, the addition of four chapters to cover a mere decade to a book of twenty-three chapters covering some three thousand years, calls for an explanation. When writing my book I was fully aware that I could not possibly hope to become an expert on all periods within the brief span of a lifetime. Being conscious of my limitations, I expressed in the Preface the hope that specialists on various periods might correct mistakes I had probably made when dealing with subjects on which they were bound to know a great deal more than I. To my disappointment, however, most reviewers confined their criticisms to the concluding section covering relatively recent periods, mainly on the ground that the chapters dealing with modern developments were 'too sketchy', while the chapters dealing with earlier periods were unnecessarily long.

I am unrepentant about the allocation of my space as between earlier periods on which very little material is easily accessible and more recent periods on which there is a surfeit of easily accessible literature. Viewed from historical perspective, recent periods are no more important than earlier periods. The former are of course more interesting to the large majority of present-day readers. But then this book was intended to be a textbook and a reference book for students and others interested in any period of Foreign Exchange history.

However, to meet my critics to some extent, I took the opportunity of the publication of this new edition for adding four chapters to cover the most recent changes – changes in the system and its practices, recent exchange movements, recent theoretical discussions, and innovations in Foreign Exchange policy. All this has

altered somewhat the balance of the book in the sense suggested
by the large majority of my critics.

There was only one reviewer who actually claimed, in so many
words, to have responded to my appeal to *specialists* in various
periods to criticise my material in so far as it relates to the periods
in which they had specialised – Mr. L. S. Presnell, a specialist on
country banking during the Industrial Revolution, who claimed
by implication to be a specialist on about a dozen periods of
Foreign Exchange history. Yet his review of my book, that
appeared in the *Economic History Review* – oddly enough, no less
than six years after its publication – amounted to little more than
a list of attacks, wasting very little time or space on trying to
justify, explain or illustrate his criticisms.

But one instance in which Mr. Presnell departed from his
method of criticism gave an idea of the extent to which his declared claim to possess expert knowledge on the various subjects
on which he criticised me is justified. Incredible as it may seem,
the journal of a learned society, the Economic History Society,
did actually publish his observation implying that there had been
credit inflation in Ancient Rome. He says that to me '. . . paper
credit looks somewhat naughty. *Thus* we have confusing account
of the alleged coincidence of inflation and deflation in later
Roman times' (my italics). Mr. Presnell, who claimed to have
criticised my chapter on Rome in response to my appeal to
specialists on Roman monetary history, showed himself unaware
that inflation during the decline of Rome assumed the form, not
of 'paper credit' (naughty or otherwise), which had barely
existed at the time, but of extreme debasement of the coinage.

The fact that a learned society went out of its way to publish a
review containing such obvious nonsense goes some way towards
confirming a remark of Julian Huxley when giving evidence in
the Mitchell-Hedges lawsuit, to the effect that learned societies
are referred to as being 'learned' only in the sense in which
all barristers are referred to as 'learned Counsel'.

Long-suffering authors have seldom the opportunity to answer
their critics, which is a pity because, by drawing attention to
flagrant instances of ill-informed criticisms such as the one denounced above, they might be able to raise the standard of
criticism. Being a hard-hitting critic myself it is not for me to
object to being hit hard – provided my critic knows what he is
talking about. Indeed I take this opportunity to repeat my in-

vitation to *specialists* in particular periods to criticise any mistakes on subjects in which they specialise. But when I say *specialists* I mean *specialists*.

120 CLIFFORD'S INN,   P. E.
  LONDON, E.C.4
January 1970

Preface to the First Edition

BOOKS on the history of Foreign Exchange covering some limited period or some special aspect of the subject would fill a fair-sized library. But, having studied the literature on Foreign Exchange for nearly half a century, I have been unable to discover a single book in any of the principal languages that would cover the entire history of Foreign Exchange in all its main aspects from its origins to our days. I feel there is a real need for filling that gap.

Anyone who realises the great importance of Foreign Exchange in our economic system is bound to agree that the task of writing its comprehensive history was well worth undertaking. I would have gladly undertaken it even for its own sake, as an intellectual exercise, even if I had felt that it would not serve any practical purpose. Actually I am convinced that my effort was fully justified also on a purely utilitarian basis, apart from the satisfaction I derived from the illusion of having made a modest contribution to human knowledge. Anyhow, to be quite candid, I have always found it difficult to resist a challenge to attempt something that has never been attempted up to now.

It may seem strange that nobody else has tried to produce such a comprehensive history of Foreign Exchange. There are histories on many less important subjects, and the importance of Foreign Exchange is now widely realised among economic historians and monetary economists. Possibly they were deterred by the difficulty of acquiring expert knowledge on all periods – from Babylonia to the present day. Evidently they were afraid of risking mistakes. They preferred to confine themselves to more limited subjects on which they were able to produce much material of outstanding merit, precisely because the self-imposed limitation of their scope enabled them to devote to their subject the study of a lifetime. They deserve the gratitude of students and practical men interested in Foreign Exchange.

But I feel that the time has now come for an effort to co-ordinate the vast material produced by a multitude of authors into a broad survey of the entire subject. It is surely to the advantage of practical experts as well as economists to possess a comprehensive account of situations and problems of past ages. Anyone really interested is of course in a position to dig out the relevant material for himself, but he may have to dig deep for it, or he may have to piece it together from a large number of books and articles. It would greatly facilitate his task to be able to find at least the outline of Foreign Exchange history within the covers of a single volume.

I purposely restricted the length of this book, even though I have accumulated enough material to make it several times longer, as I was anxious not to deter the average student, Government official, banker, business man or politician, by producing a work of formidable size. For this reason I resisted the temptation to go into all the technical details which I would have liked to include. My aim was, in addition to providing a text-book, to make it easy for the reader to find what he is interested in and to use it as a reference book; and to derive from its use encouragement and help for a more detailed study of any particular period or aspect of the subject in which he is interested. It should help him to view that limited subject from a broader perspective.

I am only too well aware that I have undertaken a very ungrateful task and I fully expect to become a sitting target for criticisms by specialists who are bound to know a great deal more about their particular periods than I could reasonably be expected to know. I should like to refer such critics to a highly authorative answer, anticipating their criticisms, contained in a passage in the Preface of Bertrand Russell's *History of Western Philosophy* (London, 1946, George Allen & Unwin) which might have been written for my special benefit. He points out that 'if books covering a wide field are to be written at all, it is inevitable that those who write such books should spend less time on any one part than can be spent by a man who concentrates on a brief period'. The alternative would be a symposium containing contributions by a number of authors specialising in particular periods. But Russell feels that 'there is something lost when many authors co-operate. If there is any unity in the movement of history, if there is any intimate relation between what goes before and what comes later, it is necessary, for setting this forth, that earlier and later periods should be synthesised in a single mind.'

A volume containing essays by specialists on various periods of Foreign Exchange history would miss the object defined above. A criticism of the *Oxford History of England* by Sir George Clark, appearing in *The Times* on November 15, 1961, indicates another disadvantage of producing a composite volume – discrepancies between the treatment of various periods by the prominent writers who are the recognised authorities on them.

Needless to say, I do not expect – as indeed it would be idle to expect – that the above defence will shield my book from criticism by specialists. Nor do I want to be shielded from criticism of any errors of omission or commission of which my book may be found guilty. To point out such faults is an essentially constructive approach. But I hope that at least some of the critics will judge the book at least partly according to whether I have succeeded in presenting the broad picture I had set out to produce, and not entirely according to whether any specific section in which they are particularly interested is up to the standard of writings by specialists on the subject of that section.

I am only too well aware of the impossibility to do full justice to such an immense range of subjects within the limited space of this book. But somebody had to make a start. To cover the whole subject really adequately would be beyond the capacity of any single individual even if he were to devote his entire working life to it. This is largely because the supply of our principal 'raw material', the record of exchange rates through the ages, is so deplorably inadequate. There is everything to be said for compiling continuous series of exchange rates for all the important exchanges in the principal Foreign Exchange markets, at least from the 16th century, but preferably also for the late Medieval Period. The material is there, in public records and business archives. But to make it accessible is a task that only some well-endowed research department could undertake.

Literature on the evolution of Foreign Exchange theory and policy is more plentiful. My task in that sphere was to try to achieve a picture of continuity which, I think, is badly needed. For instance, hardly any writer on Foreign Exchange theory or history has made any reference to the first appearance of the purchasing power parity theory in the 16th century. Yet it is important to realise that, since this theory was revived during the Napoleonic Wars and again during the first World War, there is causal relationship between its appearance and the inflationary conditions during the periods in which it appeared.

The history of Foreign Exchange presents much that is of interest to the general reader. It is mildly amusing to know that

Cleopatra financed her life of luxury partly by devaluing the drachma; that Nero financed the rebuilding of Rome after the great fire by debasing the denarius; that Plato invented the gold exchange standard and Aristophanes invented Gresham's Law; that the Papal Court of Avignon initiated the first known Forward Exchange transactions in the 13th century; that the Duke of Northumberland in 1551 forestalled Sir Stafford Cripps in officially denying an impending change in the parity of sterling which was carried out soon after his denial; that Primo de Rivera was forestalled by Philip II in resorting to borrowing through the Foreign Exchange market by the same method of renewing short-term contracts over a period of years; that Napoleon followed closely the quotation of sterling as an indication of the progress of his blockade of England; that sterling rose to 7 dollars at the beginning of the first World War; that in the early 'twenties speculators lost fortunes because they believed in the purchasing power parity theory of Foreign Exchange. A study of Foreign History reveals much that is bound to appeal to the dramatic sense of the reader. It contains an endless succession of tragedies and comedies.

I dedicate this book to the Librarians and staffs of the libraries in which I collected the material for it as a token of my gratitude for the invaluable help I received from them. Their share in facilitating research deserves more acknowledgment than it has received. Indeed, but for them this book, and a great many other books, could not have been written.

P. E.

CLIFFORD'S INN,
    LONDON, E.C.4

Contents

    1. Scope of the Book. 2. Progress *v.* Stability. 3. Relations between Theory and Practice. 4. Broader Basis for Theory. 5. Need for studying Lessons of the Past. 6. Relationship between various Aspects of Foreign Exchange History. 7. Division of the Material into Periods. 8. Quantity and Quality of the Material.

    1. Scarcity of Evidence. 2. Early Forms of External Payments. 3. Coins changing Hands by Weight. 4. Interpretation of Foreign Coin Hoards. 5. Exchanging Coins by Tale. 6. Early Bills of Exchange – Babylonia and Assyria. A Gradual Evolution.

    1. Money-Changers in the Middle East and Greece. 2. Money-Changers in Israel. 3. Arbritrage in Coins with Persia. 4. Active Market in Coins in Greece. 5. Early Bankers in Athens. 6. Roman *Argentarii*. 7. Roman Coins outside the Empire. 8. Foreign Exchange during the Debasement Period. 9. Early International Transfers in Greece. 10. Isolated Transactions. 11. Cicero's Exchange Operations. 12. The Alexandria Market. 13. Purpose of Foreign Exchange in the Ancient Period.

    1. Ratios between Monetary Metals. 2. Decline of Gold-Silver Ratio. 3. Wide Discrepancies. 4. Complications arising from 'Trimetallism'. 5. Changes in the Attic Coinage. 6. Favourite International Currencies. 7. Mint Parities and Exchange Rates in Greece. 8. Roman Exchange Rates during the Period of Expansion. 9. The Period of Roman Debasements. 10. Debasements in Egypt. 11. Metal Prices and Exchange Rates.

    1. Lack of Interest in broader aspects of Foreign Exchange. 2. Inferences from Monetary Measures. 3. Aristophanes and Gresham's Law. 4. The Greeks and Foreign Exchange Theory. 5. Plato and the Gold Exchange

CHAPTER ONE

Introductory

(1) SCOPE OF THE BOOK

A HISTORY of an institution such as the Foreign Exchange system, if it aims at being comprehensive, has to cover many aspects of the subject. It has to describe the origin and evolution of Foreign Exchange markets, of Foreign Exchange practices and techniques and of the Foreign Exchange system as it operated at its various phases of progress. It has to record basic changes in the nature and volume of Foreign Exchange transactions, and in the relative importance of at least the principal Foreign Exchanges and of the principal Foreign Exchange markets. It has to examine the influences that affected exchange rates and to describe, at least in outline, the major Foreign Exchange movements throughout the ages, indicating as far as possible their causes, their effects and their background. It has to relate their developments to economic history in general, and even to national and world history. It has to follow the contemporary theories on the evolution of the system and on the movements of exchange rates. Finally, it has to study the official attitude towards Foreign Exchange during successive periods in the principal countries, whether it manifests itself in negative restrictions on its operation or in positive policies to influence exchange rates.

But Foreign Exchange history, if it aspires at being more than a bare chronology, must go beyond giving an account of all these developments. Without being influenced in its findings by preconceived theories, it has to aim at ascertaining some theoretical pattern in the evolution of Foreign Exchange. It has to try to discover and analyse the rules that emerge from the factual evidence and from their contemporary interpretation. The economic historian must try to trace such similarities as may exist between the wide variety of practical experiences in Foreign Exhcange and between their impact on theory and policy. He also has to search for contrasts between practical experiences during various periods and between the reactions of theoretical and practical experts to them. History has a habit of repeating itself, but much more often than not it repeats itself with a difference. Such differences are apt to be as instructive as the similarities.

It is the historian's task to probe into basic causes and ultimate effects in addition to recording immediate causes and effects. He has to try to ascertain the philosophy that runs through the history of Foreign Exchange. But he must resist the temptation of using Foreign Exchange as a peg upon which to hang his own ideas of economic history and of general history, viewed from the angle of Foreign Exchange history.

(2) PROGRESS v. STABILITY

Progress towards perfection of the system, ever since the first ascertainable rudimentary attempts were made to find a solution to the problem of providing channels for payments across national frontiers, has indeed been remarkable. Like most progress, it has been achieved through trial and error, as a result of a series of successful innovations alternating with costly mistakes. In this sphere as in many other spheres progress was from time to time interrupted by sharp if temporary set-backs and also by periods of prolonged stagnation or decline. But after each interruption progress was resumed, and the system was carried to more and more advanced stages.

But, it may well be asked, has this progress necessarily been in the right direction? Has mankind, in building up a Foreign Exchange system and advancing it to the modern stage with which we are familiar today, not created a Frankenstein monster that is liable to destroy its creator? Or, at any rate, is our highly developed Foreign Exchange system not liable to cause frequent grave crises which would not occur in the absence of such a system? Is our present system, with its extensive facilities for disturbing transactions, not pregnant with dangers undreamt of in earlier days when our forerunners had to make the best of much less adequate facilities?

It is the historian's task to ascertain whether during various periods Foreign Exchange was on balance a static influence producing an equalising effect between the national economies of various countries, or whether it produced dynamic effects, either in a constructive sense or in a disturbing sense. It may be difficult to escape the conclusion that the contribution made by Foreign

Exchange towards economic progress had to be paid for dearly as a result of being exposed to destructive influences inherent in such an advanced system. Were our forerunners, who did not possess such an elaborate mechanism, more fortunate or less fortunate than our generation?

(3) RELATIONS BETWEEN THEORY AND PRACTICE

The fact that drastic changes both in Foreign Exchange practices and techniques and in Foreign Exchange theory and policy usually coincided with periods of major wars or major economic upheavals deserves attention. Was it more than coincidence that Foreign Exchange was subjected to searching investigations during unsettled periods such as that of the international inflation following the discovery of America, the wars with France towards the end of the 17th century, the Napoleonic Wars, the first World War, the crises of the 1930's, the second World War or the difficulties of sterling in the 1950's and the 1960's?

Though changes in practices and theories during such periods are undoubtedly of outstanding importance, the historian must also pay attention to the circumstances in which less spectacular changes came about during stable periods. When markets are inactive Foreign Exchange dealers endeavour to develop new practices in order to earn their bread and butter, and in doing so they are apt to change the system. This was presumably so through the ages. Economists, too, consolidate previous changes and reinterpret theories and policies developed under the influences of previous unsettled conditions, or deal more thoroughly with the chronic problems of the system, as distinct from its acute troubles which monopolise their attention during disturbed periods.

(4) BROADER BASIS FOR THEORY

The student of Foreign Exchange theory who is unfamiliar with the history of Foreign Exchange has to base his conclusions on the analysis of experience during his own period, with only occasional references perhaps to the period immediately preceeding it. He may be inclined to regard his conclusions as being founded on immutable economic laws and is oblivious of the possibility that Foreign Exchange movements may obey to some extent a different set of laws amidst totally different circumstances or against a

totally different institutional background. Knowledge of those
laws may assist the economist in ascertaining the common de-
nominator – if there is one – that is applicable to all circumstances.
Or it may at any rate enable him to be more open-minded about
the possibility of having to revise his firmly established and
dogmatically-held conclusions if and when a change in circumstances should call for such a revision.

How far does the history of Foreign Exchange confirm the
'great man' interpretation of history? The chapters on theory and
policy throughout the ages contain many names that were house-
hold words in their time. Had these experts made genuine major
contributions towards the progress of Foreign Exchange? Their
advice was occasionally followed by statesmen, and they may
have influenced market techniques. Or is it more likely that
Foreign Exchange facilities and the rules that regulated their use
developed and changed not as a result of brilliant ideas but for
the most part through an unconscious process resulting from the
combined and cumulative wisdom (or unwisdom) of generations
of practical men? The latter usually succeed in persuading themselves that they have nothing but healthy contempt for theory.
Nevertheless, subconsciously they may have allowed themselves
to be influenced by ideas of those who study their subject in its
broader aspects.

(5) NEED FOR STUDYING LESSONS OF THE PAST

Most theoretical monetary economists, even those who specialised
in Foreign Exchanges, made relatively little use of the lessons
taught by earlier periods of Foreign Exchange history. It is no
wonder that practical experts responsible for devising and execut-
ing Foreign Exchange policies so often failed to benefit by the
lessons of the past. Much theoretical knowledge and practical
experience acquired by our forerunners is being largely wasted
by being allowed to fade into oblivion. It is rediscovered from
time to time through trial and error, at the cost of mistakes which
could and should have been avoided.

To give only one outstanding instance in order to illustrate
the above criticism, the British Government's first action in 1934
on the outbreak of the second World War was deliberately to
depreciate sterling by some 20 per cent. Yet as long ago as 1569
a Memorandum prepared by the Royal Commission on Currency

made it plain that it was to the grave disadvantage to the Government and to the country to allow the exchange to depreciate at a time when large external payments had to be met with the aid of a depreciated currency. Although that Memorandum was no doubt in the archives or the library of the Treasury, it would have been little short of a miracle if anyone happened to consult it. Its common-sense conclusion was completely ignored. Possibly if a concise history of Foreign Exchange policy had been available, those responsible for shaping Foreign Exchange policy in 1939 might have been able to benefit by the accumulated wisdom of earlier experts. At any rate they would have had the advantage of being able to take their decision with the full knowledge of their forerunners' advice.

This experience, and many similar experiences that could be quoted, shows that a Foreign Exchange history should survey the past partly from the point of view of its bearing on our modern problems. Yet historians who try to view events of the distant past through modern eyes, instead of attempting to view it exclusively as it appeared to contemporary observers, are often subject to criticism. Surely there is room for both kinds of histories.

(6) RELATIONSHIP BETWEEN VARIOUS ASPECTS OF FOREIGN EXCHANGE HISTORY

Another task for the historian is to study the close reciprocal relationship between the various aspects of his subject. The evolution of the Foreign Exchange system bears close relation to changes in the nature and volume of Foreign Exchange transactions, to movements of exchange rates, to the development of Foreign Exchange theory and to the official attitude towards Foreign Exchange. One is apt to dogmatise about this relationship if one's conlcusions are based exclusively on the study of conditions prevailing in our time or during a limited recent period.

There are instances in which institutional changes are causes of trends in exchange rates, or trends of thoughts on Foreign Exchange theory and of policy. There are, however, also instances in which institutional changes are their effect. Government intervention in Foreign Exchanges was in many instances responsible for changes in Foreign Exchange practices and for the development of Foreign Exchange theory. On the other hand, in other instances it was changes in practices or progress in theoretical knowledge that induced Governments to intervene.

(7) DIVISION OF THE MATERIAL INTO PERIODS

The material in this book is divided into six historical periods. The first period begins with the earliest known experiences in Foreign Exchange and ends with the fall of the Western Roman Empire. The second period takes us to the discovery of America, which in this conjunction is an event of outstanding importance, owing to its effect on the supply of precious metals. Up to that stage our task of dividing the material into periods is simple, because we are able to follow the conventional dividing lines of general history. Our difficulties begin when we have to find landmarks for dividing into convenient periods the vast material from the end of the 15th century to our days. The French Revolution and the ensuing Napoleonic Wars provide one resonable dividing line, as they mark the opening of a relatively stable period between Waterloo and the first World War. The disorganisation caused by the first World War is again an important landmark. Finally the importance of changes in trends, practices and policies in the sixties calls for a separate section.

This division of the material is admittedly far from ideal, for practical and theoretical experience in each period is very far from homogeneous. There are, however, sufficient similarities within each period and sufficient differences between them to warrant the choice of these dividing lines for want of better.

Within each section the material is divided into chapters dealing with the Foreign Exchange system as it worked in practice, exchange rates and trends, theory and policy respectively. This division of material inevitably leads to some measure of overlapping, but it is justified because it corresponds to the four main aspects of Foreign Exchange history. It is preferable to adhering to strict chronological order and trying to record the evolution of Foreign Exchange in all its aspects in the same chapter. Moreover, it is convenient to readers, many of whom may be particularly interested in one or other aspect. It saves them time and trouble if they want to look up, say, exchange trends in the 16th century, or policy in the 18th century, as they do not have to dig out the material they need from a chapter containing much material that is irrelevant to the special point of view with which they are concerned.

(8) QUANTITY AND QUALITY OF THE MATERIAL

The material available for our purpose naturally improves in quantity and quality as and when we proceed from earlier to more recent periods. For the Ancient Period we must rely on a small number of isolated remarks in the classical literature and have to try to make bricks with very little straw. Our raw material is more plentiful for the Medieval Period, even if it is largely one-sided and patchy. From the 16th century onwards there is ample practical material, and from the 17th century onwards theoretical writings abound. As to the 19th and 20th centuries, our main difficulty is one of *embarras de richesse*.

The institutional evolution of the system can be traced to a reasonable degree. It would be a much more difficult task to produce a continuous series of exchange rates and I did not attempt it. Literature on Foreign Exchange theory as such is virtually non-existent until about the 17th century. Most of the theoretical knowledge that existed during the Ancient and Medieval Periods can only be inferred from evidence on exchange practices or policies and from writings on those subjects.

There is much evidence about the official attitude towards Foreign Exchange from a very early period. We encounter legislative measures restricting or regulating Foreign Exchange dealing from the time of Ancient Greece and Persia. Indeed, we derive our material on Foreign Exchange during the Ancient Period overwhelmingly from references to such measures. Most of them relate to intervention in a negative sense, and it was not until comparatively recent times that a reasonable volume of evidence about active official intervention in the Foreign Exchange markets and about monetary policies aimed at influencing exchange rates, became available.

One of the justifications for an attempt at comprehensive historical treatment is that it discloses the existence of gaps in our knowledge. So long as literature on the history of Foreign Exchange is confined to a number of monographs dealing with limited periods in isolation from other periods the contrast between the extent to which various periods or various aspects of the subject are covered may remain unnoticed. An attempt to present a comprehensive picture is apt to draw attention to the need for reinforcing our material in various respects, and provides ample scope for specialists who are enabled to see their chosen subject in perspective as part of the comprehensive history.

PART I

ANCIENT PERIOD

CHAPTER TWO

Origins of Foreign Exchange

(1) SCARCITY OF EVIDENCE

THE origins of Foreign Exchange, even more than those of money itself, are largely a matter of conjecture. The pre-history of money can be reconstructed at any rate to a large extent with the aid of evidence such as hoards of coins or of other objects obviously suitable for monetary use. Such hoards are often self-explanatory, or inference drawn from them can be corroborated with the aid of other evidence. But hoards of coins do not in themselves throw much light, if any at all, on the use of money for foreign payments, beyond the extent to which they suggest that, since there had been a turnover in coins outside their countries of origin, they may have been the object of transactions in exchange for local currency or payments for local goods or services. Even as far as the beginnings of the historic period are concerned, early texts that have a bearing on Foreign Exchange transactions and might aid us to build theories about the pre-historic period are very few and far between; they are often obscure or ambiguous and are seldom really informative.

Ethnological evidence on the use of primitive moneys in backward communities in modern times undoubtedly helps the economic historian to some extent in reconstructing the origins and early evolution of the monetary system. It is, however, of very little use in an attempt to elaborate a hypothesis concerning the origins and early evolution of Foreign Exchange. For trade between primitive communities in modern times was conducted mostly in the form of barter, so that it did not involve Foreign Exchange transactions. Even though in many known instances the goods employed by one community as a primitive currency were imported from, or exported to, some other community, the latter must have regarded them simply as goods given or accepted in exchange for other goods. There was, therefore, no exchange of the money of one community against that of the other.

B

(2) EARLY FORMS OF EXTERNAL PAYMENTS

Ancient history provides evidence of similar barter transactions. In some known instances, when two countries used different metals as money, both of them regarded the monetary metal of the other as a commodity. There were transactions involving the exchange of gold produced by Ancient Egypt against copper of Cyprus, copper having been the monetary metal in the former while gold may be assumed to have been that of the latter.[1] Such transactions did not really constitute Foreign Exchange, especially as they assumed mostly the form of exchanges of presents.

A relatively advanced form of foreign trade was reached with the adoption of indirect barter, with the currency of the importing country acting as intermediary. Visiting foreign merchants, when selling their goods, accepted payment in local currency and spent the proceeds on the purchase of local goods, so that there was no Foreign Exchange involved at that stage.

At an even more advanced stages the same monetary material – such as certain metals changing hands by weight – which were employed as money in two countries, were used for payment in their foreign trade with each other. This again did not constitute Foreign Exchange. It practically amounted to trading between members of a kind of monetary union using identical monetary material, for the purposes of which no Foreign Exchange was necessary.

(3) COINS CHANGING HANDS BY WEIGHT

Further progress was made towards the development of Foreign Exchange when the monetary metal came to change hands in the shape of uniform prices, bearing the seal of some banker or merchant or, in Babylonia, of some Temple.[2] Such moneys had been in circulation in the Middle East during the 2nd Millennium. There are also references in the Old Testament to numbers of pieces of silver many centuries before the final step towards the adoption of coinage was taken by King Gyges of Lydia (716–678 B.C.) by affixing his seal on dumps of electrum, giving thereby a State guarantee of their weight and fineness.

Until that stage was reached, the State authority confined itself to supervising the quality and weight of privately issued metallic money. It is just conceivable, but unlikely, that some such private coins had come to command sufficient confidence to be exchanged by tale. In that case Foreign Exchange might well have developed some time during the 2nd Millennium. There is, however, no evidence to that effect, and it seems much more likely that, while the seal of a reputable merchant or of a temple was widely accepted as a guarantee of fineness, such private coins changed hands mostly by weight, especially in international transactions.

Even when the next stage was reached, at which national coins were exchanged for foreign coins by weight, no Foreign Exchange transactions proper were involved. For although different standardised media of exchange were exchanged against each other, they were reduced to an identical unit of account by being exchanged on the basis of the quantity of their metallic content. There could be no exchange rates in such transactions, as there was no need to count the number of the units of the coins exchanged against each other and the value of one unit in terms of the other was not quoted.

(4) INTERPRETATION OF FOREIGN COIN HOARDS

The discovery of many hoards of early foreign coins all over Europe, North Africa and Western Asia does not in itself prove conclusively that there had been Foreign Exchange transactions between local and foreign coins during the period when the coins were issued. They may have been exchanged by weight. In any case old coins were apt to remain in circulation for very long periods, and quite possibly it was not until many years after their issue that they came to be used in Foreign Exchange transactions proper. But in many instances foreign coins, during the periods in which they had originated, are known to have circulated freely side by side with national coins, at a fixed ratio in relation to the latter, so that Foreign Exchange transactions proper did not necessarily arise. The foreign coins were simply a subsidiary currency. It was only when the ratio was allowed to fluctuate more or less freely that the coins became the object of Foreign Exchange.

Many of the coins discovered in hoards outside their countries of origin may have found their way abroad not as a result of Foreign Exchange transactions but through expenditure by invading or allied armies – Roman generals had the right to mint Roman coins abroad for the requirements of their legions –

through payments of tribute, or through the seizure of treasure by conquering armies. But it seems reasonable to assume that at least part of these coin hoards came to be exported and imported as a result of peaceful Foreign Exchange transactions in connection with foreign trade or travel. And even foreign coins that were originally obtained through non-commercial channels may have become sooner or later the subject of Foreign Exchange transactions against national coins.

(5) EXCHANGING COINS BY TALE

For a long time after the first adoption of coinage coins continued to be taken by weight in both domestic and international trade. Gradually, however, confidence in certain coins became sufficiently established to make it possible to exchange them against each other by tale in domestic transactions, although their weight was frequently checked and their fineness tested, especially in wholesale trade. At a more advanced stage some coins that had come to command a very high degree of confidence came to be accepted freely by tale also in international transactions.

So long as such coins were exchanged for coins which had not commanded the same confidence, so that the latter were only accepted by weight, there was no real Foreign Exchange transaction. All that happened was that the possessor of the coins that commanded confidence bought monetary metals by weight in the shape of foreign coins. It was only when the coins of both parties in transactions came to change hands by tale that a Foreign Exchange system in the real sense came into being. At last the currency of one community came to be exchanged against that of another community on the basis of an exchange rate between them, expressing the value of one monetary unit in terms of the other.

Markets in foreign coins quoted by tale in terms of each other must have developed some time during the 6th or 5th centuries B.C. and gradually exchange rates between the coins which inspired confidence must have come to be quoted regularly. Although there was already a rudimentary market in foreign coins while they still changed hands by weight, and its existence gave rise to the occupation of money-changers, they were in reality bullion deals, and only became Foreign Exchange deals when it became possible to exchange coins by tale. For a long time after that stage was reached coins continued to be tested occasionally and worn pieces were weighed.

(6) EARLY BILLS OF EXCHANGE – BABYLONIA AND ASSYRIA

Exchanging coins was not the only form in which Foreign Exchange made its appearance. The conventional formula according to which barter was followed by primitive money, which was followed by more advanced forms of money, and eventually the highest stage was reached through the adoption of various forms of credit, does not correspond to the historic sequence of development. Nor does it apply to the evolution of Foreign Exchange. From a very early period, long before the development of Foreign Exchange transactions in coins, more advanced means of payments are believed to have been used in foreign trade. Bills of exchange made their appearance in Babylonia and Assyria many centuries before the invention of coinage in Lydia, and they may possibly have been used by these two countries in trade with each other.

A document originating in the first year of Hammurabi's reign (21st century B.C.) in the Aber-Habba Sun Temple of Sippar on the Euphrates and preserved in the British Museum, authorises its bearer to receive in 15 days in the City of Eshama on the Tigris 8½ *minae* of lead deposited with the Priestess of the Temple.[3] Lead was the currency of Assyria but not of Babylonia where silver by weight and barley were the media of exchange and standards of value. Under Article 112 of the Code of Hammurabi anyone defaulting on bills of exchange was liable to a fine amounting to fivefold the amount involved. In this respect this device answered the definition of the modern bill of exchange, since default on it was liable to entail particularly strict sanctions. The only doubtful question is if, and to what extent, this instrument of credit was also an instrument of international payments.

The texts of a very large number of bills, issued by Babylonian and Assyrian merchants and others, indicating that payment was made in localities other than those in which the bills were issued, were preserved in cuneiform writing on slate tablets. Unfortunately I have not come across any clear-cut instances of bills providing for payment in another country and in another currency than that of the country in which they were issued. Nevertheless, in view of the known facts about the very close trade relations between countries of the Ancient Middle East it seems reasonable to assume that there must have been such transactions, at any rate between Babylonia and Assyria.

It is, for instance, conceivable that Babylonian merchants, about to visit Assyria in order to buy goods, may have acquired bills in terms of lead, the Assyrian currency, before their departure, against payment in their local currency, silver or barley, enabling them to receive lead in Assyria. Alternatively they may have acquired bills issued in terms of silver and on arrival in Assyria they exchanged the proceeds against lead. Admittedly it is open to argument whether transactions in bills of such a kind constituted Foreign Exchange transactions, considering that lead was looked upon as a commodity in Babylonia, while silver and barley were regarded as commodities in Assyria.

(7) A GRADUAL EVOLUTION

This instance, as that of the transition from exchanging monetary metals by weight to exchanging coins by tale, shows the essentially gradual character of the evolution of Foreign Exchange. Dealing with the origin of money, Crowther attributed its invention to some 'lazy genius' who could not be bothered with the complications of barter.[4] Similar absurd hypotheses were put forward also about the origin of Foreign Exchange, especially in the form of bills of exchange. Endemann, whose book on the origins of bills was for a long time the standard work on the subject, rightly ridiculed such theories.[5] They are indeed utterly divorced from realities. Institutions such as money, or its use in Foreign Exchange, are not invented by some genius, lazy or active, on a dull Sunday afternoon. The earliest forerunners of modern Foreign Exchange dealers with their elaborate systems of private telephone lines, telex communication to overseas centres and computers, must have drifted from one phase of evolution to the next very gradually, often without being aware of the significance of the change they were instrumental in bringing about. It would be most unrealistic to assume that Foreign Exchange was the invention of an individual who suddenly decided that it would be a good idea to exchange coins by tale, or to buy and sell drafts in foreign currencies, instead of having all the bother of weighing and testing precious metals.

The process which led to the adoption of Foreign Exchange may have varied from community to community. Some must have worked out their own solution, many others may have copied solutions adopted by neighbouring communities. In any case, it was a gradual process in which progress was made by trial and error, and in which progress was interrupted from time to time by reverses.

The diffusionist theory under which social institutions spread from race to race has more justification in respect of the origins of Foreign Exchange than in respect of the origins of money, precisely because it takes two communities to engage in Foreign Exchange which, by definition, is an international process. But the fact that the most international trading community of the early Ancient Period, Phoenicia, was very late in emulating other nations by adopting coinage or Foreign Exchange, shows that the diffusion of the system did not proceed as a matter of course, at any rate during its early phases.

NOTES TO CHAPTER TWO

1. Paul Einzig, *Primitive Money* (London, 1949), p. 204.
2. Einzig, *op. cit.* pp. 213–14.
3. R. Eisler, *Das Geld* (München, 1924), p. 191.
4. Sir Geoffrey Crowther, *An Outline of Money.* Revised ed. (London, 1948), p. 2.
5. Wilhelm Endemann, *Studien in der romanisch-kanonistischen Wirtschafts-und Rechtslehre bis gegen Ende des 17. Jahrhunderts* (Berlin, 1874), p. 76.

CHAPTER THREE

Early Foreign Exchange Markets

(1) MONEY-CHANGERS IN THE MIDDLE EAST AND GREECE

THE first Foreign Exchange markets consisted of meeting-places of money-changers functioning in commercial centres. They were familiar figures in market places and harbours in the Ancient Middle East and Greece, with their tables, scales and weights, displaying a variety of domestic and foreign coins. Even though other forms of monetary payments between countries were not unknown, their extent must have been insignificant compared with that of exchanging coins.

Money-changers usually combined their functions with those of bullion dealers, serving the requirements of international trade and finance in a dual capacity. There was no clear dividing line between the two functions, since, as we saw above, most coins changed hands by weight, especially during the early period, and also later whenever distrust developed towards coinages. Possibly many early money-changers were also goldsmiths and silversmiths, familiar with the art of assaying and smelting.

The profession of money-changers must have come into being in countries of the Ancient Middle East at a relatively early stage of their monetary evolution. Even during the period when foreign coins were only accepted at their bullion value, in centres of foreign trade there was a need for the services of specialists able to weigh the coins with a high degree of precision and to seek to ascertain their fineness by some primitive method of assaying – such as the use of Lydian stone. In all probability in the first instance it was these specialists who, on the basis of their superior experience, came to feel gradually justified in exchanging dependable coins by tale, thereby initiating the most primitive form of Foreign Exchanges.

(2) MONEY-CHANGERS IN ISRAEL

According to the Talmud money-changers functioned regularly in Ancient Israel at weekly fairs, held mostly on Fridays in smaller localities and every day in Jerusalem and other larger places. They wore coins as earrings to indicate their membership of the money-changers' guild.[1] Apart from coins that found their way to Israel through foreign trade or travel, there was a constant inward stream of foreign coins resulting from contributions to the Temple Chest of Jerusalem by Jews living in Babylonia and other foreign countries. From time to time *staters, darics* and other foreign coins that had accumulated in this reserve found their way into circulation and must have given rise to Foreign Exchange transactions.

Money-changers in the Temple of Jerusalem at a later period figure prominently in the New Testament. Their presence there is on record in the four Gospels which all describe the well-remembered scene in which Jesus cast the money-changers out of the Temple, overthrowing their tables.[2] But a passage in the Parable of the Talents, in which the master chides his servant for having failed to 'put his money to the exchangers',[3] seems to indicate that it was not their activities as such but the display of those activities on sacred premises that brought upon them their chastisement.

According to Josephus, Jewish money-dealers were systematically engaged in transferring funds between Palestine and Babylonia.[4] Owing to the remarkably high interest rates prevailing in the latter country, there must have been fair scope for transactions of some primitive form of interest arbitrage, especially as the Jews were prevented by their laws from charging interest in their own country.

(3) ARBITRAGE IN COINS WITH PERSIA

What was much more important, the artificially fixed gold-silver ratio under the bimetallist system in the Persian Empire provided opportunities for profitable space arbitrage, since for a very long time silver was undervalued in Persia, so that there must have been a constant stream of silver from that country. It seems probable, however, that discrepancies between the relative value of monetary metals prevailing at any given moment in various countries were exploited mainly by foreign merchants when choosing the means of payment for their purchases or repatriating the proceeds of their sales, rather than by professional arbitrageurs engaged in transferring coins from one country to another.

(4) ACTIVE MARKET IN COINS IN GREECE

There must have been a large turnover in foreign coins in Ancient Greece, since most important City States had their own national coinages. Trade between these small economic units was presumably active, because, with the progress of civilisation, they must have tended to become less and less self-sufficient. It was easy to transact foreign trade with neighbouring City States or even with more distant ones across the Aegean Sea. Also there must have been frequent interchanges of visits between peoples belonging to the same race and speaking the same language.

Tributes, contributions to defence funds by allies, religious contributions in Delphi and other sacred places, and frequent large-scale bribery of politicians, generals, street orators and others by foreign rulers, also resulted in substantial international movements of coins. Adverse balances of payments were settled by means of accepting payment in coins for exports. This is known to have been the case of Athens, which City State had a perennial adverse trade balance. It was settled by means of exporting its highly dependable silver coins which were willingly accepted during most of the 5th and 4th centuries B.C. throughout the greater part of Ancient Greece. According to Xenophon (c. 430–354 B.C.), if foreign merchants selling goods to Athens did not wish to take Athenian goods in exchange they were in a position to take silver coins which were acceptable everywhere.[5]

(5) EARLY BANKERS IN ATHENS

Owing to the extent to which coins found their way from other City States, and to which Persian, Macedonian and other coins of the Mediterranean sphere of civilisation were also exchanged systematically by traders and travellers, money-changing became an important profession in Athens at an early stage. Those engaged in it were kept busy also because very often foreign coins, once imported, remained in circulation side by side with the domestic currency and gave rise to frequent exchange transactions. Diphylus (4th century B.C.) describes a scene in Athens fish market where both Attic and Aeginetan *obols* were circulating. The exchange rate was $\frac{7}{16}$ Ageinetan *obol* for each Attic *obol*. Very often prices were quoted in *obols* without indicating which *obol* was meant. Sellers required Aeginetan *obols*, but having received Aeginetan currency, they often tried to give back change in Attic *obols*.[6] There must have been a lively traffic in the two currencies through money-changers.

The Athens money-changers were known under the name of *trapezitai* (*trapeza* = table) after the benches they used for their dealings. Many of them became influential members of the business community and indeed of Ancient society. In the 4th century B.C. the names of 23 *trapezitai* have been preserved for posterity.[7] Many of them were also engaged in various loan transactions, commerce and industry. What we are concerned with here is their international transfer operations transacted in addition to money-changing.

We have evidence in the speeches of Demosthenes (383–322 B.C.) before Athens Law Courts that there existed in Athens an 'exchange' which may have been similar to the *bourses* in Western European financial centres during the Middle Ages or the Royal Exchange in London from the 16th century, at which business in loans and Foreign Exchange was systematically transacted.[8] Even though the texts available to us only mention activity in loans, since they concern transactions relating to foreign trade it seems reasonable to suppose that Foreign Exchange business was also transacted at the same places. It is also probable that similar institutions existed in other centres.

The multiplicity of coinages provided ample scope for money-changers not only in Ancient Greece and in Magna Graecia and the Hellenistic world. The use of three monetary metals, gold, silver and copper, and of electrum – in which the relative gold and silver content varied widely and was changed frequently – must have made life for money-changers very complicated.

(6) ROMAN *ARGENTARII*

The system of money-changing is believed to have been adopted in Rome from about the beginning of the 5th century B.C. By the time of the second Punic War the activities of money-changers must have become fairly important. They fulfilled an increasing need, because of the large number of foreign silver coins that found their way to Rome during the period when bronze was the local monetary metal. The heavy bronze coins, the *aes grave*, were unsuitable for foreign trade requirements, and most exchange must have taken place in Roman centres. The fluctuation of bronze-silver ratio during the Punic Wars must have greatly increased activities in the Roman Foreign Exchange market.

During the centuries of Roman expansion large quantities of gold and silver coins were imported, not so much in connection with trade or visits by foreigners as through tributes or booty. A great part of such coins were usually deposited in the Temple of Saturn, but sooner or later they found their way into circulation and gave rise to exhcange transactions. But the captured coins were often distributed immediately among the victorious legions and came into circulation.

Argentarii, the Roman equivalent of the Greek *trapezitai*, were established in all parts of the Roman Empire. They made their appearance in ports and other commercial centres of any newly acquired province as soon as Roman arms had conquered it. The profession of *argentarii* carried certain privileges amounting to monopoly. On the other hand, it had been subject to official regulations which were, generally speaking, much stricter than in Greece, and which became increasingly strict during the long period of currency debasement.

The *argentarii* charged a commission for exchanging foreign coins against domestic coins at official rates. There is a reference to this in Cicero who accused Verres of having charged an exchange fee to Sicilian farmers on the payments he made for wheat bought for the Government. 'How do you justify those exchanges when all Sicilians use the same money?'[9] In addition to the *argentarii*, specialists in assaying coins and ingots, called *nummularii*, assisted in the traffic in coins.

(7) ROMAN COINS OUTSIDE THE EMPIRE

Foreign coins circulated in ample supply within the Roman Empire, judging by the number of hoards found. In particular the provinces adjoining foreign countries were in the habit of using coins from across the border as token moneys,[10] with or without official or conventional fixed exchange rates in relation to the *denarius*. On the other hand, quantities of Roman coins found their way abroad largely as a result of the perennial adverse trade balance. The large number of hoards of Roman coins found in Germany, in the countries adjoining the Black Sea, in Scandinavia, Persia, India, Ceylon and Nubia, and in many other countries outside the confines of the Roman Empire indicates the extent to which such coins must have been used in payment abroad.

The Roman gold coin, the *aureus*, was the first currency to attain world-wide fame. After the currency reforms of Augustus, the silver *denarius*, too, came to be regarded as highly acceptable abroad, even in distant China. It is a reasonable assumption that the influx of these coins in payment for oriental luxuries gave occasion for active money-changing business in those countries.

(8) FOREIGN EXCHANGE DURING THE DEBASEMENT PERIOD

The rôle played by money-changers greatly increased in importance during the centuries of debasement that was a cause as well as an effect of the decline of Rome. Beginning with Nero, most Emperors debased the silver coinage, and its secular depreciation and also its occasional temporary recoveries gave rise to much speculation in Roman gold coins and foreign coins in general, as well as in precious metals. There was a great deal of hoarding of good coins minted prior to the debasements, and also of metals, by speculators who resold them later at a profit.

One of the effects of the progressive depreciation and wide fluctuations of the Roman currency during the period of decline was that it ceased to be freely acceptable outside the confines of the Empire. Even the gold coins, whose fineness was maintained but whose weight was gradually reduced, came to be dealt in by weight. The coins issued before Nero's debasement disappeared through hoarding and export. In order to facilitate traffic with India, full-valued coins of Tiberius were minted from time to time purely for the requirements of foreign trade, in the same way as Maria Theresa dollars are still coined for trading with certain parts of North East Africa and Arabia. Germanic chiefs and others minted Roman coins with the effigy of Emperors reigning prior to the debasements, because such coins continued to command confidence and were accepted everywhere.

Byzantium was one of the leading Foreign Exchange centres of the Roman world. It retained and even increased this rôle during the decline of the Western Empire. Byzantine gold coins remained for a long time an international means of payment. They were exchangeable against Indian coins at favourable rates, long after India ceased to accept Roman silver coins.

(9) EARLY INTERNATIONAL TRANSFERS IN GREECE

There is much evidence of international transfers during the Ancient Period, side by side with dealings in coins. Reference was made in the last chapter to the early use of bills of exchange in Babylonia and Assyria. It has been suggested by historians that similar devices of international payments were used at a later phase, in Ancient Greece, in Rome and in Egypt, under Roman rule. If so, no evidence to that effect survived.

Several known instances of international transfers in Ancient Greece are recorded in classical literature. Two of them concern the Athens banker Pasion who flourished in the first half of the 4th century B.C., and who, a slave by birth, left behind a fortune of eighty talents. He owned some funds in Miletus and enabled an Athenian to receive payment there by sending instructions to his Milesian correspondent to that effect.[11] There is, however, no indication whether the payment was to be made in Attic or Milesian currency and no evidence to indicate that a bill of exchange was used.

The other instance, widely quoted by historians, concerned an Athenian merchant Stratocles who, in 394 B.C., when he was about to pay a visit to Bosporus, paid a certain amount to Isocrates on the understanding that the latter's father, who lived there, would pay him back in local currency. The transaction, which was guaranteed by Pasion, received publicity through a lawsuit in the course of which Isocrates (436–338 B.C.) stated its particulars. The text of his speech does not indicate whether the transaction involved the use of a bill of exchange, even though transactions in foreign bills were legally possible in Athens. Indeed under Solon's laws (c. 600 B.C.) the cession of claims to third parties was permissible, so that bills *could* change hands, but we have no evidence showing that they actually *did*.

(10) ISOLATED TRANSACTIONS

It would be a mistake to infer from such instances that there was a regular turnover in Foreign Exchange transfers. The exceptional nature of this transaction was indicated by the explanation that Isocrates deemed necessary to make, stating: 'I thought it would be highly advantageous not to jeopardise my money by the risks of voyage, especially as the Lacedaemonian Navy were then masters of the sea'.[12] This explanation would not have been necessary if transactions of the same kind had been carried out as a matter of daily routine.

That facilities for such transfers were not readily available may be inferred also from Plutarch's remark that, after Themistocles went into exile (471 B.C.), 'a great part of his estate was privately conveyed away by his friends and was sent after him by sea to Asia'.[13] Evidently during the 5th century B.C. exiles were not in a position to draw bills against assest they had left behind, in the way they did during the Medieval Period or in more recent times.

On the other hand, the practice of keeping balances in foreign centres was familiar in Athens in the 4th century B.C. Satyrus, King of Bosporus, deposited during the 390's a large sum with Pasion in Athens.

(11) CICERO'S EXCHANGE OPERATIONS

External payments by means of transfers must have been practised during the Roman period more frequently than in Ancient Greece, even though evidence of such transactions remained very scant. Remittances to the Eastern provinces which retained an independent coinage under Roman rule must have been a simple matter, because the exchange rates of local coins were legally fixed in relation to the *denarius*. There was the much-quoted instance of Cicero (106–43 B.C.) asking his banker friend Atticus (109–32 B.C.) whether his student son could change his allowance in Athens.[14] Some translations refer to a 'bill of exchange' or a 'draft', but the original text does not specify the means of transfer; the term used was *permutatione*, which simply means 'by exchange'.

In another letter to Atticus, Cicero said that he had in Asia (a Roman province in Asia Minor) local currency to the value of nearly 2,200,000 *sesterces*. 'Pay a bill of exchange of that amount and it will be easy for you to maintain my credit.'[15] Here again it is open to doubt whether the translator was justified in translating *permutatione* into 'by bill of exchange' instead of transfer by means of exchange. It is more likely that the payments were made not by bills but by what we would call today mail transfers.

During the period of *Pax Romana* conditions were sufficiently stable for Roman bankers and other wealthy people to maintain business relationships with correspondents not only in the Roman provinces but also in friendly border states outside the confines of the Empire. Even in the absence of actual evidence it seems reasonable to suppose that relatively frequent transfers were made between some foreign countries and Roman cities.

(12) THE ALEXANDRIA MARKET

Under the Ptolemies Alexandria played an important intermediary part in the trade relations of the Roman Empire with the East and was the leading foreign exchange market in the Ancient Period. This activity continued under Roman rule. It was favoured by the geographic position of Egypt, being on the main trade route to the East, and also by the steady demand for Egyptian coins resulting from large exports of grain. Coins from the Yemen, India, Ethiopia as well as Roman coins and the currencies which Eastern provinces of the Empire were authorised to issue, must have reached the Alexandria market regularly.

The payment of Egypt's annual tribute to Rome was supposed to have been made not in the form of bullion but 'through balances obtained abroad from exports or other credits . . . There was a considerable surplus of cereals for export. The profits derived from Eastern trade were evidently great and credits were also established by charges for transportation and by tourist travel.'[16] In other words the tribute was paid by means of buying up the proceeds of visible and invisible exports.

It is not known, however, whether this was done by means of the advanced system described above or simply with the aid of exchange control which is known to have been in force, under which foreign merchants, on their arrival in Alexandria, had to surrender their foreign coins to authorised dealers, in return for debased local coins which they used for the purchase of goods for export.[17]

The sum total of the above evidence on operations in international transfers does not amount to very much. It seems reasonable to assume, however, that the actual extent and importance of such operations was considerably greater than would appear from the occasional contemporary reference to the subject that happened to survive, in particular during the centuries in which the power of Rome was at its highest. Even so, it seems most un-likely that such transfers were at any time sufficiently frequent to provide a Foreign Exchange market with rates quoted regularly, except possibly in Alexandria and perhaps in Byzantium. The markets in coins must have been practically the only form of Foreign Exchange markets proper during the Ancient Period.

(13) PURPOSE OF FOREIGN EXCHANGE IN THE ANCIENT PERIOD

A Foreign Exchange system existed in substance during the greater part of the 1st Millennium B.C. It served substantially the same purpose as modern Foreign Exchange did in more recent times:

1. It provided means by which residents in one country were able to buy goods from other countries or sell goods to other countries.
2. It provided channels for non-commercial payments of every kind from one country to another.
3. It provided facilities for the transfer of capital abroad.
4. It provided opportunities for speculation in the national currencies or in foreign currencies.
5. It even provided a limited scope for abritrage.

On the other hand, as we shall see in Chapter 5, the early Foreign Exchange system lacked the mechanism by which the modern Foreign Exchange system is capable of playing the part of readjusting disequilibria in the internal and international economy. This was due in part to the inflexibility of foreign trade which did not respond nearly so readily to exchange movements as in more recent times, and in part to a deficiency inherent in the Foreign Exchange system at the early stage of its evolution – it relapsed too readily into the previous phase of transacting foreign trade and payments by means of metals by weight. The Foreign Exchange market was not sufficiently established to withstand the ups and downs of major crises or prolonged difficulties.

NOTES TO CHAPTER THREE

1. S. Ejges, *Das Geld im Talmud* (Vilna, 1930), pp. 73–5.
2. New Testament: Matthew xxi. 12–13; Mark xi. 15–17; Luke xix. 45–6; John ii. 13–16.
3. New Testament: Matthew xxv. 14–30; Luke xix. 12–27.

4. Josephus, *Antiquities*. Quoted by T. Frank (ed.), *An Economic Survey of Ancient Rome* (Baltimore, 1924), vol. iv, p. 225.

5. Xenophon, *On the Methods of Improving the Revenues of Athens*, iii. 2.

6. Theodore Reinach, 'L'Anarchie monétaire et ses remèdes chez les anciens Grecs', *Académie des Inscriptions et Belles-Lettres*, vol. 38, ii (Paris, 1911), p. 353.

7. Fritz Heichelheim, *Wirtschaftsgeschichte des Altertumes* (Leyden, 1938), vol. i, p. 353.

8. Demosthenes, *Private Orations*, xxxiii. 5, 6; xxxiv. 50.

9. Cicero, *Actio Secunda in Verrem*, ii. 3. 181.

10. C. H. V. Sutherland, *Coinage in Roman Imperial Policy, 38 B.C.—A.D. 68* (London, 1951), p. 11.

11. W. L. Westermann, 'Warehousing and Trapezite Banking in Antiquity,' *Journal of Economic and Business History* (Cambridge, Mass, 1930), p. 41.

12. Isocrates, *Orations*, xvii. 36.

13. Plutarch, *Lives* (Everyman ed.), *Themistocles*, vol. i, p. 184.

14. Cicero, *Letters to Atticus*, xii. 24.

15. Cicero, *op. cit.* ii. 1.

16. T. Frank, *op. cit.* vol. ii, p. 438.

17. L. C. West and A. C. Jones, *Currency in Roman and Byzantine Egypt* (Princeton, 1944), p. 80.

CHAPTER FOUR

Exchange Rates in Ancient Greece and Rome

(1) RATIOS BETWEEN MONETARY METALS

MATERIAL relating to exchange rates during the Ancient Period is very scant. In the writings of the classics there are occasional references to the ratio between the value of monetary metals and to exchange parities between the various coinages. Numismatics and metrology provided between them much useful material indicating the relative metal contents of various coin issues. There is also a certain amount of information about changes in the value of gold or silver in terms of current coins. But information about actual exchange rates and about exchange movements during the Ancient Period is highly inadequate. They can be deducted very approximately from the known facts about gold-silver ratios, mint parities and their pce of metals in terms of current coins. Actual exchange rates – that is, prices of coins of one country in terms of coins of another country – have only survived in isolated instances.

There was a variety of monetary metals in use – gold, silver, electrum of widely varying gold-silver proportions, copper and its alloys – bronze or brass – even iron and lead. Copper or bronze was for a long time the monetary metal in early Rome and other countries and copper coins were not merely fiduciary currencies or token moneys but full-valued moneys.

The ever-changing relationship between the values of the monetary metals was of course a most important factor in determining exchange rates between coins of different metals. There is no evidence to show whether the causal relationship was reciprocal. The ratios were subject to wide fluctuations. Gold-silver ratio varied roughly between 1:10 and 1:15 during the Ancient Greek period. There were also wide discrepancies between the ratios existing at any given moment in different countries, and also between official ratios and market ratios in the same country.[1] In view of the immense risk and difficulties in the way of arbitrage transactions and of the heavy transport costs – especially in the case of copper – such discrepancies were apt to persist over long periods.

(2) DECLINE OF GOLD-SILVER RATIO

For several centuries the official ratio of $1:13\frac{1}{3}$ remained in force in Babylonia and other countries of the Middle East. The Persian Empire maintained that ratio during the 5th and 4th centuries, even though during part of that period the ratio in Greece was much lower – 12:1 and even 11:1. The result was a persistent outflow of silver, so that by the time of the conquest of Persia by Alexander (336–323 B.C.) in 331 B.C. silver coins were very scarce there.

Metallic ratios were known to have been affected from time to time materially by changes in the relative supply position of the three metals. For instance, during the Peloponnesian War (431–404 B.C.) the large gold reserve that had been accumulated by Athens out of contributions by her allies had to be spent, and its return into circulation greatly increased the supply of gold available. As a result the relative value of gold to silver and copper declined.

This tendency became further reinforced when the escape of slaves working in the Laurium silver mines, accomplished with Spartan assistance, interrupted the exploitation of those mines and the issue of silver coins had to be suspended, and again when under Philip (359–336 B.C.) and Alexander gold production in Thrace increased. Above all, the redistribution of the gigantic Persian gold reserves seized by Alexander in Susa and Persepolis (331 B.C.) resulted in a depreciation of gold to 10:1. To a less extent silver also depreciated at the same time in terms of copper, probably as a result of large issues of silver coinage by Alexander, during whose reign the silver-copper ratio declined from 120:1 to between 60:1 and 80:1.[2]

(3) WIDE DISCREPANCIES

If records of exchange rates between gold, silver and copper currencies were available, they would probably show a broad tendency to follow the changes in the relative value of the three metals, allowing of course for changes in the relative weight and fineness of the coinages. All the time there must have been wide discrepancies between metallic ratios prevailing at any given moment in various parts of the Mediterranean area. For a long time the silver value of copper was much higher in Italy than in Egypt. Discrepancies attained fantastic dimensions in relation to the Far East, especially in relation to China where silver had a much higher gold value than in either Europe or the Middle East. In Sicily during the 4th century the ratio was 15:1 while in the Crimea towards the middle of that century it was 11·7:1. For a long time after the conquest of Persia the ratio remained around 10:1.

That ratio was sought to be applied also by Rome during a much later period. When the conquered Aetolians applied to Rome in 189 B.C. to be allowed to pay in gold one-third of the tribute imposed on them, the ratio was fixed at 10:1.[3] The ratio tended to rise, however, during the late Republican era and by the time of Augustus (27 B.C.–A.D. 14) the parity between the gold *aureus* and the silver *denarius* could be fixed at 12½:1.

During the long period of debasement the copper-silver ratio seems to have fluctuated between 40:1 and 100:1, while the gold-silver ratio, which declined once more to 10:1 under Trajan (A.D. 98–117) as a result of the large booty of gold seized in Dacia, and declined further to 7·8:1 under Diocletian (A.D. 284–305), rose to 18:1 under Theodosius (A.D. 378–95).

(4) COMPLICATIONS ARISING FROM 'TRIMETALLISM'

The choice of the monetary standard by countries of the Middle East and by the Greek City States, and the frequent changes made in the weight and fineness of coins, were a determining influence on their exchange rates. They formed an important part of Foreign Exchange policy and will be discussed, therefore, in Chapter 6. The fact that during the Ancient Period there were not two but three monetary metals even after the use of electrum was discontinued made matters very complicated. The system of 'trimetallism' – to use the term adopted by Giesecke – must have given rise to even more involved problems than those arising from bimetallism in more recent periods. Its operation necessitated frequent monetary adjustments in order to avoid excessive inflow

or outflow of one or other of the monetary metals at rates unfavourable to the country concerned. There were either open
measures of devaluations or revaluations, or surreptitious debasements. While during a transition period the latter yielded
certain advantages, in international transactions they seldom
escaped in the long run the vigilance of *trapezitei* who were usually
only prepared to buy debased coins at their reduced metallic
value.

A further element of complication was the changing proportion
of gold and silver in electrum coins. In addition to 'trimetallism',
'symmetallism' was also in operation for several centuries, since
electrum contained both silver and gold. There was a tendency
towards a reduction of the proportion of gold in electrum coins.

(5) CHANGES IN THE ATTIC COINAGE

The attic coinage provides some very well-known early instances
of changes in the international value of a currency through adjustments of its mint parity. In about 594 B.C. Solon devalued the
drachma, increasing the number of coins to the mina of silver from
70 to 100, at the same time as changing over from the Aeginetan
to the Euboean weight standard. Towards the middle of the 6th
century B.C. Peisistratus (–527 B.C.) raised its value by some 4 per
cent, but his son and successor, Hippias, halved it towards the end
of that century by doubling the nominal value of the *two-drachmae*
piece.

Thereafter for something like a century the coinage of Athens
remained very stable and utterly dependable, until it became
strongly debased between 407 and 393 B.C. as a result of the
troubles arising from the Peloponnesian War. After the repudiation of the debased currency, the *tetradrachma* emerged, however,
once more as a coin which commanded confidence abroad, judging
by Xenophon's remarks in 350 B.C., referred to in the last chapter,[4]
on the willingness of foreign exporters to Athens to accept silver
coins in payment.

(6) FAVOURITE INTERNATIONAL CURRENCIES

For some time the Athens *tetradrachma* commanded a premium
of 5 per cent in Delphi over its mint parity with the local currency,
because of the demand for it for the requirements of international

trade. Coins of other City States – Rhodes, Corinth, Boeotia, etc., of Persia and of Macedonia under Philip and Alexander, which took their turn as the favourite currency for international trade and became centres of monetary unions – were also overvalued during their respective periods of predominance. In Athens, for instance, the Rhodes *drachma* was at a 5 per cent premium for some time during the 2nd century B.C.

There were instances of coins used extensively in international trade which were accepted at rates well above their metallic value over prolonged periods. The electrum *stater* of Cyzicus provides one of the best-known examples of what Heichelheim describes as a fiduciary currency acceptable in international trade [5] – meaning presumably that importers from the Euxine were willing to buy them at above their metallic value on the assumption that they in turn could always get for it that higher value. Cyzican *staters* were in persistent demand for the requirements of trade with countries of the Euxine. Originally they contained 75 per cent of gold, but their silver content was subsequently increased to 40 per cent. Nevertheless, they continued to be accepted at their original value for a remarkably long time. Even after they ceased to be in demand for trade requirements they remained a favourite international unit of account, which is known to have been used for reckoning payments to foreign mercenaries. [6]

(7) MINT PARITIES AND EXCHANGE RATES
IN GREECE

A vast amount of material is available about changes in coinages, even if caution is called for against some dogmatic conclusions based by metrologists on weight figures which are bound to be undependable owing to the varying original weight of coins as well as the varying degree of their wear. Unfortunately the large number of excellent works available to economic historians, while dealing with discrepancies between metal prices and mint parities, have only very occasional references to actual exchange rates. Yet in searching for expalnations of changes in coinages they could ill afford to ignore exchange discrepancies unconnected with previous changes in the relative value of monetary metals or in the metallic contents of coins.

There must surely have been frequent and marked deviations from mint parities, owing to changes in the supply-demand relationships of various currencies through balance of payments surpluses or deficits. Any deviation of exchange rates arising from one-sided buying or selling pressure on a currency was just as liable to interfere with the smooth working of the bimetallistic or tri-metallistic system as the development of a discrepancy between gold-silver-copper ratios in two countries or between official ratios and market prices of metals.

The few references to exchange rates that survived in classical literature are separated from each other by very long periods for which we have no figures at all. For instance, according to Xenophon, at the time of the expedition against Artaxerxes, in which he participated in 401 B.C., a Persian *siglus* (*shekel*) was worth 7½ Attic *obols*.[7] In a speech by Demosthenes (383–322 B.C.)[8] it appears that a *stater* of Cyzicus was worth in Bosporus 28 *drachmae*. In the text it is pointedly stated that the *stater* was worth *there* so much, which seems to imply that it had a different value elsewhere. The existence of discrepancies between exchange rates in various places is also suggested by a story of Callisthenes, in which the poet Persinus, having taken refuge in Mytilene after his escape from the court of the tyrants of Athens, was invited to return. He replied that he was able to sell his Phocian gold coins at a better rate in Mytilene than in Athens.[9]

(8) ROMAN EXCHANGE RATES DURING THE PERIOD OF EXPANSION

The exchange rates of Roman bronze coins must have been greatly affected by changes in the relative values of monetary metals. It was not until 268 B.C. that the first Roman silver coins were issued with a fixed ratio in relation to the bronze coinage. Until then the rate at which bronze coins could be converted into foreign silver coins for the requirements of foreign trade must have been subject to wide fluctuations. Very soon after this change there began a long series of devaluations of the *aes grave*, the large bronze coin whose weight was gradually reduced from a pound to half an ounce in the course of the Punic Wars. The Roman silver coinage, too, was frequently debased during that period, and again during the social wars at the beginning of the 1st century B.C., mainly through the issue of plated coins. In foreign trade metals changed hands by weight during such periods of debasement.

The exchange rate fixed for the conquered Eastern provinces

was 3 *denarii* per *tetradrachma*, even though the weight of the *tetradrachma* was different in various countries. (An exception was made in favour of Syria whose *tetradrachma* was fixed at 4 *denarii*.) The fixing of such an arbitrary exchange rate resulted in the overvaluation of some coinages, with the inevitable result that they disappeared from circulation.[10]

It is to the credit of Augustus to have stabilised the Roman currency, establishing the rate of 25 *denarii* to the *aureus*. His immediate successors did not fully maintain the metallic content of either coin, though during the first half of the 1st century A.D. the depreciation of both of them was moderate.

(9) THE PERIOD OF ROMAN DEBASEMENTS

It was Nero (A.D. 54–68) who took the first major step to initiate the disastrous depreciation of the Roman currency that was to continue, brief respites apart, till the end of the 4th century. It could not be sheer coincidence that his recoinage, involving a reduction of the weight of both *aureus* and *denarius* as well as a reduction of the latter's fineness by some 10 per cent, was carried out very soon after by the destruction of Rome by fire in 64 A.D. The high expenditure involved in the rebuilding of the city must have been covered partly out of the profit on the recoinage.

While the fineness of the *aureus* was maintained, its weight was gradually reduced. On the other hand, the weight of the *denarius* was maintained after its reduction by Nero, but its silver content was reduced to vanishing point by a series of progressive debasements of the coinage under the successive emperors. Not only despots like Heliogabalus (A.D. 218–22) whose name had become a byword for infamy, but even some who are rightly looked upon by historians as wise and great Emperors, took part in the long series of acts leading to the extreme depreciation of the *denarius*. Thus Trajan (A.D. 98–117) with a less valid excuse than that of Nero, debased the coinage in order to finance the invasion of Dacia.

The long succession of debasements was, it is true, interrupted from time to time by well-meaning efforts by Emperors such as Aurelian (A.D. 270–5), Diocletian (A.D. 284–305), Constantine (A.D. 306–37) and other Emperors to stem and even reverse the tide. Aurelian's victories secured for him substantial treasure enabling him to attempt an improvement of the coinage. He encountered, however, even stiffer resistance to his disinflationary drive than did more recent statesmen attempting to reverse the inflationary tide. A revolt organised by the 'moneyers' who had stood to lose through his attempt to restore the State monopoly of minting had to be suppressed at the cost of 7,000 lives. The beneficial result of this sacrifice was purely temporary. The full-valued bronze coins he issued in supplementation of the over-valued plated coins disappeared from circulation after his death, because, as a result of a new depreciation of the *denarius* it became profitable to melt them down.

Diocletian and Constantine made courageous efforts to resume the issue of good gold and silver coins, but the former changed hands by weight, while the latter varied in weight too widely to form the basis of a stable exchange rate. The improved coinage issued under the Antonines (A.D. 138–80) remained popular in foreign trade, but the example was not followed. The downward trend continued, temporary interruptions apart, throughout the 3rd and 4th centuries. For reasons which are yet to be explained, adequately inflationary depreciation of Roman coins came to an end in the 5th century – presumably because the coinage became utterly discredited by then.

(10) DEBASEMENTS IN EGYPT

Even before the beginning of the Roman debasement period Egypt had a foretaste of currency depreciation under the reign of Ptolemeus Auletes, Cleopatra's father (81–51 B.C.). Having dissipated the substantial treasure accumulated by his dynasty, he embarked on the issue of large quantities of silver coinage with its silver content reduced by two-thirds. Silver coinage became discredited and its issue was suspended. Only full-weight bronze coins remained in circulation. Cleopatra herself, towards the end of her reign (51–30 B.C.) devalued that coinage by 75 per cent by calling up the face value of the *drachma* to four *drachmae*. During the early period of Roman rule the Egyptian *tetradrachma* tended to be, more often than not, at a premium against the official *denarius* rate fixed by the authorities. From the beginning of the 4th century, however, debasement and inflation in Egypt came to surpass even that of Rome, and in the course of that century it assumed dimensions comparable with paper currency infla-tions in modern times. The silver-washed copper coins came to represent very large nominal amounts of depreciating monetary units.

According to Mickwitz the value of 1 lb. of gold increased in Egypt from 1,125 *denarii* in A.D. 179 to 3,000 twelve years later, to 50,000 in A.D. 280, to 1·4 million in A.D. 319, to 108 million in A.D. 341 and to 3,300 million in A.D. 400.[11]

Jones quotes undated Egyptian documents giving the price of 54,000, 150,000, 180,000 and 275,000 *denarii* for the *solidus*, a gold coin weighing $\frac{1}{72}$ lb., during various times in the 4th century.[12] Towards the middle of the 4th century the progress of inflation reached its climax, and after the end of that century it seems to have come to an end. According to Jones, issues of copper coins almost ceased and those of silver became very rare. The price of the *solidus* – by which name the *aureus* came to be known – fell in the Western Empire, from 12,000 *denarii* in A.D. 419 to about 7,000 *denarii* in A.D. 445, when oddly enough, the Imperial Government forbade the sale of *solidi* under that price. According to Cassiodorus, writing about A.D. 510, its price was kept stable for some time at 6,000 *denarii*.[13]

(11) METAL PRICES AND EXCHANGE RATES

It seems reasonable to assume that, although such exchange rates as were quoted during the period to which the above figures refer followed approximately the movements of the price of gold and of the *solidus*, during the period of extreme inflation very wide discrepancies developed and remained in existence over prolonged periods.

The extreme scarcity of material relating to exchange rates during that period, and indeed the Ancient Period in general, is probably due to the inadequate importance attached to it. Otherwise we might possess much more documentary evidence, comparable in quantity with the evidence that has survived concerning the prices of various issues of local coins of the same community in terms of each other. The absence of exchange rates is in sharp contrast with the wealth of material economic historians have succeeded in discovering on prices of goods and services. Exchange rates are hardly ever mentioned in surviving texts of speeches or in correspondence. This is presumably because they had been looked upon as a technical matter which concerns the expert only. Exchange rates were, therefore, ignored in the same

way as were Forward Exchange rates for several generations
of economists and financial writers during the second half of the
19th century and the first two decades of the 20th century, until
Keynes drew attention to them. When I was engaged on research
into the history of Forward Exchange, I was struck by the difficulty of finding forward rates for the period before the first World
War. Yet I had at my disposal the pre-1914 volumes of newspapers. It is of course much more difficult to find exchange rates
relating to periods in which no newspapers existed.

NOTES TO CHAPTER FOUR

1. François Lenormant, *La Monnaie dans l'antiquité* (Paris, 1878), vol. i,
pp. 152–3.
2. Fritz Heichelheim, *Wirtschaftsgeschichte des Altertumes* (Leyden, 1938), vol. 1,
p. 428.
3. Walther Giesecke, *Antikes Geldwesen* (Leipzig, 1938), p. 156.
4. Xenophon, *On the Methods of Improving the Revenues of Athens*, iii. 2.
5. Heichelheim, *op. cit.* vol. i., p. 309.
6. A. R. Burns, *Money and Monetary Policy in Early Times* (London, 1927),
p. 145.
7. Xenophon, *Anabasis*, i. 5, 6.
8. Demosthenes, *Private Orations*, xxxiv. 23.
9. Callisthenes, *Ap. Porluce*, x. 93. Quoted by Lenormant, *op. cit.* vol. ii, p. 63.
10. Burns, *op. cit.* p. 104.
11. Gunnar Mickwitz, *Geld und Wirtschaft im Römischen Reich des vierten Jarhun-
dertes n. Chr.* (Helsinki, 1931), p. 27.
12. A. H. M. Jones, 'Inflation under the Roman Empire' (*Ec. Hist. Review*,
1953), p. 308.
13. Jones, *op. cit.* p. 310.

CHAPTER FIVE

Ancient Foreign Exchange Theory

(1) LACK OF INTEREST IN BROADER ASPECTS OF FOREIGN EXCHANGE

EVIDENCE indicating knowledge of Foreign Exchange theory in the Ancient Period is extremely scant. Very few texts that could help us to reconstruct an Ancient Greek or a Roman Foreign Exchange theory, or even to justify us in assuming its existence, have survived. Indeed, even the broader subject of monetary theory seems to have been neglected by both races although they had surely attained a sufficiently high stage of civilisation and intellectual progress to be reasonably expected to accomplish something in that direction. Burns, in his standard work on the subject, *Money and Monetary Policy in Ancient Times*, summed up the contribution of the Ancient Period to our knowledge on monetary theory in the following sentence: 'The Greek philosophers made passing references to money in their treatises on politics and ethics, to which the Romans had added little or nothing'.[1] Even the limited material he refers to deals mostly with policy rather than with theory, and in any case most of it concerns general aspects of money rather than Foreign Exchange.

(2) INFERENCES FROM MONETARY MEASURES

It is tempting to infer from the adoption of various monetary measures that those responsible for them must have been aware of some basic rules, although we would be taking risks if we regarded conclusions in this sphere as more than sheer conjecture. There is no clear indication that monetary measures of countries in the Middle East during the Ancient Period were based on a knowledge of any Foreign Exchange theory. It seems, however, reasonable to suppose that some administrators of Greek City States were not unfamiliar with some broader rules of Foreign Exchange. In particular they must have been aware of the relationship between the metallic contents of coins and their exchange values. Even such elementary knowledge must have been far from universal.

(3) ARISTOPHANES AND GRESHAM'S LAW

Outstanding among the instances indicating some familiarity with Foreign Exchange theory in Greece was the much-quoted remark by Aristophanes (450–385 B.C.) in one of his comedies, written towards the end of the 5th century or the beginning of the 4th century B.C. 'In our Republic bad citizens are preferred to good ones just as bad money circulates while good money has disappeared.'[2]

This passage is widely regarded as the first formulation of what is known today as Gresham's Law. It refers to the period of 407–393 B.C. during which the coinage in Athens became extremely debased and the old good silver coins disappeared from circulation. We have no means of knowing whether Aristophanes, when writing the above passage, had in mind their disappearance through export or through domestic hoarding. Only if the former was the case could we accept the view that Aristophanes was seeking to establish a Foreign Exchange theory.

(4) THE GREEKS AND FOREIGN EXCHANGE THEORY

The importance and complexity of Foreign Exchange problems in Ancient Greece, with the multitude of frequently changing coinages and with active foreign trade and other international transactions between City States, was considerable. It seems, therefore, unlikely that none of the many monetary authorities possessed the minimum of theoretical knowledge that made the difference between stumbling on some solution or aiming deliberately at it. Faced with the frequently recurrent problems arising from the working of bimetallistic or trimetallistic systems, they must have noticed that the exchanges had obeyed to some rules amidst identical or similar circumstances. Persia was not the only country which became depleted of one of the monetary metals as a result of its overvaluation in terms of other monetary metals. Many an administrator or advisor must have learnt that lesson over and over again at the expense of some other country, or, failing that, at the expense of his own country.

It is conceivable that these administrators and experts were only thinking in terms of discrepancies between metallic ratios and overlooked the importance of discrepancies between exchange rates and their metallic parities. Nevertheless, the chances are that at least some of them realised that deviations of exchanges from their metallic parities were often at the root of the trouble and, as a result of a recurrence of identical situations, worked out theoretical rules relating to the operation of the system.

(5) PLATO AND THE GOLD EXCHANGE STANDARD

What is remarkable is that Plato (427–347 B.C.), Aristotle (384–322 B.C.) and Xenophon (c. 430–354 B.C.), who did show an interest in the monetary system, should have devoted so little attention to its broader international aspects. Admittedly Plato's proposal to use currency of no intrinsic value for domestic purposes and to confine the use of precious metals for transactions with foreign countries[3] does provide some rudiments of the theoretical foundations of the gold exchange standard. It was quoted in that sense by the Report of the Royal Commission on Indian Finance and Currency in 1914. Since it concerns policy rather than theory it will be dealt with in the next chapter.

The subject of the debasement of coinage received much attention by the author (or authors) of the pseudo-Aristotelian *Oeconomica*. But if there were attempts at any analysis of the effect of debasement on foreign trade, in the 4th century B.C., we have no evidence of them. On the other hand, it is practically certain that experience with many instances of debased coins had taught practical experts the rule which even a layman, Aristophanes, was able to figure out.

(6) NO CONCERN ABOUT ADVERSE BALANCE OF PAYMENTS

There is no indication that any Greek author, politician or administrator was acquainted with the balance of trade theory of Foreign Exchange. The leading financial expert of Ancient Greece, Xenophon, writing in the 4th century B.C., seems to have taken pride in the fact that Athens was in the enviable position of being able to finance a perennial trade deficit by exporting silver coins. Indeed the tendency in Athens was to discourage exports rather than encourage them.[4] Under Solon's legislation olive oil was the only product that was allowed to be exported. It was the Archon's duty to curse publicly anyone who exported fruit. A special class of informers on clandestine fig exporters named 'sycophants' came into existence and gained notoriety.[5]

Evidently there was no particular desire to eliminate the chronic import surplus which did not appear to have worried the Athens authorities. This was presumably because it did not affect the exchange value of the *drachma*. Otherwise exchange problems arising from the trade deficit might have induced Xenophon or others to give some thought to Foreign Exchange theory. The outflow of the bulk of the output of the Laurium silver mines did not appear to have caused concern, any more than does the export of the bulk of gold output in South Africa in our time. But while the South African Governments keep a watchful eye on the balance of payments, its very existence appears to have been ignored in ancient Athens.

(7) ROMAN ATTITUDE TOWARDS TRADE DEFICIT

Although the theoretical aspects of Foreign Exchange received even less attention in Rome than in Greece, several Roman statesmen and writers showed themselves aware of the importance of the adverse trade balance of the Roman Empire with the East, estimated by Pliny at 100 million *sesterces*, of which 50 million was with India.[6] It did not occur to them, however, to try to establish causal relationship between the import surplus and exchange rates. Indeed, there appeared to be no such relationship. During the period of debasement foreign trade was transacted with the aid of bullion changing hands by weight, or of old full-valued coins, so that the question of exchange rate between the debased *denarius* and foreign currencies could not often arise.

The adverse trade balance may have been, nevertheless, one of the causes of the disastrous depreciation of the *denarius*. It produced this effect not through influencing supply and demand in Foreign Exchange markets but through accentuating the shortage of precious metals which must have contributed towards compelling the successive Emperors to debase the silver coinage to an increasing extent and to reduce the weight of the gold coins.

(8) BULLION PRICES WERE MORE IMPORTANT THAN EXCHANGES

In Republican Rome Foreign Exchange difficulties figured from time to time prominently, and from early times they were among the major economic problems for prolonged periods. They assumed immense importance during the late centuries of the Empire. Yet practically nothing had been written about them by contemporary authors, not even during the long period of debasement in the 3rd and 4th centuries when such problems entered into the economic life of the community to a very considerable extent. They were not regarded as Foreign Exchange problems but primarily as problems of the appreciation and fluctuation of full-valued Roman gold and silver coins or of bullion in terms of debased Roman silver coins.

A fair amount has been said and written about speculation in good coins and in bullion during that period. On the other hand, the appreciation of foreign coins in terms of Roman currency was hardly referred to at all in contemporary literature. This was because of the technical character of the subject, but also because dealing in foreign coins was confined to a small fraction of the population, while dealing in Roman coins entered into the everyday life of most people. This in itself is no excuse for the absence of any attempt to analyse the Foreign Exchange situation. After all, in the Napoleonic Wars, too, it was the public concern felt in Britain over the high price of bullion and not over the depreciation of Foreign Exchanges that gave rise to the bullionist controversy. Nevertheless, we are indebted to that controversy for an important progress of Foreign Exchange theory. But it seems that Romans had very little inclination towards economy analysis in general.

(9) ROMAN DEBASEMENTS WERE NOT BASED ON THEORETICAL CONSIDERATIONS

It would be a mistake to read into policy decisions in general, and into debasement decisions in particular, any profound theoretical considerations. A. H. M. Jones is right in rejecting the suggestion put forward by Heichelheim and Mickwitz according to which Trajan deliberately debased the silver *denarius* in order to adjust it to the lower price of gold which declined as a result of the seizure of large gold hoards in Dacia.[7] He pointed out that

C

this theory put the cart before the horse. The *denarius* was debased to cover Trajan's war expenses incurred in connection with the conquest of Dacia, so that the decline in the price of gold after the end of that war did not precede but succeed the debasement as the effect of the release of the Dacian booty.

This fall in the price of gold is referred to in a letter written around A.D. 110 by one Heliodorus in Egypt to his brother. He says that officials in Egypt had bought gold at a high price on the assumption that a prolonged war would cause its price to rise. When the campaign ended sooner than expected the price of gold dropped from 15 to 11 *drachmae* (no weight unit given).[8] The volume of Trajan's booty was estimated at some 500,000 lb. which was a large enough quantity to account for the fall at some 30 per cent in its price.

Jones is probably right also in assuming that in the majority of instances debasements in Rome were simply the consequences of budgetary deficits and had therefore no bearing on Foreign Exchange theory. It seems possible that at least some of the Greek devaluations and debasements could safely be explained on the same ground. Among others, it may be assumed that the calling up of the *drachma* by Hippias at the end of the 5th century B.C. was done for that reason. Nor was the earlier and more moderate devaluation by Solon due to theoretical considerations connected with encouragement of exports though an undervaluation of the exchange was suggested in modern literature. Such considerations would presuppose familiarity with the purchasing power parity theory or at least with the balance of payments theory. But, as we saw above, it is conceivable that some of the late Roman debasements were inspired to some extent by a desire to mitigate the scarcity of precious metals.

(10) PURCHASING POWER PARITY THEORY WAS UNKNOWN AND INAPPLICABLE

Neither Greek nor Roman writers gave any indication of having discovered even the most rudimentary form of purchasing power parity theory. There was indeed no reason why they should. Amidst the then prevailing conditions it would be clearly absurd to entertain any notions that purchasing power parities had any influence on exchange rates. Exports of any country were confined to a relatively small number of goods, and imports depended not on relative prices but on requirements. Romans imported oriental luxuries not because they were produced cheaper in Arabia, India or China than at home, but because they were not produced at home. Cost of transport and profit margins amounted to a much higher proportion of the sale price of goods than in modern times. According to Pliny (A.D. 23–79), merchants importing Indian goods sold them in Rome at a hundredfold of what they had paid for them.[9]

Since the luxuries produced abroad were in strong demand and since the buyers could afford to pay for them, they were imported regardless of whether they were expensive. And if the foreign goods were not wanted the fact that, owing to an undervaluation of the producing country's currency, they could be bought cheaply did not stimulate their purchases. According to Gibbon, the countries of the East were largely self-sufficient and did not want to buy any goods that Rome would have been in a position to supply.[10]

During the early phases of the debasements the exchange value of the *denarius* remained well maintained. It was not until the reign of Commodus (A.D. 180–192) that there was a sudden rise in the price of gold and silver in terms of *denarii*. This fact did not mean, however, that the previous overvaluation of the *denarius* necessarily aggravated the balance of payments deficit of the Empire. If, as Pliny stated, the margin between the price of luxuries in their countries of origin and in their countries of destination was anything like 10,000 per cent, no conceivable overvaluation of the *denarius* could have made much difference.

(11) UNCONVINCING THEORETICAL EXPLANATIONS

Moreover, it must be remembered that during the 3rd and 4th centuries A.D. the Empire relapsed to a large extent into a state of natural economy in which barter played a prominent part and payments were made largely in kind. This was the case especially in Egypt, so much so that the price of the *solidus* came to be quoted in wheat. It was not the wheat which was sold against payment in coins but the coins that were sold in payment against wheat, so many measures per coin.[11]

The attempt made by Burns to apply the purchasing power parity theory in retrospect to conditions between the 1st and 4th centuries A.D. appears to me quite unconvincing.[12]

Nor is the suggestion, put forward by Burns, that the object of the moderate revaluation of the *drachma* by Peisistratus was to prevent a rise in prices that threatened to develop as a result of a fall in the value of silver, acceptable.[13] It implies familiarity with the impact of exchange movements on domestic price levels in the 5th century B.C. Administrators may have been aware of the effect of debasements on prices, but they must have surely attributed it to the changes in the metal content of the coins and not to the resulting changes in their exchange value.

(12) NO AUTOMATIC ADJUSTMENT

Roman writers and administrators can hardly be blamed for being unfamiliar with the theory of automatic adjustment of monetary supplies and price levels through the mechanism of the Foreign Exchange market. Under the economic system prevailing during the period of debasements Foreign Exchanges could not possibly operate in that sense, seeing that foreign trade was financed by bullion changing hands by weight, and debased coins were not accepted abroad in payment for imports. We pointed out above that imports and exports were largely independent of considerations of relative prices. They were far from elastic and for this reason alone a depreciation or undervaluation of the *denarius* could not produce any automatic adjustment by stimulating exports or discourage imports.

In any case, the automatic adjustment of payments through the mechanism of Foreign Exchange would have been prevented by the curious situation prevailing during a great part of the 3rd and 4th centuries A.D. by which inflation and deflation were running concurrently. Inflation resulted in an expansion of the consumer purchasing power through ever-increasing issues of silver-plated or silver-washed coins. At the same time the growing scarcity of gold and silver bullion used for the financing of production and wholesale trade tended to handicap production. There was, therefore, no surplus available for export even if prices had been favourable for it, and even if there had been a demand for it.

(13) METALLISTIC THEORY *v.* QUANTITY THEORY

Contemporary educated opinion must have been aware of the link between debasements and the fall in the external value of the Roman currency, as expressed by the rise in the price of gold and silver. For a long time the prevailing metallistic theory must have attributed the depreciation to the reduction of the silver content of the *denarius* through the successive debasements. But by the 3rd century it must have become obvious that this metallistic explanation was no longer adequate. Between A.D. 301 and 323 for instance the price of the *solidus* rose from 50,000 to 160,000 *denarii*, even though the silver content of the *denarius* was only halved, having been reduced from 4 to 2 per cent. And when the stage was reached that the silver content could not be reduced any further since it was virtually nil – the copper coins were merely treated to a silver wash – the *denarius* continued to depreciate, both in terms of precious metals and in terms of goods, at a rapidly accelerating pace.

This should have led to the discovery of the quantity theory of money. Possibly it did, judging by the fact that in the 5th century inflation was eventually checked by discontinuing the issue of coins. Possibly administrators of the Eastern Empire may have realised that the metallic value of the current coinage – and therefore its external value – depended on the volume of demand for metals or for good coins in relation to the volume of their circulation. But we have no evidence that such a conclusion was ever reached by any conscious process of inference. Quite possibly the policy to stop inflation was an instinctive reaction to its disastrous effect, without any theorectical foundations.

NOTES TO CHAPTER FIVE

1. Burns, *Money and Monetary Policy in Early Times* (London, 1927), p. 314.
2. Aristophanes, *The Frogs*, 717.
3. Plato, *Laws*, v. 12.
4. Xenophon, *On the Methods of Improving the Revenues of Athens*, iii. 2.
5. Plutarch, *Lives* (Everyman ed.), *Solon*, vol. i, p. 137.
6. Pliny, *Natural History*, vi. 26.
7. A. H. M. Jones, 'Inflation under the Roman Empire' (*Ec. Hist. Review*, 1953), p. 294.
8. Frank, *op. cit.* vol. ii, pp. 443-4.
9. Pliny, *op. cit.* vi. 28.
10. Edward Gibbon, *Decline and Fall of the Roman Empire* (Everyman ed.), vol. i, p. 55.
11. A. H. M. Jones, 'Inflation under the Roman Empire', *op. cit.* p. 308.
12. Burns, *op. cit.* p. 417.
13. Burns, *op. cit.* pp. 357-8.

CHAPTER SIX

Ancient Foreign Exchange Policy

(1) DELIBERATE POLICY OR 'MUDDLING THROUGH'?

EVIDENCE on the basis of which Foreign Exchange policies in the Ancient Period could be reconstructed is much more plentiful than the material on ancient Foreign Exchange theory. We must guard ourselves, however, against reading too much into such evidence. When dealing with contemporary or recent examples of official action in the spheres of Foreign Exchange one is inclined to assume too readily that certain decisions were taken as a matter of deliberate policy, whereas in reality the authorities may have drifted into a certain line of action for considerations of immediate expediency without being aware of its broader implication. In this sphere, as in other spheres, the right thing was often done for the wrong reason. 'Muddling through' was by no means an exclusively modern British practice.

When it comes to reconstructing monetary policies that were supposed to have been practised something like 2000 years ago, we are faced with the additional difficulty of inadequate factual knowledge and background knowledge. While in some instances we may be satisfied that the known facts suggest deliberate policy, in many other instances the motives behind the actions are a matter of guesswork. We would have to know a great deal more about the circumstances in which decisions were taken before we could form any definite opinions about their motives and objects.

(2) CHOICE OF MONETARY STANDARDS

Foremost among the category of Foreign Exchange policy decisions about many of which there is ample factual evidence are those concerned with the choice of, or changes in, the monetary standards, determining the monetary metal and the weight and fineness of the coinage. The choice of the weight standard was of particular importance, precisely because in the Foreign Exchange

market most coins changed hands by weight. It simplified trade
between two countries if their coinages were based on the same
weight standard. The choice of weight standard may have served
commercial aims of encouraging trade with certain countries and
discouraging it with other countries, or it may have served political
aims – joining or leaving one of the monetary areas, membership
in which usually had political as well as commercial and financial
implications.

(3) PERSIA'S MONETARY POLICIES

The Persian Empire was practically the only country in the
Ancient Middle East where the authorities appear to have followed deliberate policies other than that involved in choosing and
changing the weight standards of coinages. The central government allowed various conquered provinces to retain their national
coinage, and for a long time there appears to have been no attempt to fix exchange rates between these coins and the royal gold
coin, the *daric*. The provincial coins were subject to fluctuations
against each other as well as against the royal coinage. The latter
had the advantage of being accepted by the central Treasury and
the provincial Treasuries at its face value, while provincial coins
were only accepted by weight. According to Brandis this discrimination resulted in a premium in favour of the royal coinage.[1]

A much more important device, by which the exchange value
of the *daric* in relation to silver currencies was sought to be bolstered up was the fixing of the gold-silver ratio at $1:13\frac{1}{4}$ over
a prolonged period. It was maintained at that level long after it
ceased to correspond to the ratio prevailing outside Persia, following on the depreciation of gold referred to in Chapter 4. It
seems probable that this policy was not due to any economic
consideration but to considerations of prestige. The kings of Persia
regarded the supremacy of their gold coin as a symbol of their
own personal supremacy. Towards the middle of the 6th century
B.C. the *daric* was actually revalued to a slight extent. A downward
adjustment of the gold-silver parity would have been considered
an undignified act and they refrained from it, even though as a
result of the depreciation of gold in terms of silver during the 5th
and 4th centuries the disadvantages of their policy of prestige must
have been obvious. But the same considerations of prestige were
also responsible for the maintenance of the high quality of the *daric*.

(4) LYDIA'S DOUBLE STANDARD

Lydia, the birthplace of coinage, may conceivably have practised a form of Foreign Exchange policy consisting of making up her primitive punch-marked coins to two different weight standards, for eastward trade by the caravan routes towards Mesopotamia, and for westward trade to the Ionian coastal towns.

This had the advantage of facilitating the financing of trade both with the countries whose currencies conformed to Babylonian weight standards and with the countries whose coinage was based on Aeginetan weight standards.[2]

(5) PLATO'S MONETARY PLAN

In Ancient Greece exchanges were on the whole allowed to take care of themselves to a reasonable degree, but we encounter, nevertheless, many instances of exchange control. An inscription found at Olbia, dating from the beginning of the 4th century, places on record that the exchange rate for the Cyzicus *stater* was legally fixed there. During the same period there was a monopoly of Foreign Exchange business in Byzantium. Various cities which coined their money adopted a restriction to protect their coinage without suppressing free dealing in them.

Reference was made in the last chapter to the policy of watertight exchange control advocated by Plato who came out in favour of a system under which a fiduciary currency used within the country would be isolated by means of stringent exchange restrictions. He recommended the issue of coins which were to be of no intrinsic value outside the issuing State. Private citizens were to be forbidden to own gold or silver, but the State would have to possess a reserve in such coins for the requirements of wars and the expenditure of foreign embassies. It should be made compulsory for private individuals returning from abroad to sell their foreign coins to the State against payment in domestic currency.[3]

(6) EXCHANGE CONTROL IN SPARTA

Even though Plato made no reference to the system operating on somewhat similar lines in Sparta, it seems reasonable to assume that he was familiar with it, and presumably it was Sparta's practical example that had inspired his proposal. The only major difference between the system advocated by Plato and the one introduced in Sparta by Lycurgus (*c.* 825 B.C.) – which was actually in operation long before and also during Plato's lifetime – was that instead of coins, Sparta used clumsy and cumbersome iron bars, rendered useless for industrial purposes by a special treatment of the metal described by Plutarch and other writers of the ancient period.[4]

In Sparta there were severe penalties on unauthorised holders of precious metals. The threat and frequent application of these penalties created a very strict system of exchange control. That it was not watertight is indicated by references in various ancient writings to the discovery of private hoards of foreign, especially Athenian, coins (named 'owls' nests' because of the design of these coins). Possession of such coins was often regarded as evidence of treasonable relations with foreign States as well as an offence against the law on exchange control.

The degree of severity and efficiency with which these exchange restrictions were enforced tended to decline some time after their adoption by Lycurgus, but from time to time attempts were made to reinforce them. For instance, in the 5th century under the reign of Agis (427–398 B.C.) gold and silver was allowed to flow into Sparta, and it did flow in on a large scale thanks to the rich war booties secured by Lysander.[5] Efforts were made to check the acquisition of gold and silver by private citizens, but it was of no avail.

(7) EXCHANGE CONTROL IN EGYPT

Plato's advice was also applied in Egypt under the Ptolemies and also under Roman rule. The authorities endeavoured to ensure the surrender of full-valued coins by residents and only debased local coins were allowed to be used in local circulation.[6] The foreign coins were used for external payments only and foreign merchants had to surrender their coins on arrival in Egypt, against payment in Egyptian coins. There is no evidence to show whether the Egyptian authorities followed Plato's suggestion deliberately, though the chances are that, in common with all educated people of the period, they were at any rate familiar with his writings.

C 2

(8) POLICY OF STABLE CURRENCY

Although according to the evidence of *Oeconomica*, debasements were frequent occurrences in Hellas and in Magna Graecia, the more important among the City States such as Athens and kingdoms such as Macedonia and Persia, and even some lesser City States, attached considerable importance to maintaining the value of their coinage. The text of the civic oath in the State of Chersonnesos, a Greek colony on the Euxine, contained an undertaking to maintain the value of the coinage.[7] And in an agreement concluded between Mytilene and Phocia in 400 B.C. any official guilty of debasing the coinage was liable to severe penalties.[8] The governments of the period were undoubtedly aware of the practical advantages and prestige value of a stable currency, though some tyrants could not resist the temptation of deriving immediate financial benefit from debasement. Even some enlightened and public-spirited governments were apt to be forced by circumstances to resort to debasement or devaluation.

(9) DEVALUATION BY SOLON

The best-known early instance of a deliberate devaluation of the coinage as a matter of policy by a government not inspired by motives of immediate financial gain was that of the devaluation of the *drachma* in Athens from 70 *drachmae* to 100 to a *mina* of silver by Solon, already referred to in Chapters 4 and 5. According to one interpretation this was done largely or partly for the sake of stimulating the export trade of Athens. There is no reason to suppose, however, that the reduction of the metallic value of the *drachma* made any difference from the point of view of the competitive capacity of Athens exporters, seeing that during that early period, long before the Attic coins became an international currency, foreign trade must have been transacted largely against payment in bullion or coins by weight. It was not until much later that the Athens silver coins came to inspire sufficient confidence to become an international currency and to change hands by tale in international as well as domestic trade transactions.

In all probability Solon's object was purely or overwhelmingly social – to reduce the burden of the domestic indebtedness. In any case, Athens had been in a position to pay for her trade deficit thanks to her resources of silver. As we pointed out in the last chapter, the chronic import surplus was not viewed with much concern, and there was no evident desire to reduce it.

The subsequent upward adjustment of the *drachma* by 4 per cent under Peisistratus may have served considerations of prestige, since the *daric* was revalued to a comparable extent about the same time. This was one of the rare instances of competitive currency appreciation. Burns favours the theory that the revaluation was connected with the increase in the output of the Laurium mines, causing a fall in the value of silver, and that the increase in the weight of the coins was meant to obviate a rise in prices.[9] The widely shared explanation of the 50 per cent devaluation by Hippias is that he wanted to make a profit on the transaction whereby half of the coins which had been called in on the excuse that they were bad, were retained and the nominal amount of those returned to their owners was doubled.

(10) ROMAN DEVALUATIONS DURING THE PUNIC WARS

Foreign Exchange policy played a subordinate part during the period of the greatness of Rome. Since the Roman Empire covered most of the known civilised world and Roman currency was freely accepted by countries outside its confines, there was for a long time no inducement for paying much attention to Foreign Exchange problems. Tampering with the coinage, resorted to even by some of the greatest statesmen and Emperors was not done in any desire to influence the exchange value of the Roman currency.

It is necessary to resist the temptation of interpreting scant factual material in a sense that would suit our modern conditions but would not suit those prevailing in Ancient Rome. In particular it would be a mistake to attribute a deliberate Foreign Exchange policy either the devaluation of the bronze coinage during the Punic Wars or the debasement of the silver coinage during the period of decline. The repeated devaluations of the bronze coins, the *aes grave*, aimed not at stimulating exports but at facilitating the domestic financing of war expenditure of the Republic. The debasements of the *denarius* under the Empire were necessitated primarily by scarcity of precious metals and especially by budgetary deficits caused by the cost of maintaining large armies even in time of peace.

(11) RESTRICTIONS IN ROME

Official Foreign Exchange policy in Rome was much more restrictive than it had been most of the time in most parts of Greece. The trade of money-changers was subject to much closer regulation and official interference. Long before the beginning of the debasement period authorised money-changers in Roman provinces were given a monopolistic position, for the sake of securing Foreign Exchanges needed for official requirements.

This fact emerges from a document quoted by Rostovtzeff concerning measures taken at the beginning of the 3rd century B.C. by the city of Mylassa, in Caria (Asia Minor), to prevent illicit dealings in exchanges. The document states: 'The security of the city is shaken by the malice and villainy of a few people who assail it and rob the community. Through them speculation in exchanges has entered our market place and prevents the city from securing a supply of the necessities of life, so that many of the citizens and indeed the community as a whole suffer from scarcity. And on this account also the regular payment of the taxes to the Emperor is delayed.'[10]

The language of this indictment foreshadows the style in which during the Medieval Period, and also in more recent times, speculative dealings in exchanges were to be frequently denounced as the root of all evil. The quotation also suggests that exchange control in the Roman Empire was adopted largely for the purpose of enabling the provincial administration to accumulate the exchange necessary for the payment of the tribute due to Rome.

Arbitrage, too, was occasionally subject to restrictions. An edict issued in A.D. 356 limits the amount of copper coins which merchants were allowed to transport from one province to another, to prevent their making a profit on the difference between their prices.[11]

(12) MAINTAINING ARTIFICIAL RATES

There is a fair amount of information available about the working of exchange control in Egypt under Roman occupation. Like a number of other Roman eastern provinces, Egypt was allowed to issue her own coinage, but the value of the Egyptian *tetradrachma* was fixed in terms of the Roman *denarius*. The money-changers in Egypt were under an obligation to accept Roman coins at the official exchange rate, even though the debasement of the latter proceeded from time to time faster than that of the local coinage. In A.D. 260 in Oxyrhynchus the money-changers made an attempt to defy the regulations. They closed their doors in order to avoid having to accept an official rate on the Roman silver coins issued recently under the reign of Gallienus (A.D. 260–8) because they were even more debased than previous issues and at the official parity they were overvalued against Egyptian currency. The Roman authorities ordered the exchange dealers, however, to reopen and to accept the Roman coins at the official rate, with the exception of counterfeit coins. The decree referred to penalties enacted on previous occasions, which clearly implied that difficulties of that kind had been a familiar phenomena of the period.[12]

A sophisticated method of securing a gain on Foreing Exchange transactions was applied by the Egyptian authorities under the Ptolemies. Having forced visiting foreign merchants to exchange their foreign moneys against debased local coins, they imposed a ban from time to time on the export of wheat. The unfortunate merchants thus caught had no choice but to re-sell their Egyptian money at a loss.[13] There was a royal bank in Alexandria with extensive privileges in respect of Foreign Exchange.[14]

(13) FUTILE EFFORTS TO PREVENT EFFECTS OF DEBASEMENTS

The main object of the official Foreign Exchange policy during the debasement period was to maintain the value of the debased silver coins at an artificially high level. This effort was of course of no avail in the long run. It was entirely useless in relation to foreign exporters who were in a position to insist on payment in full-valued money or in metals by weight. And since Roman importers had to procure such means of external payment they had to pay higher unofficial prices for gold coins or bullion.

The *argentarii* were under obligation to surrender to the Treasury any gold coins they were able to collect from the public, and were paid the officially fixed price which was left unchanged for years, even though the market value of the gold coins increased as and when silver coins became more and more debased. Symmachus, prefect of Rome in a report to Valentinian II in A.D. 384 or 385, pointed out that since the price of the gold coins had risen, the *collectarii* (as the money-changers came to be named), were losing on the transactions. He appealed to the Emperor to increase the official price.[15]

In the Eastern Empire, too, drastic controls had been adopted to prevent the outflow of precious metals. To that end Persian merchants were forbidden to bring their goods across the river that constituted the border.

(13) DEFENDING MONETARY SUPPLIES BY CHANGING THE COINAGE

It is a pity we know so little about the way in which bimetallism and trimetallism operated in the Ancient Period. The authorities of various countries must have known a great deal about defending the monetary circulation of their countries – in those days the question of having to defend official reserves did not arise – by means of adjusting their mint parities. But we can seldom be certain that such changes were in fact made for the purpose of preventing an outflow of a high-valued coinage. For instance, Burns' theory that Nero's object in debasing the *denarius* was to readjust the gold-silver ratio[16] is hardly more than conjecture.

There are no known instances of active official intervention in the Foreign Exchange market to influence exchange rates. Yet the relative narrowness of the market would have provided good opportunities for successful intervention, though any attempt at bolstering up a currency against the consequences of its debasement or inflation would have been foredoomed to failure. The authorities sought to influence exchange rates in a number of instances by trying to impose official rates, but this attempt was often unsuccessful.

NOTES TO CHAPTER SIX

1. J. Brandis, *Das Münz-, Mass- und Gewichtswesen in Vorderasien bis auf Alexander den Grossen* (Berlin, 1866), p. 263.
2. A. R. Burns, *Money and Monetary Policy in Early Times* (London, 1927), p. 196.
3. Plato, *Laws*, v. 12.
4. Plutarch, *Lives* (Everyman ed.), *Lycurgus*, vol. i, p. 68.
5. Plutarch, *op. cit. Lysander*, vol. ii, p. 116.
6. L. C. West and A. C. Jones, *Currency in Roman and Byzantine Egypt* (Princeton, 1944), p. 189.

7. Fritz Heichelheim, *Wirtschaftsgeschichte des Altertumes* (Leyden, 1938), vol. i, p. 310.

8. Burns, *op. cit.* pp. 64 and 92.

9. Burns, *op. cit.* pp. 357–8.

10. M. Rostovtzeff, *The Social and Economic History of the Roman Empire* (Oxford, 1926), pp. 420–1.

11. Theodore Mommsen, *Histoire de la monnaie romaine* (Paris, 1873), vol. iii. p. 420.

12. Mommsen, *op. cit.* vol. iii, p. 421.

13. West & Jones, *op. cit.* p. 92.

14. M. Rostovtzeff, *The Social and Economic History of the Hellenistic World* (Oxford, 1941), p. 402.

15. A. H. M. Jones, 'Inflation under the Roman Empire' (*Ec. Hist. Review*, 1953), p. 302.

16. Burns, *op. cit.* pp. 412–13.

PART II

MEDIEVAL PERIOD

CHAPTER SEVEN

Medieval Foreign Exchange Markets

(1) SETBACK DURING THE DARK AGES

THE Foreign Exchange system did not escape the general setback in civilisation that followed the end of *Pax Romana*. Facilities other than the exchange of coins for effecting international transfers must have disappeared long before the actual collapse of the Western Empire, owing to unstable financial and political conditions from the 3rd century A.D. Even the less advanced form of Foreign Exchange, exchanging coins by tale, which had suffered a setback during the debasement period, must have declined further in the Dark Ages, owing to the general contraction of foreign trade and to lack of confidence in most coinages.

To a large extent foreign trade, which during the 3rd century reverted to its original primitive form, continued in that form in the early Middle Ages. A large proportion of commercial payments abroad were made mostly in the form of bullion or coins by weight.

(2) REIGN AND DECLINE OF BYZANTINE COINAGE

Gold coins of the Eastern Empire and some other coins continued to be taken by tale during the early Middle Ages, so that Foreign Exchange in the form of money-changing continued. In Byzantium and Alexandria there were many money-changers, as there were also in countries established on the ruins of the Western Empire. The exchange of coins against each other came to be referred to by early medieval writers – mostly ecclesiastics – as 'manual' exchanges.

With the debasement of the Byzantine coinage during later centuries there was in Byzantium an increase in the turnover in foreign coins, owing to speculative anticipation of further depreciation. Gold coins of Michael VII (1071–8), which were the last full-valued coins of the Eastern Empire, continued to be minted for the requirements of foreign trade, because they commanded confidence abroad as well as at home.[1] But as and when current Byzantine coinage became discredited, foreign coins, especially those of Genoa and Venice, came increasingly into circulation even in Constantinople itself.

Full-valued Byzantine gold coins, and also Arab *dirhems*, and later the *denarius* of Charlemagne, circulated in Europe, Western Asia and North Africa. At the same time, a growing variety of local coins issued by succession States of the Western Empire came into circulation outside their countries of origin.

(3) EXPANSION OF MANUAL EXCHANGES

The expansion of manual exchanges in medieval Europe owes much to the absence of political unity in Italy, Germany and Spain. As in the City States in Ancient Greece, the multiplicity of coinage systems in those advanced countries led to a large turnover in Foreign Exchange between the independent political units. Crusades, too, caused an increase in the inter-change of coins throughout Central and Eastern Europe and the Levant.

By the 11th century money-changing became once more an important profession everywhere. Those engaged in it were variously described in contemporary writings as *cambiatores*, *campsores*, *bancari* or *tabulari*. Even the ancient Greek term *trepezitai* reappeared in an 11th-century French document. The name 'banker' originated from the benches used by money-changers in Genoa and other Italian cities. In most countries these money-changers formed associations which achieved some influence in medieval commercial life and even in political life. One of their ranks became a Byzantine Emperor – Michael IV (1034–41). Many money-changers combined their functions with those of goldsmiths and silversmiths. The gradual extension of their activities to loan and deposit business further increased their importance.

(4) MONEY-CHANGING IN EUROPE AND ASIA

Rome, and Avignon during the residence of the Papal Court in that city, became an important Foreign Exchange centre. Visitors from all parts of the Christian world exchanged there a wide variety of coins brought from their countries, and this gave rise to a regular traffic in most of the known foreign coins of that period. Owing to the resulting active turnover, exchange rates must have been quoted fairly regularly.

In Spain, too, exchange rates for foreign coins must have been of importance, judging by a 13th-century law in Valencia, which permitted the settlement of obligations contracted in foreign moneys by means of payment in local coins at the current exchange rate.[2] In Aragon and Navarre foreign coins came into circulation in large quantities, and gave rise to regular exchanges, in connection with domestic as well as international transactions.[3]

Money-changing developed to a considerable degree also in Flanders. Medieval English coins found their way there in large quantities, judging by the number and size of hoards of English silver pennies found in the Low Countries. These pennies had good markets also in Germany, France and other countries in Western and Central Europe.

There is much information available about money-changing during the Middle Ages also outside Europe – in the Middle East, in India and in China. Pegolotti, writing in the 14th century, advised merchants trading with China to exchange their silver coins for Chinese paper money at Quinsay rather than Peking. Apparently there was a free market in the former place with an active turnover. There is also information about Medieval money-changing in Japan.

(5) TRANSFERS, EXCHANGE CONTRACTS AND BILLS OF EXCHANGE

With the gradual recovery of trade from the setback that resulted from the decline and collapse of the Roman Empire, manual exchanges became increasingly inadequate to meet expanding commercial requirements. The development of an international banking system, with merchant banking houses maintaining branches or correspondents in foreign centres, provided additional methods of Foreign Exchange by means of notarial contracts, bills, letters of credits and the equivalent of modern mail transfers, the cost of which, and the risks involved, were much less than that of dispatching specie or bullion. The adoption of a system of bank deposits greatly assisted the development of transfers as a means of making external as well as domestic payments.

From the 13th century onwards exchanges by means of notarial exchange contracts, and later by bills of exchange, gradually took the place of manual exchanges as the main form of Foreign Exchange. The declining importance of exchanging coins is indicated by the adoption of the term *cambium minutum* (petty exchange) by scholastic writers of the later Medieval Period. It implied that transactions in foreign coins were intended to serve relatively unimportant requirements, in contradistinction to *cambium per litteras* (exchange by bills), which served the requirements of trade. Hence the English name 'merchant exchange', or 'merchandising exchange' for bills of exchange that appeared later, implying a decline of the use of coins in foreign trade.

(6) ORIGINS OF BILLS OF EXCHANGE

During the early Middle Ages the Arabs are said to have been familiar with the use of bills from the 8th century A.D., but its use must have been handicapped by the strict Mohammedan law against interest, and there is no evidence for their international use. The initiative for international payments by means of bills of exchange, or at any rate its early development, has been variously attributed to the Jews, to Crusaders and to Italian merchant bankers. When in the 12th century the Ghibellines were driven to Amsterdam by the Guelphs, and when Jews, having been expelled from one country after another – in particular by Philip Auguste (1180–1223) and Philip the Tall (1316–22) from France – found refuge in Italy, they were said to have tried to realise at least part of the possessions they had had to leave behind, by drawing bills on those in whose charge these possessions had been left. They sold such bills to merchants wanting to buy goods in the countries concerned. Various early writers even suggested that this practice developed already in the 7th century when Dagobert (*c.* 602–39) expelled the Jews from the Frankish kingdom.[4] Whether this was really the origin of the medieval bills of exchange is, however, a matter of conjecture. Nor is there confirmation for claims that they were in use in Venice in the 9th century, indeed that there were, in fact, any bills before the 12th or 13th century.

(7) TEMPLARS' FINANCIAL OPERATIONS

More concrete evidence is available about early international payments in connection with Crusades. The two powerful Orders of Knights, the Templars and the Hospitallers of St. John, developed systems under which it was possible, primarily for participants in Crusades but also for others, to effect international transfers, not only between the West and the Levant but also between various European countries. These orders were favourably placed for transporting specie or bullion, thanks to their ability of providing strong escorts at a relatively low cost and at short notice. Moreover, since they owned fortified and well-guarded bases in many countries and possessed substantial financial resources of their own in addition to those deposited with them for safe keeping, they were often able to make international payments without having to move specie.[5]

Sayous quotes an instance of the rôle played by the Templars in international financial transactions arising from the late Crusades. On May 12, 1249, a group of Italian traders in Cyprus remitted 10,000 Syrian gold *bezants* to Yolande de Bourbon on instruction from the Templars who undertook to repay the equivalent in *livres tournois* in Paris on the date of the next fair of Lagny. In another document Yolande de Bourbon undertook to repay the Templars on the same date.[6]

There is much evidence for Foreign Exchange operations through the use of notarial contracts or letters of credit by Crusaders. Richard Cœur de Lion (1189–99), while on crusade, is claimed to have made transfers through ordinary trading channels. St. Louis (1226–70) drew *mandats* on his Paris Treasury in payment to his creditors in the Levant. They were cashed by Genoese bankers who converted the proceeds into Genoese money.[7]

(8) LETTERS OF CREDIT

Italian merchant bankers had branches or correspondents in those places of the Levant which were in Christian hands, and also in European countries whence crusaders came or through which they had to pass. They were able to make payments on letters of credit in various local currencies, debiting the guarantors of such credits on the basis of the current exchange rates. For instance in 1219 de Montmorency guaranteed a letter of credit of 300 *livres tournois* for nine knights on their departure for the Holy Land.[8]

To quote an instance of letters of credit issued for non-military requirements, Guillaume Durand, Bishop of Mende (1237–96) in his *Speculum Juris* gave particulars of a letter of credit received by a French student who went to study at the University of Bologna.[9]

(9) NOTARIAL CONTRACTS

Before exchange operations assumed technically the form of bills they were transacted by means of contracts drawn up by notaries. Genoese notarial records contain a great many early instances of such contracts, a large proportion of which included provisions for the re-change of the amount payable abroad, in case of non-payment, at a fixed exchange rate. This provision may have indicated the absence of genuine commercial transaction behind such arrangements, and there can be no doubt that in a great many cases the exchange-re-change deal merely concealed an interest-bearing loan. It is conceivable, however, that in many instances both parties simply wanted to safeguard themselves against adverse exchange movements if the borrower should find himself unable to meet his liability through the loss of the consignment.

The first known Foreign Exchange contract dates from June 8, 1156. Two brothers, having received 115 Genoese pounds, in a contract concluded before a Genoa notrary, promised to reimburse 460 *bezants* one month after their arrival in Constantinople or in any other city where the Emperor held his Court. There was a provision under which in case of non-payment the creditor could claim 500 *bezants* in the Levant on All Saints Day, and in case of default of that obligation the debtor had to pay 250 Genoese pounds before August 1 of the following year.[10]

Another instance of exchange contract, following closely on the one quoted above, dates from 1157. It concerns the payment of 10 Genoese pounds in Tunis against payment received in Genoa. In this instance the place of payment is in a foreign country but the currency is the local unit.[11]

(10) ADVANTAGES OF TRANSFERS BY BILLS

At the next stage in the evolution of bills of exchange there were, in addition to notarial contracts, also letters notifying the party concerned about the contracts. Such letters eventually replaced altogether the clumsy and cumbersome contracts. Endemann, who gives an account of this evolution lays stress on its slow pace.[12]

The advantage of transfers by bills in preference to conveying bullion or specie were manifold. It took less time to send a courier with bills than to dispatch specie under the guard of a heavily armed convoy. Renouard quotes an instance in which in 1338 it took twenty-one days to deliver at Avignon coins collected at Rouen, while eight days were sufficient for the courier to deliver a bill.[13] In the 14th century a Papal collector named Gelhard suggested to the Papal Court that one of the Bruges bankers should appoint an agent in Cracow, because transfers effected through such channels would only take ten months while it took a full year for specie consignments to reach their destination.[14]

It was also incomparably safer to remit by bills, for even if couriers were robbed the illicit possessors of the bills were unable to collect the money. In one instance the fleet of Louis IX recovered from captured pirates quite a number of letters of credit which the latter had been unable to use.

It was difficult for arbitrage to take advantage of the wide discrepancies that existed most of the time between the prices of coins in various countries at any given moment. Apart from official restrictions – to be discussed in Chapter 10 – which handicapped arbitrage, the cost of transport for coins was extremely high, largely because they could only be conveyed under strong armed escorts. It was at times possible to combine the transport of bullion or specie with journeys of important personages who would have to travel heavily escorted in any case. When this was not possible, the delay caused by having to accumulate sufficiently large consignments to make the employment of strong escorts worth while meant risk of changes in the exchange rates and certainty of loss of interest. Another major obstacle to arbitrage was the high seignorage and minting charges levied in every country, which discouraged the export of specie for the purpose of selling them to the mints of the importing countries.

(11) PAPAL COURT'S FOREIGN EXCHANGE TRANSACTIONS

The Church played an important rôle in the development of active markets in foreign bills. The transfer of the proceeds of

Papal collections from all Christian countries gave rise to a regular demand for means by which such transfers could be effected without having to move specie. And the ban on interest payments under the strict application of the Church law against usury gave rise to systematic circumvention of this ban by means of transactions in foreign bills.

Much documentary evidence is available about the transactions between the Papal Court of Avignon and Italian banking houses concerning the transfer of Papal collections. The Papal Court sold regularly to these bankers the proceeds of collections in England and other countries against payment in Avignon in florins. The bankers transferred the moneys to Avignon largely by means of purchases of bills. In the case of England the flow of Papal revenues provided a counterpart for the demand for sterling in connection with wool purchases by Italian merchants, largely through the intermediary of the Bruges market.

On June 9, 1317, the Papal Chamber concluded with the banking houses Bardi and Peruzzi a contract covering a period of twelve months, during which the Papal Nuncio in England was to pay over to their London branches the proceeds of the Papal collections for remittance to Avignon. These agreements were renewed year after year.[15] In some contracts with these and other bankers the exchange rates were fixed in advance for a whole year. By this arrangement the Papal Chamber safeguarded itself against losses through exchange depreciation – an interesting early instance of Forward Exchange transactions, even though the amounts to be transferred and the dates of the transfers could not be fixed in advance.[16] The detailed lists of transfers from London and from other centres to Avignon contained in Renouard's standard work on the subject of Papal foreign financial transactions give an idea of remarkable extent of these operations.[17]

Part of the funds received by the Papal Chamber in Avignon or in Rome were used for international purposes, such as covering the expenses of Papal Nuncios, subsidising crusades, supporting Christian colonies in the Near East, or financing princes engaged in wars approved by the Pope. Such transactions, too, were carried out by Italian bankers, so that the international movements of funds in connection with the Papal financial transactions and the operations in bills resulting from them were by no means unilateral.

(12) HOW ANTI-USURY LAWS HELPED
FOREIGN EXCHANGE

An even more effective if unintentional way in which the Church contributed to the development of the Foreign Exchange market was through the adoption of strict rules against lending money on interest. There was a ban on the discounting of domestic bills and on other forms of credit on which interest was charged. Disregard of the anti-usury law was liable to entail the penalty of excommunication. The ban contained, however, a major loophole. Under a rule, endorsed by most if not all scholastic writers, it was permissible to buy and sell bills issued in terms of a foreign currency and payable in a foreign country. This made it possible to disguise a domestic credit transaction in the form of a Foreign Exchange transaction.

In order to provide facilities for such operations fairs were specially organised abroad towards the end of the 15th century. They were held at regular intervals – usually four times a year – largely for the purpose of being able to issue bills payable there. For a long time the Champagne fairs served that purpose. Much later, the banking community of Genoa organised the fairs of Besançon and the banking community of Florence organised the fairs of Lyons mainly for the purpose of providing opportunities for credit transactions which were technically legitimate because interest was concealed in the form of exchange rates.

(13) HOW ANTI-USURY LAW HINDERED
FOREIGN EXCHANGE

In spite of the many loopholes in the anti-usury laws, their severity did often hinder Foreign Exchange. As is usually the case, while they were unable to prevent the types of deals against which they were directed, they handicapped legitimate business. They certainly discouraged the development of Forward Exchange – apart from those referred to above – because of the views the Church took of transactions involving no exchange risk.

Foreign Exchange was emphatically outlawed under Mohammedan law which was even more severe than the Christian anti-usury laws. Under Mohammedan law coins of the same metal were not allowed to be exchanged except on the basis of strict equivalence. Any discrepancy between value given and received

70   MEDIEVAL PERIOD

was condemned as usury. To quote the relevant text: 'The Messenger of Allah said: Sell not gold for gold except in equal quantity . . . nor silver for silver except in equal quantity . . . nor sell anything present for that which is absent.'[18] The exchange of gold for silver was lawful, but only if the delivery of both was effected on the spot.[19] Compared with these laws of Draconian severity the anti-usury laws in the Western world were positively mild.

(14) FICTITIOUS *v.* GENUINE BILLS

The procedure followed by those wishing to evade anti-usury laws was that the borrower sold the lender a bill drawn on a fair to be held in a foreign centre and issued in terms of a foreign currency. Contrary to modern practice, these bills were not discounted, but the exchange rate at which the bankers bought them allowed for the interest involved. Of course, in many instances the sale of the bill genuinely anticipated the collection of the proceeds of goods to be sold at that fair, or at any rate in the country where it was held. But a large proportion of bills was not connected with any international goods transactions. It was tacitly understood between the two parties that the bill would not be met on maturity. The dishonoured bill was protested as a matter of form and was returned to its place of issue. The debtor was then under obligation to repay its amount at the current rate of the re-change, or at a rate agreed in advance, which allowed to the creditor a high interest disguised in the form of exchange difference. Repayment was usually guaranteed, or the creditor received adequate security. Moreover, since the text of bills began with the sentence '*Al nome di Dio*', default on them was looked upon as blasphemy.

The popularisation of the use of foreign bills was very fortunate from the point of view of economic progress during the last three centuries of the Middle Ages. Trade was expanding, but until the discovery of America the output of monetary metals was unable to keep pace with growing requirements. Moreover, the Eastward flow of gold and silver in payment for the import of oriental luxuries continued during a great part of the Medieval Period. Thanks to the increasing use of bills for financing trade, the resulting scarcity of money which would have checked progress was mitigated to some extent. The facilities of the Foreign Exchange markets during the 13th, 14th and 15th centuries rendered, therefore, a great service to the cause of progress.

(15) THE SYSTEM THAT EMERGED DURING THE
13th CENTURY

The Foreign Exchange system that developed during the 13th century remained essentially unchanged until the French Revolution. It was first and foremost a market in bills, though the market in coins survived. The two types of Foreign Exchange markets were largely interrelated, even though transactions in coins and bills of exchange were not necessarily conducted by the same people.

In addition to the active markets operating during the quarterly fairs, there were also permanent markets operating all the year round in important commercial centres in Italy, France, the Low Countries, Spain and England, where a large proportion of the bills originated or came to be paid.

Most bills drawn on foreign centres were not issued in the currencies of their countries of origin, because under the anti-usury laws it was essential to issue them in terms of a foreign currency. Buyers of such bills sold against payment in terms of their national currencies dispatched them to their agents at the fairs or in the centres where they were payable. The proceeds were either repatriated in the form of goods or of specie, or they were applied for buying a 're-change' bill on the centre where the bills had originated, issued in terms of that centre's currency. On many occasions the re-change was effected through the intermediary of a third centre. Very often the transaction was carried forward with the aid of bills maturing at later dates.

Bills were not necessarily payable in terms of the paying centre's currency. Very often they were issued in a third currency, or in fictitious units. For instance, bills drawn on the Champagne fair could be issued not only in Paris *deniers* but also in other currencies, or in a fictitious unit, the *écu de marc*. Or in Genoa during the 15th century a florin of account equivalent to 25 *soldi* was introduced. owing to the almost uninterrupted appreciation of the actual gold florin. Bills issued in such fictitious units were usually paid by means of a book transfer in terms of that unit. Only the balance of the transactions was paid in an existing currency at the current exchange rate of that currency in terms of the fictitious unit.

Very often triangular transactions were more profitable than direct transactions. The Datini archives contain evidence showing that remittances from Venice to Bruges were often effected *via* Barcelona.[20]

(16) THE PRINCIPAL MARKETS

Foreign Exchange markets developed during the 13th century in the Italian cities – mainly in Venice, Genoa, Florence, Lucca, Milan, Bologna, Siena and Rome. Markets in other parts of Europe were also run almost entirely by Italian merchant-bankers. Such Italian-controlled markets existed in the centres of the great fairs – the Champagne centres (Bar, Lagny and Troyes), Lyons, Besançon, Paris, Avignon and Rouen in France, Seville and Valladolid in Spain – and also in Bruges (gradually replaced by Antwerp towards the end of the 15th century), London, and Constantinople until its capture by the Turks. London lagged behind other important Western European financial centres. The development of Foreign Exchange business in the Hanseatic cities, advanced as they were in many other respects, was even slower, though there is some evidence of bill transactions between Danzig, Cologne and Nuremberg during the 15th century.[21] The Foreign Exchange markets in Bruges and London were created entirely by Italian merchant-bankers; Flemish and English bankers did not begin to take a really active part until the 16th century.

Some of the Foreign Exchange markets were concentrated in certain streets, such as Lombard Street in London, or the Exchange Street in Kyoto, Japan,[22] or on bridges such as the Rialto in Venice (which was originally called *Ponte della Moneta*), or the *Pont du Change* in Paris. In many instances Foreign Exchange business was transacted in a building used especially for that purpose. There was a *Loggia di Cambio* in Bologna and other cities. This was the origin of most continental *bourses*. During the Middle Ages, and for a long time after, transactions in securities were negligible, and foreign bills constituted the object of most of the activity in the early *bourses*. This tradition has survived in France in the name of stockbrokers who are still called *agents de change*, even though they have long ceased to deal in Foreign Exchange. A certain amount of Foreign Exchange business continues to be transacted by bankers even in our days in the special section of the Paris *bourse* and of other continental *bourses*. In addition to Foreign Exchange, the *bourses* played an important part also in loan and credit transactions, just like in ancient Athens.

For a long time there was no dividing line between merchants and bankers, because the former had to transact a great deal of Foreign Exchange in connection with their commercial business, and the latter were actively engaged in import and export trade. Most early banks in Western Europe owed their origins to Foreign Exchange dealings. The change of goldsmiths into bankers in England is a much later development; it dates from the 17th century.

(17) THE RÔLE OF FAIRS

Bills matured at specific fairs, or at sight or so many days after sight, or at 'usance' which meant a period varying according to the distance between the place of their issue and that of their payment. During the 15th century the usance was one month between London and Flanders, two months between London and Hamburg and three months in relation to the Italian cities. Some bills were payable at half usance or at double usance. The period of usance tended slowly to become shorter with the improvement of communications, though its length was partly due, not to the time required for the bill to reach its destination, but to the combination of a credit transaction with a transfer transaction.

There was always an active turnover in bills maturing at fairs, so that buyers and sellers could easily find counterparts. Some bills matured at the next fair but one, or even at the third or fourth fair. A large and increasing proportion of bills had, however, no connection with fairs. For instance, bills connected with English wool exports were usually payable at the staples a certain number of weeks or months after their date of issue, determined by custom.

During the course of fairs themselves many commercial and financial transactions were concluded which originated further bills. Towards the close of each fair a day was set aside for clearing the various claims and counter-claims arising from the purchase and sale of bills or from other transactions debited or credited to the accounts of the participants.

Business in bills was usually transacted through the intermediary of brokers who charged a commission based on a fixed tariff. There was a great deal of arbitrage between the various markets. A regular service of fast couriers was maintained by banks between the financial centres with the object of ascertaining exchange rates, or of securing early information on changes in coinages or other events that were liable to affect the exchanges. They also conveyed the bills to their place of destination. Many banks kept balances with their branches or correspondents in foreign centres, and a large proportion of the turnover in the Foreign Exchange markets aimed at increasing or reducing such balances.

(18) FINANCING GOVERNMENTS BY MEANS OF BILLS

Invisible trade was also financed largely with the aid of bills. Apart from the transfer of Papal collections referred to above, there were also political payments such as subsidies to foreign princes or others, transfers of funds needed for military expenditure, etc. Wars waged abroad were largely financed by means of bill transactions. Ehrenberg quotes a letter of a Sienese trading company to their agents at the Champagne fair informing them that they had sold bills in Siena for the next fair as a means of raising money for prosecuting the war against Florence.[23]

All Foreign Exchange markets depended for their turnover largely on various types of fictitious bills. At times the volume of such business was much larger than that of the genuine business. According to de Roover, the books of medieval merchants show many more bills than commercial transactions. The borderline between genuine and fictitious was not very distinct, but in many instances the fictitious character of the transactions was quite obvious.

By the close of the 15th century, and even much earlier, Europe and the Mediterranean regions of Asia and Africa possessed a well-developed Foreign Exchange system. There were also markets in India, China and Japan. Even though the system did not work smoothly and was liable to break down, its development greatly assisted economic progress. It provided a mechanism that was available after the end of the Medieval Period, through which to finance the distribution of the large influx of precious metals to Spain after the discovery of America.

NOTES TO CHAPTER SEVEN

1. Steven Runciman, *Byzantine Trade and Industry*, Cambridge Economic History, vol. ii, pp. 115–16.
2. Earl J. Hamilton, *Money Prices and Wages in Valencia, Aragon and Navarre, 1351–1500* (Cambridge, Mass., 1936), p. 7.
3. Hamilton, *op. cit.*, pp. 82, 119–20, 137.
4. Samuel Ricard, *Traité général du commerce* (Amsterdam, 1700), p. 89.
5. Léopold Delisle, *Mémoire sur les opérations financières des templiers*, Académie des Inscriptions et Belles-Lettres, vol. 333 (Paris, 1888), p. 20.

6. André-E. Sayous, 'Les Mandats de Saint Louis sur son trésor et le mouvement international des capitaux pendant la septième croisade, *1248–1254'*, *Revue Historique*, vol. 167, 1936, p. 266.
7. Sayous, *op. cit.*, p. 284.
8. Hans Prutz, *Kulturgeschichte der Kreutzzüge* (Berlin, 1883), p. 366.
9. Raymond de Roover, *L'Évolution de la lettre de change, XIVe–XVIIIe siècle* (Paris, 1953), p. 182.
10. de Roover, *op. cit.* p. 27.
11. E. L. Jäger, *Der Traktat des Lucas Paccioli von 1494 über den Wechsel* (Stuttgart, 1878), p. 9.
12. Wilhelm Endemann, *Studien in der romanisch-kanonistischen Wirtschafts- und Rechtslehre bis gegen Ende des 17. Jahrhunderts* (Berlin, 1874), p. 76.
13. Yves Renouard, *Les Relations des papes d'Avignon et des compagnies commerciales et bancaires de 1316 à 1378* (Paris, 1941), p. 555.
14. Max Neumann, *Geschichte des Wechsels im Hansagebiet bis zum 17. Jahrhundert* (Erlangen, 1863), p. 30.
15. Renouard, *op. cit.* p. 130.
16. Paul Einzig, *A Dynamic Theory of Forward Exchange* (London, 1961), p. 1.
17. Renouard, *op. cit.* pp. 131–4.
18. Anwar Iqbal Qureshi, *Islam and the Theory of Interest* (Lahore, 1945), p. 69.
19. Qureshi, *op. cit.* p. 70.
20. Raymond de Roover, *Money, Banking and Credit in Medieval Bruges* (Cambridge, Mass., 1948), p. 66.
21. Neumann, *op. cit.* pp. 176–7.
22. Yosoburo Takekoshi, *The Economic Aspects of the History of the Civilization of Japan* (London, 1930), p. 28.
23. Richard Ehrenberg, *Capital and Finance in the Age of the Renaissance* (London, 1928), p. 57.

D

CHAPTER EIGHT

Medieval Exchange Rates and Trends

(1) RATES BETWEEN COINS

ALTHOUGH in the Middle Ages quotations of exchange rates were encountered much more frequently in literature, in public discussions or correspondence between business houses than during the Ancient Period, not nearly enough has been done to compile from business archives and other sources any continuous series that could be of use for analysing trends. Even de Roover, a very thorough student of the Medieval Period, complained that there were almost no statistical data available on Medieval exchange rates.[1] Moreover, in many instances it was not clear whether the rates quoted referred to fictitious units or actual currencies.

During the early Medieval Period rates between coins must have been the only exchange rates. Markets in bills of exchange did not develop till later, and notarial exchange contracts had no market. Such mail transfers as may have occurred during the Dark Ages must have been too few and far between to give rise to regular quotations. It was not until a fairly advanced phase of the Middle Ages – possibly from the 13th or 14th century – that exchange contract rates and bill rates were encountered regularly.

Exchange rates between coins must have been quoted regularly in the Byzantine Empire throughout the Medieval Period. As we saw in the last chapter, in Constantinople and a number of other big markets in Europe and the East there was an active turnover in foreign coins. The prices at which they changed hands must have been fairly representative as an indication of supply-demand relationship, because competition among rival money-changers must have been very keen in markets where there was no tariff of officially fixed rates.

(2) DISCREPANCIES BETWEEN RATES FOR BILLS AND COINS

After the development of an active market in foreign bills two sets of exchange quotations came to exist side by side in each

important financial centre – rates for coins and for bills. Even
if bills were payable in the actual coins in use, the rates were
hardly ever identical. There was usually a discrepancy between
the price of, say, English coins in terms of florins in London or
Florence on the one hand and the bill on Florence quoted in
London or the bill on London quoted in Florence on the other. In
this respect the position was similar to that prevailing in our days
when there are usually different quotations for foreign bank-notes
and for transfers, even if this difference is moderate in normal
conditions. In the old days discrepancies were apt to be wider
because, apart from many other reasons, transactions in coins
were cash transactions, entailing loss of interest for a relatively
brief period only, while exchange rates of bills usually included
interest for longer periods.

There were also different rates quoted according to the borrower's standing. This practice continued right into the 19th
century. So long as interest had to be included in the exchange
rate it was not possible to discriminate between good and bad
names otherwise than by quoting different exchange rates for
their bills. There was, so to say, one exchange rate for the rich
and another exchange rate for the poor.

The importance of the exchange rates of bills gradually overshadowed that of coins, even though the latter basically influenced
the former, since they tended to fluctuate around the approximate
mint parities of the time, within the approximate specie points
of the time. Uncertainty of specie points was particularly marked
when payment was due in current coins, since they were usually
a mixed lot. Recipients had to expect to receive a fair average
assortment that necessarily included worn coins, even if clipped
and counterfeit coins were rejected. Occasionally several exchange
rates were quoted, according to the proportion of certain types
of coins to be included in the payment.

The practice of quoting rates for bills payable at fairs in terms
of fictitious units, to be dealt with below, reduced the relative
importance of exchange rates between coins. They only played
a direct part when payment had to be made in actual coins
instead of effecting transfers of money by means of book entries
in terms of the fictitious unit. But dealers in bills payable in
fictitious units had to bear in mind the exchange rate between
the fictitious unit and the local coinage.

The rates for foreign bills were naturally influenced by the length of their maturity. But there were apt to be marked discrepancies in addition to those justified on that ground. Apart from considerations of loss of interest, the conveyance of bills to their destination took less time than that of coins, and the cost of transport was also lower. The supply-demand position necessarily affected the discrepancy. If, for instance, the supply of English coins in Bruges exceeded demand for them, buyers would only be prepared to pay a price that allowed for the cost of transporting these coins to London where they could be used for making payments there, or for accumulating balances to be used for making payments eventually. If money was needed urgently for making payments in London, Bruges merchant bankers were willing to pay more for a sight bill than for coins, precisely because it was possible to remit the money more speedily by means of bills. On the other hand, if the supply of English coins in Bruges fell short of demand it was liable to go to a premium against sight bills on London, because of the delay involved in sending the bills to London and shipping the proceeds in specie to Bruges.

(3) FIXING EXCHANGE RATES AT FAIRS

We have a number of detailed accounts of the way in which exchange rates were quoted at some of the fairs. There was a system of fixing of exchange rates by a representative body of merchant bankers. At the Genoa Fairs, for instance, on the third day of each fair the exchange rates were determined by the bankers. All brokers, through whose intermediary bills were bought and sold, had to leave the room where the 'fixing' took place, and only bankers of recognised standing were allowed to remain. Each of them suggested an exchange rate and eventually the rate which received the largest number of votes, and at least half of the total votes, was adopted.[2]

At the Lyons fairs there were first separate meetings of the Florence, Genoa and Lucca bankers, and it was the average of the rates suggested by the three groups that became the 'official' rate.[3] Crude as this method may appear, it commanded much confidence, and prior to the fixing a large proportion of the business transactions was concluded on the basis of the rates, as yet unknown, which were about to be fixed. The high standing of the participants in this exercise inspired confidence in their good faith.

They were relied upon not to submit biased or frivolous rates.

In Genoa exchange rates were fixed also in between fairs. As soon as the banker returned from the latest fair a committee of six, appointed by the Senate, fixed the rate for bills maturing at the next fair.[4]

(4) ATTITUDE OF THE CHURCH TOWARDS EXCHANGE RATES

The rates fixed at fairs were not official in the sense of being compulsory; they only served for guidance. A list of them was immediately dispatched to other centres for the information of branches and correspondents. Merchants and bankers were at liberty to deal on the basis of other rates, and indeed with the ever-changing supply-demand position the official rates were often superseded almost immediately. But if dealers departed too far from the official rates they exposed themselves to investigation by the Church authorities, in order to ascertain whether the rates were usurious.[5]

It was an acceptable defence that the rates, though not identical with the official rates, were the freely negotiated current market rates. We shall see in the next chapter that scholastic writers, expressing the views of the Church, believed in the fairness of exchange rates arrived at in the open market, as these rates were looked upon as representing the 'common estimation' of the value of one currency in terms of another. In theory it was therefore advisable to transact exchanges at rates reasonably near the official rates, unless some new development or some special consideration such as speculative anticipation of a change obviously justified a departure from them. Indeed, the main reason for the adoption of the whole system of fixing exchange rates was presumably to satisfy the Church that the rates were in accordance with the requirements of its anti-usury laws.

In addition to determining the exchange rates for current transactions, the fair committees also determined the rates for bills maturing at the next fair. Balances which remained outstanding after the claims and counterclaims in a particular currency had been offset against each other at the end of each fair were often carried forward in the form of bills maturing at the next fair. According to Usher, the exchange rates for such deferred transactions included interest that was usually of the order of 8 to 12 per cent per annum.[6]

(5) ARTIFICIAL MANIPULATIONS OF EXCHANGE RATES

There were very frequent allegations of artificial manipulations of exchange rates by interested parties. It was, for instance, a perennial complaint in medieval England that Florentine bankers or Flemish merchants were supposed to keep sterling at an artificially unfavourable rate to the detriment of English wool exporters. The fact that on one occasion during the 14th century the florin rate remained rigidly stable at 3 shillings for five years indicated its artificial character.[7] The setting up of the staple at Calais was decided upon mainly on the ground that as a result of the arrangement the exchange took place on a territory under the control of the King of England who had there the power to protect sterling against hostile influences. There was much written about speculative activity of skilful and sinister syndicates which were supposed to influence exchange rates to their advantage by spreading false rumours or by other methods.

(6) CHANGING GOLD-SILVER RATIO

Exchange rates were largely affected by changing relationship between the value of gold and silver and by changes in the respective metallic contents of coins. Most of these latter changes were in a downward direction, though in many instances the metallic value of coins was raised at any rate temporarily. The relative value of gold to silver coins, too, was subject to considerable changes. Although silver was the principal monetary metal most of the time, in most countries in Europe bimetallism of varying form and degree was in operation over prolonged periods.

Whenever and wherever gold and silver coins that were in circulation had a fixed ratio in relation to each other in law or in practice, this provided opportunity for profitable operations by arbitrageurs each time that ratio differed from the market ratio or from the official ratio abroad. Such a situation occurred frequently enough. Exchange dealers had to be constantly on the look-out for discrepancies that developed or were liable to develop between the ratios in various countries.

(7) SECULAR EXCHANGE DEPRECIATION

It was most important to be informed about changes and prospective changes in the gold or silver content of coins. The history of medieval exchange trends is a history of secular depreciation caused by cuts in metal contents of coins, relieved from time to time by periods of stability and by temporary appreciations. Even the best currencies provided no exception from this rule in the long run. The *bezant* began to depreciate in the 12th century, at first slowly and later at a more rapid pace. Venetian *denars* at the end of the 12th century were only worth about a quarter of Charlemagne's *denarius* on which they were originally based. The Genoese pound, too, took its turn in the secular downward trend. While the Florentine gold florin which was for a long time the byword of stability maintained its weight and fineness throughout the Middle Ages, its value in terms of *soldi* rose from 20 in 1252 to 111 in 1480.

In England debasements were relatively few and far between before Henry VIII, thanks largely to the early development of Parliamentary control over finances. Although changing the coinage was an ancient royal prerogative, again and again kings of England had to give an undertaking to refrain from exercising it, in return for granting of supplies by Parliament which was made conditional on that promise. Even before the advent of Parliament, despotic monarchs such as William the Conqueror (1066–87) promised to his feudal council to refrain from exercising his prerogative in respect of the debasement of coinage – profits which had formed an important part of the revenue of the Duchy of Normandy – in return for the imposition of the hearth tax. Although such promises were often dishonoured, the fact that Parliament had the control of supply grants did restrain most English monarchs from abusing their prerogative to anything like the extent to which it was regularly abused in France, Spain and Germany – to mention only those countries.

In many of the splinter States of Germany, and also in some of the more important States, devaluation through calling in the coins and re-issuing them with a reduced metallic content formed a regular revenue of the rulers and was repeated every year during a great part of the 12th century. In some countries, such as Bohemia and Silesia, this was done in some instances several times in a single year.[8] This process of depreciation continued during the 13th and 14th centuries, relieved by temporary recoveries. In 1358 Archduke Rudolf IV of Austria came to an understanding with his Estates to refrain from tampering with the currency in return for a 10 per cent duty on all drinks.[9] The silver mark of

Cologne was worth 55 *groschen* in 1226 and 91 in 1350, declining to 70 in 1378 and rising to over 100 by 1459.[10]

The Spanish kingdoms of Aragon, Castile and Valencia experienced frequent and extensive debasements. Henry II of Castile (1369–79) reduced the silver content of the *real* to a fraction of its original content. Henry III (1390–1406) restored the coinage to the tale and standard that prevailed before Henry II, but under his successors the depreciation resumed its course and continued during the greater part of the 15th century. It was not until the Ordinance of Medina del Campo, issued in 1497 under Ferdinand and Isabella (1475–1516), that the monetary chaos was brought to an end.[11]

In France one of the reasons why Louis IX (1226–70) earned his claim for being known in history as Saint Louis was that he maintained a relatively sound currency. His son and immediate successor, Philip the Bold (1270–85), did not dare to depart unduly from the high standard established by his father. On the other hand, Philip the Fair (1285–1314) resorted to frequent changes in the value of the coins. Between 1295 and 1305 he reduced the value of the currency by some 79 per cent, but in the following eight years he carried out a number of revaluations, so that at the end of his reign the value of the coins was substantially the same as in 1295.[12] It was mainly these manipulations that inspired the criticisms of Oresme, in his *Tractatus Monetarium*, on whose advice Charles V (1364–80) endeavoured to emulate Louis IX in pursuing a sound policy.

(8) SPECULATIVE ANTICIPATIONS OF CHANGES

The records of most other continental countries show similar trends. Having regard to the frequency of debasements and devaluations during the Middle Ages, it is only natural that speculative anticipation of such events should have frequently disturbed the Foreign Exchange markets and influenced exchange rates to a considerable extent. The degree of uncertainty was high during most of the time – possibly even higher than in modern periods when exchanges came from time to time under the influence of devaluation or revaluation rumours. The slowness with which news of changes travelled in those days provided ample scope for uncontradicted false reports. The time lag between the acquisition of bills and the collection of their proceeds was very long, and facilities for covering exchange risks were far from adequate.

Apart altogether from official changes in mint parities, exchanges were also liable to be affected by progressive deterioration of the coinage through the widespread practice of counterfeiting and clipping, in addition to normal wear and the disappearance of full-weight coins. Even though the direct effect of these factors affected the value of coins only, it affected indirectly bill rates, too, by causing a feeling of distrust in the value of currencies in which the bills were ultimately payable.

(9) DEALING IN TERMS OF FICTITIOUS UNITS

It was mainly in order to escape the effects of incessant changes in the value of coins on bill rates that merchants adopted the device of issuing bills in terms of some fictitious unit of stable value. This practice was largely confined to bills drawn on fairs. As a result, other bills, drawn in actual currencies, were usually quoted at a discount against fictitious units, and they fluctuated more widely. The relative stability of exchange rates in terms of fictitious units was in sharp contrast with the instability of such units in terms of the actual currencies of the countries concerned.

Between the middle of the 13th century and the end of the 15th century the Genoese silver currency depreciated to one-sixth of its value, the Florentine silver currency to one-seventh of its value, but the fictitious gold units in which their Foreign Exchange transactions were conducted retained the weight and fineness of the metal they were supposed to represent. Only on rare occasions did actual currencies remain stable over prolonged periods. For instance, the Milanese florin remained stable from 1340 till the end of the 14th century, the Venice gold *ducat* during the second half of the 15th century. English coins remained more stable than most continental coins, owing to the absence of debasements or devaluations over long periods as pointed out above. Their value was affected, however, by their erosion.

A very large proportion of international payments were transacted in terms of fictitious units. In many instances the value of the fictitious units was officially fixed in terms of the national currency and this official rate was adjusted from time to time to the market rate. Whenever the official rate of a fictitious unit became divorced from reality, 'black market' rates developed.

D 2

(10) INCLUSION OF INTEREST CHARGES

In addition to the fluctuations due to the changing metallic contents of the coins, the exchange value of bills was affected by a
set of influences which did not operate in exchange rates between
coins. Because of the inclusion of interest charges in exchange
rates, the latter were affected not only by the length of their
maturity but also by the level at which interest rates would have
been quoted if it had been allowed to quote them openly. Tight
or easy conditions of money supply was liable to affect exchange
rates not only through affecting the amount of interest included
in exchange rates but also through affecting supply and demand
in foreign bills. More will be said about this in the next chapter.

The exchange value of a bill in terms of the creditor's currency
against the debtor country's currency tended to be lower in the
debtor centre than in the creditor centre, precisely because the
exchange rate included interest charge. The creditor could not
have earned interest on his money unless he had been able to
effect the re-change at a more favourable exchange rate than the
one at which he originally bought the bill from his debtor. Equilibrium rate was not mint parity, but mint parity plus or minus
the prevailing interest rate, in the same way as in modern conditions equilibrium rate of Forward Exchanges is not parity with
spot rate but spot rate plus or minus interest differential. The
discrepancy had to be wide enough to cover not only the interest
but also the risk of a change in the exchange rate to the detriment
of the creditor that was liable to occur between the moment he
bought the bill and the moment he was able to complete the
re-change. It tended to be wider for long maturities than for short
maturities, not only because more interest was included but also
because the risk of an adverse change was greater.

Since the Middle Ages, and for a long time after, exchange
rates roughly allowed for interest charges, for all practical purposes during that period they played a part not dissimilar to that
of the modern forward rates. Because the separate existence of
the interest element in the transactions had to be concealed, the
practice of discounting bills was not adopted until the 17th
century in Protestant countries and much later in Catholic
countries. Today when business is transacted in foreign bills
exchange rate and the discount to be added to or deducted from
the amount are treated apart. But during the Middle Ages interest

charges were no more separated from exchange rates than they are today in respect of forward rates. And even when it became possible to discount bills, this new practice remained confined to inland bills. The old practice continued to be applied for foreign bills for centuries right to the 19th century.

(11) PREDICTABLE FLUCTUATIONS

As a result of this discrepancy – to which we propose to return in the next chapter – bankers made a profit on their Foreign Exchange transactions, unless it was wiped out by an adverse movement in the exchange rate. The chance of increasing their profit in case of a favourable movement in the exchange rate tended to balance this risk. Indeed, their superior knowledge of seasonal and other predictable influences loaded the dice in their favour, though they were of course exposed to unpredictable events.

Judging by the chart published by de Roover covering the fluctuation of the Bruges-London exchange rate between 1436 and 1439, there was a sharp decline of the *écu* in the summer in 1436, 1438 and 1439.[13] Fifteenth century dealers in Foreign Exchange, like their modern successors, must have felt reasonably safe in relying on the recurrence of such seasonal movements. There were also predictable fluctuations due to temporary local influences such as the imminent departure of ships which meant an increase in the advance sales of bills representing the proceeds of the goods. Experienced merchants, anticipating the nature and extent of such tendencies, made their arrangements in good time.

(12) UNPREDICTABLE EXCHANGE MOVEMENTS

Exceptional factors were liable to upset the calculations even of experienced dealers. They had to be on the look-out for economic, political, etc. developments liable to affect exchange rates. Medieval business correspondence is full of information of that nature. For instance, a letter written by a Siena merchant from Troyes to Lombardy in 1265 warned his friend to expect a depreciation of the French exchange in Italy in consequence of a military expedition to be undertaken by Charles of Anjou.[14] Major credit operations by princes were liable to affect exchange rates – favourably when the credit was granted, adversely when it had to be repaid or renewed. Advance information about any such operations and, above all, about impending changes in coinages, was useful to enable bankers and merchants to anticipate the effect on exchange rates.

In view of the possibility that exchange rates might be affected by unpredictable influences, cautious merchants endeavoured to make sure of their profits on commercial transactions by covering the exchange risk on goods they dispatched to their agents abroad, the more so if the goods were not sold immediately. This was one of the reasons why merchant-bankers sold in advance the bills representing the proceeds of their exports, apart altogether from any need for financing the transaction. Otherwise they would have had no means of being certain of their profit until the goods were actually sold and the proceeds were actually exchanged for their own currency.

Bankers endeavoured in many instances to safeguard themselves against exchange risk by selling in advance the proceeds of the bills they had bought, to avoid having to carry 'open positions' until the re-change had been effected. Such transactions may be regarded as the primitive forerunners of modern Forward Exchange. The price of the re-change bills was in some instances fixed in advance so that bankers and merchants knew in advance how they stood.

Such prudent covering of the exchange risk had to be concealed in those days, because under the ban on usury a profit on the purchase of bills was only justified on the ground of the exchange risk involved. Transactions which involved no such risk were viewed by the Church as interest-bearing loans pure and simple.

(13) LOANS DISGUISED AS SPECULATIVE TRANSACTIONS

Non-commercial exchange transactions constituted an important source of activity in the Foreign Exchange markets during the late Middle Ages. Of outstanding importance among them were those between Florence and Venice. In outward form these transactions were supposed to be speculative. Actually they concealed interest on loans or deposits. In normal conditions the Venetian pound commanded a higher value in Venice than in Florence because the former was a borrower while the latter a lender. This meant that the Florentine purchaser of a bill on Venice in Florence was able to make a profit, provided that during the period between the issue of the bills and its maturity the exchange rate between the florin and the *ducat* did not go against them to such an extent as to wipe out the discrepancy. According to medieval writers describing this practice, there was in fact a regular profit on these operations.

Actually the practice constituted a pretext for paying interest in disguise both on commercial credits and on deposits. Merchants or private individuals in Florence, having liquid funds at their disposal, deposited them with banking houses on the understanding that the latter would use them for speculation in Venetian exchange on their own account. Alternatively, the banks carried out such operations on account of the owners of the funds. In either case, judging by documentary evidence dating from 1415, the owner of the fund received between 7 and 8 per cent per annum. As de Roover remarked, these dealings in Venetian exchange only concealed the true character of interest-bearing loans and were designed to placate theologians.[15] To us it may seem strange that straightforward commercial transactions had to be disguised as speculative transactions in order to be made acceptable to the Church authorities. But that was in accordance with the spirit of the times.

Speculation in exchanges was not confined to professionals. Owners of funds had the means of taking a hand in such operations and did so on a number of known occasions, at a time when gambling facilities in stocks and shares were non-existent. Speculative activity was bound to influence exchange rates, especially when prohibition of specie movements made normal specie points inoperative as the cost of illicit specie exports and the risk involved in smuggling specie made operations unprofitable unless discrepancies were particularly wide.

(14) 'CERTAIN' AND 'UNCERTAIN' QUOTATIONS

A very large proportion of the space in contemporary practical guides to operations in exchanges, and of books on commercial arithmetic which dealt with Foreign Exchanges, was devoted to the method of quoting foreign currencies. Writers dwelt at considerable length on the difference between 'certain' and 'uncertain' quotation – that is, whether it was the unit of the domestic currency that was quoted in terms of variable amounts of foreign currency, or the unit of the latter that was quoted in terms of variable amounts of domestic currency. The subject was of a minor matter of simple arithmetic, but it was looked upon as a matter of first-rate importance. We shall return to it when dealing with its theoretical aspects in the next chapter.

NOTES TO CHAPTER EIGHT

1. Raymond de Roover, *Money, Banking and Credit in Medieval Bruges* (Cambridge, Mass., 1948), p. 58.
2. Richard Ehrenberg, *Das Zeitalter der Fugger* (Jena, 1896), vol. ii, pp. 234–5.
3. Henri Lapeyre, *Une Famille de marchands, les Ruiz* (Paris, 1955), p. 285.
4. Wilhelm Endemann, *Studien in der romanisch-kanonistischen Wirtschafts- und Rechtslehre bis gegen Ende des 17. Jahrhunderts* (Berlin, 1874), pp. 218–19.
5. Endemann, *op. cit.* p. 219.
6. A. P. Usher, *The Early History of Deposit Banking in Mediterranean Europe* (Cambridge, Mass., 1943), p. 123.
7. Sir John Craig, *The Mint* (Cambridge, 1953), p. 63.
8. Richard Gaettens, *Inflationen* (Munich, 1955), p. 50.
9. Gaettens, *op. cit.* p. 40.
10. W. A. Shaw, *The History of Currency, 1252 to 1894* (London, 1895), p. 30.
11. Shaw, *op. cit.* pp. 324, 328.
12. René Sédillot, *Le Franc. Histoire d'une monnaie* (Paris, 1953), p. 67.
13. de Roover, *op. cit.* p. 64.
14. Robert S. Lopez, *The Trade of Medieval Europe.* Cambridge Economic History (Cambridge, 1952), vol. ii, p. 342.
15. Raymond de Roover, *Cambium ad Venetias – Contribution to the History of Foreign Exchange.* Studi in onore di Armando Sapori (Milan, 1957), pp. 635–40.

CHAPTER NINE

Medieval Foreign Exchange Theory

(1) CONTRIBUTIONS BY SCHOLASTIC WRITERS

PROGRESS of Foreign Exchange theory during the advanced Middle Ages did not keep pace with that of the evolution of the Foreign Exchange system itself. It is true, there was no longer any lack of interest in broader aspects of Foreign Exchanges. While in Greek and Roman literature we can find only very occasional references to broader Foreign Exchange problems, medieval literature from the 13th century onwards abounds in material on that subject. But the overwhelming majority of such material is concerned exclusively with the ethics of Foreign Exchange operations, viewed from the angle of the Church laws against usury, which term was synonymous with charging interest at no matter what rate.

In spite of their one-sided character and self-imposed limitations, the contributions of scholastic literature towards the progress of Foreign Exchange theory must not be underrated. We must bear in mind that, had it not been for the discussion of the subject from the point of view of the anti-usury doctrine, its other aspects might have received even less attention. As it was, in between long moral arguments, futile and irrelevant as they may have been both from a practical angle and from the point of view of Foreign Exchange theory, some interesting factual material was provided, and it is at times possible to deduct from the arguments the existence of some theoretical notions – even though some of these were wholly or largely misconceived.

(2) THE CHURCH FAVOURED GENUINE COMMERCIAL BILLS

It is very easy to point out inconsistencies between the writings of various scholastic writers, and indeed between writings of the same writer, or to criticise them for their inability to realise or admit openly that anything short of a complete ban on exchange transactions was bound to leave wide loopholes through which the anti-usury law could be evaded with impunity. To understand the attitude of ecclesiastic writers, we must bear in mind the conflicting considerations of trying to safeguard the defenceless from exploitation and ruin by usurers and, at the same time, abstaining from blocking necessary and essential Foreign Exchange business. All but the most rigid dogmatists felt impelled to try to reconcile these requirements by turning a blind eye towards the true character of some practices.

Many scholastic writers were fully aware of the great advantages of using bills for legitimate commercial purposes and wrote about them in extravagant terms. Such bills were compared by several of them to water on which ships carry goods, without which there could be no trade. Writing in 1494, Luca Paccioli voiced an oft-repeated scholastic view in declaring that if bills of exchange were abolished it would destroy the foundations of commercial structure, the community could not be maintained and mankind could not be fed.[1] It is an open question whether he and other scholastic writers expressing identical views simply meant that the use of bills encouraged international trade by providing a device that is more convenient than the cumbersome and costly device of specie movements, or whether they realised the broader advantages of monetary expansion, made possible by the use of bills, on the whole economy during a period when inadequacy of the supply of monetary metals was the chief obstacle to progress.

(3) FICTITIOUS BILLS CONDEMNED

In sharp contrast to the emphatic approval of genuine bills (*cambio reale*) by most scholastic writers, fictitious bills drawn specially for the purpose of evading the anti-usury laws were frequently and emphatically condemned by all scholastic writers. Such bills were called 'dry exchange' (*cambio sicco*) or 'fictitious exchange' (*cambio fittito*). The difference between the two is defined in various ways, but it is not important, seeing that both were equally condemned. It was often difficult if not impossible, however, to ascertain the borderline between them and genuine commercial bills, notwithstanding the efforts of many generations of 'Doctors' to define it.

Rather than impose highly harmful restrictions on the legitimate use of bills, many scholastic writers were prepared to pretend to ignore some loopholes, even if their toleration meant risking some evasion of the anti-usury law. It was a choice between evils. An uncompromising attitude would have had the merit of consistency but it would have effectively blocked economic progress for centuries. A more liberal attitude might have stimulated progress, but it would have given free hand to usury, and open concessions for considerations of expediency would have discredited the Church. De Roover may be right in saying that because of their legal bias, the 'Doctors' became so involved in fastidious discussion of technicalities that they lost sight of more pertinent facts.[2] But their efforts to explain the facts of the situation in a way as to bring them in conformity with the anti-usury laws yielded some useful results from the point of view of Foreign Exchange theory.

(4) EXCHANGE RATES ARRIVED AT BY 'COMMON ESTIMATION'

To answer the question whether or not exchange rates concealed interest charges, scholastic writers had to give careful thought to the influences affecting exchange rates. One of the results was the emergence of a principle of considerable importance – that exchange rates were just and legitimate if arrived at by 'common estimation' (*publica aestimatio*) of the market. Grice-Hutchinson interpreted this frequently recurring term as meaning that ecclesiastic authorities 'thought it fairer to rely on the impersonal forces of the market which reflected the judgment of the whole community'.[3] She regards Laurentius de Rodolphis (c. 1360–1442), himself not a cleric, as the originator of this important theory. Transactions at rates different from current market rates were condemned as usurious. This rule suggests by implication that the free play of supply and demand necessarily produced the correct rate.

The theory of market mechanism, which was to influence Foreign Exchange theory from the 18th century right to our days, is based on that principle. Those who, in our days, are in favour of floating exchange rates are subconscious disciples of the medieval ecclesiastic writers who had conceived the notion that in matters of exchanges – as indeed in matters of prices in general – the collective wisdom behind the sum total of individual buying and selling orders must necessarily produce the right price, or at any rate the fair price.

Although the adoption of this principle by the Church provided a powerful argument against official attempts at controlling exchange rates, in practice this was not the way in which it came to be interpreted. Indeed it did not even prevent the development of a diametrically opposite theory blaming speculation for embarrassing exchange movements. Any inconsistency between trusting the collective wisdom of market operators and condemning them for exercising their power to their advantage was sought to be disposed of by condemning 'conspiracies' between operators, the spreading of false rumours and the use of other methods to influence the rates artificially.

(5) ORIGINS OF THE PSYCHOLOGICAL THEORY

Admission by scholastic writers of the obvious and generally known fact that exchange rates included interest charges would have necessarily entailed the condemnation of the entire practice. Some 'Doctors' did in fact adopt such an uncompromising attitude. Others, however, preferred to convey the impression that they were unaware of the inclusion of interest charges. Thus they sought to explain the effect on exchange rates of the distances between the two financial centres concerned on the ground of the extent of risk of loss through a depreciation of exchange, a risk which was necessarily higher the longer it took for the buyer to collect the bills and to repatriate the proceeds.

The same explanation was also used to account for the difference between rates for long bills and short bills. The lower price paid for bills of more distant maturity dates made it obvious that the parties allowed for interest charges for a longer period. But scholastic writers, anxious to avoid having to outlaw the entire practice, accounted for the difference between rates of bills according to the length of their maturities on the ground that the longer the period involved the higher the risk of an exchange movement adverse to the buyer of the bill. This was implied by Alessandro Lombardo (d. 1314) who said in his *Tractatus de Usuris*, that it was unlawful for bills in *tournois deniers* to be cheaper in Genoa on account of their distant maturity at the Champagne fair, unless there was a speculative anticipation of its depreciation.[4]

By admitting that the extent of risk is a legitimate cause for exchange movements, the scholastics have laid the foundations of the psychological or subjective theory of Foreign Exchange.

It was re-stated many times in more recent periods, whenever there were wide fluctuations of exchange rates.

(6) 'PRESENT MONEY' v. 'ABSENT MONEY'

There was further the question of a discrepancy between rates at a given moment in two centres. Henry of Ghent, who wrote in the 13th century, considered it justified for coins to be more valuable within their own areas of circulation than abroad and regarded any profit derived from transporting coins to those areas as legitimate.[5] This principle was carried further by Aegidus Lessinus who, writing towards the end of the 14th century, first enunciated the doctrine that present money is worth more than absent money.[6] This rule may be interpreted as indicating approval of profits on Foreign Exchange on the ground of the expense and labour incurred in conveying absent money to the centre concerned. It justified wider margins for exchange between distant centres, owing to the higher cost of converting absent money into present money. This may be looked upon as amounting to a primitive attempt to apply the cost of production theory of prices to the prices of currencies in terms of each other.

(7) DIFFERENCE BETWEEN BILL RATES IN TWO CENTRES

The discrepancy between exchange rates in different centres received more attention later in connection with the curious phenomenon, referred to in the last chapter, of a difference between bill rates in the lending and borrowing centres at any given moment. The fact that the price of bills drawn in Florence on Venice in terms of Venetian currency were higher in Venice than in Florence gave rise to much controversy. Some scholastic writers suspected usury, while others were prepared to accept the transactions in the sense their initiators intended them to accept.

Some modern writers on early Foreign Exchange attributed the difference to the 'certain' and 'uncertain' quotation of bills to the concealment of interest in exchange rates and believed that the exchanges which quoted 'certain' – one of their units quoted in fluctuating numbers of foreign units – were quoted at a higher price abroad than at home. Actually there was no difference from that point of view. The discrepancy described above was necessary, because the only way in which a creditor could make a profit on a Foreign Exchange transaction was by obtaining a more favourable rate on the re-change than the one which he accepted when he bought the bill. This again was only possible, apart from unpredictable changes in the exchange rates in his favour, if there was a permanent margin in his favour.

(8) EFFECT OF MONEY SUPPLY ON EXCHANGE RATES

Scholastic writers noticed the effect of the scarce or plentiful money supplies on exchange rates. Dealing with the discrepancies between exchange rates at a given moment in various centres, Paccioli explained them on the ground of a different degree of excess or scarcity prevailing in them.[7] But this subject was adequately dealt with by earlier writers of practical guides for merchants. Outstanding among them was Pegolotti's book, written about 1340,[8] and Uzzano's book, written about a century later.[9] Both of them were aware of the influence of the monetary scarcity (*strettezza*) or ease (*larghezza*) on exchange rates. But while Pegolotti gave merchants the advice to avoid having to make payments at fairs where money was easy, Uzzano appears to have held the opposite view and warned merchants against remitting money to centres where money was scarce and withdrawing it from centres where it was plentiful. He based his advice – described by de Roover as 'paradoxical' – on the assumption that by the time the money had reached its destination conditions were liable to have changed. For markets where money was stringent attracted specie, with the result that conditions became easy.[10] The realisation that tight money attracted specie constituted an important step towards the theory of automatic adjustment. Moreover, Uzzano was aware that the mechanism of adjustment operated through the specie points. He knew that at certain exchange rates it became profitable to export or import specie.[11]

(9) BALANCE OF PAYMENTS IGNORED

Neither the practical experts nor the scholastic writers indicated any knowledge of the effect of the balance of payments on exchange rates. Yet, it seems reasonable to infer from some of their observations that a rudimentary balance of payments theory may have existed in their minds, even though they were not sufficiently articulate to put it into words. Judging by the 'common estimation' principle they may have been aware of the impact of supply and demand on the exchange rates, and the influence of an import or export surplus on supply and demand must have been self-evident. But it seems that an adverse balance of payments held no more terror for some experts in the 14th century than it did for Xenophon in the 4th century B.C. This at any rate may be inferred from the advice given by Pierre Du Bois to Philip the Fair in 1302, opposing debasements on the unexpected ground that they would tend to increase exports.[12] He was concerned by the adverse effect of a favourable balance on domestic prices and disregarded its beneficial effect on exchanges.

Benedetto Cotrugli, in a book written in 1458,[13] showed himself aware of the seasonal variations of exchanges, which he may have attributed, consciously or otherwise, to changes in supply and demand. A few decades later Paccioli mentioned the effect on the money market – and therefore on the exchange rates – of departures of ships from Venice.[14]

(10) RESTRICTIVE MEASURES BASED ON FALLACIES

Let us now examine one or two instances, pointing towards theoretical knowledge, or absence of it, implied by Foreign Exchange policies pursued by various Governments during the Middle Ages.

Ignorance of the effect of exchanges on specie movements is clearly implied in some Government measures. In England in 1307 a ban was imposed on the export of money by Papal agents without special licence, 'except by way of exchange'.[15] There was, apparently, no objection to the withdrawal of the proceeds of Papal collections by means of providing the counterpart to Italian payments for English wool exports. Those responsible for the measures were not aware that the effect of the operations on the supply of specie was substantially the same as if the Papal agents had been allowed to transfer their money in cash. For an appreciation of sterling through a demand for bills on London or the sale of foreign bills in London, arising from the wool export surplus, would have tended to cause an influx of specie or a mitigation of an efflux that would have taken place otherwise. The acquisition of part of such bills for the purposes of remittances by Papal agents was bound to affect specie movements adversely in a positive or negative sense. But the advisers of Edward I were oblivious of the balance of payments theory which would have safeguarded them from such a fallacy. Yet a year earlier a law was enacted to the effect that 'religious persons shall send nothing to their superiors beyond sea under the name of Exchanges'.[16]

On other occasions a restrictive measure by which pilgrims leaving for Palestine or Rome were only allowed to buy bills for covering their expenses on the undertaking that they would export English products of a corresponding value was repeatedly enacted. It shows that in these instances the authorities were fully aware of the effects of meeting such invisible imports out of the proceeds of additional visible exports. Likewise a law was passed under Richard II and renewed under Henry IV, enacting that merchants remitting to Rome or elsewhere had to give an undertaking to buy within a certain number of months 'merchandises of the Staple or other Commodities of the Land, to the value of the sum so exchanged'.[17] This implied knowledge that a reduction in the supply of foreign bills through purchases by pilgrims or through remittances abroad would be detrimental to the supply of specie in the country.

(ii) RICHARD AYLESBURY'S THEORY

With regard to theoretical knowledge of dealers in Foreign Exchange, the much-quoted observation made by Richard Aylesbury in 1381 that the way to prevent a drain on the supply of specie was to prevent imports from exceeding exports lends itself to more than one interpretation. It is at least possible that, knowing as he did the Foreign Exchange system as it operated, he may have implied that, in the absence of a depreciation of sterling beyond specie point through an import surplus, the country would not lose specie so long as imports were balanced by exports, even if there was no ban on the export of specie, because such an outflow would result in a surplus of demand for sterling bills over their supply, and the resulting appreciation of sterling would reverse the flow of specie.

It was because Aylesbury was some four centuries ahead of his time that the bullionist policy, which ignored the balance of trade theory, continued to reign supreme throughout the Middle

Ages and for a long time after. It is indeed curious that while the effect of monetary supplies on exchange rates was duly grasped in the Middle Ages, the effect of an import or export surplus did not appear to have been realised by most Medieval writers on Foreign Exchange.

(12) FOREIGN EXCHANGE MARKETS AND MONEY MARKETS

Modern economic historians dealing with the medieval Foreign Exchange market usually refer to it as the 'money market'. This is because during the Medieval Period – and some time after – there was no separate discount market or market in short loans. All short-term funds that were available – apart from money lent to princes or municipalities – were employed in foreign bills. In any case, as we already pointed out, credit business as well as Foreign Exchange business was transacted at the medieval *bourses*. For this reason the impact of the supply of short-term funds on exchange rates was even more direct in those days than it is in modern conditions when usually a bare fraction of the banks' funds is employed in the Foreign Exchange market, and the bulk is used in domestic credit transactions.

There is no indication that anybody was aware of any reciprocity in the relationship between exchange rates and interest rates. Yet if, for reasons unconnected with the local supply of money or changes in interest rates, there was a depreciation or appreciation of exchange rates, it tended to affect the supply of money and interest rates to a considerable extent, precisely because money market and Foreign Exchange market were virtually identical, and the requirements of the latter constituted the predominant influence on the former. During the Middle Ages, and for some time after, the yield on Foreign Exchange transactions competed with that of domestic loan transactions even more actively than in our days when most banks are only prepared to divert a small proportion of their resources for use in interest arbitrage.

(13) OPERATION OF SPECIE POINTS

The operation of specie points must have been evident to contemporary writers. Fluctuations were roughly limited by rates at which it was more profitable to make payments in specie. Although these specie points were incomparably wider than those operating in more recent times, and, owing to the uncertainty of the quality of coins received in payment or of the cost of moving specie, they were also even less definite, their existence must surely have been recognised by contemporary experts, even if most of them made no reference to it. They must have been aware that specie points were affected not only by transport costs but also by the seignorage, minting charges and the additional cost and risk of smuggling specie from countries where the export of specie was prohibited, or the alternative cost of export licence.

Medieval experts may also have been familiar with the difference between specie points according to whether or not the coins to be transported circulated in both countries, as was frequently the case. The difference between specie points for coins which were not in circulation in the importing country and those which were in circulation was of considerable importance both from a theoretical and a practical point of view.

(14) INFLUENCE OF TERMS OF TRADE REALISED

The influence of the terms of trade appears to have been more clearly realised, at any rate in isolated instances, in the Middle Ages than in much more recent times. In England in 1347 the Commons complained that the exchange was so adverse in Flanders to English exporters that they lost one-third or more of their money.[18] By exchanges being 'adverse' to exporters it was obviously not meant that an unduly high exchange value of sterling was handicapping exports, but that an unduly low value of sterling was reducing the sterling proceeds of exports. This consideration was overlooked during the competitive currency depreciation period in the 'thirties. It was not re-discovered until after the second World War.

(15) OPERATION OF MARKET MECHANISM

The Foreign Exchange system was sufficiently developed, at any rate by the 14th and 15th centuries, to allow for the operation of the market mechanism, tending to result in automatic adjustments. It is true, the market mechanism could not operate smoothly. The wideness of specie points and the uncertainty of their whereabouts, together with the existence of various exchange restrictions and

bans on specie movements, made it difficult and at times impossible for exchange rates to cause specie movements to an extent
necessary for achieving an automatic elimination of discrepancies
between countries. But the system was much more effective during
the late Middle Ages than during previous periods.

In the experience of Ancient Rome the relapse into the use
of metals by weight for payments in foreign trade prevented
the depreciation of the *denarius* from causing a reduction of the
perennial adverse balance of payments. By the 14th century
the widely established practice of exchanging coins by tale,
the development of a good market in foreign bills and the use of
fictitious units in international transactions, made it possible for
exchange depreciation to stimulate exports and handicap imports.
In the case of fictitious currencies, it was the ups and downs of
those units in terms of local currencies that was liable to affect
imports and exports. This function of the exchanges was not to be
discovered, however, for several centuries. Most medieval experts
appeared to have been oblivious of its existence, presumably
because for a long time imports and exports were too rigid to
respond readily to exchange movements.

(16) PRICE LEVELS AND EXCHANGE RATES

Scholastic writers may conceivably have had an inkling of the
purchasing power parity theory in its most rudimentary form.
The view that exchanges were determined by the difference
between the 'common estimation' of money in two countries may
possibly indicate anticipation of the view that purchasing power
parities were capable of affecting exchanges, though the notion of
price levels was non-existent in the Middle Ages. What is perhaps
even more important, exports and imports were largely inelastic
and unresponsive to changes in prices or exchanges.

On the other hand, medieval Foreign Exchange theory anticipated modern theory in respect of its realisation of the effect of
exchange rates on price levels. We saw above that in 1302 Du Bois
referred to the effect produced by debasements through stimulating exports. Six years later, he advised Philip the Fair that
debasements caused prices to rise because foreigners valued the
currency only according to its content of precious metals.[19] He
and other medieval experts who were aware of the effect of debasements on domestic prices were ahead of experts of the early

'twenties who, having just re-discovered that exchanges were affected by price levels, overlooked for a long time the reciprocal character of the relationship.

NOTES TO CHAPTER NINE

1. E. L. Jäger, *Der Traktat des Luca Paccioli von 1494 über den Wechsel* (Stuttgart, 1878), p. 12.
2. Raymond de Roover, *Cambium ad Venetias – Contribution to the History of Foreign Exchange*. Studi in onore di Armando Sapori (Milan, 1957), p. 640.
3. Marjorie Grice-Hutchinson, *The Salamanca School* (Oxford, 1952), p. 27.
4. Raymond de Roover, *L'Évolution de la lettre de change, XIVe–XVIIIe siècle* (Paris, 1953), p. 172.
5. Edmund Schreiber, *Die volkswirtschaftliche Anschauungen der Scholastik seit Thomas v. Aquin* (Jena, 1913), p. 134.
6. Wilhelm Endemann, *Studien in der romanisch-kanonistischen Wirtschafts- und Rechtslehre bis gegen Ende des 17. Jahrhunderts* (Berlin, 1874), pp. 110–11.
7. Jäger, *op. cit.* pp. 16–18.
8. Francesco Baldussi Pegolotti, *La pratica della mercatura*. Medieval Academy of America (Cambridge, Mass., 1936).
9. Giovanni di Antonio da Uzzano, *La pratica della mercatura*, p. 152 *et seq.*, quoted by Raymond de Roover, *Money, Banking and Credit in Medieval Bruges* (Cambridge, Mass., 1948), p. 77.
10. de Roover, *ibid.*
11. de Roover, *op. cit.* p. 92.
12. Henri Lapeyre, *Une Famille de marchands, les Ruiz* (Paris, 1955), p. 304.
13. Adolphe Landry, *Essai économique sur les mutations des monnaies dans l'ancienne France de Philippe le Bel à Charles VII* (Paris, 1910), pp. 208–9.
14. Jäger, *op. cit.* p. 16.
15. *Rolls of Parliament*, vol. i, p. 222b.
16. *Rolls of Parliament*, 35 Edward I, vol. i, p. 217a.
17. *Statutes*, vol. ii, pp. 210–11.
18. *Rolls of Parliament*, vol. ii, p. 116a.
19. Schreiber, *op. cit.* pp. 188–9.

CHAPTER TEN

Medieval Foreign Exchange Policy

(1) SAFEGUARDING THE SUPPLY OF SPECIE

DELIBERATE and systematic actions taken by Governments with the object of influencing the Foreign Exchange situation had become more easily discernible during the Middle Ages than during the Ancient Period. They received publicity in contemporary writings, in acts of legislation and in records of public discussions. There was little evidence of any depreciation of exchanges being brought about as a matter of deliberate policy for the sake of its economic effect, as distinct from accepting it as an incidental and mostly unwanted result of deliberate reductions in the metallic equivalent of monetary units undertaken for other considerations.

Such changes were in most countries even more frequent during the Middle Ages than during the Ancient Period. Most of them could not be regarded, however, as means of a deliberate Foreign Exchange policy, even if they inevitably affected exchange rates. The main object of most debasements and devaluations – in so far as they were decided upon as a matter of policy instead of being forced into it by shortage of monetary metals – was either to secure a profit on the re-coinage or to safeguard the supply of specie against a drain through export. In the latter respect their rôle was similar to that of Bank Rate changes in modern times.

(2) DEVALUATION OR DEBASEMENT TO CHECK SPECIE DRAIN

Whenever the metallic value of coins exceeded their official value they tended to disappear from circulation and the mints were idle. The disappearance of coins through their export was often due to a depreciation and undervaluation of the exchange as a result of which it became profitable to export specie. The authorities were not in a position to defend their exchange by means of high interest

rates or credit squeeze – indeed their main trouble was scarcity of
currency – so they resorted to devaluation or debasement. The
first meant an open act calling up the nominal value of the coins,
or re-issuing the coins with a declared reduction of their metal
content per unit. The second was usually a surreptitious act reducing the metal content of the newly minted coins.

In one instance at any rate, debasements are suggested to have
possibly pursued deliberate Foreign Exchange policy. According
to Le Blanc, during the Hundred Years War the Dauphin
deliberately lowered the metal content of the French coinage in
order to attract bullion and thereby to embarrass the English.[1]
If this interpretation is correct it would imply that he and his
advisers were aware of the effect of the overvaluation of the
coinage during the time lag that followed each debasement,
before exchange rates adjusted themselves to the lower metallic
value of the coins. It seems more likely, however, that the coinage
was debased simply as a means for raising funds to finance the war.

(3) CHANGES AND DISCREPANCIES IN GOLD-SILVER RATIO

As W. A. Shaw pointed out, in many ways the currency problem
before medieval Governments was even more difficult than that
which besets the modern world. The frequent and substantial
changes in the fixed gold-silver ratio in particular coinages – in
France for instance it fluctuated between $14\frac{1}{4}$ and $19\frac{1}{2}$ during the
ten years ended 1313 – created unsettled conditions. Moreover,
Governments had to cope with the absence of a uniform ratio
between gold and silver in various countries at any given moment.[2]
For instance at the same date it was between 7 and 8 in Moorish
parts of Spain and 12 in Christian parts. In 1474 the rates were
11·15 in England, 11 in France, $10\frac{1}{2}$ in Italy and under 10 in
Spain.[3]

It was in order to prevent the exploitation of such discrepancies
by international arbitrage, and by merchants who naturally made
all their payments in the cheaper coins, that exchange rates for
foreign coins were fixed and often changed by proclamation. The
frequent changes in the metallic contents of the national coinages
aimed not merely at protecting the domestic supply of money from
depletion through outward arbitrage but also at increasing it
through making inward arbitrage worth while.

(4) BULLIONIST POLICIES

Bullionist policies, which were in force in most countries during the Middle Ages, implied ignorance of the fact that an overall import or export surplus was apt to influence specie movements through its effect on exchange rates. Administrators in most countries aimed at maintaining the supply of coins mainly by direct physical controls – bans on the export of specie, compulsion to spend on local goods the payment received for imported goods. They even sought to balance each individual transaction, instead of aiming at an overall balance and disregarding losses on individual transactions, relying on the effect of a favourable trade balance on the exchanges and, through the exchanges, on specie movements.

(5) STRICT REGULATION OF MANUAL EXCHANGES

There was in most countries a noteworthy difference in the degree of Government control over manual exchanges and over the market in foreign bills. The latter market had been virtually non-existent in the Roman Empire and the strict control of the late Roman period had not come to be applied to it as and when the new system developed in the Succession States of the Empire. Exchanging of coins, on the other hand, was strictly controlled in the Roman Empire, and it was subject to drastic regulations in medieval Europe. Money-changers had to obtain concessions or licences from the ruler. In most countries they had to conform to tightly drawn official market regulations the infringement of which entailed severe penalties.

In some countries licensed money-changers were at liberty to deal in coins at exchange rates determined by free market influences, but in most instances the authorities fixed a tariff for coins by proclamation and money-changers were under an obligation to buy and sell on the basis of the official exchange rates. Their remuneration consisted of a fixed commission they were authorised to charge. In many instances they had to surrender to the authorities the gold coins – and at times the silver coins of high metal content – obtained in the course of their activities, in return for payment in current coin at the official rates.

There is, for instance, much detailed evidence about the terms of concessions granted by the Counts of Flanders in the 13th century to individuals, authorising them to exchange bullion and coins. Such concessions were granted mostly for a limited number of years but in some instances 'in perpetuity'.[4] Foreign citizens were usually disqualified from obtaining such concessions, or even from being employed by money-changers, as far as manual exchanges were concerned. By contrast there were in Flanders no such limitations on dealing in bills of exchange, which activity was overwhelmingly in foreign – especially Italian – hands.

(6) BAN ON PRIVATE MONEY-CHANGING IN ENGLAND

Although England was to become in more recent times the chief advocate of freedom in exchange dealings, she applied during the Middle Ages much stricter exchange controls than most continental countries. From the early 12th century, and possibly even before, the monopoly of manual exchanges was exercised by the Royal Exchanger. That office survived right into the 17th century.

Henry I (110–35) placed a ban on all private dealings in coins.[5] No one but the officially appointed moneyers were allowed to exchange coins, and for some time even they had to confine their activities to their own respective counties. Any offender against exchange regulations was treated as counterfeiter and was subjected to the horrible extreme penalties applied for that crime.

The nature and extent of restrictions were subject to frequent changes. In 1223, for instance, the Foreign Exchange centres of Flanders were officially advised that in England they could only exchange money in London or in Canterbury. Later this regulation was relaxed somewhat and other towns were ordered to elect officials for their local Mints, including a Keeper of the Exchange.[6] Presumably the reason why dealing in coins was subject to stricter control in England than on the Continent was that for geographical reasons the import or export of coins was more easily enforceable. Even in England it was, however, very far from watertight. The large number of statutes passed to reaffirm or reinforce it were only partly effective.

(7) FIXING EXCHANGE RATES BETWEEN COINS

Throughout the Middle Ages there was in most countries a permanent ban on the export of national coins even during periods when the export of bullion or of foreign coins was permitted. Very often the import of foreign coins in general, or of certain foreign coins, was forbidden. There was usually a ban on the imports of debased coins, and of national coins minted abroad.

A frequently applied Foreign Exchange policy device was the regulation of the prices of foreign coins in terms of local coins. This was a widespread practice during the Middle Ages when in most countries certain foreign coins were allowed to circulate side by side, especially when the local coins disappeared as a result of the cost of Crusades or other wars, or through hoarding or exports and over a long period no metals were taken to the Mint, the toleration of foreign coins became necessary. When there was an artificially fixed ratio between them and the national coins money-changers were under an obligation to effect exchanges at the official rates, but in other instances the exchange rates between them were allowed to fluctuate, and debts were discharged on the basis of the current exchange rates.

In 1373 a statute was passed in England, on the initiative of Parliament, providing that 'four pence Scottish money should go for no more than three pence English, and if the Scottish money should be diminished on that account its exchange rate in English money should again be brought down in proportion'. But, according to Ruding, the Ordinance to that effect seems not to have been sufficiently respected, and in 1387 all the sheriffs were commanded to issue weekly proclamations declaring that Scottish coins must not be received or paid at more than their official rates.[7]

On the Continent, too, frequent attempts were made at determining exchange rates for coins. For instance, in France proclamations were issued in frequent intervals during the early part of the 14th century, crying down the rates of those foreign coins which were permitted to circulate.

Yet another suggested reason why the authorisation or toleration of foreign coins was looked upon at best as a necessary evil and during periods of adverse pressure as an unqualified evil, was that specie points for such coins were much narrower than for either national coins or for bullion. Exporters of, say, French coins which circulated at a fixed rate in Spain did not have to pay seignorage or minting charges, nor did they lose on worn coins. This meant that foreign coins accepted at a fixed rate were exported long before it became profitable to export national coins or bullion, so that the monetary circulation was apt to become reduced well below essential requirements. But the same risk existed also when domestic coins were in circulation abroad, and yet that practice was encouraged by many Governments.

(8) BAN ON CIRCULATION OF FOREIGN COINS

In Valencia in 1247 holders of foreign coins were ordered to surrender their holdings within 40 days against payment in local vellum coins on the basis of the official exchange rate.[8] In 1398 a proclamation was issued in Spain prohibiting the circulation of foreign coins except at their bullion value.[9]

In England and in most continental countries on many occasions complete bans were imposed on the circulation of foreign coins. As in Ptolemian Egypt, it was compulsory for travellers to exchange their foreign coins for national coins on their arrival, and the operation was reversed on their departure. In many instances on the Continent the object of such attempts at isolating the local coinage was to ensure the circulation of the debased local currencies which were accepted for want of better. Thus in Portugal, Alphonso V (1432–81) placed a ban on foreign coins to ensure acceptance of the debased and overvalued domestic coins.

On other occasions prohibition of foreign coins was a device of economic warfare, directed against the currency of the enemy. English money was barred from France during part of the Hundred Years War.

Control of manual exchanges was not confined to Europe. According to Pegolotti the exchange of coins into Chinese paper money at Peking had to be affected through an official body whose decisions about the exchange rate were apt to be subject to delays.

(9) CONTROL OVER TRANSACTIONS IN BILLS

In respect of transactions in bills, restrictions were imposed both by the Church and by the State. We saw in earlier chapters that the former's sole concern was to prevent usury. Apart from that it was to the interest of the Papal Curia to ensure freedom of transfers in order to be able to gain possession of the proceeds of Papal collections. The greater part of exchange control measures in England, France and other countries aimed at the prevention of unduly heavy withdrawals of such proceeds. There were, therefore, frequent clashes between Church and State on matters relating to exchange restrictions. In one recorded instance in 1255, Pope Alexander IV threatened with excommunication English Bishops and Prelates who, in compliance with the ban placed on such payments by Henry III (1216–72), refused to meet bills drawn upon them by merchant banks acting on his authority. Thereupon the bills were met.[10]

Bill markets in some Western European countries enjoyed a reasonable degree of freedom from Government interference. In Flanders in particular dealings in bills were free during the 14th and 15th centuries. This must have been a reaction to the attempt made in 1299 to do away altogether with private exchanges. The Regent of Flanders ordered the demolition of all *bourses*, but there is no evidence that this was carried out.[11] On the other hand, in 1315 the Duke of Brabant authorised Genoese merchants to transact Foreign Exchange with whoever they wanted to.[12]

Another form of exchange control, adopted in Spain in 1438, was to put the Barcelona Bank of Deposits in charge of clearing all bills of exchange.[13] The ban on private clearing was deemed necessary for the defence of the exchange rate. Money-changers were ordered to wind up their business.

On the other hand, French kings went out of their way to encourage dealings in bills, and to that end they granted to the Lyons fairs unlimited freedom of exchange, subject only to a ban on dealing with a hereditary enemy of France, England.[14]

(10) STRICT EXCHANGE CONTROL IN ENGLAND

In England restrictions on transactions in bills, as on those in coins, were on the whole stricter than in most continental countries. From time to time dealings in bills were only permitted to mer chants regularly engaged in bill transactions for their trade. At times a ban was placed on direct transactions even between merchants who had to buy and sell bills through the Royal Exchanger. But when in 1381 Richard II (1377–99) passed a statute to that effect it gave rise to strong protests by the Italian merchants directly concerned. Parliament, too, objected and submitted a petition saying that this restriction was damaging the King and his realm, because English exporters of wool and other merchandise were at a disadvantage compared with the exporters of other countries. The royal reply indicated that the merchants

E

could ask for the Chancellor's permission to deal with each other and if the request was reasonable he might grant it.[15]

One of the characteristic measures of exchange control was the law passed in 1487 under Henry VII (1485–1509), called the Act Against Usury and Unlawful Bargaining. Under this Act any transactions based on 'dry' exchanges were considered void, those responsible were liable to fine and confiscation, 'reserving to the Church this punysshement notwithstondyng, the Correction of their Soulles accordying to the lawes of the same'.[16]

(11) FIXING METHOD OF PAYMENT

Official interference with exchanges took an unusual form in 1399 in Bruges. An Ordinance prescribed that all bills payable in Bruges must be paid in actual specie instead of being credited to the holder's account. A gradually increasing proportion was to be payable in gold. The resulting tightening of money conditions affected exchange rates considerably, sterling depreciating from 25 to 27 per *écu*. From January 1401 bills had to be paid wholly in gold. Exchanges moved further in favour of the Flemish currency, but owing to the undervaluation of gold coins it was not profitable to import them. In September 1401 the Ordinance was repealed.[17] But the lesson taught by this experiment was forgotten. The same mistake was repeated in 1410 and, as we shall see in the next section, it was applied on more than one occasion in Antwerp during the 16th century.

From an early stage the English authorities made efforts to enforce the repatriation of at least part of the proceeds of exports in the form of specie. It was partly to that end that staples were established in Calais and elsewhere for handling wool and other 'staple' exports. From time to time it was decreed that the whole or a large part of such goods had to be paid for in specie. This policy naturally reduced the demand for sterling bills. On the other hand, the various Statutes of Employment that followed each other during the late Middle Ages, under which foreign merchants were forced to spend in England the proceeds of their goods sold there, tended to reduce the supply of sterling bills.

(12) NO OFFICIAL OPERATIONS IN THE MARKET

There was no evidence of any official intervention in the Foreign Exchange market in the form of operations on Government account for the purpose of influencing the exchange rates until the 16th century.

One of the reasons why exchange control encountered so much opposition even during a period of extensive economic controls was the fear that in the interest of its efficient enforcement the authorities would not hesitate to resort to mail censorship. According to de Roover this was actually done, judging by merchants' letters found in Antwerp archives and in the Datini archives, showing that merchants resorted to the use of codes in their correspondence. The authorities made this practice unlawful. Evidently, they could not have known that codes were used, and they could have had no reason for objecting to the practice, unless they were in the habit of opening merchants' letters.

(13) INTERNATIONAL POLICIES

The system of monetary unions which assumed considerable importance during the Ancient Period was not much in evidence in the Middle Ages. It took a long time before countries as closely connected as Flanders and Brabant came to decide to establish a monetary union. The Spanish kingdoms had independent currencies, and so had the various German States, even though the Emperors ensured some degree of loose monetary association between the latter. Nor was there a monetary union between England and Scotland until after political union had first been achieved, though Scottish coins had circulated freely in England and vice versa.

On the other hand, even in the absence of any formal arrangements, coinages of various States very often sought to conform to the same standard. The *denarius* of Charlemagne influenced coinages for centuries. Governments deemed it advisable to adopt units identical with some foreign unit that had established an international prestige. Agreements were concluded between Governments concerning the circulation of each other's coins on each other's territories, at a fixed price. In 1345 an agreement was made with Flanders providing for the coining of English gold *nobles* in Flanders, which were to circulate there at the same value as in England.[18] In 1478 an agreement was reached with Flanders as to the rates of exchange.

Agreements to reconcile conflicting national interests arising from exchange control measures are contained in various international treaties. Thus in a representation made by Edward II (1307–27) to Philip the Fair of France (1285–1314) in 1311 against the seizure of English merchants' money on leaving France, reference is made to a provision in the peace treaty concluded under Edward I permitting them to bring any kind of money out of France.[19]

NOTES TO CHAPTER TEN

1. Albert Despaux, *L'Inflation dans l'histoire* (Paris, 1923), p. 132.
2. W. A. Shaw, *The History of Currency, 1252 to 1894* (London, 1895), p. 17.
3. Shaw, *op. cit.* p. 17.
4. Georges Bigwood, *Le Régime judiciaire et économique du commerce de l'argent dans la Belgique du Moyen Age* (Brussels, 1921), pp. 391–4.
5. Sir John Craig, *The Mint* (Cambridge, 1953), p. 29.
6. Craig, *op. cit.*, pp. 31–3.
7. Roger Ruding, *Annals of the Coinage of Britain* (London, 1819), vol. ii, p. 240.
8. Earl J. Hamilton, *Money, Prices and Wages in Valencia, Aragon and Navarre* (Cambridge, Mass., 1936), p. 70.
9. Shaw, *op. cit.* p. 24.
10. Hartley Withers, *Money Changing* (London, 1913), pp. 120–2.
11. Raymond de Roover, *Money, Banking and Credit in Medieval Bruges* (Cambridge, Mass., 1948), p. 234.
12. Jules Finot, *Les Relations commerciales entre la Flandre et la République de Genève au Moyen Age* (Paris, 1906), p. 290.
13. A. P. Usher, *The Early History of Deposit Banking in Mediterranean Europe* (Cambridge, Mass., 1943), pp. 313–16.
14. Ordinance of Louis XI, March 8, 1463. Quoted by Frederic Borel, *Les Foires de Genève au 15ᵉ siècle* (Geneva, 1892), p. 137.
15. *Rolls of Parliament*, vol. iii, p. 138b.
16. *Statutes*, ii, 514.
17. de Roover, *op. cit.* pp. 78–81.
18. Ruding, *op. cit.* vol. ii, p. 174.
19. Ruding, *op. cit.* vol. ii, p. 133.

PART III

EARLY MODERN PERIOD

CHAPTER ELEVEN

Foreign Exchange Practices from the 16th Century

(1) NO IMMEDIATE CHANGES

By the 15th century a relatively advanced system of Foreign Exchange was in operation. Although the next three centuries covered by this section witnessed many basic changes, de Roover is right in saying that no spectacular changes came about immediately after the end of the Medieval Period. Even many of the changes that occurred during the 17th and 18th centuries were largely a matter of degree.

Because from about the middle of the 16th century the Foreign Exchange system came to receive much more attention, we have much more material about its operation than during the Middle Ages. Although it seems possible that some techniques described in detail and commented upon extensively in the 16th century or after had existed already in the 15th century or even before, in the absence of adequate concrete evidence to that effect one is inclined to attribute to the 16th or 17th century progress that may have been achieved in earlier centuries. On the other hand, we must avoid falling into the other extreme by underrating the significance of the evolution of the Foreign Exchange system during the early Modern Period. They were gradual but some were of great importance.

(2) SUMMARY OF NEW DEVELOPMENTS

The following is a summary of the new developments that occurred between the discovery of America and the French Revolution:

1. The Church ban on exchange transactions that were suspected of concealing loan transactions was gradually relaxed and disappeared eventually.
2. Bills of exchange became transferable during the 17th century.

3. The volume of Foreign Exchange transactions expanded considerably.
4. Official Foreign Exchange transactions increased in importance.
5. International loan transactions became more frequent.
6. Movements of funds for investment in foreign centres increased in importance.
7. The monopolistic position of Italian bankers in non-Italian centres weakened and ceased eventually.
8. New leading Foreign Exchange centres developed, and some old ones declined.
9. The importance of fairs as Foreign Exchange markets declined during the 17th century and eventually ceased to play any part in Foreign Exchange.
10. The importance of mail days in permanent Foreign Exchange markets increased.
11. Development of Forward Exchange facilities became noticeable.
12. The importance of bank transfers increased.
13. The relative importance of domestic credit transactions compared with Foreign Exchange transactions increased.

(3) CHURCH BAN GRADUALLY RELAXED

For a very long time the progress of the Foreign Exchange system consisted largely of improving the existing facilities without changing them basically. For one thing, the anti-usury laws remained in force throughout the 16th century and for a long time after. They were reaffirmed and upheld again and again even in some Protestant countries, presumably because Protestant Churchmen, statesmen and scholars did not want to appear to be less zealous than the Roman Catholic Church in their efforts to protect debtors against exploitation through 'usurious' lending. Foreign Exchanges continued, therefore, to be used as a device for evading these laws. Protestant writers, such as Milles, blame the Popes for having invented that device for the purpose of facilitating the transfer of Peter's pence.[1] And a Protestant schoolman, Thomas Wilson, was more Catholic than any Pope in his uncompromising condemnation of Foreign Exchange.

Even after the abandonment of the absolute ban on interest in Protestant countries – in England it was abandoned in 1571 – a maximum limit was fixed for permitted interest charges. Foreign Exchanges continued to be used as a device for evasion wherever and whenever the current rate of interest was in excess of the legal maximum. In England, for instance, interest rates remained for a long time above the statutory limit of 10 per cent, so that lenders continued to find it necessary to conceal their interest charges in exchange rates. Not until the middle of the 17th century did the development of the domestic bill obviate the necessity for concealing inland credits behind Foreign Exchange transactions.

While criticism of Foreign Exchange operations on ethical grounds abated – it came to be focused largely on the transaction of business at rates differing from market rates – they remained subject to criticism on economic grounds. Apart from the universal condemnation of speculative transactions, arbitrage was also often attacked. Dealers in Foreign Exchange were unpopular almost everywhere – apart from other reasons, because in most countries they were mostly foreigners or Jews. Even in France, where the official attitude towards Foreign Exchange was liberal during the Middle Ages, many complaints were made towards the middle of the 16th century against foreign dealers in Foreign Exchange in Lyons, who were accused of mopping up in France all the available funds and exporting them.

(4) BILLS BECOME TRANSFERABLE

The main significance of the change by which bills became transferable from about the middle of the 17th century was that it greatly facilitated the expansion of the turnover in the market, as the same bills could change hands many times before they matured. This assisted in the development of a good active market in which rates no longer depended to such an extent as before on the volume of bills that happened to be issued at a given moment.

The practice of re-change, which was such a prominent feature of the Medieval Foreign Exchange market, continued for a long time, but it was applied less and less for the purpose of circumventing anti-usury laws. It became the normal procedure for covering exchange risk. Curiously enough, even Malynes, with all his remarkable knowledge of Foreign Exchange practices, was under the impression that re-change was necessarily a device for circumventing the anti-usury laws. In reality the practice continued long after the necessity for such manœuvring ceased. It

E 2

was described and discussed in some detail by Adam Smith who quoted in *The Wealth of Nations* an instance of transactions between London and Edinburgh.[2] Although the anti-usury laws had not operated in the Netherlands, Amsterdam Foreign Exchange dealers transacted re-change business to the same extent as those in other centres, simply as a means of covering their open positions, or those of their customers.

During the 16th century the volume of transactions increased considerably. This was largely due to the influx of gold and silver from America, which facilitated an expansion of foreign trade and of international financial operations of every kind. The rise in prices caused by the influx of precious metals had also contributed towards increasing the nominal amount of the turnover in Foreign Exchange.

(5) OFFICIAL OPERATIONS

Official Foreign Exchange operations in particular increased in volume and importance during the 16th century. The various representatives of the Fuggers, Gresham, Spinola, the Schetz brothers, Ruiz, etc. – mostly Italians, South Germans, Spaniards or Portuguese – carried out official Foreign Exchange transactions on an unprecedented scale. Princes financed their allies, or collected subsidies from them, by means of Foreign Exchange operations. Above all they used and misused the Foreign Exchange market for raising or remitting funds required for their military operations abroad.

During the early part of the 16th century Jacob Fugger gained prominence through his foreign bill operations on behalf of the Emperors, the best-known of which was the one carried out for the purpose of financing the election of Charles V (1520–58) in 1519.[3] Even earlier, in 1509, he was able to secure the remittance of a subsidy granted by the Cambrai League to Emperor Maximilian (1493–1519), amounting to 170,000 *ducats*, from the Italian cities, Antwerp, etc., to Augsburg within a few weeks by means of bills of exchange.[4] Under the reign of Mary (1553–8), in 1554 Gresham was instructed to buy bills in Antwerp and to go to Spain to collect 200,000 *ducats*. The conclusion and repayment on Government loans abroad came to play an increasingly important part in the Foreign Exchange markets.

The Kings of Spain financed their prolonged and costly military operations in the Low Countries and elsewhere largely by means of bill transactions, because of the difficulties and risk involved in the transport of specie, whether by land or by sea. In 1584, for instance, the Fuggers transferred to the Netherlands 250,000 gold *ducats* on account of the King of Spain in the form of bills from Venice, Augsburg and Nuremberg or Frankfurt.[5] Most of the transfers of money were arranged through Genoa by means of bills on Antwerp. When in 1526 the English subsidy of £20,000 to finance the pay of Swiss mercenaries of Charles V, who won the victory of Pavia that year, was sent by Henry VIII (1509–47) in the form of bullion the transaction was criticised on the ground that a 10 per cent economy could have been achieved by remitting it through the Foreign Exchange market.

(6) BORROWING THROUGH THE FOREIGN EXCHANGE MARKET

Borrowing operations abroad by princes were a prominent feature of the Antwerp Foreign Exchange market where Emperor Charles V, Philip II of Spain (1556–98), Henry VIII and his successors and other contemporary rulers frequently appeared as borrowers. Gresham's correspondence contains a number of references to the effect of such transactions on exchange rates. While many of these transactions assumed the form of outright loans, in other instances Government agents took up money 'by exchange'. The Spanish Government made arrangements with financiers such as Simon Ruiz to carry out transactions in *asientos* – Treasury bills issued by Philip's Government – which could be sold abroad, in Antwerp, Genoa, etc., at rates different from the officially fixed rates.[6]

In 1598 the Fuggers granted Philip II a credit of 200,000 *écus* and the transaction was financed through sales by the Spanish agent of the Fuggers of bills drawn on various branches or agents in Genoa, Venice, Naples, Rome, Florence and Piacenza. These bills were met out of the proceeds of the re-change in the centres concerned, and were repaid every three months out of the proceeds of the sale of new bills until the balance was repaid in 1606. The average charge was about 15 per cent p.a. Here was a flagrant instance of borrowing by means of 'kite-flying' fictitious exchange transactions.[7] History repeated itself in our century when, during the 'thirties, the Spanish authorities borrowed a substantial amount by means of swap transactions which were renewed every three months over a period of years.

(7) NEW FOREIGN EXCHANGE CENTRES

The pre-eminence of the Italian cities and of Italian bankers who had been established in all European Foreign Exchange markets gradually declined during the late 16th century and the 17th century. Although Italian bankers continued to play an important part in Foreign Exchange operations in London and other markets right to the 18th century, English, German, Flemish, Dutch, Spanish, Portuguese and French bankers gained increasing prominence. In particular Spanish and Portuguese Jews, banished from their countries, established themselves in Antwerp, Amsterdam and other Foreign Exchange markets.

Genoa remained a most important Foreign Exchange centre for clearing and arbitrage right until the 18th century; it came to 'live by exchange', having lost its commerce with the Levant.[8] It handled the bulk of the Spanish silver shipments from America. Most other Italian cities declined in importance. Their place was taken by Antwerp – which displaced Bruges as the financial centre of the Low Countries – Cologne and later Frankfurt, Hamburg and Lübeck, Paris – which came to overshadow Lyons during the second half of the 16th century – and Spanish cities such as Seville, Vallodolid and Medina del Campo.

In the 17th century Amsterdam achieved supremacy as a Foreign Exchange market. One of the reasons for its rise was that in the Netherlands the export of bullion and specie was completely free of any restriction. It continued to hold its lead until its occupation by the French army in 1795, even though during the decades preceding that event some bank difficulties weakened its position and strengthened that of London, Paris and Hamburg. Italian bankers continued to play an active part in all these centres, but they were unable to retain their former monopolistic position. Markets of importance were created under official patronage in Berlin and Vienna during the 18th century.

It was not until the 16th century that Germany entered the field of Foreign Exchange operations on an appreciable scale. Frankfurt and, much later and to a less extent, Hamburg and Lübeck, assumed considerable importance. Simultaneously the influx of gold and silver from the Spanish colonial empire secured for Spain a very important position in the sphere of Foreign Exchange operations. Later, in the 18th century, Lisbon gained in importance, mainly through operations arising from shipments of Brazilian gold.

(8) STERLING'S INCREASING IMPORTANCE

London also increased its turnover during the 16th century, though it continued to transact Foreign Exchange business almost entirely with and through Antwerp. During the 17th century London's direct contacts with other markets increased, but even in the 18th century it transacted through Amsterdam a very large proportion of its Foreign Exchange business, especially with Scandinavian and Baltic centres.

The relative importance of sterling increased considerably from the 16th century. By the beginning of the 18th century it came to be quoted 'certain' even against important exchanges such as those on Amsterdam, Antwerp and Hamburg, though not against Paris, Lyons, Genoa and Venice. But almost to the end of the 18th century the importance of bills on Amsterdam overshadowed that of bills on London.

(9) DECLINING IMPORTANCE OF FAIRS

A large proportion of Foreign Exchange continued to be transacted at fairs. Indeed during the 16th century the importance of fairs as Foreign Exchange markets further increased. Some of them did very little else than transact Foreign Exchange. The Besançon fair, which was subsequently transferred to Piacenza, was established and maintained for the sole purpose of providing facilities for Genoese Foreign Exchange dealers. From the 17th century, however, business came to be diverted gradually from the fairs. Those of Spain, which became particularly important after the discovery of America, remained important long after fairs in other countries ceased to dominate Foreign Exchange business. The system of quarterly settlements became increasingly inadequate. It was often not convenient to time the maturity of bills to coincide with the dates of fairs. For this reason the development of permanent Foreign Exchange markets with a more or less active turnover throughout the year made good progress during the 17th century. In the 18th century fairs virtually ceased to play any part in the Foreign Exchange system, except in Spain where they continued for some time.

Mail days took the place of fairs as important dates from the point of view of Foreign Exchange. There was relatively little activity during the days or weeks between mail days and rates usually remained relatively stable in the intervals. Very often operators preferred to await a future mail day in the hope of being then able to get a more favourable rate. With the improvement of communications usances for bills became gradually reduced somewhat, though they still remained rather long by modern standards. Days of grace, too, remained long by modern standards.

(10) EARLY TYPES OF FORWARD EXCHANGE

One of the important 16th-century developments was the appearance of a system of 'betting' on future exchange rates which became very prevalent in the Low Countries and in Spain. The parties concerned made forecasts of exchange rates that would prevail at a certain date, and the discrepancy between these rates and the actual rate on the date in question determined who won the bet and how much the loser was to pay to the winner.[9] This primitive form of Forward Exchange was strongly condemned by the authorities. The Netherlands Government banned such transactions in 1541 and on various other occasions, and other Governments, too, did their best to discourage them. Nevertheless, the practice flourished, presumably because it was used not only for gambling but also for covering exchange risk.

There is no actual evidence of Forward Exchange business of a more advanced type until the early part of the 18th century, but this does not necessarily mean that none was transacted in earlier centuries. It seems highly probable that such operations had existed from an early period but had escaped the attention of contemporary observers.

The first 'modern' Forward Exchange transactions of which I was able to find concrete evidence occurred in 1702 in connection with the financing of Marlborough's army on the Continent. The Treasury Book registers an agreement under which Mr. Santigny's Company was to deliver sight bills on Amsterdam during seven months for sums not exceeding £50,000 a month at 10 *guilders* 17 *stuyvers* per £1, and also £20,000 immediately at 11 *guilders*.

There was thus a premium of 3 *stuyvers* per £1 on bills to be delivered at future dates.[10] It represented an average premium for seven different maturity dates.

Even though little was said in contemporary literature about speculation by means of such forward transactions, Foreign Exchange speculation in general was evidently proceeding on a large scale on many occasions. It was frequently denounced by scholastic writers, Government spokesmen and experts throughout the 16th and 17th centuries, less frequently during the 18th century. Possibly official pronouncements on the subject were inclined to exaggerate the extent of such speculation, in order to divert attention from the part played by official policies in bringing about a depreciation. But even discounting such exaggerations, a great deal of speculative business must have been transacted· during unsettled periods, and must have been a major cause as well as a major effect of the unstable conditions. More will be said about this subject in Chapter 13.

(11) TRANSACTIONS IN *BANCO* MONEY

Very little is said in works on early Foreign Exchange about the practice of international transfers without the use of bills, but it seems probable that, with the creation and expansion of an international network of branches and representatives by leading banking houses, it had gradually increased. The development of clearing of international transactions through the operation of banks such as the Bank of Amsterdam must have greatly stimulated Foreign Exchange without the use of bills. To reduce the inconvenience caused by the lack of uniformity of coins, a high proportion of bills was made payable either in terms of fictitious units, whose use was described in Chapter 7, or by transfers of credit balances in *banco* money, payable not in cash but by means of book transfers by the Bank of Amsterdam and similar banks.

As a result of such improved facilities, speculation must have increased not only in volume but also in relative importance. Likewise, the volume of arbitrage must have benefited by this convenient device as well as by the improvement of communications. Much of the professional speculation must have taken the form of uncovered arbitrage. This developed in Antwerp from 1540 on a large scale. Operators, in addition to trying to take advantage of discrepancies in space, also endeavoured to speculate on future discrepancies.

(12) INTERNATIONAL CAPITAL TRANSFERS

From the 16th century we encounter much evidence of Foreign Exchange transactions in connection with international private investment and the flight of national capital. For instance, in 1546 pessimism about the outcome of the war in Germany induced many people in the Low Countries to send their money to Lyons, Venice, England, etc., with the result that there was an acute scarcity of funds in Antwerp.[11] During the Commonwealth Sir Thomas Violet complained about the effect of the withdrawal of foreign funds and the transfer of national capital abroad.[12] After the Restoration Sir Thomas Culpeper remarked that 'much money of foreigners, by Reason of the high rate of Usury, is brought over here'.[13]

By the late 17th century the importance of transfers of funds among the factors affecting the exchanges came to be widely realised. Writing in 1772, Beldam says that foreigners had lodged much money in English funds, so much that the annual payment of interest to them was estimated at about £1½ million.[14] Movements of foreign funds assumed from time to time considerable importance among the factors influencing exchange rates. In the 18th century, fluctuations of interest differentials between London and Amsterdam gave rise to important movements of funds affecting the Foreign Exchange market. London attracted Dutch money whenever the yield was at least 1 per cent higher than in Amsterdam.[15] The export of capital to India, too, became from time to time substantial and affected the exchange value of sterling.

(13) FOREIGN EXCHANGE BROKERS' ROLE

Various Foreign Exchange practices described in the previous section gradually became more refined. The large number of books published for the guidance of merchants and bankers showed familiarity with a wealth of technical details. Economists, too, showed an increasing interest in the practical side of Foreign Exchange. For instance, Sir James Steuart, writing in the 18th century, explains why brokers were used in the Foreign Exchange market. He pointed out that the party which took the initiative for a Foreign Exchange transaction was always at a disadvantage because the rate was liable to move against him. To minimise this effect, if a London merchant had to make a payment in Paris he kept it secret by operating through the intermediary of a broker.[16] To ensure the impartiality of brokers, in many countries they were forbidden to transact Foreign Exchange on their own account. Thus Louis XIV (1643–1715), in his ordinance of 1673, reinforced the ban on *agents de change* functioning as bankers.[17]

We saw in Chapter 3 that already in Ancient Athens the Foreign Exchange market was combined with a market for loans. This system was revived at the medieval Fairs and other Foreign Exchange markets, though its development had to conform to the anti-usury laws. Borrowers on the various continental *bourses* were primarily rulers and municipal authorities. It was not until the second half of the 17th century that the use of domestic bills increased the relative importance of the money market for private domestic lending. Right to the end of the 18th century the Money market remained in most countries a section of the Foreign Exchange market.

Notwithstanding all the above changes and progress since the end of the 15th century, even by the end of the 18th century the Foreign Exchange system was still substantially medieval in many essential respects. Transactions in coins continued to play an important part. Usances were still very long, and this, together with the high cost of transporting coins or bullion and the uncertain quality of most coins, made for relatively wide fluctuations even during periods of stability. Interest continued to be included in exchange rates, and re-change was practised.

Another medieval practice which was still in force in the 18th century was the use of imaginary monetary units, both in domestic and international transactions. Very often foreign bills continued to be made out in such units rather than in currencies that were in actual use, even if actual payments had to be made eventually in coins.

The most important change affecting Foreign Exchange was the decline in the frequency of alterations in mint parities during the 18th century, though there were many notable exceptions to this rule, and the adoption of paper currencies in Russia, Portugal, the North American Colonies and other countries introduced a new major element making for instability.

NOTES TO CHAPTER ELEVEN

1. Thomas Milles, *The Customer's Replie* (London, 1604), pp. 11–12.
2. Adam Smith, *An Inquiry into the Causes and the Nature of the Wealth of Nations*, ed. J. R. McCulloch (Edinburgh, 1863), pp. 135–6.
3. Richard Ehrenberg, *Das Zeitalter der Fugger* (Jena, 1896), vol. i, pp. 133–134.
4. Ehrenberg, *op. cit.* vol. i, p. 93.
5. Ehrenberg, *op. cit.* vol. ii, p. 245.
6. Henri Lapeyre, *Simon Ruiz et les 'asientos' de Philippe II* (Paris, 1953), *passim*.
7. Fernand Braudel, *Le pacte de ricorsa au service du roi d'Espagne*. Studi in onore di Armando Sapori (Milan, 1957), vol. ii, pp. 1119–21.
8. A Justice, *A General Treatise of Monies and Exchanges* (London, 1707), p. 76.
9. Ehrenberg, *op. cit.* vol. ii, pp. 19–20.
10. *Calendar of Treasury Books*, 1702, vol. xvii, Part I, p. 21.
11. *Tudor Economic Documents*, vol. ii, pp. 140–1.
12. *State Papers, Domestic*, 1650, vol. ix, p. 179.
13. Sir Thomas Culpeper, *A Tract against Usury* (London, 1668), p. 31.
14. — Beldam, *Consideration on Money, Bullion and Foreign Exchange* (London, 1722), p. 38.
15. T. S. Ashton, *An Economic History of England – The 18th Century* (London, 1955), p. 193.
16. Sir James Steuart, *An Inquiry into the Principles of Political Economy* (London, 1767), pp. 313–14.
17. Germain Martin, *L'Histoire du crédit en France sous le règne de Louis XIV* (Paris, 1913), vol. i, p. 186.

CHAPTER TWELVE

Exchange Rates and Trends

(1) PREMIUM ON *BANCO* MONEY

THERE was no fundamental change in the method of exchange quotations between the discovery of America and the French Revolution. We saw in the last chapter that exchange rates for bills continued to include interest charges and varied, therefore, at any given moment according to the maturity of the bills. For instance, in Lyons in 1515 bills on Rome were quoted at $59\frac{1}{2}$ for the Easter Fair and $60\frac{1}{2}$ for the August Fair; bills on Medina del Campo at 336 for the Easter Fair and 342 for the August Fair.[1] Reduced to percentages per annum the discrepancies between rates for different maturities usually varied widely, because anticipations of changes in the exchange rates for different dates were liable to be affected by different sets of considerations, seasonal or otherwise.

Rates for payment in *banco* money always differed from the rates for payment in current coin. There was always a premium on *banco* money against the more or less deteriorated local coinage. It tended to be wide on many occasions, though at times of wars when cash was urgently needed it was inclined to contract. In the early 18th century the premium on *banco* money against payment in coins was of the order of 4 to 5 per cent in Amsterdam, 5 to 14 per cent in Hamburg, around 18 per cent in Frankfurt and 20 per cent in Venice.[2]

(2) DIVERSITY OF PARITIES

Exchange rates between fictitious units depended on their relative metallic value which was seldom changed, but they had a fluctuating value in terms of the local currencies in which actual payments were made when cash payments were required. Postelthwayte distinguished between 'real' parities – the ratio between real moneys – and 'political' parities – the ratio between fictitious units.[3] There were usually discrepancies between the official prices of foreign coins fixed by Governments and the fluctuating market ratios. In many instances bills drawn on centres where a fictitious unit existed were issued, quoted and paid also in terms of real currency units.

The calculations of mint parities continued to present a major problem during the 16th and 17th centuries, owing to the frequent difference at a given moment between the metal content of coins of various denominations belonging to the current coinage of the same country. Indeed, in spite of the improvement of the minting technique towards the end of the 17th century, there were often wide discrepancies even between the metal contents of newly minted coins of the same denomination and of the same issue.

As we pointed out in Chapter 8, it was usually profitable to export foreign coins to their countries of origin, or to import national coins, long before it became profitable to export local coins or bullion or to import bullion or foreign coins. Such transactions were largely influenced by the high level of seignorage and minting charges in the importing country, and also by the officially proclaimed rates for foreign coins which were often artificially favourable to the importing country.

(3) GOLD-SILVER RATIO

Since silver coins were in most countries the most important currencies in common use, the parities which were of the greatest practical importance were those relating to their metallic contents. As Malynes observed, 'It is more proper to make Exchanges upon the Silver Coins, for the price of Commodities is most ruled thereby in all places'. He quoted an instance in which, in 1611, gold went to a 10 per cent premium over silver, but domestic prices remained unaffected. 'But if silver were enhanced presently the Prices would follow, and the Price of Exchange would fall more.'[4]

Frequent changes in the official gold-silver ratio, and fluctuation in the relative market value of gold and silver made it difficult to ascertain the metallic ratio between the gold coins of one country and the silver coins of another. In arbitrage the parities between gold coins were of some importance but it was not until the 18th century that they came to assume decisive importance as far as sterling was concerned.

During the 16th and 17th centuries there were very frequent

changes of parities, specie points and exchange rates as a result of debasements and recoinages, and through calling up or down the face value of coins. As during the Medieval Period, the operation of bimetallism called for frequent adjustments of the official metallic value of the gold coins or silver coins in order to adjust the gold-silver ratio. Not only did that ratio continue to fluctuate widely but the market discrepancies that existed at any given moment between the gold-silver ratio in various countries during the Middle Ages continued to prevail also during sub-sequent centuries. For instance, in 1601 the ratio was 11 to 1 in England and 12 to 1 in neighbouring countries, according to the Report of the Royal Commission headed by Sir Richard Martin.[5]

The uneven influx of gold and silver from America tended to affect the ratio between the two metals. Attempts by Charles V and other Governments to resist natural adjustments of the rates – to be discussed in Chapter 14 – produced only temporary results. During periods of transition the discrepancies between official ratios and market ratios affected exchange rates to a considerable extent.

(4) EFFECT OF DETERIORATED COINAGE ON PARITIES

In his correspondence Gresham repeatedly referred to his difficulty in ascertaining the 'true exchange' (parity) between England and Flanders. On two occasions during the 16th century, in 1564 and 1576, Royal Commissions were set up mainly in order to ascertain the parities of sterling. In 1576 the various parities arrived at according to the various methods of calculation differed within a range of over 16 per cent.

What was even worse, these vague and elusive multiple parities could not be looked upon as the real parities for practical purposes. For the relative value of currencies in terms of each other depended not on the official parities but on the rates between the average metal content of the coins actually in circulation, in which payments were made. As during the Middle Ages, the circulation contained most of the time, even during the 18th century, a high if varying proportion of debased, worn coins, though improved minting technique made clipping more difficult.

It will give an idea of the effect of this on the real 'parity' if we recall that before the British re-coinage of 1695 sterling was quoted in Paris at a discount of between 20 and 25 per cent compared with its theoretical parity, owing to the deteriorated quality of the English coinage. Although conditions improved in the 18th century, before the British recoinage of 1774 average gold coins were some 2 per cent below their official weight. Uncertainty about the metal content of the coins to be received in payment made buyers inclined to err on the safe side and was a major cause of erratic fluctuations and discrepancies.

(5) CALCULATION OF SPECIE POINTS

When it came to specie points, their calculation, or rather estimation, was even less dependable. Transport conditions were better than in the Middle Ages; conditions of security improved – at any rate in times of peace – and communications became more frequent. Nevertheless, owing to the ever-present possibility of a change in parities to the disadvantage of the exporter or importer of bullion or specie, in the 16th and 17th centuries such transactions always involved a fairly high exchange risk. Moreover, the medieval bans on the export of bullion and specie continued in most countries during the 16th and most of the 17th centuries. Those violating the law ran the risk of confiscation and other even graver penalties, so that it was not worth their while to take such a risk unless the profit margin was sufficiently wide to make it appear worth their while.

The stricter the penalties, and the more efficiently the ban was enforced, the wider the profit margin had to be before bullion or specie was moved. Thus in practice each revival or reinforcement of old statutes against bullion and specie export widened the specie points, and led to wider exchange movements. Owing to the difference in the degree of efficiency of the embargo on bullion and specie, and in the degree of risk involved in breaking the law in various countries, the margins between parities and specie points varied widely according to country.

The first known calculation of specie point was given by Gresham in his letter to Elizabeth I (1558–1603) in 1558. He gave the rate of 21s. 4d. as the gold import point from Flanders, so that at the then prevailing rate of 22s. there was a profit of 8d. in the import of bullion in preference to making payments by exchange.[6]

Towards the end of the 17th century the cost of specie shipments between England and Ireland was 6 per cent. Cary remarked in

1696 that this made it unprofitable to send guineas in payment, even though they commanded a premium of 12 per cent in Dublin. It was more profitable to buy bills on Dublin at 15 per cent discount.[7] Writing in the 'thirties of the 18th century, Cantillon reckoned the costs of specie shipments as being just over 2 per cent in time of peace between London and Amsterdam and to 6 per cent between Paris and Amsterdam. The cost between London and Spain was 5 per cent. It was something like 10 to 12 per cent between England and India.[8]

(6) COST OF SPECIE EXPORT LICENCES

Shipping costs for gold and silver were particularly high between Spain and her American colonies, judging by the fact that in Seville in 1520 the discount was 10 per cent on bills on Haiti, 15 per cent on bills on Mexico, 25 per cent on bills on Peru and 35 per cent on bills on Chile.[9]

The influence of the cost of licence for the export of specie from Spain on specie points was illustrated by a report of Philip II's agent, Ruiz, quoted by Lapeyre, according to which, at an exchange rate of 420 *maravedis* per *écu* it was preferable to remit money by exchange, but if the rate rose above 425 it became more advantageous to secure a licence.[10]

Rules adopted from time to time in some countries, under which payments had to be accepted in part in certain currencies other than those in terms of which the bills were issued, necessarily affected the exchange rates. About this more will be said in Chapter 14.

There were also frequent changes in seignorage and minting charges. Uncertainty of transport costs and insurance premiums, changes of which were unpredictable, was added to frequent changes in parities, or to the absence of ascertainable parities, as a cause of wide fluctuations in specie points. In such circumstances bullion or specie arbitrage was indeed far from being the near-exact science it is in our times.

Banks which had their own branches in foreign centres were of course at a slight advantage, because at any rate they did not have to allow for commission when reckoning the costs. It had been largely the possession of a network of branches that secured for the Italian banks, and later for some South German banks, a strong position in the Foreign Exchange markets.

(7) DISCREPANCY BETWEEN RATES IN CREDITOR AND DEBTOR CENTRES

While during the Middle Ages the Flemish currency was quoted 'uncertain' in London and sterling was quoted 'certain' in Bruges, during the 16th century sterling came to be quoted both in London and in Antwerp in a fluctuating number of Flemish currency units. The same rule applied to the exchange on Hamburg. As Malynes put it, London was 'the head of exchange' in relation to these cities. On the other hand, the French *écu* and the Venetian *ducat* continued to be quoted 'uncertain' both in London and Antwerp. The practice in this respect changed from time to time.

The medieval system under which there was always a marked discrepancy between the rate of creditor centre's exchange quoted in debtor centres and the rate of the debtor's exchange quoted at the same time in the creditor centres, in favour of the latter, continued during the 16th century. In respect of *maravedi* the discrepancy was at times remarkably wide, largely owing to the existence of strict exchange control measures in Spain. With the decline of interest rates and the reduction of the cost of specie shipments, however, the secular trend was towards a contraction of discrepancies.

(8) CAUSES OF INSTABILITY

The instability of exchange rates that characterised the Middle Ages continued during the 16th and 17th centuries. In the majority of instances wars or civil wars were its main cause, with bad administration as a poor second. Court extravagance and lavish expenditure on the proverbial 'foreign favourites' of kings, which had played an important part in bringing about many medieval devaluations or debasements, almost ceased to figure among the causes from the 16th century, though the endless succession of Spanish devaluations, and also English devaluations under Henry VIII, were attributable partly to extravagant and incompetent administration.

Increased international financial activities of Governments in the 16th and the 17th centuries introduced an additional element of instability, owing to the effect of the raising and repayment of loans abroad on exchange rates. Last but not least, active intervention by Government agents in Foreign Exchange markets were as often as not influences making for instability, and the possibility of such intervention decidedly made for uncertainty.

But the most important factor making for uncertainty, the power of Governments to change the metal content or the nominal value of their coins, lost a great deal of its importance as an influence on exchange rates by the 18th century, at any rate as far as the leading exchanges were concerned. Such changes came to be much less frequent.

The following is a broad outline of major trends in the principal Foreign Exchanges during the period covered in this section:

(9) CHANGES IN PARITIES UNDER THE TUDORS

After a period of stability under Henry VII, the wars of Henry VIII with France that began in 1523 resulted in a depreciation of sterling, the exchange rate of Venetian *ducats* and of Flemish pounds *groat* in London rising sharply. There was a heavy outflow of specie, and to check it the face value of coins was enhanced in 1526 by 10 per cent. Again between 1543 and 1551 the metallic content of coins was repeatedly reduced, causing a depreciation of sterling by something like 60 per cent. All the time there were frequent complaints about the 'undervaluation' of sterling (meaning its depreciation to a discount) as the cause of the outflow of specie.

Anticipations of changes in parities influenced exchange rates considerably. For instance, in 1551 when the tide turned in favour of sterling and testoons were called down from 12d. to 9d., there were persistent rumours of a further change. Although firm denials were issued, and an official proclamation threatened the rumour-mongers with pillory and with the loss of one of their ears, the exchanges were affected by the rumours. The administration ended by calling down the testoons by another 3d., only a month after the denial.

Sterling depreciated temporarily in Antwerp at the time of Wyatt's revolt in 1554, but it recovered when that revolt was suppressed. Soon after the accession of Elizabeth I there was a successful recoinage and thenceforth sterling commanded more confidence abroad. This was due not only to the improvement of the coins in circulation and the absence of any further tampering with the coinage, but also to the cessation of borrowing abroad. References to sterling being 'undervalued' recurred from time to

time, however, in Gresham's correspondence and other contemporary material. It often depreciated below specie points. For
instance, in 1564 there was an outflow of bullion, sterling having
depreciated to 19s. 8d. *groat*.

(10) STERLING AND ARMADA THREAT

The behaviour of sterling under the menace of a Spanish invasion
during the 1580's can be followed from a series of exchange rates
quoted at the Lyons fairs. While in 1580 the *écu de marc* was around
73, sterling gradually depreciated, the rate reaching 79 in 1586
and 1587. During 1587 it gradually recovered and, oddly enough,
this trend continued also in the Armada crisis year of 1588. At each
successive quarterly fair sterling was better in spite of the imminent
threat of a Spanish invasion. After the destruction of the Armada,
at the August fair the rate was down at 70½ compared with 74
early in the year.[11] During that troubled period there were so
many conflicting influences, military, political and economic – the
Low Countries had their own difficulties and so did France[12] –
that it would be difficult to find an acceptable explanation of the
improvement that preceded the victory.

During the last quarter of the 16th century England frequently
suffered grave disadvantages through the fixing of the official
tariff of foreign coins by the Government of the Low Countries
in a way as to draw specie to the Netherlands. The frequent
adjustment of the official rates in Antwerp caused much concern
to Gresham and Burghley, because of its effect on sterling.

(11) STERLING OVERVALUATION AND ENGLISH TRADE

In 1601 an ill-advised change in the gold-silver ratio resulted in
an appreciation of sterling, and this caused a depression in the
cloth export trade at the beginning of the reign of James I.

Adverse exchange was a frequently recurrent complaint under
the early Stuarts, as it led to a persistent outflow of specie. The
upheaval on the Continent during the early part of the Thirty
Years War caused sterling to appreciate in Hamburg and other
German cities, with the result that English exports were handicapped and imports were stimulated. During the 1630's there was

a persistent outflow of specie, mainly to France, but also to Holland, the exchanges of both countries making shipments often profitable. The drain continued much of the time during the Civil War and the Protectorate, as sterling was affected by the withdrawal of foreign capital and the flight of British capital.

(12) STERLING AFFECTED BY DETERIORATED COINAGE

Towards the end of the 17th century sterling weakened, owing to the deterioration of the coinage under the late Stuarts. After the Revolution of 1688, the war against Louis XIV accentuated that weakness, because of the cost of maintaining the British armies on the Continent. During 1695 the Dutch exchange rose to a premium of over 30 per cent, and it was generally expected that sterling would be devalued. The Government rejected, however, Lowndes' advice to adjust the legal parity to the low value of the deteriorated coinage. Thereupon a gradual recovery set in and it became accentuated towards the middle of 1696 through the delayed effect of the re-coinage decided upon at the beginning of that year, under the terms of which the coinage was restored to its full face value at the Government's expense. By November sterling rose for a very short time to a premium. But, as a result of the war, it soon went to a discount again.

The newly created Bank of England had to draw bills on Amsterdam in order to finance the British forces abroad and this tended to keep sterling at a discount throughout the War of the Spanish Succession. Matters were made worse by the ill-advised method of giving certain firms the monopoly of supplying the Government with Foreign Exchange.

(13) EFFECT OF WAR OF SPANISH SUCCESSION

The end of the war left sterling overvalued (in the modern sense) in relation to the *livre*, for the same reason as in the 1920's – the more extensive depreciation of the French exchange was not accompanied by a corresponding increase in wages in France. This affected the balance of payments and caused sterling to weaken temporarily in Amsterdam. Since, however, the coinage was not tampered with, fluctuations of exchange rates remained more or less within the approximate specie points. It is true, in the course of the following decades the coinage was inclined to deteriorate, but silver coins lost more of their metallic value than gold coins, and since by this time gold came to be more important in England than silver, exchange rates were not affected to a very large degree.

Strange as this may sound, in 1715 and again in 1745 the Jacobite Revolt caused sterling to appreciate temporarily in Amsterdam. According to Ashton this was because of the assumption that a restoration of the Stuarts would have affected Holland's political position adversely.[13]

(14) MOVEMENTS OF DUTCH FUNDS

A few years after the end of the War of the Spanish Succession the decline of interest rates in England caused sterling to weaken, owing to withdrawals of Dutch funds invested in London. This influence of the movements of Dutch funds to and from London continued from time to time to play an important part in determining the sterling-*guilder* exchange throughout the 18th century. In 1759, for instance, the favourable terms of a new Government issue attracted Dutch funds and made sterling appreciate. On the other hand, there were Dutch withdrawals on each occasion when Amsterdam experienced a financial crisis. Indeed on such occasions support of Dutch banks from London tended to accentuate the effect of Dutch withdrawals on the exchange.[14]

Notwithstanding wars and other disturbing influences, the sterling-*guilder* rate remained remarkably stable during the 18th century. According to Ashton the initial effect of wars was an appreciation of sterling, because there was a demand for cash leading to selling of foreign bill holdings. But subsequent progress of the wars led to a depreciation of sterling owing to the cost of British forces on the Continent and of subsidies paid to allies. Sterling declined to low levels in the war years of 1710, 1743, 1760 and 1777.[15] It never declined to a level comparable to the one reached in 1695–6, because the coinage was not allowed to deteriorate to a comparable extent. Post-war booms caused sterling to appreciate temporarily. The undertone of sterling became firm between the Peace of Paris and the Wars of the French Revolution, largely owing to the favourable effect of the Industrial Revolution on the balance of payments.

(15) FRENCH EXCHANGE AFFECTED BY WARS AND CIVIL WARS

The French exchange was affected by a series of devaluations during the 16th and 17th centuries, beginning with the reduction in the metal content of the coinage during the wars of Francis I (1515–47), and ending with the cuts resulting from inflationary financing of extravagant expenditure by Louis XIV. On rare occasions there were attempts at revaluation. Outstanding amongst them was the reform of 1577 following on the pronouncement by the Estates of Blois in 1574. After each effort, however, the secular downward trend reasserted itself, usually as a result of wars or civil wars. During the wars of the *Fronde* the *livre* was repeatedly devalued in order to prevent the efflux of specie through the depreciation of the exchange.

The two major wars of Louis XIV, in 1688–97 and 1701–13, were accompanied by further depreciations caused partly by the new device of paper money inflation. Under a Royal decree 25 per cent of each payment had to be accepted in paper money. Since the notes were at a substantial discount this rule necessarily affected the exchange value of the French currency.

John Law's inflationary experiment in 1720–1 temporarily unsettled the French exchange which depreciated considerably in Amsterdam and in London. But the reform of 1726 put an end to the policy of debasements and thereafter official mint parities remained unchanged right to the Revolution. Even though exchange fluctuations resulting from major wars and the ups and downs of the French balance of payments were relatively wide, having regard to the stability of mint parities, they were incomparably narrower than during any previous period of French history.

(16) GERMAN CURRENCY CHAOS DURING THE THIRTY YEARS WAR

Absence of political unity in Germany was one of the causes of the currency chaos that reached its climax during the early years of the Thirty Years War between 1618 and 1623. Even before that disastrous period, Germany experienced much currency trouble. Imperial decrees relating to currency were often disregarded by most German States which issued inferior coins depreciating rapidly in terms of the *rix-dollar*. The trade balance of many of these States was adverse during a great part of the 16th century and there were frequent complaints about the outflow of specie. In the course of an investigation of the heavy outflow of coins in 1586 merchants giving evidence stated that there was a profit of something like 10 per cent on such arbitrage.[16]

The depreciating trend became strongly accentuated after the outbreak of the Thirty Years War. Although the worst currency chaos came to an end in 1623 – by which time the *kreutzer* declined to one-twentieth of its original value – it was not until after the conclusion of the Peace of Westphalia in 1648 that it became possible to attempt monetary reforms. That treaty weakened, however, the Emperor's control over the currencies of the German States.

While the 18th century was a period of relative stability for the British and French exchanges, in Germany the currencies of Prussia and other German States suffered gravely as a result of the Seven Years War. Frederick the Great (1740–86) felt compelled to debase his currency, and other German rulers followed his example. In Hamburg the premium on *banco* money over current coin widened considerably. In 1763 re-coinages were carried out, but it took a long time for Prussia and other German States to restore the soundness of their currencies.

(17) DEBASEMENTS IN SPAIN

Spain experienced a prolonged series of debasements and devaluations throughout the late 16th century and the 17th century, as a result of expensive wars abroad, the perennial adverse trade balance and inflation in the form of over-issues of base vellum coinage, in addition to the inflation caused by the heavy influx of gold and silver from America. The gold and silver coins retained their high quality under Charles V and Philip II, but the adverse trend of the exchanges and the rigidity of gold-silver ratio, together with the high cost of wars abroad, resulted in a constant outflow of precious metals. The depreciating trend of the *maravedi* continued during the 18th century, though not at the same rate as before.

(18) DUTCH EXCHANGE ACHIEVES STABILITY

The exchange of the Low Countries depreciated during the last quarter of the 16th century as a result of the prolonged wars with Spain. Between 1574 and 1590 repeated devaluations caused the

Antwerp exchange to depreciate by 48 per cent. Brulez observed that after each devaluation there was a partial recovery,[17] with the exception of 1585, when the sack of Antwerp by the Spanish Army prevented a recovery after the devaluation. Evidently speculators, having discounted the devaluations covered when they materialised, Brulez was unable to discern either seasonal movements or cyclical trends during that period.

While in 1575 the *rix dollar* was 32 *stuyvers*, in 1586 it was 45 and in 1620 it was 52. Thereafter it became more stable for most of the 17th century. During the 18th century the *guilder* was one of the most stable currencies of Europe.

The Swedish currency experienced major depreciations during the wars of the 17th century and those of Charles XII (1697–1718), owing to inflation by means of the issue of copper coinage. The Russian *rouble*, too, was depreciated from time to time, largely as a result of excessive issue of copper fiduciary currency. Under Peter the Great (1682–1725) the *rouble* rate depreciated by some 50 per cent.

NOTES TO CHAPTER TWELVE

1. Karl Otto Müller, *Welthandelsbrauche, 1480–1540* (Stuttgart, 1939), p. 68.
2. William Forbes, *A Methodical Treatise Concerning Bills of Exchange* (Edinburgh, 1718), p. 4.
3. Malachy Postlethwayt, *The Universal Dictionary of Trade and Commerce* (London, 1776).
4. Gerald Malynes, *Lex Mercatoria*, 3rd ed. (London, 1686), pp. 264–5.
5. *State Papers, Domestic*, 1601, 279, p. 97.
6. J. W. Burgon, *The Life and Times of Sir Thomas Gresham* (London, 1889), p. 485.
7. John Cary, *An Essay on the Coyn and Credit of England* (Bristol, 1696).
8. Richard Cantillon, *Essai sur la nature du commerce en général*, Trs. Henry Higgs (London, 1931), p. 253.
9. André Sayous, 'Les changes de l'Espagne sur l'Amérique en 16e siècle', *Revue d'Économie Politique*, Nov.–Dec. 1927, p. 1439.
10. Henri Lapeyre, *Une Famille de marchands, les Ruiz* (Paris, 1955), p. 288.
11. Lapeyre, *op. cit.* pp. 468–70.
12. Lapeyre, *op. cit.* p. 455.
13. T. S. Ashton, *An Economic History of England – The 18th Century* (London, 1955), p. 194.
14. Ashton, *op. cit.* p. 193.
15. Ashton, *op. cit.* p. 196.
16. W. A. Shaw, *The History of Currency* (London, 1895), p. 102.
17. W. Brulez, *De Wisselkoersen te Antwerpen in het Laatste Kwart van de 16e. Eeuw* (The Hague, 1956), pp. 84–5.

CHAPTER THIRTEEN

Emergence of a Foreign Exchange Theory

(1) PROGRESS FROM THE 16th CENTURY

A FOREIGN Exchange theory, in the sense of a deliberate analysis of causes and effects of Foreign Exchange movements and the rôle of Foreign Exchange in the economic system, was almost unknown until the 16th century. Its origin and progress during the 16th and 17th centuries was mainly due to contributions by scholastic writers concerned primarily with the ethics of Foreign Exchange, by experts advising Governments on Foreign Exchange policy and by writers of textbooks on commercial arithmetic or of practical guides for merchants. Not until the late 17th century and the 18th century did economists assume full control of the subject.

The following are the principal Foreign Exchange theories that originated or were developed during the 16th, 17th and 18th centuries:

1. The speculation or 'conspiracy' theory.
2. The trade balance theory.
3. The balance of indebtedness theory.
4. The theory of specie point mechanism.
5. The theory relating to the effect of exchange rates on prices.
6. The supply and demand theory.
7. The quantity theory.
8. The purchasing power parity theory.
9. The terms of trade theory.
10. The interest theory.

(2) THE SPECULATION OR CONSPIRACY THEORY

Throughout the ages it was a widespread and firmly held belief that speculative activities, conspiracies, or intervention by hostile Governments were to blame for exchange depreciations. The popularity of this one-sided, exaggerated and over-simplified theory – which was seldom applied in reverse, for speculators

were hardly ever given credit for causing exchanges to appreciate
– must have been partly responsible for the slow development of
more scientific explanations of Foreign Exchange trends. But even
in the absence of any sinister designs, speculation on future
changes – whose anticipation produced a psychological effect on
the market – could often account for exchange movements.

Beyond doubt there was a great deal of truth in the frequent
complaints about deliberate action by greedy merchants or
bankers, or by hostile Governments, to bring about a depreciation
of exchanges, much more than modern writers, influenced by more
recent experience, are prepared to admit. In a relatively narrow
market it was easier to carry out speculative manœuvres and to
engage in malevolent machinations causing the exchanges to
depreciate. Moreover, the Foreign Exchange markets operated
overwhelmingly in foreign bills maturing in several months, and
there was therefore ample scope for conspiracy or for official
action to cause a depreciation of an exchange by the simultaneous
effect of artificially increasing the supply of the bills in the currency
concerned and, at the same time, reducing the demand for them
by mopping up the liquid financial resources available for that
purpose.

In modern conditions the scope for conspiracy is much more
limited. For anyone selling spot exchanges has to deliver them in
two days, while anyone selling forward exchange receives no cash
until he has delivered them on maturity. Selling short is, therefore,
not nearly as effective as it was in the 16th century. Furthermore,
four centuries ago speculators had the additional temporary
advantage of using profitably the funds they mopped up by their
bear operations.

The much quoted successful manœuvres by Gaspare Ducci who,
in 1540, cornered liquid funds in Antwerp, and thereby influenced
exchange rates to the detriment of the Portuguese Government
agent, was only one of the innumerable instances in support of
the conspiracy theory. But speculation and sinister manœuvring
was frequently suspected even in instances when exchange rates
merely adapted themselves to changes in their parities, or were
obviously influenced by an adverse balance of payments.

The primitive speculation theory, and the conspiracy theory
that went with it, was revived on each occasion when exchanges
were weak. Usually it was the favourite defence of inefficient
Governments. Thus towards the end of the 16th century the

F

Hanseatic League, which was by then on the decline, accused the Merchant Adventurers of influencing the exchanges against its exchange.

(3) CHANGES IN PARITIES AND CHANGES DUE TO SUPPLY AND DEMAND

Gresham has been criticised by modern historians for his alleged inability to discriminate between exchange movements due to changes in mint parities and those due to other causes affecting the supply and demand of bills. Admittedly, in a letter written to Elizabeth I in 1558, Gresham claimed credit for having raised the value of sterling in Antwerp from 16s. to 22s. *groat* in 1551–1552,[1] even though its recovery was quite obviously caused by a change in the intrinsic value of sterling resulting from the reform measures of the Northumberland administration. But, considering that his correspondence and memoranda disclose a remarkably high degree of familiarity with Foreign Exchange theory and practice, it seems reasonable to assume that his claim was simply inspired by his understandable desire to emphasise the importance of market influences and, by implication, of his rôle in controlling them. In any case, in the very same letter he clearly stated that the devaluations by Henry VIII caused sterling to depreciate, so that it seems most unlikely that he should have been unaware of the operation in reverse of the principle implied in his remark.

Scholastic writers were able at an early stage to draw sharp distinction between the changes in the intrinsic value of exchanges and changes in their valuation in the Foreign Exchange markets caused by other legitimate influences. An outstanding analysis of the causes of deviation of exchange rates from their mint parities was provided by Azpilcueta Navarro, a Professor of canon law at the Salamanca University. He stated that the exchange value of the moneys may diverge from their relative intrinsic values, among other reasons, because of anticipations of debasements; or because money is worth more where it is scarce and less where it is plentiful; or because one money is absent and the other present.[2]

(4) EFFECT OF ADVERSE TRADE BALANCE

Neither he nor other Spanish writers of the 16th century contributed anything noteworthy on the effect of the trade balance on exchange rates. In this respect English writers of the same period were much more advanced. Gresham's Memorandum to Elizabeth I in 1559, indicates awareness of the effect of an adverse trade balance by suggesting that one of the ways of improving sterling would be 'by making more Englissh commodities by a full third parte in value or more to be caryed owt yerely from hence then be browght yerely of forrayne commodities hither'.[3] The Memorandum of the Royal Commission of 1564 also indicated familiarity with the theory by recommending devices to reinforce the customs control and thereby reduce imports that found their way into England.[4]

While a number of early Mercantilist writers recognised that exchange rates were determined by supply and demand – or, as they frequently put it, by the relationship between the supply of bills and that of funds – many of them failed to make it adequately clear that supply and demand were in turn largely determined by the trade balance, including invisible items. They merely stated that an adverse balance caused an outflow of specie. The clarification of the way in which an adverse balance operated through exchange rates and the specie point mechanism was the result of the controversies in England at the beginning and end of the 17th century, about which more will be said below.

(5) INVISIBLE ITEMS AND CAPITAL ITEMS

The importance of invisible items such as military expenditure abroad, subsidies to foreign Governments, the expenses of ambassadors and other travellers, etc., and remittances of Papal collections, was realised by many early writers on Foreign Exchange, even though the effect of these items, like that of visible trade, was discussed from the point of view of specie movements rather than exchange rates. It was to the credit of Mun to have listed the above items and some others besides as factors in international payments. Petty, writing in the 1660's about the abnormal discount on the Irish exchange, went into details of the effect of invisible import items, both on current and capital account, on the exchange rate between Dublin and London.[5] Later Cantillon added expenditure on secret service to the list.

By the 18th century the balance of trade theory had taken such deep roots that many experts came to rely upon exchange rates as a barometer indicating the state of the trade balance. It was realised, however, by some of them that, in addition to the current trade items, capital items were also liable to affect exchanges.

(6) BALANCE OF INDEBTEDNESS THEORY

Dutot stated that 'the exchange rate indicates from day to day the indebtedness of our nation against another'.[6] Here we have the beginnings of the balance of indebtedness theory. Ten years later, Montesquieu put forward a static theory, revived in the controversies of the early 1920's. According to him, so far from determining exchange rates, there could be no balance of indebtedness, since international accounts must always be balanced.[7]

For a long time the impact of an import or export surplus on exchange rates was always understood in a bilateral sense. It was widely assumed both by practical experts and theoretical commentators that the exchange rate between two countries was determined by the surplus of deficit on trade and of capital movements between those two countries in isolation from the rest of the world. The fact that, owing to triangular and mutlilateral trade, and to the highly developed international exchange arbitrage, such effects were liable to spread to all markets and to all exchanges in addition to those of the two countries immediately concerned, so that it was the overall surplus or deficit that mattered, appears to have been ignored until it was first clearly stated by Mun.

(7) THE MALYNES-MISSELDEN-MUN CONTROVERSY

Malynes, writing in the 1620's, sought to create scientific foundations for the theory blaming speculators for all the economic trouble of which England was suffering during the early period of the Stuart régime. They were held responsible for the undervaluation of sterling and the resulting loss of silver, as a result of which there was a chronic shortage of money to the grave detriment of trade.

This theory provided a starting-point of one of the most important controversies in the history of Foreign Exchange theory, between the three 'M's' – Malynes on the one hand and Misselden and Mun on the other. Both antagonists of Malynes maintained that the loss of specie was due to the adverse trade balance, but while Misselden believed that the outflow could and should be checked by devaluation, Mun adapted the static theory that change in the value of the coinage would not affect the trade balance which should be improved by other means.

Although Malynes was greatly superior to his two antagonists in respect of his knowledge of theoretico-technical aspects of Foreign Exchange, his basic views were unsound. Mun emerged easily victorious from the triangular controversy and gained immense authority with his theory that exchanges, and therefore specie movements, depended on the trade balance. His influence was largely responsible for the subsequent decision to free the coinage from seignorage, to remove the ban on bullion and foreign specie exports, and to abstain from using changes in parities as a deliberate device of Foreign Exchange policy.

Almost simultaneously with the above controversy the problem was argued out also in Naples between De Santis and Serra. During the early part of the 17th century Naples suffered considerable hardships through the persistent outflow of specie. De Santis attributed this to speculation, while Serra maintained that it was due to the adverse trade balance.

Mun's victory established the trade balance theory as the accepted Foreign Exchange theory. Its one-sided and exaggerated interpretation was criticised by Nicholas Barbon and later by Sir James Steuart.

(8) SPECIE POINT MECHANISM DISCOVERED

By far the most important achievement of early Foreign Exchange theory was the discovery of the rôle played by Foreign Exchange in the readjustment of discrepancies between specie supplies in particular countries. The first step in that direction was the discovery by economists of the specie point mechanism that had long been familiar to merchants. We saw in the last chapter that in his letter to Elizabeth I, Gresham alluded to the influence of the cost of specie shipments among the factors influencing the international flow of specie.[8] Even earlier, in 1553, in a letter to the Council, he said that as a result of the appreciation of sterling in Antwerp to 22 *groat* the specie that had left England during the debasement period was likely to return. While he was concerned with the specie import only, Malynes, writing about half a century later, was concerned with specie export points only. Writing in the 1690's, Locke and Clement referred to the cost of shipments as a factor in the exchange position.

Some half a century later Hume and Cantillon advanced the theory further. Hume observed that an import surplus causes the exchange to turn against us and this becomes a new encouragement to export 'as much as the charge of carriage and insurance of the money would amount to'.[9] This was an allusion to the automatic adjustment of the trade balance through the operation of specie points. Some two decades before its publication, Cantillon wrote on similar lines, but it was not published until 1755, some years after Hume's work appeared.

(9) ORIGINS OF STATIC THEORY

The main significance of the Hume–Cantillon theory is that it is the first indication of a theory of an automatically balancing international economy, and it establishes an important link between Foreign Exchange theory and general economic theory. Indeed it formed an essential part of the static theory which was to be developed further during the 19th century. Other links were established with economic theory by earlier writers who observed the effect of exchange movements on prices and of price movements on exchanges, and the impact of terms of trade on balances of payment and exchanges.

Another static concept, which overlooked or underrated the existence of a time-lag between a rise and fall of the external value of a currency and the corresponding adjustment of its internal value, appeared on the scene at an early stage. We saw above that Mun opposed devaluations on the ground that the prices of imported and exported goods would change to a corresponding degree.[10] It seems that disregard of the dynamism of time-lags is almost as old as Foreign Exchange theory itself.

(10) HOW EXCHANGES AFFECT PRICES

Early writers were much more concerned with the effect of exchange movements on prices than with the effect of price movements of exchanges. Writing in 1549, Hales referred to the effect of debasements on domestic prices.[11] The Memorandum of the Royal Commission of 1564 applies this theory in no uncertain terms to prices of goods that are subject to foreign trade transactions. 'The Exchange is the gouernere of prices of all warres

interchangublye vented between this Realm and the Low Coun-
treyes.'[12] This view is a great advance on the bullionist conception
according to which the reason why debasements caused a rise in
domestic prices was not because of their effect on exchange rates,
but because the metal content of coins was lower. Even such a
prominent monetary economist and enlightened expert on Foreign
Exchange as Davanzati accepted that theory,[13] and so did a
number of English Mercantilist writers throughout the 17th century.

(11) HOW PRICES AFFECT EXCHANGES

Again and again we come across remarks in 16th and 17th century
scholastic literature to the effect that exchange rates depend on
the ease or scarcity of funds, or on the plentiful or scant supply of
bills. This theory was first put forward clearly in 1512 by John
Major (or Mair), a Scottish theologian living in Paris,[14] in a work
published about 1521. The same idea found very clear expression
in the following passage of Gresham's Memorandum of 1559:
'The waye to rayse th'exhaunge for England . . . by making
money scante in Lumbard Strete'.[15] Contemporary Spanish official circles, too, realised this truth. Margaret of Parma wrote to
Philip II from Brussels in 1562 that the Antwerp *bourse* was tight
and consequently Foreign Exchanges were low.

The quantity of money which Gresham and other writers of
the period had in mind was obviously the supply of cash available
in the Foreign Exchange market for the purchase of bills. Most
of them did not make it clear whether they had in mind that
supply of funds or the entire supply of coinage in circulation in
the country concerned.

(12) ORIGINS OF THE PURCHASING POWER
PARITY THEORY

From this point of view the Salamanca School and some other
Spanish scholastic writers of the 16th and 17th centuries were well
ahead of their contemporaries. While some of their writings
merely expressed the familiar supply and demand theory as it
applied to Foreign Exchange, others expressed distinctly the view
that exchanges were influenced by the effect of the relative quantities of money in the whole country on the relative price level in

the country concerned. Clearest of all was Domingo de Banez who, writing at the end of the 16th century, stated: 'In places where money is scarce goods will be cheaper than in those where the whole mass of money is bigger, and therefore it is lawful to exchange a smaller sum in one country for a larger sum in another'.[16]

What most other Spanish scholars appeared to have had in mind was merely the relationship between the prices of goods exported from Spain to the West Indies. The prices of these goods, by the time they reached their destination, was very high, owing to the cost and risk of their transport. Naturally enough, the purchasing power parities representing the difference between the prices of these goods in Spain and in Mexico or Peru were strongly in favour of the Spanish exchange. During the early Colonial period there was very little export of goods other than precious metal from the colonies to Spain, so that the prices of local products did not enter into the picture.

(13) ITS LIMITED APPLICATION

The theory in the above sense merely amounted to a recognition of the truism that if goods actually exported to France cost so-and-so much in sterling in England and cost so-and-so many *livres* in France then the sterling-*livre* rate represented the arithmetical ratio between the English and French prices of these goods, allowing for the cost of transport. The recognition of such arithmetical relationship by Mercado among others, between the relative prices of Spanish goods in Spain and in her colonies and the exchange rates of bills on those colonies[17] did not amount, therefore, to a recognition of the influence of relative average price levels on exchange rates.

The one-sided nature of foreign trade between Spain and her colonies made for a strong demand for bills on Spain, which were always at a considerable premium. The more distant were the colonies the higher was the premium, which corresponded to the higher cost and risk of gold and silver shipments to Spain and the loss of interest for longer periods. As I pointed out in Chapter 9, the theory according to which exchange rates varied according to distances between the two centres concerned may be regarded as a form of cost-of-production theory, since the rates were determined by the cost of the operation.

(14) ITS ADVANCED APPLICATION

The controversy around the recoinage of 1696 contributed much towards the progress of Foreign Exchange theory. Outstanding amongst them is a combination of the purchasing power parity theory in a broader sense and the trade balance theory, put forward by Locke. According to him, money 'is the most worth in that country where there is the least money in proportion to its trade. . . . The over-balance of the trade must be taken into consideration. These two together regulate the exchange.'[18]

Already by the middle of the 17th century the purchasing power parity theory attained in one respect a degree of refinement which has remained unsurpassed right to our days. Henry Robinson, writing in 1641, was able to discriminate between the effect of an undervalued exchange in a sellers' market and in a buyers' market. According to him, the reason why the undervaluation of sterling was not an advantage to English exporters was that 'all other Nations now almost make cloth of their owne'.[19]

(15) EFFECT OF TIGHT AND PLENTIFUL MONEY SUPPLY

Practical experience amply confirmed the theory that exchange rates depended on the relative supply of funds in the money market. For instance, paradoxical as this may seem, the arrival of gold and silver fleets from the New World to Seville affected adversely the exchange value of the *maravedi* because it enabled Spanish operators to increase their demand for foreign bills. The first impact of this influx of monetary metals was felt on the Seville Foreign Exchange market; after each arrival of gold or silver fleets there was a discrepancy between exchange rates quoted in Seville and Medina del Campo, in favour of the latter. It took a little time before the effect of the increase in the volume of money spread over other Spanish Foreign Exchange markets. Owing to the ban on the export of gold and silver from Spain, the effect of monetary ease on the *maravedi* was not offset by an automatic efflux, but in due course its depreciation beyond specie points did result in an outflow, with or without licence.

When money was tight in Flanders as a result of war, or in France as a result of Civil War, the early effect was an appreciation of the Flemish or French exchange. At one stage during the Civil

F 2

War in England sterling was firm, because loss of specie through payments for munitions from abroad and outflow of refugee capital resulted in an acute scarcity of funds in Lombard Street, and caused a reduction of the demand for foreign bills. It was not until later stages of wars and civil wars that inflationary expenditure through debasements began to produce an adverse effect on exchanges.

(16) THE TERMS OF TRADE CONCEPT

Some writers in the 16th and 17th centuries showed themselves aware of the terms of trade concept. One of the frequently raised grievances of the period was that prices abroad were higher than in England. Hales expressed the view that domestic prices should rise in the interest of improving the trade balance, for since we must buy dear, we must also sell dear, 'or else we should make ill bargaynes for ourselves'.[20] Gresham's Memorandum pointed out in 1559 that if sterling appreciated English merchants could buy more foreign goods for the same amount of sterling.[21]

In France, the Estates General of Blois in 1574 indicated a familiarity with the adverse effect of exchange depreciation on the proceeds of exports. Arguing against a further devaluation of the coinage, they pointed out that, as a result of its depreciation, France now received less gold and silver for her exports. They suggested that the prices of goods should be raised in order to get more gold and silver for French exports.[22]

(17) EXCHANGE OPERATIONS CANNOT AFFECT ADVERSE BALANCES

It is to the credit of Raleigh and Mun to have alluded to the fact that in the long run specie supply in a country could only be affected by the balance of payments. But it did not find really clear expression until the late 17th century and the 18th century. Locke stressed the absurdity of the notion that an international debt could be settled by issuing bills unless they were drawn on the proceeds of actual goods exports. He also pointed out that imported silver would only be re-exported unless its import was due to an 'overbalance'.[23] Melon observed that if we have an adverse trade balance we shall owe that balance until we repay it either by an export surplus or by sending specie. Conversely, in the absence of an adverse trade balance the counterpart of an outflow of bullion or specie is simply represented by an increase of privately owned foreign assets. He also said that if the Government tried to support the exchange by selling foreign bills at rates favourable to the buyers, the country does not settle thereby its external debts. 'We shall remain debtors until we pay, and we cannot pay with new bills, as this merely amounts to a renewal of the debt.'[24]

(18) HOW 'DRY' EXCHANGES AFFECTED RATES

On the face of it 'dry' exchanges were supposed to affect exchange rates, because they were simply sold to the 'deliverer' on the understanding that the 'taker' would default on it and would pay after the re-change operation was completed. Actually, as de Roover observes, these exchanges did influence exchange rates through their influence on the interest rates that are included in the exchange rates for bills representing genuine international transfers.[25] If an increase of demand for domestic credits disguised in the form of dry exchanges caused a rise in interest rates, 'deliverers' buying genuine bills expected to earn similar interest on such bills. De Roover might have added that when as a result of an increase in the supply of dry exchanges the liquid resources of the market were mopped up, the resulting scarcity would also materially affect exchange rates.

The reciprocal character of the relationship between exchange rates and interest rates emerges from some early writings. Thus, Malynes realised that the outflow of bullion resulting from adverse exchange rates leads to a rise in interest rates.[26]

(19) GRESHAM'S LAW

The famous 'Gresham's Law', as it is generally understood, states that bad money is in the habit of driving out good money, without making any refernce to the vital rôle exchange rates play in the operation of the law. Yet in many situations good money was able to remain in the country because, as Davanzati pointed out, owing to the favourable exchange rate it was not profitable to export coin or bullion. Gresham himself stated that the debasement by Henry VIII caused an outflow of gold because the exchange depreciated from 22s. 8d. to 13s. 4d. [27]

But if two moneys of different intrinsic value were in circulation in a country and their relative face value did not correspond to the ratio between their intrinsic value, then the overvalued coins were apt to disappear. And if the exchange rates are based on the value of average coins received in payment, then it was obviously worth while to export the heavy coins.

(20) PROGRESS IN THE 18TH CENTURY

Progress in Foreign Exchange theory achieved during the 17th century was consolidated and carried forward during the 18th century. Many writers were concerned with a more detailed elaboration of the trade balance theory, with special regard to invisible items and capital movements. We saw above that Cantillon and Hume carried the basic analysis further by laying stress on the self-regulating mechanism of international reallocation of monetary metals. In his *Essai sur la nature du commerce en général*, Cantillon foreshadowed the theory of international solidarity of prices working through the specie point mechanism.[28]

Amidst the more stable conditions of the 18th century the purchasing power parity theory was forgotten, or at any rate the emphasis in contemporary literature drifted to other theories. During the greater part of the 18th century, notwithstanding some very costly wars, fluctuations of the principal exchange rates seldom exceeded specie points to any considerable extent for any considerable length of time. The improved version of the trade balance theory, which took into account invisible items, capital items, and the multilateral character of international payments, was deemed therefore adequate.

(21) ADAM SMITH'S CONTRIBUTION

Adam Smith's contribution to Foreign Exchange theory bears no comparison with his contribution to various other branches of economics. Even so, Viner and Angell were inclined to underrate it, because their primary concern was not Foreign Exchange theory as such, but the rôle played by Foreign Exchange in international trade theory or in the theory of international prices. Viewed from those angles *The Wealth of Nations* largely confined itself to re-stating Lockes' formula under which specie movements tend to adjust the volume of money in each country to the ratio between the quantity of money in the country concerned and monetary requirements of trade, or, as Adam Smith put it, 'effectual demand' for money.[29] He accepted the view that Government action could not increase the volume of currency beyond the requirements of the economy. Even though he went a step further by stating that an increase in the quantity of paper money tended to cause an outflow of a corresponding amount of gold or silver,[30] he made no attempt to analyse the process. Nor did he carry further the progress achieved by his forerunners towards integrating Foreign Exchange with general economic theory.

Nevertheless, Foreign Exchange theory is indebted to Adam Smith in many respects. A contribution of importance was his analysis of international transfers connected with major wars abroad.[31] His detailed examination of the difference between 'real' and 'computed' exchanges in the case of worn coins and transactions in *banco* money, easily surpassed anything written before him on the subject. His view that the value of an inconvertible currency depended on the prospects of its convertibility was the forerunner of the scientific psychological theory.[32]

(22) DEVELOPMENT OF DYNAMIC THEORY

The evolution of Foreign Exchange theory during the three centuries covered by this section provides a fascinating example – to use Schumpeter's telling phrase – of 'how a theory struggles into existence'. Progress was indeed so gradual that the task of allocating the credit for it was extremely difficult. What mattered, however, was that while at the beginning of the 16th century Foreign Exchange theory was virtually non-existent, on the eve of the French Revolution there existed a fairly comprehensive set of doctrines, even if it had to be pieced together from the writings of many generations of economists.

Some of the ideas of early contributors to Foreign Exchange theory attained a remarkable degree of refinement. Unfortunately they faded into oblivion and were not re-discovered until quite recently. More recent Foreign Exchange theory could and should have benefited, for instance, from Davanzati's analysis in 1582 of the effect produced on exchange rates by forced buying or selling in the Foreign Exchange market by merchants, or by princes having to finance wars.[33] He led the way towards dynamic process-analysis by explaining that a counterpart was attracted by the profit possibilities created through deviations of exchange rates from their parities. Even earlier, in 1512, Mair set an example for process-analysis by describing how the exchange rates arose in Antwerp or Bruges.[34] And Montesquieu set an example for dynamic Foreign Exchange theory in the form of analysing the self-aggravating character of changes in the terms of trade by his shrewd finding that if more money had to be remitted as a result of an adverse change in the terms of trade, it caused a depreciation of the exchange, which in turn accentuated further the deterioration of the terms of trade.[35]

These are only a few instances to show that contemporary authors on Foreign Exchange theory miss a great deal by confining their interest to contemporary or recent literature, and that there is no justification to refer to the period before Adam Smith as 'pre-history of economics'.

NOTES TO CHAPTER THIRTEEN

1. J. W. Burgon, *Life and Times of Sir Thomas Gresham* (London, 1839), vol.i, pp. 483–6.
2. Azpilcueta Navarro, *Comentario resolutori de usuras* (Salamanca, 1556), quoted by Marjorie Grice-Hutchinson, *The Salamanca School* (Oxford, 1952), p. 92.
3. Raymond -de Roover, *Gresham on Foreign Exchange* (Cambridge, Mass., 1949), op. 304.
4. *Tudor Economic Documents*, vol. iii, pp. 358–9.
5. C. H. Hall (ed.), *The Economic Writings of Sir William Petty* (Cambridge, 1899), vol. i, pp. 185–6.
6. F. C. Dutot, *Réflexions politiques sur les finaces et le commerce* (Paris, 1738). In Eugène Daire (ed.), *Economistes-financiers du 18ᵉ siècle* (Paris, 1843), p. 970.
7. Charles de Montesquieu, *L'Esprit des lois* (Geneva, 1748), book xxii, chapter x, p. 374.
8. *Tudor Economic Documents*, vol. ii, pp. 148–9.
9. David Hume, *Political Discourses*, 1782. *In Essays, Moral, Political and Literary* (London, 1875), p. 186.
10. Thomas Mun, *England's Treasure by Forraign Trade* (1664). In J. R. McCulloch (ed.), *Early English Tracts on Commerce* (Cambridge, 1952), p. 151.
11. John Hales, *Discourse on the Common Weal*, in *Tudor Economic Documents*, vol. iii, pp. 305–6.
12. *Tudor Economic Documents*, vol. iii, p. 347.
13. Bernardo Davanzati, *A Discourse upon Coins* (trsl. John Toland, London, 1696), pp. 21–2.
14. Louis Vereecke, 'La Licité du "cambium bursae" chez Jean Mair (1469–

1550)', *Revue Historique de Droit Français et Étranger* (Paris, 1952), 4. sér., vol. 30, p. 128.

15. De Roover, *op. cit.* p. 303.

16. Domingo de Báñez, *De Justitia et Jure* (Venice, 1594), quoted by Grice-Hutchinson, *op. cit.* p. 57.

17. Tomás de Mercado, *Tratos y contratos de mercadores* (Salamanca, 1569), quoted by Grice-Hutchinson, *op. cit.* pp. 99–100.

18. John Locke, *Considerations of the Consequences of lowering the Interest and raising the Value of Money*, in *The Works of John Locke* (London, 1812), vol. v, p. 50.

19. Henry Robinson, *England's Safety in Trade Encrease* (London, 1641), in W. A. Shaw (ed.), *Select Tracts* (London, 1896), pp. 62–3.

20. *Tudor Economic Documents*, vol. iii, p. 305.

21. De Roover, *op. cit.* p. 305.

22. Albert Despaux, *Les Dévaluations monétaires dans l'histoire* (Paris, 1936), pp. 364–5.

23. John Locke, *Further Considerations concerning raising the Value of Money*, in *The Works of John Locke*, vol. v, p. 148.

24. Jean François Melon, *Essai politique sur le commerce* (Paris, 1734), in E. Daire, *op. cit.* pp. 789–902.

25. De Roover, *op. cit.* p. 163.

26. Gerald Malynes, *Lex Mercatoria*, 3rd ed. (London, 1686), p. 272.

27. *Tudor Economic Documents*, vol. ii, pp. 146–9.

28. Richard Cantillon, *Essai sur la nature du commerce en général* (Paris, 1785), trsl. H. Higgs (London, 1931), pp. 263–5.

29. Adam Smith, *An Inquiry into the Causes and Nature of the Wealth of Nations*, ed. J. R. McCulloch (Edinburgh, 1863), pp. 128–30, 190–1.

30. Adam Smith, *op. cit.* pp. 126–7.

31. Adam Smith, *op. cit.* pp. 193–5.

32. Adam Smith, *op. cit.* p. 144.

33. Bernardo Davanzati, *Dei cambia*, in *Le opere di Bernardo Davanzati*, ed. E. Bindi (Florence, 1853), vol. ii, pp. 429–30.

34. Vereecke, *op. cit.* p. 128.

35. Montesquieu, *op. cit.* pp. 377–8.

CHAPTER FOURTEEN

Progress of Foreign Exchange Policy

(1) PROGRESS DURING THE 16TH AND 17TH CENTURIES

PROGRESS in Foreign Exchange practice and in theoretical knowledge during the 16th and 17th centuries was accompanied by comparable progress in the sphere of Foreign Exchange policy. This was a consequence of the growing importance of Foreign Exchange in the national and international economy, of the increasing familiarity with the technique and theory of the subject, as well as of the growing realisation of its importance by princes and their advisers. We saw that already during the Middle Ages many of them appeared to be vaguely aware of the bearing of the Foreign Exchange position on the depletion or replenishment of monetary supplies in their countries. But it was not until the 16th century that ideas on the subject were beginning to become clarified. Administrators became gradually aware of the direct effect of exchange rates on domestic prices, in addition to their indirect effect through bringing about changes in the quantity of money by means of causing specie movements.

Important practical considerations led to the conclusion that the Governments must intervene in order to make Foreign Exchanges behave in a way that would suit the requirements of their countries. The disturbing effect of speculation, arbitrage and malevolent manipulations of exchanges reinforced the case for official measures. Last but by no means least, the growing importance of the Government's own international financial operations – borrowing, repayment, transfers of funds to finance military expenditure and subsidies abroad – made it appear expedient to take more active interest in Foreign Exchange.

(2) ENDS AND MEANS

The ends of Foreign Exchange policies pursued during the period covered by this Section may be summarised as follows:

 1. Retaining or attracting bullion and specie.
 2. Preventing or reversing a rise in domestic prices resulting from a depreciation of the exchange.
 3. Safeguarding the interests of national industries by stimulating exports or handicapping imports.
 4. Keeping down or reducing the cost of Government remittances abroad.
 5. Causing difficulties to hostile Governments.

The principal means applied to attain one or several of the above ends may be summarised as follows:

 1. Ban on the export of bullion and specie.
 2. Export licence fee on bullion and specie.
 3. Ban on the import of foreign coins.
 4. Fixing exchange rates for foreign coins.
 5. High import duties or import restrictions.
 6. Ban on unauthorised exchange transactions.
 7. Ban on exchange transactions at unfavourable rates.
 8. Tax on Foreign Exchange transactions.
 9. Compulsory surrender of coins or foreign bills.
 10. Devaluations or debasements.
 11. Revaluations or recoinages.
 12. Adjustment of gold-silver ratio.
 13. Official Foreign Exchange operations.
 14. Altering of the spread between specie points through handicapping or facilitating the circulation of the same coins in two countries.

Other means that had been advocated – some of them from highly authoritative quarters – but not adopted, included the creation of an exchange stabilisation fund, the creation of artificially tight money conditions in the domestic money market, etc.

(3) BANS ON EXPORT OF BULLION AND SPECIE

Bans on the export of bullion and specie, with their incidental effect on specie points, and, through it, on exchange rates, continued to be resorted to systematically for a long time after the end of the Medieval Period. In most countries they remained permanently on the Statute Book, even if the extent of their actual enforcement varied. After long periods of relatively slack enforcement the old statutes came to be remembered again and again in times of difficulties and were revived and reinforced. Even if such measures were not adopted with the object of influencing exchange rates, those responsible for them must have been aware of their effect on exchange rates, so that in a negative sense their decisions constituted acts of Foreign Exchange policy, inasmuch as they decided to accept such effects for the sake of the benefits they hoped to derive from the measure in other directions.

From the point of view of the ban on bullion and specie export, the Netherlands and some Italian States enjoyed a more liberal régime during the 16th and 17th centuries than England, Spain, France or Germany. The prohibition was particularly strict in Spain, in spite of the large influx of precious metals during the 16th century and the first half of the 17th century.

As and when it came to be recognised that bullion and specie movements were normally determined by the trade balance, the futility of attempts at the direct physical control of their export was accepted. Government after Government came to the conclusion that, in trying to stop the outflow of their monetary metals by means of embargoes, they would merely fight symptoms instead of dealing with fundamental causes. Accordingly, gold and silver movements became increasingly liberalised. This was done in England during 1663 and by France about a century later. Nevertheless, the ban on the export of national coinage remained in force in most countries long after the export of gold and silver in every other form was freed.

In the 16th century and after, the Spanish Government sought to discourage the outflow of precious metals, without actually banning it, by making their export subject to licence for which a fee was charged. This device failed to achieve its object, for, given the perennial adverse trade balance and the drain caused by wars abroad, the *maravedi* tended to depreciate to a level at which it was profitable to pay the licence fee, or at which it was deemed worth while to take the risk attached to smuggling.

(4) ATTITUDE TOWARDS FOREIGN COINS

Foreign coins circulating outside their countries played largely the rôle of international currencies. From time to time bans were imposed, however, on their import and on their circulation, either because Governments were anxious to safeguard their coinage against the competition of a more attractive rival coinage or because they wanted to protect the national economy against being flooded with inferior foreign coins.

Conceivably, in some instances at any rate, the ban on the import and circulation of foreign coins may have been imposed with the object of applying a device, similar to the one advocated by Keynes in the 1920's, of widening the margins between specie points. Conversely, measures to encourage the circulation of foreign coins at home, or of national coins abroad, may have served the opposite end – that of narrowing the margins between specie points. The possibility of importing or exporting coins which circulated in both countries concerned caused the margin between specie points to contract because it eliminated the cost of coinage in the importing country. That device was advocated by the Royal Commission of 1564 which suggested an arrangement providing for the circulation of English coins in the Low Countries and France, with the declared object of defending the exchange against depreciation.[1] The commission took the view that, by raising the exchange, this device would change the terms of trade in favour of England to an extent that would more than compensate for the additional loss of specie.[2]

Under Mercantilist influences, statesmen and administrators came to attach so much importance to maintaining favourable exchange rates that their whole economic policy came to serve that end in the 17th century and after. They endeavoured to ensure a favourable trade balance at all costs; they encouraged the creation and expansion of industries making for national self-sufficiency in goods formerly imported. Even though the ultimate object may have been the attraction of more bullion and specie, the securing of a favourable exchange became a recognised intermediate aim to that end.

(5) RESTRICTIONS ON FOREIGN EXCHANGE OPERATIONS

Restrictions on Foreign Exchange operations had its ups and downs during the 16th and 17th centuries. They had never been as continuous as the restrictions on bullion and specie movements. All Tudor monarchs from Henry VII onwards repeatedly revived this medieval device, in particular in 1487, 1537, 1551, 1559 and 1576. From time to time a Royal Exchanger, or a Keeper of the Exchanges, was put in control of private transactions in foreign bills. The fact that under the Tudors men of the prominence of Sir Thomas Boleyn (1509), Sir Thomas Moore (1520) and Lord Burleigh himself (1575) were given that post – the latter held it for twenty-three years – indicates the importance attached to it.

On one occasion, at any rate, Elizabeth I chose the comptrollers for their expert knowledge rather than for their political usefulness. In 1576 she put two haberdashers and a grocer in charge of the exchange control, her Proclamation stating that they were men well acquainted with the manner of exchanges and re-changes to and from the City of London, and to and from foreign parts. Notwithstanding this well-advised choice, this experiment with exchange control, like all previous and subsequent experiments during that early period, proved to be a total failure and was soon abandoned.

(6) UPS AND DOWNS OF EXCHANGE CONTROL

On each occasion when exchange control was adopted or reinforced, there was a wave of protests on the part of merchants and bankers. Their warnings about the adverse effect of the measures proved invariably to have been well founded. The control proved to be ineffective, and, as on each previous occasion, the authorities reached eventually the conclusion that it was more trouble than it was worth. According to the argument used by the Italian merchants in London in their petition in 1576, apart from its damaging effect on private trading interest, it accentuated the direct loss of specie rather than preventing it, for one of the consequences of restricting remittances by means of Foreign Exchange was an increase of the evasion of the ban on bullion and specie exports.

In 1539, after another abortive attempt at restoring control, Henry VIII issued a Proclamation authorising all persons to make exchanges and re-changes in as large and ample a manner as hitherto from the date of the Proclamation (July 30) until the Feast of All Saints, on the ground that restraints upon exchanges 'would be to the great hindraunce of traffick'.[3] Which realisation and admission did not prevent his Government from restoring the ban again soon after.

From time to time the Tudor administrations went so far as to revive one of the most drastic forms of medieval exchange control – the Statute of Employment, compelling foreign exporters to England to spend the proceeds on English goods within a short time limit. More moderate forms of exchange control were also resorted to at times. Instead of appointing Royal Exchangers, exchange was only allowed to be transacted through the intermediary of sworn brokers who were authorised to grant licence to known merchants for *bona-fide* commercial purposes.

In continental countries, too, severity in exchange control alternated with liberalism. In France, during the period of relative stability under Henri IV (1589–1610), controls were relaxed, but during the subsequent period of troubles they sought to be reinforced.

(7) DISAPPEARANCE OF EXCHANGE CONTROL

So long as it remained the prevailing conception that Foreign Exchange speculation or sinister manipulations of exchange rates were the root of all evil, there was bound to be strong inducement to apply exchange control whenever things were going wrong. This policy continued under the early Stuarts, but when in 1628 Charles I put forward the claim that exchange control was a royal prerogative Parliament passed a resolution that it constituted a grievance. No further Royal Exchanger was appointed after that date.

Even the Commonwealth Government, authoritarian as it was, abstained from adopting exchange control, disregarding the advice it received to this effect from Sir Thomas Violet and others. By that time the more enlightened expert opinion that emerged from the controversy between Malynes, Misselden and Mun was beginning to influence the official attitude.

An alternative to exchange control was the imposition of a tax on exchange transactions. This was attempted in England under Elizabeth. In 1586, when sterling was weak, a tax was introduced up to a maximum limit of 5 per cent, though the actual rate applied was $2\frac{1}{2}$ per cent only. Since it was a flat rate regardless to the maturity of bills, its burden was intolerably high for relatively short bills. For one month's usance bills on Antwerp it was 30 per cent p.a. It is no wonder there was an outcry of protest and the device was soon dropped.

(8) OFFICIALLY FIXED EXCHANGE RATES

Another alternative form of exchange control to the creation of an exchange monopoly was the official fixing of exchange rates. It was applied in a number of countries to a very large degree right to the eve of the French Revolution, in the form of fixing the prices of foreign coins and changing their tariff by means of relatively frequent proclamations. In some countries, especially in the Netherlands, this was a very important device of Foreign Exchange policy during the late 16th and early 17th centuries, as it tended to influence specie movements and exchange rates for bills. There were bound to be discrepancies between the official prices of foreign coins prevailing at any given moment in various countries, and also between official prices and market prices in any one country. Governments were unable to make the official prices effective whenever they differed substantially from the market prices.

Somebody was always bound to complain, whether Governments fixed the price of foreign coins too high or too low. If they overvalued the national coins in terms of foreign coins, merchants complained that they were at a disadvantage when competing with their foreign rivals at home or abroad. If they overvalued the foreign coins foreign Governments complained that this was a Machiavellian device to attract specie from their country. Raleigh, in his otherwise brilliant Memorandum to James I, said that because French coins were too highly valued in France English merchants were bound to lose when bringing their money home. But he also said that in Poland the current English gold coin, the Jacobus, was worth 27s., while at home it was only worth 24s., and he strongly advised James I to raise the value of that coin to a similarly high level.[4] In fairness to Raleigh, the possibility that, just as the 1695 edition of his Memorandum contained some obvious interpolations, quite conceivably the publishers of the 1653 edition, too, attributed to him views he had never held, must be borne in mind.

In 1586 the Royal Exchanger was instructed not to authorise exchange transactions if sterling was sold at less than its 'just value'. It was a favourite idea of Malynes that merchants and others engaged in Foreign Exchange should be forbidden to sell foreign bills at above Mint parity. Long before him, the Royal Commission of 1564 showed itself aware of the disadvantages of allowing the exchange to depreciate.[5]

(9) ACTIVE OFFICIAL INTERVENTION

Some of the known instances of forcing exporters to sell their Foreign Exchange to the Government at an unfavourable rate occurred under the reign of Elizabeth I. On two recorded occasions, in 1552 and in 1553, the cloth fleet of the Merchant Adventurers was detained, on Gresham's instructions, in English ports until the exporters agreed to sell the Government a certain amount of Flemish currency at rates less favourable to them than the market rates prevailing at the time in Antwerp or in London. The object of these drastic measures was to secure for Gresham the exchange needed for paying the Government's external debt and for supporting sterling in the Antwerp market.

These operations provided an early instance of active official intervention in the Foreign Exchange market. There were, however, many other less publicised instances during the 16th and 17th centuries. According to modern historians the extent to which Gresham actually succeeded in influencing the exchanges in Antwerp by means of such intervention – as distinct from protecting sterling by regulating the arrival and sale of English cloth and by managing intelligently his Government's borrowing, renewal and repayment operations – had been overrated by earlier historians.

Among others, Buckley expressed doubts whether such intervention could really produce beneficial effects. He pointed out that, since Gresham depleted the market's normal supply of bills, English importers had to bid for a reduced volume of these bills.[6] On the other hand, de Roover holds the view that Gresham's operations were effective in the short run, but not in the long run, and that in any event they could not be repeated very often.

Both Gresham's Memorandum and the Royal Commissions of 1564, and of 1586, emphatically advised Elizabeth to create what we would call today an Exchange Equalisation Account. The same suggestion was revived by Henry Robinson under the Commonwealth. Lack of funds hampered Gresham and other Royal agents from trying to prove the possibility of raising the exchange to the desired level by means of systematic intervention. It is highly doubtful whether they would have been able to get very far if Gresham's request for a fund of £10,000 – a very modest amount even for those days – had been met.

Steuart quotes an unsuccessful attempt at official support of the exchange in the 18th century. After the recoinage of 1726 the French *livre* was weak and Cardinal Fleury supported it on the assumption that the weakness was due to an adverse trade balance. He found, however, that the support resulted in a very heavy loss of gold, many times more than the amount of the import surplus. Eventually he came to realise that the demand for bills on Amsterdam was due to the unfavourable prices paid by the Mint for coins to be surrendered for re-coinage, as a result of which holders of coins preferred to buy Foreign Exchanges. He thereupon raised the Mint price, and the premium on the bills on Amsterdam disappeared.[8]

(10) CHANGING OF PARITIES

Changes in parities were by far the most drastic device with which to affect exchange rates. In a great many instances they were resorted to for other purposes and their effect on exchange rates was merely incidental. They could only serve the purpose of stopping an outflow of specie and of bringing about an inflow to the extent to which a reduction of the metallic content of coins was not followed immediately by a corresponding depreciation of the exchanges.

When the object of changes in the metallic content or nominal value of coins was to adjust official mint parities to a previous actual deterioration of the national coinage in circulation then it was not supposed to lead to changes in exchange rates, since they had already adapted themselves prior to the change of the official metallic parity to the approximate real value of the coins. In the absence of such previous depreciation, however, changes in the metal content of the monetary unit was supposed to produce more or less prompt and roughly corresponding changes in exchange rates. In practice a speculative anticipation of the impending change, and the covering of positions after it had materialised, reduced the extent to which the change affected the exchange rates. We saw in the last chapter that this was what happened repeatedly in Antwerp in the late 16th century.

Yet another form of official Foreign Exchange policy consisted of changing or suspending the seignorage. Any change in the seignorage affected the specie points and therefore it affected the exchange rates. In the Low Countries it was the practice in the 17th century to refund the seignorage in order to attract metals from abroad. In England seignorage was abolished in 1666 and in France it was suspended for six years in 1679. During the 18th century seignorage was materially reduced in most countries.

(11) CHANGING OF GOLD-SILVER RATIO

Reference has already been made in Chapter 10 to the effect of changing the official gold-silver ratio, or of maintaining it in face of a change in the market ratio or in the official rates abroad. This device was liable to affect exchange rates both directly and indirectly, but the main object of its application was usually outside the sphere of Foreign Exchange policy. A striking instance was provided by an attempt of Charles V in 1527 to resist an appreciation of gold against silver by some 10 per cent. An ordinance reduced the official ratio between gold and silver coins in Flanders to its level of 1521. As a result the official price of English *angels* in Antwerp was reduced from 65 to 57 *stuyvers*, and of the French *écu* from 40 to 36 *stuyvers*. There was a heavy outflow of gold from the Low Countries. By 1538 the ratio was restored to where it was prior to the change of 1527, but later the price of gold coins was once more officially called down by 10 per cent. The Regent announced that the object of the measure was to lower the price level. Rumours of an impending second cut of 5 per cent brought business to a standstill. When this cut was carried out there were no buyers at the lower rates. It took over a year before conditions became normal.[9]

Another device, referred to in Chapter 10, was the official determination of the currencies in which bills had to be paid. By compelling debtors to pay in undervalued currencies, or creditors to accept payment in overvalued currencies, exchange rates were bound to be affected. But it was not the main object of the measures to bring about such effects.

(12) SUGGESTIONS OF MONETARY SQUEEZE AND INTEREST RATE POLICY

One of Gresham's favourite ideas was to resort to the highly advanced device of raising sterling by creating artificial monetary stringency at home. We saw in the last chapter that he advised the administration of Elizabeth, in his Memorandum of 1559, to keep money tight. There is no evidence if, and to what extent, his advice was acted upon and with what result, but it seems unlikely that such an advanced form of Foreign Exchange policy was applied on occasion in England and elsewhere in the 16th century. Yet while the device advocated by Gresham may appear to have been well ahead of his time, we saw in Chapter 12 that it was actually applied by private interests. Gresham must have derived his idea from accounts of the cornering of funds in Antwerp carried out by Ducci shortly before his time.

During the second half of the 17th century the influence of interest rates on the movements of foreign capital came to be realised. Among others, Locke pointed out that the lowering of interest rates induced foreigners to call home their money.[10] It seems unlikely, however, that any official action was taken to adjust interest rates for the sake of influencing exchange rates, until well after the establishment of the Bank of England.

(13) FOREIGN EXCHANGE IN THE SERVICE OF ECONOMIC WARFARE

Foreign Exchange policy often served the purpose of economic warfare, or at any rate of the prevailing beggar-my-neighbour policy. Gresham strongly advised the Governments he served to adopt his proposals, and held out as inducement the prospect of being able to impoverish all other princes in Christendom by doing so. Machiavelli had nothing on Gresham when the latter set out to advise his Government 'to undoe realmes and Princes',[11] by Foreign Exchange manipulations and the accumulation of export surpluses in the form of foreign balances. It is no wonder mutual suspicion prevailed. In England the Spanish Government or its offshoot in Brussels was often suspected of such sinister designs. Louis XIV is said to have done more harm to the Netherlands with currency manipulations than with his armies. But it is difficult to form an opinion to what extent Foreign Exchange operations that tended to damage the interests of other countries were taken deliberately with that object in mind, or whether their damaging effect was merely incidental to their main object of defending the national currency.

A device of economic warfare that was applied in some known instances was a ban on Foreign Exchange transactions with the enemy. It was applied on occasions even before hostilities actually broke out. Thus, during the prolonged conflict between Charles V and Francis I, merchants in Antwerp were forbidden to transact Foreign Exchange business with the King of France. The downfall of Gaspare Ducci, who was able to dominate the Antwerp Foreign Exchange market for a long time in his capacity of agent of Charles V, was due to the discovery in 1550 that he had offended against this ban by continuing his active arbitrage transactions with Lyons.[12]

Throughout the 16th and 17th centuries the Kings of France were in a position to influence the Spanish exchange rate in accordance with French political or economic requirements, by the simple device of granting or withholding their *laisser passer* for consignments of specie from Spain to the Low Countries. A ban on such specie movements entailed a fall in the *maravedi* and an appreciation of bills on Antwerp.

An outstanding instance of the use of Foreign Exchange in the service of economic warfare was provided in 1587 by English operations to corner bills drawn on Genoa banks, thereby exhausting their liquid resources and making it more difficult for them to meet the requirements of Philip II for the financing of the Armada.[13] But the claim that it was thanks to these manœuvres that the expedition against England had to be deferred until the summer of 1588, is probably grossly exaggerated.

(14) INTERNATIONAL CO-OPERATION

In sharp contrast with such beggar-my-neighbour policy, Robinson, who was the first monetary internationalist, laid stress on the disadvantages of depleting the specie supplies of other countries through an overvaluation of sterling, stating that it was to our benefit if money was plentiful in other countries.[14]

In 1523 an attempt was made at international monetary co-operation. Henry VIII concluded a treaty with Charles V, providing for an agreed tariff of exchange rates between the most important coins. There is not enough information to indicate whether this arrangement had operated satisfactorily, but it seems probable that exchange rates continued to fluctuate in the market and that merchants took full advantage of discrepancies. Again in 1575 and 1576 agreements were reached with the Low Countries for fixing exchange rates for a number of coins. There were other similar agreements during the 16th century and early 17th century. The report of the Royal Commission of 1601 stated that the rates fixed in 1576 did not allow for the true gold-silver ratio, and that in the Low Countries coins were allowed to circulate at a higher rate than the one decreed in the Proclamation.[15]

(15) OFFICIAL REMITTANCES ABROAD

Owing to the increased financial requirements of the armed forces operating abroad, and to subsidies to allies, official remittances continued to play an important part in Foreign Exchanges during the major wars of the 18th century. There was much criticism in England of the methods by which the necessary foreign bills were acquired. In the entries of the Treasury Books relating to such transactions we encounter the same names over and over again, showing that certain financiers had practically the monopoly of supplying the Government. The absence of competitors must have necessarily meant unfavourable rates.

Under Walpole the bills were supplied by the Bank of England, the East India Company and the South Sea Company, but even that arrangement was far from satisfactory. From time to time the Government of the day was criticised by the Opposition of the day, but most Governments failed to take advantage of the free play of supply and demand in the open market or alternatively to call for competitive tenders. Nor did they appear to realise that since payments abroad caused a deterioration of the balance of payments they necessarily caused an outflow of bullion or specie, so that the official operations merely meant that the shipments of monetary metals were made on private initiative and those undertaking them, instead of the Government, reaped the benefit of the difference that made the transactions worth while.

(16) THE POLICY OF *LAISSER-FAIRE*

Two leading French economists of the 18th century, Melon and Dutot, pointed out the futility of any form of official intervention in Foreign Exchanges other than by taking the initiative for shipping specie whenever this was necessary to provide the balance, before a depreciation of the exchange leads to an outflow through private arbitrage; and by borrowing abroad to meet an adverse balance. In fact, the extent of official actions in pursuit of Foreign Exchange policies abated during the 18th century, partly because conditions were more stable and partly because the spirit of *laisser-faire* was gaining ground.

The policy of *laisser-faire* came to be applied in the sphere of Foreign Exchange even before Adam Smith. Many of the devices used during the 16th and 17th centuries had fallen in disuse, so that during the new period of instability arising from the Wars of the French Revolution the authorities concerned were without experience to guide them in the Foreign Exchange policy measures.

NOTES TO CHAPTER FOURTEEN

1. *Tudor Economic Documents*, vol. iii, p. 354.
2. *Op. cit.* vol. iii, p. 355.
3. Roger Ruding, *Annals of the Coinage of Britain* (London, 1819), vol. ii, p. 432.
4. Sir Walter Raleigh, *Observations touching Trade and Commerce with the Hollanders and other Nations* (London, 1658), pp. 38–9, 55–6.
5. *Tudor Economic Documents*, vol. iii, pp. 348–9.
6. H. Buckley, 'Sir Thomas Gresham and the Foreign Exchange', *Economic Journal*, 1924, vol. 34, p. 398.
7. Raymond de Roover, *Gresham on Foreign Exchange* (Cambridge, Mass., 1947), pp. 222–3.
8. Sir James Steuart, *Political Oeconomy* (London, 1767), pp. 340–1.
9. F. Edler, 'The Effect of the Financial Measures of Charles V on the Commerce of Antwerp – 1539–40', *Revue Belge de Philologie et d'Histoire* (Brussels, 1937), vol. xvi, pp. 668–70.
10. John Locke, *Considerations of the Consequences of lowering of Interest and raising the Value of Money*, in *Complete Works* (London, 1912), vol. v, p. 29.
11. De Roover, *op. cit.* p. 301.
12. Richard E. Ehrenberg, *Das Zeitalter der Fugger* (Jena, 1896), vol. i, p. 316.
13. E. Lipson, *The Economic History of England*, 4th ed. (London, 1947), vol. i, p. 242. See also W. Cunningham, *The Growth of English Industry and Commerce*, 3rd ed. (Cambridge, 1903), vol. ii, pp. 146–7.
14. W. A. Shaw, *Select Tracts* (London, 1896), p. 66.
15. *State Papers, Domestic*, 1601, vol. 279, pp. 47–8.

PART IV

THE NINETEENTH CENTURY

CHAPTER FIFTEEN

Practices in the 19th Century

(1) MANY IMPORTANT CHANGES

FOR the purposes of our Foreign Exchange history, as indeed for many other purposes, the 19th century began with the French Revolution and ended with the outbreak of the first World War. Although both landmarks are very distinct, the unity of the period between them is imperfect, because of the striking difference between the disturbed conditions in Foreign Exchanges during the French Revolution and the Napoleonic Wars and the subsequent period of relative stability that characterised the more important exchanges, at any rate most of the time, during the rest of the 19th century and right up to 1914.

Nevertheless, the unstable initial period had closer resemblance to the modern system than to the system of the 18th century. Indeed, the advanced paper currency inflation in France during the Revolution and the fluctuation of the inconvertible pound during the period of suspension may be regarded as the first meaningful experience in Foreign Exchange movements under inconvertible paper currency systems.

The following were the most important changes between 1789 and 1914:

1. Parities became better defined.
2. Specie points became narrower.
3. Active markets developed in foreign bank-notes.
4. All the time there were a number of inconvertible exchanges.
5. There were many changes in the list of currencies quoted.
6. The method of including interest charges in exchange rates changed.
7. Differences between bill rates according to the seller's standing became more marked.
8. 'Usance' no longer determined the maturity of bills but was the basis of calculating the difference between market quotations and actual amounts paid for bills.
9. The importance of mail days increased, but later it declined.

G

10. Paris and London became the leading markets.
11. The New York market developed and increased in importance.
12. Finance bills became more important.
13. Mail transfers became an increasingly important form of Foreign Exchange.
14. They were beginning to be replaced by telegraphic transfers.
15. Closer relationship was established betwen foreign banks.
16. Markets became continuous, dealers being in contact every day throughout business hours.
17. Forward Exchanges came to be widely transacted.
18. The volume of commercial transactions increased.
19. The volume of capital transfers increased.
20. The volume and variety of arbitrage transactions increased.

(2) PARITIES BECOME MORE DISTINCT

The establishment of a new well-defined monetary unit in France in 1803, after the end of the paper currency inflation, heralded the advent of firmer and better-defined new exchange parities than those of earlier centuries. During the 19th century Mint parities were defined by unequivocal texts in Acts of Parliament and their calculation became largely a matter of simple arithmetic, at any rate as far as currencies based on the same metal were concerned. Owing to the increased importance of paper money and bank credit, the relative state of the various coinage no longer affected the effective parities to the same extent.

It took many a decade, however, before complications arising from the absence of fixed parities between gold and silver currencies, or between metallic currencies and paper currencies, had become reduced as a result of the wider adoption of the gold standard in an increasing number of important countries.

(3) NARROWING OF SPECIE POINTS

Another change that occurred very gradually was the narrowing of the spread between specie points. It was brought about by the improvement of transport conditions leading to a gradual lowering of transport costs, interest charges and insurance after the end of the Napoleonic Wars. This caused a considerable narrowing of the range of fluctuations of exchanges based on the same metallic standard. It was not until the concluding decades of the 19th century and the early years of the 20th century, however, that the spread between gold points narrowed to figures comparable to those that came to prevail during the period of stability in the inter-war period.

In any case, right up to the first World War, specie points of the majority of exchanges remained less clearly defined than is assumed by our generation in retrospect. Strictly speaking, the only exchanges with really narrow gold points were those between countries on a really effective gold standard. There were only three countries which actually allowed gold to be exported with absolute freedom during the decades preceding 1914 – Britain, the United States and Holland. Other countries with currencies based legally on gold frequently resorted to various technical devices circumventing their own currency legislation, in an endeavour to discourage, if not prevent, gold withdrawals from their official reserves, or to encourage gold imports by artificial means. More will be said about this in Chapter 18. Here let it be sufficient to point out that the specie points of the majority of exchanges remained flexible and were liable to important adjustments as a result of the application of such tactics. It was never possible to foresee for certain if, and to what extent, French, German or other monetary authorities would fall back upon devices that would shift the specie points.

Moreover, specie points were also affected by certain private practices. For instance, the absence of a good market for dollar drafts in London during the greater part of the 19th century tended to widen the gold export point from Britain to the United States, because gold shippers in London had to await the return remittance instead of being able to sell immediately a dollar cheque drawn on the firm entrusted with selling the gold consignment. The margin between par and gold import point from New York to London was in practice wider than the margin between par and gold export point. With the development of a good market in dollars in London this difference disappeared.

(4) DEALINGS IN PAPER CURRENCIES

One of the most striking changes in Foreign Exchange practices, brought about by the French Revolution almost from the very outset, was the development of a very active market in paper money, both for spot and forward transactions. Even though Foreign Exchange business was transacted in notes to some extent at various times and places during the 18th century, and in some countries already during the late 17th century, systematic dealings on a large scale date from the French Revolution. Most Foreign Exchanges dealings with countries on an inconvertible paper currency basis were in terms of bills payable in paper currency. A buyer of a bill on Paris in Hamburg during the Revolution acquired a claim payable in rapidly depreciating *assignats* or *mandats*. During the period of suspension in Britain, any buyer of a bill on London bought a claim payable in inconvertible Bank of England notes. Likewise, a bill on Vienna or St. Petersburg was payable in paper *gulden* or *roubles*, and its value in Hamburg largely depended on the degree of the depreciation of the paper *gulden* or *rouble* in terms of silver, which remained the basis of currency in Hamburg.

After the liquidation of the financial aftermaths of the Napoleonic Wars, the principal currencies became based once more on gold and/or silver, and metallic parities came into their own again. There remained, however, a number of paper currencies which were subject to active Foreign Exchange dealing. At one time or other wars, civil wars or revolutions caused the suspension of the convertibility of the gold or silver currencies of France, Russia, Italy, Austria-Hungary, Spain, the Balkan States, and outside Europe the United States and various Latin-American countries.

The market in foreign notes was overshadowed most of the time by the market in foreign bills which, until about the last quarter of the 19th century, constituted the major part of the Foreign Exchange market. Dealings in bills, together with mail transfers, financed practically the entire rapidly expanding volume of international trade. The relative importance of mail transfers, and later of telegraphic transfers, increased considerably during the concluding decades of the 19th century, and even more during the years immediately preceding the first World War.

(5) CHANGES IN THE LIST OF QUOTATIONS

As a result of the expansion of foreign trade with the new continents, a wider variety of exchanges came to be quoted. During the second half of the century this increase in the number of exchanges was offset by the political unification of countries such as Germany and Italy, which until then had a large number of independent currencies. But for a long time after the unification of currencies the separate quotations of exchanges on cites of formerly independent States continued to appear in Foreign Exchange lists. Writing in 1893, Clare criticised the survival in the London list of quotations of rates of exchanges on four German cities, even though these rates were always identical, also on four Italian cities and, 'for some occult reason', for no less than nine Spanish cities with identical exchange rates.[1] The explanation of this curious practice is that some three-quarters of a century earlier there were discrepancies of anything up to 8 per cent at a given moment between rates of bills on various Spanish cities, owing to the risk of robbery to which consignments of money from one Spanish city to another were exposed.[2] Although by the end of the 19th century conditions of security in Spain improved, the tradition of quoting separately for each Spanish city lingered on.

(6) HOW FOREIGN BILL RATES WERE QUOTED

Exchange rates for bills continued to include interest charges, but for some time these charges were allowed for only approximately. Towards the middle of the 19th century it was stated in one of the practical reference books for merchants: 'In the actual negotiations of bills any small difference of time is not taken into consideration, a bill at 90 days' date frequently bringing in as good a price as one at 75 days' date'.[3] Gradually the practice became more refined, however, especially as and when the increased use of finance bills made it easier to transact business in the market in large round amounts.

By the 'seventies the practice of the market was that the rates were quoted for 'usance' maturities, regardless of the actual maturities of the bills. The 'usance' was thirty days for bills on Paris or Geneva, one calendar month for Germany and Holland, two months for New York, three months for Italy and South America, etc. If a bill was shorter, discount for the difference was allowed to the seller. If it was longer, discount for the difference was allowed to the buyer.[4] This practice simplified for dealers in the market the speedy transaction of business in batches of bills maturing on various dates, without having to waste time on reckoning out price differences due to differences in maturities. Claims and counterclaims arising from such differences could be settled subsequently and their reckoning did not hold up the business which had to be transacted within one single hour on the afternoon of mail days.

(7) DIFFERENTIAL RATES FOR CLASSES OF BILLS

Another refinement was the development of distinction between different classes of bills. During the early decades of the century the practice in this respect was the same as in earlier centuries, namely, the exchange rates quoted in the market applied to commercial bills, while what would be called today prime bills or fine bank bills commanded a more favourable exchange rate. In the course of evidence given before the Secret Committee of 1819, witnesses stated that there was usually a difference varying between $\frac{1}{2}$ per cent to $1\frac{1}{2}$ per cent in favour of first-rate names. In times of crises the discrepancy was apt to widen considerably. During the brief panic following on the news of Napoleon's return from Elba in 1815, it widened to 5 per cent.[5]

In the case of inland bills the differentiation according to the credit-worthiness of a drawer, endorser or acceptor had been expressed all along in the different discount rates applied. In the case of foreign bills, interest charges were included in exchange rates. The resulting difference according to the debtor's standing was naturally larger for long bills than for short bills, owing to the higher risk involved in holding bills of a dubious quality for a long period. It was virtually non-existent, or at any rate very moderate, in respect of cheques or bills payable at sight drawn on centres at a short distance.

At the beginning of the 19th century the printed list contained the exchange rates for ordinary commercial bills. The rates for bank bills or for bills of first-rate commercial firms were not published. By the close of the century this practice changed. According to Clare, the twofold price quotation appearing in the lists of exchange rates published in London in 1891 did not indicate the highest and lowest rates of the day, nor the turn of the market as on the Stock Exchange. It represented the difference between rates for first-class bills and for ordinary trade bills.[6] There were separate quotations for mail transfers.

(8) PAYMENTS ON 'POST DAYS'

The practice of making bills payable either on definite dates or so many days or calendar months after their issue or after sight became universal during the latter part of the 19th century. The days of grace for bills on various centres became shorter and more uniform during the second half of the century.

In London during the period when business in foreign bills was transacted on the two 'post days', Tuesdays and Fridays (later Thursdays), it had long been the custom that the buyer had to pay for bills bought on one 'post day' on the next 'post day'. Since, however, in a number of instances payment was stopped between the 'post days', it was arranged in 1879 that henceforth all transactions must be settled on the following morning. Later the settlement was fixed for the second clear day after the conclusion of the deal, which practice is still in operation.

(9) RISE AND DECLINE OF FOREIGN EXCHANGE CENTRES

While during the 17th and 18th centuries Amsterdam reigned supreme among the Foreign Exchange markets, following on its occupation by the French revolutionary army in 1795 its supremacy came to an end. During the Napoleonic Wars Hamburg took its place as the leading Foreign Exchange market, but immediately after Waterloo, London and Paris came to share that rôle, with Amsterdam as a good third. Even though between 1815 and 1821 sterling remained inconvertible while the *franc* and several other continental currencies were convertible, London was nevertheless a very active Foreign Exchange centre. Paris had the advantage of a favourable geographical position in relation to the Continent, in addition to the advantage of a convertible currency, but London was well placed for acting as intermediary in relation to other continents. While all continental exchanges were quoted 'certain' in London, most exchanges of other continents were, and still are, quoted 'uncertain'.

Other Foreign Exchange centres of importance during the 19th century were Amsterdam, Antwerp (subsequently Brussels), Frankfurt, Hamburg, and later Berlin, Vienna and the Austrian port of Trieste, Stockholm, various Italian and Spanish cities, Lisbon, St. Petersburg, Istanbul, Zurich and other Swiss places.

Outside Europe New York and other American cities, in Africa Alexandria, and among Latin-American centres Valparaiso, Buenos Aires and Rio de Janeiro had active Foreign Exchange markets. In the Far East Bombay, Calcutta, Shanghai and Hong Kong and towards the close of the century Tokyo and Yokohama developed Foreign Exchange markets. The countries of the British Empire transacted most of their Foreign Exchange business with and through London, except Canada which always had close contacts with the New York market.

(10) THE U.S. FOREIGN EXCHANGE MARKET

The New York Foreign Exchange market developed very slowly after the United States became independent. Its progress was helped by the practice inherited from the colonial period, during which no business in dollar bills was transacted in London, so that trade with Britain was financed exclusively by transactions in sterling bills on the other side of the Atlantic. For a long time most Foreign Exchange transactions were negotiated direct between American importers and exporters, largely through advertising in newspapers the bills they wanted to buy or sell. Even during the early decades of the 19th century such advertisements appeared from time to time.

The establishment of branches of London banks in New York helped the progress of the Foreign Exchange market. Nevertheless, it was a slow process. De-centralisation of commercial and financial activity was a handicap, as it dispersed the Foreign Exchange business between several centres. A large proportion of the transactions in sterling bills was done in New Orleans where bills drawn by cotton exporters to Britain were sold. Boston, too, had a Foreign Exchange market, and for a long time during the early years of the century the rates of sterling bills quoted there tended to be up to 1 per cent lower than those quoted in New York.[7] Baltimore was also a market of some importance. San Francisco became a Foreign Exchange centre for a while in connection with the Californian gold rush, and again during the Civil War when it was safer to ship bullion from that port.

Progress of the American Foreign Exchange market was assisted by the Civil War, because of the large volume of speculative business resulting from the wide fluctuations of the dollar, even though most of the speculation was in gold at a fluctuating premium. After its termination – and more especially after the adoption of the gold standard – increasingly close relations between London and New York bankers had led to a very active market in sterling bills in New York. The London market in dollar bills was for a long time much less active, because of the prevailing practice of quoting prices in sterling.

(11) EFFECT OF CLOSER BANKING RELATIONS

The relative importance of finance bills greatly increased long after the cessation of the ban on interest charges which had been originally responsible for their adoption. Such bills continued to be looked upon with disfavour by ill-informed critics. Yet, as Goschen pointed out, they played a highly constructive part in bridging seasonal gaps between imports and exports, which would otherwise have had to be settled by sending bullion backward and forward.[8]

The development of mail transfers was a natural consequence of the increasingly settled conditons under *Pax Britannica*. There was an all-round increase of confidence, and banks in the leading Foreign Exchange centres gradually acquired the habit of keeping permanent balances with each other for the requirements of their Foreign Exchange business. They came to trust each other sufficiently to accept informal transfers from such balances as a basis of Foreign Exchange transactions, and to grant each other overdraft facilities in their own currencies, instead of insisting on receiving bills of exchange from the borrower.

(12) CABLE TRANSFERS

A further stage in this development was the progress achieved through the adoption of the telegraph and the laying down of an increasing number of overseas cables. This change was not so very significant between London and the Western European centres which could be reached by mail communications in a day or two during the latter half of the century. It was very important in the case of communications with the United States nad other distant countries. The first transatlantic cable was completed in 1866, and it is reasonable to assume that from the very outset banks on both sides of the Atlantic made much use of it for transfers. The first actual evidence of the practice of cable transfers was contained in a report appearing in the *Commercial and Financial*

Chronicle of November 1, 1879.[9] By the 'nineties telegraphic transfers were used regularly and on a large scale for making payments, especially between distant countries.

(13) CHANGE IN METHOD OF DEALING

One of the effects of the development of mail transfers and of telegraphic transfers was the decline of the relative importance of Foreign Exchange dealings at the Royal Exchange and at similar formal meeting places of Foreign Exchange dealers and brokers in continental financial centres. An increasingly large proportion of the business came to be transacted every day outside these formal markets, between banks through the intermediary of brokers in the same banking centre, and through direct contact of banks between different centres. In the early years of the 20th century a number of Foreign Exchange markets in the modern sense, consisting of a number of Foreign Exchange departments and brokers linked with each other by means of a network of private telephone lines, came into existence, even though the obsolete system survived in other centres side by side with the modern system right to our days. The increasing use of the telephone within the same market contributed towards the transformation of Foreign Exchange business, though it was not until after the first World War that overseas telephone lines assumed first-rate importance.

In the circumstances the continued meetings of formal markets became an anachronistic survival. In London in particular, where the meetings at the Royal Exchange were limited to the two post days of the week, the facilities obviously did not satisfy the requirements arising from the increasing volume of transactions. The rates fixed at those meetings at the beginning of each session served only as a guidance, and the bulk of the business that was concluded elsewhere, either before or after the fixing of the rates, was transacted at fluctuating rates in conformity with supply and demand. On frequent occasions these rates departed considerably from the 'fixed' rates immediately after their fixing.

(14) DEVELOPMENT OF FORWARD EXCHANGE

By far the most important change during the 19th century was the development of regular and active Forward Exchange dealing. It was already active in bills in Paris and in *assignats* during the

inflationary period of the French Revolution.[10] There is reason
to believe that similar markets existed also in some other fluctuating currencies during the Napoleonic Wars. It is equally probable
that on various occasions, whenever during the earlier part of the
19th century some exchanges became unsettled as a result of wars
or civil wars, forward dealings developed, partly by merchants
wanting to cover the exchange risk, and partly by speculators and
arbitrageurs. Currencies such as the Austrian *gulden* or the *rouble*
had active forward markets though concrete evidence about regular dealings is only available for the last three decades of the 19th
century.

Before Forward Exchange facilities became available the exchange risk was covered by means of long bills. A merchant or
banker, having to make payment in a foreign currency in a foreign
centre at some future date, was usually able to buy foreign bills
of the required maturity if it was not too distant a date. Likewise,
a merchant or banker expecting to receive payment in a foreign
currency at some later date was able to safeguard himself against
the risk of a depreciation of that currency by drawing a bill in
terms of that currency for the required maturity and selling it.
As a result of the increase in the turnover in Foreign Exchanges,
however, the disadvantages of this method of covering must have
manifested themselves to an increasing extent.

The purchase of long bills required an immediate capital outlay
or a bank loan, while the purchase of Forward Exchanges required
neither a cash outlay – except in some instances relatively small
deposits – nor a credit transaction – unless the buyer wanted to
cover the exchange risk by obtaining an overdraft in the currency
concerned repayable on the date on which the forward contract
matured.[11] In any case the buyer or seller of the bills, while anxious
to cover the exchange risk, may often have found it inconvenient
to borrow or lend at the prevailing discount rate.

Moreover, unless the bills were of the highest quality they had
to be sold on relatively unfavourable terms, while the forward rates
were the same, though unsatisfactory names were not taken for
forward transactions.

(15) EARLY FORWARD MARKETS

It seems probable that Vienna was the first modern market where
Forward Exchange business was transacted systematically and on

a large scale during various periods when the Austrian currency was subject to fluctuations from the middle of the 19th century till the 'nineties. *Mark* and *rouble* notes are known to have been actively dealt in for forward delivery on the Vienna *bourse* throughout the 'eighties and 'nineties, and there was also a market in forward sterling and other bills and for mail transfers. Most forward dealings were for end-of-month settlements, in accordance with the custom on continental Stock Exchanges. For instance, most business was transacted in *mark* notes in Vienna for delivery at the end of the current month or of the third, fourth or sixth month. A Forward Exchange market was functioning also in Berlin during the 'eighties. There was keen interest arbitrage between Vienna and Berlin, with the exchange risk covered, in view of the instability of the Austrian *gulden*. Much forward business was transacted in *rouble* notes before the stabilisation of that currency. Sterling bills had a good forward market in Vienna and Trieste, Berlin, St. Petersburg, Valparaiso and many other centres.[12] Even after the stabilisation of the Austro-Hungarian and Russian exchanges, they remained inconvertible and arbitrageurs deemed it safer to cover their operations.

The development of mail transfers and later of telegraphic transfers greatly assisted the development of Forward Exchange markets. It made it easier for merchants and bankers to cover by means of Forward Exchange the risk arising from fluctuations between gold and silver currencies, especially in relation to the Eastern markets. American produce exporters covered their exchange risk by selling sterling bills for forward delivery. In Valparaiso it was customary to deal in sterling bills maturing on fortnightly mail arrival dates up to twelve months ahead.

(16) LONDON'S SLOW DEVELOPMENT

For a long time this development of the forward market, as indeed of the Foreign Exchange market itself, by-passed the London market almost completely. Although, as we saw earlier, London became one of the two leading Foreign Exchange markets after the end of the Napoleonic Wars – in fact later it became the principal Foreign Exchange centre for a while, when the *franc* came under a cloud in 1870 – during the concluding decades of the 19th century its relative importance declined. This was because the overwhelming majority of foreign trade transactions in

Britain were conducted in terms of sterling, so that the necessary Foreign Exchange transactions, whether spot or forward, were completed abroad. There was no need for British importers or exporters to cover exchange risk, since they made and received payments in sterling. Importers and exporters abroad were able to cover their exchange risk in the highly developed forward markets in sterling that existed in their own centres. Their bankers, in turn, covered their risk by corresponding adjustments of their sterling balances or overdrafts on their *nostro* account with London banks.

This state of affairs gave rise to the paradoxical situation that, even though sterling was by far the most important international currency and London was by far the most important international financial centre, the turnover of the London Foreign Exchange market was distinctly smaller than that of a number of less important international financial centres. This state of affairs continued to some extent right until the eve of the first World War, even though the growing need for Foreign Exchange business in London induced a number of foreign banks to open branches in London for that purpose, and several London merchant banking firms – mostly of foreign origin – came to specialise in Foreign Exchanges.

(17) INVISIBLE ITEMS AND CAPITAL ITEMS

In addition to the increase in the turnover of Foreign Exchanges resulting from the expansion of international trade that accompanied the industrial revolution and the opening up of new continents, there was a considerable increase in the turnover arising from invisible items, especially shipping freights, insurance charges, interest and dividends on foreign investment, etc. In their evidence before Parliamentary Committees during and after the Napoleonic Wars, witnesses referred to expenditure by British travellers abroad as constituting an important factor affecting exchange rates. An even more important source of Foreign Exchange transactions was the lavish expenditure by Russian noblemen who visited Paris or other fashionable places in Western Europe.

The capital transfers involved in the reopening of British branch establishments on the Continent, which had to be closed down as a result of Napoleon's decrees, were mentioned as being amongst the major sources of Foreign Exchange operations during the concluding years of the suspension period.[13] Moreover, there was a considerable increase in the turnover arising from issues of foreign loans in London, Paris and Amsterdam, and in other forms of foreign investments during the years after the end of the Napoleonic Wars.

Indeed, the 19th century witnessed a considerable increase in the volume of investment abroad, both in the form of loans for foreign Governments and other public authorities and public utility services and in the form of direct capital investment. From time to time Foreign Exchange operations arising from such capital movements overshadowed those generated by current visible and invisible trade, but in the long run the latter provided the 'bread-and-butter' of the markets.

(18) VARIOUS TYPES OF ARBITRAGE

Later in the century the popularisation of Stock arbitrage gave rise to additional large volumes of Foreign Exchange transactions on capital account. Bullion arbitrage, too, became increasingly important in volume. From time to time these operations influenced exchange rates considerably. For instance in 1888 stock arbitrage in international securities between the Paris Bourse and the London Stock Exchange caused sterling in Paris to rise to 25·44, the highest rate for years.[14] The establishment of closer relations between banks in various centres led to a considerable increase in the volume of exchange arbitrage to take advantage of discrepancies in rates quoted in various centres, and also in the volume of interest arbitrage.

Large-scale emigration that took place during the 19th century added to the turnover in Foreign Exchanges, first through capital transfers and later through emigrants' remittances. With the expansion of international trade shipping freights and insurance premiums, too, provided an increasing volume of Foreign Exchange transactions.

By the early years of the 20th century the Foreign Exchange system reached a very advanced stage. While in London the market was largely confined to banking firms specialising in Foreign Exchange and to branches of foreign banks, abroad most banks, big and small, took part in this activity. The technique of the operations became highly refined and was described in detail in innumerable practical books and articles. In each market there were a number of highly skilled Foreign Exchange operators. By the outbreak of the first World War the modern Foreign Exchange system was well in operation all over the five continents.

NOTES TO CHAPTER FIFTEEN

1. George Clare, *The A.B.C. of the Foreign Exchanges* (London, 1893), pp. 45–7.
2. *Evidence before the Secret Committee of the House of Commons on the Expediency of the Bank resuming Cash Payments* (London, 1819), p. 114.
3. William Waterston, *A Manual of Commerce*, 2nd ed. (Edinburgh, 1844), p. 196.
4. Arthur Crump, *The English Manual of Banking* (London, 1879), p. 176.
5. *Secret Committee of* 1819, p. 160.
6. Clare, *op. cit.* p. 41.
7. *Evidence before the Select Committee on the High Price of Gold Bullion* (London, 1810), p. 108.
8. George J. Goschen, *The Theory of the Foreign Exchange*, 2nd ed. (London, 1863), pp. 38–91.
9. Arthur H. Cole, 'Evolution of the Foreign Exchange Market of the United States', *Journal of Economic and Business History*, May 1929, p. 415.
10. Paul Einzig, *A Dynamic Theory of Forward Exchange* (London, 1961), p. 94.
11. Einzig, *op. cit.* p. 6.
12. Einzig, *op. cit.* pp. 8–9.
13. *Secret Committee of* 1819, p. 44.
14. George Clare, *A Money Market Primer* (London, 1900), p. 102.

CHAPTER SIXTEEN

Foreign Exchange Tendencies

(1) STABILITY WAS FAR FROM PERFECT

THE nostalgia with which, amidst the unsettled conditions in Foreign Exchanges during and after the two World Wars, our generation has come to look back upon the 19th century as the ideal period of stability, had not been fully justified. For, apart altogether from the abnormal fluctuations during and immediately after the Napoleonic Wars, the world had ample experience in wide exchange movements even in those 'good old days' between 1815 and 1914. Although the fluctuations of the various inconvertible paper currencies – even those of Latin-America – were moderate compared with the spectacular movements of more recent decades, in their time they gave rise to many a difficult and complicated problem. There were also endless complications arising from the co-existence of gold and silver currencies, especially during the depreciation of silver in the last quarter of the 19th century. A book written in 1894 by René Théry, dealing with that period, bears the telling title *La Crise des changes*, which only goes to show that even a relatively stable period in Foreign Exchange history is considered uneventful in retrospect only.

(2) SLUMP OF THE *ASSIGNATS*

In at least part of the last decade of the 18th century and the first two decades of the 19th century most exchanges were subject to abnormal fluctuations as a result of abnormal conditions created by the French Revolution and the Napoleonic Wars. The early years of that period witnessed the extreme depreciation of the French *livre*, caused by the ever-increasing inflationary issue of inconvertible paper currency. Already by the end of 1791 the *assignats* depreciated to some extent both internally, as indicated by the increase in the premium on gold and by the rise in prices, and externally, as indicated by the decline of the Amsterdam quotation of bills on Paris from 52½ *stuyvers* in July 1790 to 39 *stuyvers* in December 1791.

During the next two years the exchange on Paris in Hamburg and Amsterdam had some very violent ups and downs, largely in accordance with changes in the military position and prospects of the French revolutionary armies. The victories of 1792 caused a recovery of the Paris rate in Amsterdam from 30 *stuyvers* in May to 37 *stuyvers* in November. Having regard to the non-stop increase of the note issue, this appreciation was entirely unwarranted. It was followed by a relapse in consequence of the French defeats during the first half of 1793, but the victories during the second half of that year resulted in another sharp recovery. The downward trend was soon resumed and became accelerated from 1794, the Hamburg quotation declining to 1·4 in August 1795 and to 0·2 in March 1796.[1] Nor was it stopped, except quite temporarily, by the substitution of the *mandats territoriaux* for the utterly discredited *assignats* under the *Directoire* in June 1796.

The depreication of the French exchange was for some time relatively moderate in the United States, partly because there was more confidence in the future of the French Republic in America than in the European countries fighting against it, and partly as a result of the repayment of some of the loans granted by France to America during the War of Independence.[2] Its depreciation in Basle, too, was for a long time more moderate than in London or Hamburg, because of better facilities for smuggling gold from France to Switzerland in defence of the ban imposed on gold exports.[3]

(3) STABILITY OF NAPOLEON'S *FRANC*

The *franc* was introduced in 1803 to replace the *livre* as the monetary unit, and it was given a metallic parity which was to remain unchanged for 125 years. The new currency remained remarkably stable throughout the Napoleonic Wars. In 1807 for instance, when sterling fluctuated within a range of 4 per cent, the movements of the *franc* against other currencies on a metallic basis were within ½ per cent. It was at a premium even in the Hamburg market. Its stability and firmness was due to the sound policies pursued under the influence of the natural revulsion of French opinion against inflationary financing, and to Napoleon's determination to maintain a sound currency. It was, of course, helped

by his success in wars, which enabled his armies to live largely on
the invaded countries and to collect substantial war indemnities.
But even the series of reverses during 1812–15 and the final overthrow of the régime after Waterloo failed to cause any noteworthy depreciation of the *franc*. Giving evidence before the
Secret Committee of 1819, N. M. Rothschild said that the extent
to which reparations paid by France to the Allies affected the
franc was 1 to 1½ per cent.[4] Even that depreciation was purely
temporary. Just as, after the second World War, the currency of
the vanquished nation was for a long time stronger than that of
its victorious opponents.

(4) SUSPENSION OF SPECIE PAYMENTS IN BRITAIN

In the early years of the Wars of the Revolution sterling was well
maintained. In 1793 the trade balance was favourable and in
July sterling was quoted above par in Hamburg – at 37 against
the par of about 35. Paradoxically enough, the deflationary effect
of the series of bank failures also helped, because it prevented
domestic prices from rising. Even though subsidies to continental
allies were a heavy burden, this was more or less offset by the
export surplus. It was not until towards the end of 1795 that
sterling began to depreciate, its quotation in Hamburg declining
at one time to 31. Large subsidies had to be paid to Austria and
the bad harvest necessitated abnormal imports of corn. Distrust
in sterling became accentuated with the Austrian defeats of 1797,
and there was a growing demand for gold.

In such circumstances the Government deemed it advisable
to authorise the Bank of England to suspend the convertibility
of its notes. It is true, following on the conclusion of peace by
Austria there was no need for further subsidies and sterling became
firmer.[5] Nevertheless, in view of the general situation, the decision
to suspend cash payments was endorsed by most sections of expert
opinion and public opinion.

(5) STERLING DURING THE NAPOLEONIC WARS

In spite of the suspension, sterling rose in Hamburg above 37
in 1797 and was well maintained till the spring of 1799. But at
the end of that year the formation of a new coalition against

France made it necessary to resume subsidies to continental allies, and in anticipation of this sterling weakened as soon as the coalition was announced. By January 1800 it was down again at 32 and by October it declined to 30. During the following year the effect of the subsidies became aggravated by an adverse change in the balance of payments and by the psychological effect of the long series of French victories on the continent.

The peace of Amiens in 1802 brought temporary relief to sterling, because there was no further need for paying subsidies. The harvest, too, was good, so that there was an export surplus and sterling improved. Nor did the renewal of the war in 1803 revive heavy pressure on sterling immediately. Even though in 1805 the resumption of subsidies on a large scale made matters worse, the news of the crushing defeat of Britain's allies at Austerlitz caused sterling to recover in anticipation of the end of subsidy payments.[6] For some time it was quoted above 34 in Hamburg, and in 1808 it rose above 35. Thereafter, however, it came under prolonged pressure, largely owing to the blockade imposed by Napoleon's Berlin and Milan decrees on trade between Britain and the Continent. In November 1808 it was down to 31, and during the following year it was around 29.

The depreciation of sterling would have been even more pronounced if it had not been mitigated by the outflow of bullion and specie. Transport costs to Hamburg were between $1\frac{1}{2}$ and 2 per cent, and insurance premium fluctuated widely around 4 per cent, so that the specie point varied between 5 and 7 per cent, reckoned not from the nominal Mint parity but from the London market price of gold in relation to the Hamburg price of silver.[7]

Evidence given before the Bullion Committee of 1810 confirmed the strange state of affairs that, although Britain was at war with Napoleon, there were large imports of French wines and brandy, which was given as one of the causes of sterling's weakness.[8] In 1809 the Hamburg quotation of sterling averaged $27\frac{1}{2}$, and in 1810 it was down at $24\frac{1}{2}$. There was an even more pronounced appreciation of the Paris exchange rate, a quotation of which was resumed regularly in London since the Peace of Amiens, and which continued to be quoted in spite of the resumption of hostilities.

Military expenditure on the Peninsular Campaign aggravated pressure on sterling. The resumption of subsidies to Russia and other continental allies, together with the cost of British forces in the campaigns that led to Napoleon's ultimate defeat, and the cost of the war with the United States, brought that pressure to its climax between 1813 and 1815. After Napoleon's banishment to Elba sterling recovered, but on the day that the news of his return to France became known in London there was a temporary slump of some 10 per cent.[9]

(6) RESUMPTION OF SPECIE PAYMENTS

Following on Waterloo the discount on sterling contracted, and par was actually reached in 1816. Legislation was passed establishing the gold standard, and for a short time sterling went even to a premium both in Hamburg and in Paris. The Government did not, however, dare to decide in favour of a resumption of cash payments. The continued excessive note issue, the adverse trade balance, foreign loans issued in London and the investment of British capital on the Continent between them resulted in a fresh depreciation in 1817. Most of the time sterling was at a discount in relation to the *franc*, which widened in 1817–19 as a result of the expansion of the note issue. In Hamburg it was quoted once more under 34.

In compliance with recommendations by two Parliamentary Committees in 1819 it was decided that the note issue should be deflated and cash payments should be resumed. In 1820 sterling rose to a premium and in the following year its convertibility into gold was restored.

From that time onward sterling was subject to more or less normal fluctuations. During the next ten years it was mostly at a premium both in Hamburg and in Paris. Apart from seasonal ups and downs, it was inclined to weaken from time to time as a result of adverse trade balances or of some unusually heavy capital export, especially to Latin-American countries following on their liberation. Economic crises at home and political trouble abroad tended to cause sterling to depreciate from time to time. For instance, the revolutions in France and Belgium of 1830 led to a depreciation of sterling as a result of withdrawals of funds due to the feeling of uncertainty.

All the time the movements of sterling in both directions were restricted by the operation of the specie point mechanism which functioned, however, more effectively in respect of gold exports than in respect of gold imports in relation to countries which were on the silver or a paper basis, or which, though on a gold basis, were inclined to discourage exports. Even in respect of gold exports, at times of acute crises the lack of adequate shipping facilities to cope with increases in shipments caused the effective gold points to widen from time to time temporarily.

(7) FLUCTUATIONS OF THE DOLLAR

In the early part of the French Revolution the dollar was adversely affected by the repayment of American war debts to France, to which reference was already made above. Later the favourable balance of payments resulting from the neutrality of the United States caused an appreciation. The dollar was at a discount against sterling up to 1807, but in 1808 British exports to America declined and the dollar went to a premium of between 6 and 10 per cent. This was well in excess of the transport cost of specie, which amounted to above 5 per cent. It became profitable from time to time to import gold in spite of the official undervaluation of its ratio to silver. Later, however, the exchange turned against the dollar and it remained frequently adverse in relation to sterling during the concluding years of the suspension in Britain, and even more so in relation to convertible currencies.

The curious system of quotation by which the dollar was reckoned as being equivalent to 4s. 6d. and its rate was quoted in terms of a 'premium' or 'discount' against this fictitious rate – when the dollar was actually at par its so-called 'premium' was quoted as being $9\frac{1}{2}$ per cent – was maintained almost to the end of the 19th century.

The New York market in bills on London was rather narrow during the early part of the century, which accounts for the wide and irregular fluctuations of the exchange rate. During 1813–15, for instance, the rate fluctuated between a 'discount' of 18 per cent and a 'premium' of 11 per cent. When peace was concluded between the United States and Britain in 1815 sterling depreciated from par to a discount of 4 per cent, but within six months it was at a premium of 11 per cent, which was equivalent to a real premium of $1\frac{1}{2}$ per cent.[10] With the broadening of the market the fluctuations became narrower. From the resumption of cash payments in Britain sterling tended to be firm in relation to the dollar.

Domestic banking difficulties in the United States caused the

dollar to weaken from time to time. The operation of the bimetallistic system, too, worked against it during the 1820s and 1830s.
The official gold-silver ratio encouraged heavy silver imports from
time to time, until the ratio was changed in 1834 in a sense so as
to encourage gold imports whenever the dollar was firm in relation
to sterling. In 1837 there was a moderate downward adjustment
in the metallic content of the dollar. Most of the time during the
1830s the dollar was at a substantial discount against sterling and,
even though it recovered to a premium for some time in the 'forties,
it was once more at a discount during the greater part of the
'fifties.

(8) THE AUSTRIAN DEVALUATIONS

The Austrian *gulden* was one of the chief victims of the Napoleonic
Wars. The convertibility of notes into silver was suspended in
1797 and the note issue gradually increased. The exchange on
Vienna depreciated and fluctuated at times violently, its movements reaching occasionally 20 per cent or more from one day to
another. By 1811 its quotation in Hamburg declined to less than
one-eighth of its parity, which fall was not excessive in view of
the increase of the note issue from 74 million *gulden* at the time of
the suspension to over 1000 million *gulden* in 1811. In that year
the *gulden* was officially devalued by 80 per cent, and this was
followed in 1817 by another devaluation of 60 per cent, so that
100 *gulden* in 1811 became first 20 and then 8 *gulden*. After the
second devaluation, however, successful efforts were made to deflate the note issue in order to restore the *gulden* to its new parity
with silver.

(9) HOW OTHER GERMAN CURRENCIES WERE AFFECTED

Among the German States, Prussia felt impelled to inflate as a
result of her defeat by Napoleon in 1806 when the convertibility
of her Treasury notes had to be suspended. By 1811 the discount
on her exchange declined considerably, but war expenditure
between 1812 and 1815 led to fresh inflation and currency depreciation. The exchange fluctuated in accordance with the changes
in the military outlook. After Waterloo the Government adopted
a firm deflationary policy leading to the recovery of the *thaler*.

In Hamburg the imaginary unit, the *banco* money, being based on a definite weight of silver, remained steady throughout the upheavals. Its *agio* against the defective silver coinage actually in circulation fluctuated within relatively narrow limits, between 24 and 25 per cent. For a long time the Hamburg quotations of all exchanges were looked upon as the measuring rod of their respective depreciation.

(10) DEPRECIATION OF THE *ROUBLE*

Russia adopted a paper currency during the reign of Catherine the Great – oddly enough she anticipated France in naming the notes *assignats* – and shortly before the French Revolution the ceiling of the note issue was raised. There followed a prolonged period of inflation. During the ten years ended 1796, the *rouble* exchange depreciated in Amsterdam from 39 *stuyvers* to 29 *stuyvers*. Its depreciation became accentuated as a result of Russia's repeated participation in the Napoleonic Wars, and by 1814 it was down to 10 *stuyvers*. After the war, however, a recovery of the *rouble* made it highly profitable from time to time to send gold to St. Petersburg. At one time the profit margin on gold from Paris was between 8 and 10 per cent.[11] This was the result of a sudden speculative anticipation of deflationary measures on the exchange. Between 1816 and 1818 the *rouble* appreciated from 9½d. to 12d. Progress was made towards its convertibility during the 'twenties and 'thirties, in spite of the abnormal expenditure incurred in connection with the Polish insurrection and the War with Turkey.

During the Napoleonic Wars the Swedish paper currency depreciated by some 70 per cent. Exchanges were quoted in *banco* money which remained steady until it was devalued in 1835. The Danish exchange, too, depreciated considerably during the war, but by the 1840's it was nearly at its metallic parities.

(11) STERLING IN THE SECOND HALF OF THE 19TH CENTURY

In the second half of the 19th century and the early years of our century, sterling remained fundamentally stable. As a result of the overvaluation of gold in the United States from 1834, there were frequent westward gold movements across the Atlantic, and the sterling-dollar rate assumed first-rate importance in the Foreign Exchange market. Its fluctuations, apart from crises and the period during and after the American Civil War, were largely under the influence of the normal seasonal demand for dollars to pay for crop exports. From time to time the routine was disorganised by some major economic or financial crisis in Britain or in the United States. Moreover, owing to London's rôle as the world's banker, sterling was frequently exposed to pressure resulting from withdrawals of foreign funds unrelated to any changes in its intrinsic strength or to the domestic economic situation in Britain. During the second half of the century sterling became increasingly sensitive to booms or crises or extraordinary financial strains or political upheavals of various kinds in any part of the world.

(12) EFFECT OF THE U.S. CIVIL WAR

The outbreak of the Civil War in the United States in 1861 gravely disturbed the relatively stable sterling-dollar relationship. Its anticipation and initial effect was, strangely enough, a sharp appreciation of the dollar, leading to heavy gold shipments from London to New York. This was largely because, owing to the uncertainty of the outlook, American holders of sterling bills realised their holdings regardless of losses, and there were also heavy forced exports from the United States to Europe in order to raise cash.[12]

With the progress of the Civil War, however, the situation soon became reversed. The dollar was adversely affected by the inflationary issue of 'greenbacks' and by the cessation of the supply of sterling bills resulting from cotton exports. The exchange and the premium on gold in New York fluctuated largely in accordance with the changing prospects of an early victory for the Northern States. There was a sharp and lasting recovery after the end of the Civil War, but not until 1879 was it deemed advisable to resume convertibility. The gold standard, enacted in 1873, became actually operative six years later.

From that time till the outbreak of the first World War the fluctuations of the sterling-dollar rate remained within relatively narrow limits, in conformity with the rules of the classical gold standard. There were, it is true, occasional 'violations' of gold points, to use Morgenstern's term.[13] In 1884, for instance, a sharp increase of interest rates in New York caused sterling to depreciate by 3 per cent in two days.[14] But on the whole the behaviour of the sterling-dollar rate conformed to the 'rules of the game' and kept within gold points for some thirty-five years prior to 1914. Even the American banking crises of 1873 and 1893 and the Baring crisis of 1890 had no extraordinary effects on it.[15]

(13) THE *FRANC* AND THE FRANCO-PRUSSIAN WAR

The French *franc* depreciated temporarily as a result of the revolutions of 1830 and 1848; but on both occasions its discount narrowed down considerably and disappeared before long. Its convertibility, which was suspended in 1848, was restored in 1850. The Franco-Prussian War of 1870–71 led once more to the suspension of its convertibility, but in spite of this, of the lost war and of the short-lived Communist régime in Paris, its discount remained remarkably narrow, the highest sterling-*franc* rate being 26·18 in October 1871, against a parity of 25·22. Nor were the heavy war indemnity payments after the war able to upset its stability. Convertibility was restored in 1878.

France legally abandoned silver in 1873 and five years later she adopted the effective gold standard. In spite of this the fluctuations of the *franc* were at times wider than those of sterling or the dollar, because during periods of strong adverse pressure the Bank of France sought to discourage gold withdrawals. About this more will be said in Chapter 18.

(14) STABILISATION IN GERMANY AND AUSTRIA

The unification of the German currency after the political unification of the German Empire in 1871 resulted in the creation of an important and strong exchange. The *mark* gained initial strength thanks to the indemnity received from France. But, as will be seen in Chapter 18, the Reichsbank often chose to protect its gold reserve by unofficially discouraging the German banks from withdrawing gold, preferring the alternative of a depreciation of the *mark* slightly beyond its theoretical gold export points.

As a result of the Austrian wars of 1848–49 in Italy and Hungary, convertibility of the *gulden* had to be suspended once more

The premium on metallic currencies rose in Vienna to something like 50 per cent. In the 'fifties there was a recovery, but the war with Italy and France in 1859 and with Prussia in 1866 caused the discount on the *gulden* to widen again to a considerable extent. Thereafter it gradually rose to parity with silver – though this was largely due to the depreciation of silver against gold. The *gulden* remained at a discount in relation to gold currencies until the early 'nineties when it came to be based on gold, even though it remained inconvertible. While during the years that preceded that reform the *gulden* fluctuated within a range of up to 7 per cent, thereafter the new currency, the *krone*, remained reasonably stable even in the absence of an automatic operation of the gold points.

International political tension that developed on repeated occasions during the years before the first World War caused the *krone* to weaken, but its depreciation remained moderate and under control on each occasion.

(15) UNSTABLE EUROPEAN EXCHANGES

After its gradual recovery from the effects of the Napoleonic Wars, the *rouble* relapsed in 1849 as a result of expenditure on the Russian military intervention to assist Austria against Hungary. Before it had a chance to recover completely from the effects of that war, the Crimean War caused fresh inflation and exchange depreciation. The Turkish War in 1878 revived this trend. All this time the *rouble* was the object of heavy speculation in Berlin and Vienna and continued to fluctuate widely until its stabilisation by the reform measures adopted by Count Witte in the 'nineties. In the early years of this century the Russo-Japanese War, and the revolutionary unrest that followed it, caused the *rouble* to weaken once more, but its depreciation was moderate.

In Italy the political unification of the country was followed by its monetary unification. She joined the Latin Monetary Union, but the war with Austria in 1866 brought about an appreciation of gold currencies against the *lira* by some $13\frac{1}{2}$ per cent. Its recovery was followed by another depreciation in 1873 and again in 1879. In 1884 it reached par, but during the early 'nineties its discount crept up once more, reaching 11 per cent in 1894. There followed a gradual recovery, and for the first time in 1903 the *lira* went to a premium.

The new Spanish currency, the *peseta*, adopted in 1868, remained at a moderate discount during the 'seventies and 'eighties, but depreciated considerably during the 'nineties. As a result of the Spanish-American War its discount in relation to gold currencies exceeded 50 per cent in 1898. A partial recovery followed, but the exchanges remained adverse and fluctuated widely right to the outbreak of the first World War. In Portugal a crisis in 1846 resulted in a sharp depreciation of the exchange and the inconvertible paper money continued to fluctuate.

(16) FLUCTUATIONS IN LATIN-AMERICA

Latin-American countries witnessed frequent periods of uncontrolled inflation and currency depreciation. The Chilean *peso* depreciated from 37d. in 1878 to 12d. sixteen years later, the parity being 36d. The premium on sterling in Valparaiso rose again considerably during the early years of the 20th century reaching a maximum of 132 per cent in 1908.

The exchange value of the Argentine paper *peso* depreciated very considerably during the 'sixties and was maintained round its low level for some years until 1876 when it resumed its depreciation and wider fluctuations. In 1899 it was stabilised once more at a lower level where it was maintained until 1914. In the Argentine and in some other Latin-American countries, exchanges were quoted mostly in gold *pesos* and the major fluctuations took place between the gold *peso* and the paper *peso* whenever the Conversion Office suspended its operations. Gold currencies were at a premium of several hundred per cent during the latter part of the 19th century and the early part of the 20th century.

The history of the Brazilian currency provides a characteristic instance of the long series of depreciations and successive devaluations to which most Latin-American exchanges were subject. From its original parity of 5s. 7½d. it depreciated to 3s. 11d. in 1823. As a result of foreign loans it recovered to 4s. 8d. two years later, but by 1830 it was down at 1s. 6d. A new parity was fixed in 1833 at 3s. 7½d., but in 1846 it was devalued to 2s. 3d. During the early 'sixties it remained relatively stable, and in the 'seventies it was at gold import point for some time. Its original parity was re-established after a devaluation, but between 1883 and 1896 it depreciated from 5s. 7½d. to 10d.[16] There was a particularly sharp fall following on the overthrow of the monarchy in 1889, from 27d. to 5d.

Wars and civil wars played havoc with most Latin-American exchanges from time to time. Their secular trend was downward, in spite of the support they received through the large influx of capital from Britain and other countries. Even in time of peace the disordered state of public finances resulted in perennial exchange difficulties.

(17) EASTERN EXCHANGES

The Japanese exchange, too, had its ups and downs during the 'seventies and 'eighties and only became consolidated during the concluding pre-1914 years. Before the *rupee* was pegged at 16d. in 1893 its depreciation was accentuated by the secular influx of silver to meet industrial and hoarding demand. Even on occasions when a depreciation of the *rupee* made it theoretically profitable to export silver, all that happened was that the influx came to a halt.[17]

The Indian example of stabilising the exchange by adopting the gold exchange standard was followed by several countries such as the Straits Settlements, Siam, the Philippines, Mexico, etc. Other silver exchanges, especially Shanghai, remained subject to wide fluctuations. The problem of gold-silver relationship, which figures so prominently during the greater part of the 19th century, remained unsolved by 1914 and continued to be the source of exchange instability in an important part of the world right to the eve of the first World War.

(18) STABILITY WAS CONFINED TO RELATIVELY FEW EXCHANGES

From the above outline of exchange trends it appears that even during what has now come to be regarded as the Classical Period of exchange stability under the gold standard, a large number of exchanges were anything but stable. Stability was largely confined to exchanges based on gold – whether or not on an effective gold standard – and even some of these were at times unstable, while the rest fluctuated widely most of the time. It is an open question whether, taking the world as a whole, the 19th century was by and large more stable than the 18th century had been between the end of the War of the Spanish Succession and the beginning of the French Revolution.

However, as far as Central, Western and Northern Europe, the European possessions on other continents and the United States were concerned, progress towards a higher degree of stability was undoubtedly made during the concluding decades of the 19th century and in the years before the first World War. With the adoption of the gold standard by the United States, Germany, France and a number of other important countries, with the creation of the Latin Monetary Union and the Scandinavian Monetary Union, and with the adoption of the gold exchange standard in many countries, a number of stable exchange relationships were created. Even inconvertible currencies such as the *rouble*, the Austrian *krone* and the *lira* settled down to stability during the last decade or two before 1914.

Generally speaking, as far as a substantial part of the Western world was concerned, the years immediatley before 1914 constituted the most stable period in the history of Foreign Exchange since Augustus and his immediate successors. Moreover, the trend pointed towards the stabilisation of the remaining unstable currencies. It seems highly probable that, had it not been for the two World Wars, this progress would have continued.

NOTES TO CHAPTER SIXTEEN

1. S. A. Falkner, *Das Papiergeld der französischen Revolution, 1789–1797* (München, 1924), *passim*.
2. Seymour E. Harris, *The Assignats* (Cambridge, Mass., 1930), p. 240.
3. Harris, *op. cit.* p. 260.
4. *Evidence before the Secret Committee of the House of Commons on the Expediency of the Bank resuming Cash Payments* (London, 1819), p. 17.
5. G. Browning, *Domestic and Financial Conditions of Great Britain* (London, 1834), p. 436.
6. Browning, *op. cit.* p. 440.
7. *Report of the Committee on the High Price of Bullion* (London, 1810), p. 25.
8. *Op. cit.* p. 66.
9. *Evidence before the Secret Committee of 1819*, p. 92.
10. William H. Crawford, *Report on Currency* (Washington, 1820), reprinted in the *Proceedings of the International Monetary Conference of Paris, 1878* (Washington, 1879), p. 552.
11. *Secret Committee of 1819*, p. 79.
12. George J. Goschen, *The Theory of the Foreign Exchange*, 2nd ed. (London, 1863), p. 49.

13. Oskar Morgenstern, *International Financial Transactions and Business Cycles* (Princeton, 1959), p. 241.

14. Arthur H. Cole, 'Evolution of the Foreign Exchange Market of the United States', *Journal of Economic and Business History*, May 1929, p. 410.

15. K. E. Davis and J. R. T. Hughes, 'A Dollar-Sterling Exchange, 1803–1895', *The Economic History Review*, August 1960, p. 62.

16. J. P. Wileman, *Brazilian Exchange* (Buenos Aires, 1896), *passim*.

17. Goschen, *op. cit.* p. 179.

CHAPTER SEVENTEEN

Good Progress of Theory

(1) STIMULATING EFFECT OF EXCHANGE FLUCTUATIONS

THE ill-wind of the French Revolution and of the Napoleonic Wars that disrupted the international monetary system for a quarter of a century had blown a great deal of good in the sphere of Foreign Exchange theory. The wide fluctuations of exchange rates between 1791 and 1821 greatly increased the concern of economists with broader aspects of Foreign Exchange. That interest, once thoroughly aroused, did not disappear altogether during the more stable period that followed. Dramatic developments similar to those which gave rise to the bullionist controversy did not recur in countries with an advanced literature on Foreign Exchange theory until during and after the first World War. But the material produced by that controversy was itself sufficient to keep generations of economists occupied. As a result, the period between 1801 and 1914 in the history of Foreign Exchange theory was one of consolidation as well as of unspectacular progress, even if much of the progress achieved during the bullionist controversy was forgotten later.

(2) 19TH-CENTURY DEVELOPMENTS

The following were the main developments in Foreign Exchange theory between the French Revolution and the first World War:

1. The purchasing power parity theory was rediscovered and was brought to a high stage of refinement, only to be allowed to fade into almost complete oblivion during the period of stability.

2. Attempts to reconcile the purchasing power parity theory with the balance of payments theory led to broader analysis of the latter.

3. The classical theory of the automatic international adjustments of national monetary supplies and price levels

through the Foreign Exchange mechanism was fully developed.

4. The speculation theory was revived on occasions of abnormal exchange trends; it was given a more scholarly form in the psychological theory.

5. Relationship between exchange rates and interest rates received closer attention, leading to the theory of international solidarity of Money markets.

6. The static 'barter' theory of Foreign Exchange was restated more clearly.

7. The effect of large Government payments abroad was analysed.

8. The effect of changes in the volume of credit as well as that of currency on exchange rates was studied.

9. A rudimentary theory of Forward Exchange made its appearance.

(3) THE BULLIONIST CONTROVERSY

The depreciation of sterling during the concluding years of the 18th century and the early years of the 19th century gave rise to the so-called 'bullionist' controversy which was probably the most important Foreign Exchange controversy for all time. It was waged over explaining the high price of bullion, to which contemporary opinion had attached much greater importance than to the weakness of sterling in the Foreign Exchange markets. Hence the name of the movement which, incidentally, had nothing in common with the Medieval bullionist school.

During the long interval between the mercantilist Malynes-Misselden-Mun controversy and the bullionist controversy associated mainly with the name of Ricardo, Foreign Exchange theory had advanced appreciably. The participants in the bullionist controversy started at a higher level of theoretical knowledge and were therefore in a position to engage in more penetrating and refined analysis, with results that have not been surpassed in some aspects even in the 20th century. Indeed, when following on the first World War the purchasing power parity theory was rediscovered, its early supporters failed in some important respects to derive the full benefit of 19th-century literature on the subject, and missed altogether some of the interesting points that had emerged from the bullionist controversy.

The main issue between 'bullionists' and 'anti-bullionists' was whether the rise in prices in Britain was the cause or the effect of the high price of bullion and the depreciation of sterling abroad. The anti-bullionists believed that import surpluses due to a series of bad crops and to Napoleon's measures against imports from Britain, and invisible imports represented by heavy transfers of subsidies to allies and expenditure on British forces abroad, were responsible for the rise in the price of gold and the adverse movements of exchanges, and that these in turn were the main cause of the rise in domestic prices. The bullionists believed that the rise in prices was caused by excessive issues of paper money, and that it was in turn responsible for the rise in the price of bullion and of the low quotation of sterling abroad. During the course of the controversy, both trade balance theory and purchasing power parity theory were thoroughly examined and the result paved the way for the modern Foreign Exchange theory.

(4) *ASSIGNATS* DEPRECIATION EXPLAINED

Even before the initiation of the bullionist controversy in 1801, new interest in theoretical aspects of Foreign Exchange was aroused by the *assignats* inflation in France as a result of which the purchasing power parity theory was rediscovered. Speaking in the Convention of 1791, Mosneron stated that, there being too much money, its value declined in terms of goods and, 'since the Foreign Exchanges merely enable us to exchange our money for the money of foreigners, our exchange depreciated correspondingly'.[1]

Here we have the rudiments of the purchasing power parity theory. Mosneron was not the only Frenchman to hold this view, but the voice of this school of thought was drowned in the storm of denunciations of speculators and of Pitt's manœuvrings aimed at a deliberate depreciation of the revolutionary currency. That line had a much stronger appeal in the prevailing atmosphere, and its popular approval effectively prevented a more scholarly analysis of the French inflationary experience in its bearing on Foreign Exchange theory.

In England little notice was at first taken of the causes and effects of sterling's weakness. For one thing, during the early part of the Revolutionary Wars, the specie point mechanism continued to operate – even if the margin between specie points

H

widened materially – so that no new explanation appeared to be
necessary. It was not until the opening years of the 19th century
that a further depreciation of sterling drew attention to the subject.

(5) BOYD AND THORNTON

The first shot in the battle of arguments which was to continue
for two decades, was fired in 1801 by Walter Boyd, a practical
expert on Foreign Exchange. He claimed that the excessive note
issue, through causing rise in prices, was responsible for the depreciation of the exchange.[2] Boyd realised the stimulating effect
on exports of an undervaluation of the exchange due to a depreciation unaccompanied by a corresponding rise in the domestic price
level.[3]

He was soon followed by Henry Thornton. 'It is obvious', the
latter wrote in 1802, that 'in proportion as goods are rendered
dear in Great Britain, the foreigner becomes unwilling to buy
them . . . and therefore . . . our exports will be diminished,
unless we assume, as we find it necessary to do, that some com-
pensation in the exchange is given to the foreigner for the disadvantage attending the purchase of our articles. . . . Our imports will also increase, for the high British price of goods will
tempt foreign commodities to come in nearly in the same degree
in which it will discourage British articles from going out.'[4] Since
the balance of trade must turn against us, the result is a depreciation of sterling which will encourage exports and discourage imports.

This distinctly suggested that higher prices in England affected
the exchanges through their effect on the trade balance, and that
the depreciation of the exchange tended to carry its own corrective
through its effect on the trade balance. Thornton thus tried to
apply to paper currency the classical theory of automatic readjustment of differences between price levels through the operation of
the exchanges.

(6) WHEATLEY'S PURCHASING POWER
PARITY THEORY

It was in John Wheatley's writings – the first of which appeared
in 1803 – that the purchasing power parity theory first emerged

really clearly and articulately. Indeed, he was the first to find in a later work a name for ratio between the price levels, calling it the 'par of produce'.[5] In his first book he declared that if the currency of one country increased above the required quantity (in the sense in which Hume and Adam Smith defined it) commodity prices would increase, and the same quantity of money 'would no longer be the measure of equivalency between the two countries for the same quantity of produce'. As a result, drawers of bills against that country would become more numerous and the bill rate would depreciate.

Wheatley stated his theory in a much more elegant form four years later. 'A bill of exchange is an order for a receipt of a given sum of money in a foreign country and must therefore be estimated according to the value of money, that is, its domestic purchasing power in the country upon which the order is given and the value of money where it is presented for sale.[7]

In his earlier work Wheatley tried to reconcile the purchasing power parity theory with the trade balance theory by suggesting that in the short run changes in prices might produce their effect on exchanges through the trade balance, but he does not recognise this effect in the long run. By 1807 he arrived at the conclusion that adverse balances, or even Government remittances, were unable to affect the exchange, provided that the note issue was kept down.[8] He came to believe that even in the short run a rise in prices in one country affected the exchanges immediately, before even it had time to affect the trade balance, simply because merchants abroad soon became aware of it and adjusted their valuation of the exchange accordingly.[9]

(7) RICARDO'S INFLUENCE

Horner – who was to become eight years later chairman of the Bullion Committee – forestalled Ricardo and Cassel in suggesting that a mere anticipation of a rise in prices was liable to affect the exchanges.[10] He thereby initiated a psychological Foreign Exchange theory.

Not until 1809 did Ricardo enter the arena. In a letter on 'The Price of Gold', published in the *Morning Chronicle*, he argued in favour of a reduction of the note circulation, on the ground that commodity prices would then experience a similar reduction and that this would bring back the exchanges within specie points.[11] With the publication of his pamphlet *The High Price of Bullion* in 1810 Ricardo assumed leadership of the campaign to make the Government realise that the depreciation of the exchange and the premium on gold was the effect of an excessive note circulation. He said that, while an unfavourable trade balance could account for a depreciation of the exchange by between 4 and 5 per cent, a depreciation of between 15 and 20 per cent was clearly due to the excessive note issue.[12]

'The exportation of the coin', he said, in *The High Price of Bullion*, 'is caused by its cheapness [by which he meant high commodity prices] and is not the effect but the cause of an unfavourable balance.'[13]

As Viner observed, Ricardo was not interested in process analysis and frequently confined his analysis to the end result, ignoring the intermediate stages.[14] This is the main reason why he did not carry the purchasing power parity theory further from the stage reached by Thornton, Wheatley and other bullionists. His influence on contemporary theory and policy was mainly through the weight of his prestige as the leading economist of the period. His views expressed in his evidence before the Bullion Committee strongly influenced the findings of that Committee.

(8) THE BULLION COMMITTEE'S REPORT

The purchasing power parity theory finds full expression in the Bullion Committee's Report. 'In the event of the prices of commodities being raised in one country by an augmentation of its circulating medium,' states the report, 'while no similar augmentation in the circulating medium of a neighbouring country has led to a similar rise in prices, the currencies of those two countries will no longer continue to bear the same relative value to each other as before. . . . The exchange will be computed between those two countries to the disadvantage of the former.'[15]

The conclusion of the Report was that there was an excess of paper money in circulation; that this was responsible for the high price of bullion and the adverse exchanges; and that no adequate provisions could be made against such excess except convertibility. The Bullion Committee failed, however, to convince the Government and the Parliamentary majority, the Bank of England and a large section of the business world. The motion introduced in the House of Commons by Horner to approve the Report was rejected by a large majority. The economists favouring the Report continued their campaign for a while, but it soon lost its force, because amidst the momentous events of the following years the depreciated state of the exchange came to be looked upon as a relatively minor matter and as a small sacrifice to accept as a price of defeating Napoleon.

(9) ITS DELAYED INFLUENCE ON THEORY

When it was found, however, that the conclusion of peace did not prevent a new depreciation of sterling a few years later, the campaign was revived and led to the appointment of 'Secret' Committees by both Houses of Parliament in 1819 to re-examine the question. Most of the evidence given by banks and business men before these Committees indicated that in the years intervening since the Bullion Committee there had been a fairly widespread change of heart and that the existence of a connection between the volume of paper currency and exchange rates had come to be widely accepted. By 1832 even essentially practical men such as N. M. Rothschild admitted that when commodities were cheap in England there was a tendency to turn the exchanges in her favour.[16]

The opposite view, that a depreciation of the exchange was due to an adverse balance of commercial payments, to subsidies to allies and to war expenses abroad, was voiced with much vigour throughout the controversy, among others by Sir Francis Baring, C. W. Bosanquet and Thomas Smith. The latter maintained with much emphasis in 1807 that the exchange rate could not have been against the country without an adverse balance.[17] In the course of time the balance of payments school gained reinforcements. Outstanding amongst its later supporters was John Fullarton who, writing during a period when Britain's experience with inconvertible paper money was beginning to fade into oblivion, while the effects of deflation were very much in evidence, stated that in most instances specie outflow was self-correcting and was liable to come to an end before the reserve was exhausted.[18] Nevertheless, the bullionist view was also restated with great vigour, among others, by George Warde Norman.

This subject was discussed very thoroughly in the course of the controversies over the renewal of the Bank charter in 1832, and again during the debates over the Bank Act of 1844. But in the prolonged argument between the 'Currency school' and the 'Banking school' considerations that came within the sphere of Foreign Exchange theory played a subordinate part and the controversy did not carry Foreign Exchange theory appreciably further.

(10) J. S. MILL AND SPECIE POINT MECHANISM

It was left to J. S. Mill to produce the classical theory, at any rate as far as metallic or convertible currencies were concerned. Without breaking new ground, he marshalled the views of his forerunners into an elegant theory of the 'self-adjusting power in the variations of the exchange'.[19] In his opinion those variations were in themselves sufficient to balance minor discrepancies between exports and imports, but they would have to lead to specie movements in order to restore equilibrium in case of major discrepancies, or disturbances arising from a permanent cause such as the general state of prices. Equilibrium was restored not through their direct effect, but through their effect on specie movements and through their effect on prices both at home and abroad.[20]

When analysing the situation under inconvertible paper currency, however, Mill was unable to elaborate a self-balancing system. Having accepted the purchasing power parity theory, he applied it in an entirely static sense. He suggested that the internal depreciation of a currency and its external depreciation in the form of adverse exchange occurred simultaneously and tended to be identical, so that the depreciation provided no encouragement whatever to export or a handicap to imports.[21]

Mill also revived the static theory that, from the point of view of international trade, there was no essential difference between trading by means of barter and by means of Foreign Exchanges. According to him, in the absence of a Foreign Exchange system the country with an adverse balance would have to reduce the price of its products in order to induce the country with unfavourable balance to accept a large quantity. He said that this same process was performed in modern conditions by means of a depreciation of the exchange of the country with an adverse balance, as a result of which the prices of the goods were reduced in terms of the currency of the country with the favourable balance.[22] This static conception was subsequently endorsed by Jevons and by other prominent British economists. It was rejected by Pareto who drew distinction between the dynamic transitional periods and the static state which terminates them. 'The static problem is complicated by the dynamic problem,' he observed.[23]

(11) GOSCHEN'S *THEORY OF THE FOREIGN EXCHANGES*

Although Goschen's great contribution to Foreign Exchange theory did not concern purchasing power parities, he touched upon that subject when dealing with exchanges under inconvertible paper currency. He remarked that fluctuations caused by trade balances, interest differentials, panic, long-distance remittances, etc., between them seldom exceeded a few per cent. But as soon as the element of a domestic depreciation of the currency was introduced we had had variations of the order of 50 per cent.[24] The bills on a given country fluctuated in proportion to the extent to which prices of all purchasable articles – bullion included – were affected by the depreciation of the currency.[25]

Notwithstanding this conclusion, the publication of Goschen's *Theory of the Foreign Exchanges* may be looked upon as the turning-point in the tide of the purchasing power parity theory which had been rising for the previous sixty years. Writing long after Goschen, Macleod felt justified in declaring that the principle that an abnormal fall of the exchange was a proof and measure of the depreciation of the paper money 'was so universally admitted now, and so perfectly evident, that there was no use in wasting more words to prove it'.[26] Yet long before he wrote this, Goschen had already shifted the emphasis from price levels to interest rates as the main factor through which equilibriating forces in the international economy operate.

It was largely because of Goschen that during the last few decades before the first World War the accepted text-book theory of Foreign Exchange was the balance of payments theory and not the purchasing power parity theory – with much emphasis laid on the effect of international movements of funds caused by interest rate differentials. This was possibly because the principal exchange movements remained within specie points – and there was no obvious call for theoretical explanations based on price differentials. The purchasing power parity theory was virtually forgotten by 1914.

(12) MARSHALL AND EXCHANGE UNDERVALUATION

There were, it is true, further contributions to the purchasing power parity theory after Goschen diverted attention from it. But they were not of major importance, with the possible exception of that of Alfred Marshall which consisted mainly of his analysis of the overvaluation or undervaluation of exchanges in relation to their purchasing power parities. He took the view that a bounty to exporters through an undervaluation of the exchange could only continue while the process of depreciation – e.g., through capital withdrawals due to political apprehensions in the case of Russia – continued. Once that process came to an end the readjustment of the exchange to its purchasing power parities was 'almost instantaneous'.[27]

The fluctuations of the *rouble* and the Austro-Hungarian *gulden* during the last two decades of the 19th century gave rise to extensive literature on the Foreign Exchange problems involved, especially in Germany and Austria, but it was largely confined to practical aspects and policy proposals. In his book on the paper *rouble* Adolf Wagner stated that inflation affected the value of the *rouble*, partly through its effect on confidence, and partly through the increase in the volume of money available for buying specie.[28]

(13) FRENCH SCHOOL REJECTS AUTOMATIC ADJUSTMENT THEORY

Among French economists interested in Foreign Exchange, Cournot restated the classical theory of automatic adjustment. He endorsed the view that the exchange rates depended on relative price levels, on the ground that goods must flow from the cheaper to the dearer market until the discrepancy between prices is reduced to transport costs.[29] But French economists in general were inclined to reject that theory on the ground that persistently adverse exchange rates caused by a perennial import surplus need not necessarily set in motion the self-correcting specie flow mechanism. The adverse balance of payments could be met by means of exporting securities. The French school went so far as to deny the existence of a tendency towards an equilibrium.

But amidst conditions of prosperity and stability that prevailed in Western Europe and North America before 1914, the optimistic Foreign Exchange theory relying on *laisser-faire* easily held the ground. This was largely because much of the writings by Spanish, Italian, Russian, etc. authors, dealing with totally different conditions, remained largely inaccessible to Anglo-American, French and German economists, so that the main stream of Foreign Exchange theory made no adequate use of their factual and statistical material or of their conclusions relating to wide exchange fluctuations. That speculation was able to cause Latin-American exchanges to deviate from their 'parities' based on relative note circulations was stated in great detail by Subercaseaux shortly before the first World War.[31] But his book did not appear in French translation until 1920 and was seldom referred to in Anglo-American literature on Foreign Exchange.

(14) SPECULATION AND THE PSYCHOLOGICAL THEORY

We saw above that the speculation theory and the conspiracy theory were revived in France during the *assignats* period. Likewise, in Britain during the period of suspension, a great deal was said and written about the part played by speculation in bringing about a depreciation of sterling. The literature of Austria and other continental countries, too, abounded in similar instances. Again during the American Civil War and during the period of Russian inflation in the second half of the 19th century, speculation was often held, rightly or wrongly, respbonnsible for aormal exchange movements. Instances, authentic or otherwise, of acts of economic warfare – to be dealt with in the next chapter – revived the conspiracy theory from time to time.

What was much more important from the point of view of the progress of Foreign Exchange theory, the attacks on speculation came to be supplemented by more scholarly views on the effect of the anticipation of various changes by speculation. This psychological theory reached a fairly advanced stage already during the bullionist controversy.

(15) EFFECT OF REPARATIONS TRANSFERS

In the course of controversy the effect of Government remittances on exchanges received much attention. Both Wheatley and

H 2

Ricardo took the line that the subsidies to allies and the cost of British forces abroad did not in themselves necessarily affect exchange rates because, in the absence of an expansion of the currency, the trade balance would have adjusted itself in a sense as to offset the effect of such payments.[31] Their essentially static analysis failed to allow for the immediate effect of such additional pressure on sterling, and for the immediate effect of its depreciation on the domestic price level. Most other bullionists were in this respect less dogmatic.

Abnormal international transfers were again subject to theoretical examination following on the payment of the French War indemnity to Germany after the defeat of 1871. The unexpected ease with which amounts that were substantial for those days had been transferred with a minimum degree of disturbance to Foreign Exchanges both after the Napoleonic Wars and after the Franco-Prussian War led to the rediscovery of Wheatley's theory by French economists – that an international transfer of capital tends to result in a corresponding transfer of goods. The adoption of this view in French literature, especially by Colson,[32] must have been largely resposible for the grave mistake made in the Treaty of Versailles in disregarding the Foreign Exchange problems involved in large non-commercial international transfers of reparations payments.

(16) INTEREST RATES AND EXCHANGE RATES

One aspect of Foreign Exchange theory which did not receive adequate attention during the bullionist controversy was the relationship between interest rates and exchange rates. Thornton did remark that when foreigners distrust sterling it is necessary to raise interest rates to a very high level in order to attract foreign capital, so as to compensate them for the risk of a depreciation of sterling.[33] Mill stated in his *Principles* that international movements of precious metals are determined much more than was formerly supposed by the state of the loan market in different countries, and much less by the state of prices, and that, therefore, 'gold might be brought back, not by a fall of prices, but by the much more rapid and convenient method of a rise of the rate of interest'.[34]

Mill was the first to apply in detail the specie point mechanism theory to the system established in Britain under the Bank Act of 1844.

(17) GOSCHEN'S CONTRIBUTION

But in spite of these and other claims to priority, it is to Goschen we are indebted for having produced a detailed analysis of the way interest rates in general, and the Bank rate in particular, affected exchange rates. His was by far the most important contribution to Foreign Exchange theory throughout the 19th century. *The Theory of the Foreign Exchanges* is still the standard work on certain aspects of the subject. Even if he had done nothing more than re-define and clarify principles stated in writings of earlier authors and arrange them into a system, he would have earned our gratitude for the thoroughness and lucidity of his remarkable exposition. Actually those who maintain that there was little or nothing really original in his book do him less than justice.

The influence of interest rates on exchange rates had been obvious to authors ever since the 16th century as far as long bill rates were concerned. But it was Goschen who pointed out that even an anticipation of changes in interest rates was liable to affect exchange rates, because it affected the rate at which buyers of bills would be able to have them discounted.[35] He also dealt in much greater detail than any previous writer with the effect of interest rates on bills payable on demand, an effect produced through the attraction of capital from abroad.[36]

Goschen explained with much clarity the relation between interest differentials and the margin between specie points. In this respect he prepared the ground for Weill's theory on the international 'solidarity' of Money markets – the most important German contribution to Foreign Exchange theory before the first World War – which presents a detailed analysis of the way in which interest arbitrage and the specie point mechanism between them tended to mitigate discrepancies of interest rates between centres with a good Money market and a good Foreign Exchange market.[37]

Goschen had immense influence on Foreign Exchange theory throughout the world. Right to our days he is among the most widely quoted authors in the literature on the subject. His first disciple was de Laveleye who elaborated his theory of the relationship between specie movements and economic crises,[38] and who represented Goschen's main theory in a more streamlined form.

(18) MARSHALL ON INDIAN EXCHANGE

The depreciation of silver in terms of gold during the last quarter of the 19th century and the resulting depreciation of the exchanges of silver-using countries drew fresh attention to Foreign Exchange problems. Outstanding among those who took an active part in the resulting controversies was Marshall. He was the first to differentiate clearly between the effect of exchange depreciations according to whether they were initiated abroad or at home – a differentiation that was remarkably ignored by subsequent writers. Dealing with the Indian exchange, he said that a fall in the *rupee* gave a bounty to Indian exporters if it was caused by a fall in the value of silver as a result of an international decline of demand for silver or an increase of the production of silver outside India. But if the fall of the *rupee* was caused by its depreciation within India through some discovery of silver mines in India or through de-hoarding of silver, that would give a bounty to European exporters to India.[39]

Marshall was also the first to appreciate the importance of movements of international Stock Exchange securities as a major factor in the operation of the Foreign Exchange system.[40]

(19) FORWARD EXCHANGE THEORY

Almost all writers on Foreign Exchange theory during the 19th century confined themselves to dealing with spot exchanges, even though during the second half of the 19th century there must have been in practical banking circles a fairly widespread knowledge of the Forward Exchange market, especially in Austrian *gulden* and Russian *roubles*. It was not until the early 'nineties that we encounter an isolated attempt at elaborating a Forward Exchange theory. Not surprisingly the first economist to deal with it was a German economist, Walter Lotz, who showed himself aware of the relationship between interest differentials and forward rates. He even realised that the forward rate was determined not by one interest rate but by several.[41] Even during the early years of the 20th century hardly any theoretical writers on Foreign Exchange showed themselves aware of Forward Exchange. Weill's book makes no reference to it, although Forward Exchange plays an all-important part in connection with the equalisation of interest rates in Money markets analysed in his standard work.[42] The Austrian economist and financial editor Walther Federn wrote a number of articles on Forward Exchange in conjunction with the intervention by the Austro-Hungarian Bank in support of the *krone*.[43] But his writings and those of other contemporary authors on Forward Exchange were confined almost entirely to its practical and policy aspects.

Knapp, writing in 1905, did not attempt to apply to exchange rates the basic principle of his State theory of money according to which money is a legal institution and its value is determined by the State. He duly admitted that the Governments' writ did not run beyond the borders of their respective States, and that the value of the national currency in terms of foreign currencies was determined by the supply and demand position. Fluctuations of exchange rates were 'the necessary consequence of the independence of States and their standards. Mint parities are determined by Governments but actual exchange rates are not fixed at their Mint parities.'[44] Only exchange control could prevent fluctuations. Knapp ignored the purchasing power parity theory and contributed nothing new to the balance of payments theory beyond his peculiar terminology which never found its way into non-German literature.

(20) CONFIDENCE IN STABILITY

Under the predominant influence of English economists, most text-books looked upon the self-regulating character of the specie point mechanism under the gold standard as axiomatic. Any exceptions from the rule, such as the fluctuation of the exchanges with the remaining silver-using countries or the instability of paper currencies, had come to be looked upon as temporary or relatively unimportant from the point of view of Foreign Exchange theory.

Even though the optimistic picture presented by Foreign Exchange theory on the eve of the first World War was fully in keeping with the general optimism of the classical economic theory inherited from the 19th century, Foreign Exchange theory did not form an integral part of general economic theory. Many text-books on economics either ignored it or dealt with it in a brief chapter or section running on conventional lines. It took an upheaval even more violent than that of the Napoleonic Wars to make economists realise once more the importance of Foreign Exchange.

NOTES TO CHAPTER SEVENTEEN

1. *Archives parlementaires*, vol. 40, pp. 497–8, quoted by Seymour E. Harris *The Assignats* (Cambridge, Mass., 1930), p. 236.
2. Walter Boyd, *A Letter to the Rt. Hon. William Pitt on the Influence of the Stoppage of Issue of Specie* (London, 1801), pp. 8–10.
3. Boyd, *op. cit.* p. 37.
4. Henry Thornton, An *Enquiry into the Nature of the Paper Credit of Great Britain* (London, 1802), p. 200.
5. John Wheatley, *Report on the Reports of Bank Committees* (Shrewsbury, 1819) pp. 20–1.
6. John Wheatley, *Remarks on Currency and Commerce* (London, 1803), p. 54.
7. John Wheatley, *An Essay on the Theory of Money and Principles of Commerce* (London, 1807), p. 60.
8. Wheatley, *Essay*, p. 175.
9. Wheatley, *Essay*, p. 64.
10. Francis Horner, review of Thornton's Book in the *Edinburgh Review*, 1802, vol. i, p. 184.
11. *David Ricardo's Works* (Sraffa ed.), vol. iii, p. 21.
12. Ricardo, *op. cit.* vol. iii, p. 85.
13. Ricardo, *op. cit.* vol. iii, p. 61.
14. Jacob Viner, *Studies in the Theory of International Trade* (London, 1937) p. 139.
15. *Report of the Committee on the High Price of Bullion* (Cannan ed.), (London, 1925), p. 17.
16. *Evidence before the Select Committee on the Bank of England's Charter* (London, 1832), p. 386.
17. Thomas Smith, *An Essay on the Theory of Money and Exchange*, 2nd ed. (London, 1811), p. 137.
18. John Fullarton, *On the Regulation of Currency* (London, 1845), p. 135.
19. J. S. Mill, *Principles of Political Economy* (1876 Popular ed.), p. 378.
20. Mill, *op. cit.* p. 374.
21. Mill, *op. cit.* pp. 384–5.
22. Mill, *op. cit.* pp. 375–6.
23. Vilfredo Pareto, *Cours d'économie politique* (Lausanne, 1897), vol. ii, p. 216, quoted by James Angell, *Theory of International Prices* (Cambridge, Mass., 1926), p. 207.
24. George J. Goschen, *The Theory of the Foreign Exchanges*, 2nd ed. (London, 1863), p. 62.
25. Goschen, *op. cit.* pp. 69–70.
26. H. D. Macleod, *The Theory of Credit* (London, 1890), vol. ii, p. 450.
27. Alfred Marshall, *Official Papers* (London, 1926), p. 173.
28. Adolf Wagner, *Die Russische Papierwährung* (Riga, 1868), pp. 86–8.
29. A. Cournot, *Principes de la théorie des richesses* (Paris, 1828), p. 311.
30. G. Subercaseaux, *Le Papier-monnaie* (Paris, 1920), *passim*.
31. Wheatley, *Remarks*, pp. 52–7, *Essay*, pp. 67–71, *Report*, pp. 20–1, quoted by Viner, *op. cit.* pp. 138–9.
32. C. Colson, *Cours d'économie politique* (Paris, 1901–7), quoted by Charles

Gide and Charles Rist, *A History of Economic Doctrines* (2nd English ed.), (London, 1948), p. 664.

33. Thornton, *Enquiry*, pp. 130–40.
34. Mill, *op. cit.* p. 407.
35. Goschen, *op. cit.* p. 54.
36. Goschen, *op. cit.* pp. 120–1.
37. Goschen, *op. cit.* pp. 140–4.
38. Émile de Laveleye, *Le Marché monétaire et ses crises* (Paris, 1866), pp. 138–44 and 175–6.
39. Marshall, *op. cit.* p. 195.
40. Marshall, *op. cit.* pp. 303–4.
41. Walther Lotz, 'Die Währungsfrage in Österreich Ungarn', *Schmollers Jahrbuch*, vol. 13 (1889), pp. 34–5.
42. N. E. Weill, *Die Solidarität der Geldmärkte* (Frankfurt, 1903), *passim*.
43. Paul Einzig, *A Dynamic Theory of Forward Exchange* (London, 1961), chapter 34.
44. G. F. Knapp, *The State Theory of Money* (trsl. J. Bonar) (London, 1924), pp. 218–19.

CHAPTER EIGHTEEN

Foreign Exchange Policy under *Laisser-faire*

(1) ENDS OF FOREIGN EXCHANGE POLICY

FOREIGN Exchange policy became more refined and more deliberate but less direct during the 19th century. The spirit of *laisser-faire* which developed during the 18th century grew even stronger. Most Governments continued to refrain most of the time from drastic direct intervention of the kind that characterised the Foreign Exchange policies before the 18th century. On the other hand, monetary policies which produced a strong indirect effect on exchanges came to be adopted partly with the deliberate object of producing such effects. Such intervention was not deemed to be incompatible with *laisser-faire*, even though its devices – Bank rate changes and the control of the volume of currency and credit – interfered very effectively with automatic trends that would have developed if the official policy had been one of strict neutrality.

The following were the main ends of Foreign Exchange policy during 1789–1914:

1. To maintain the stability of the exchange, or to minimise its depreciation, or to assist in its recovery.
2. To maintain or increase the coinage in circulation and the official metallic reserves or Foreign Exchange reserves.
3. To maintain as complete a freedom of Foreign Exchange transactions as was compatible with the above aims.
4. To keep down the cost of Government remittances abroad.

The main difference between these ends and the ones pursued in earlier centuries was a shift of the emphasis from safeguarding the supply of precious metals to safeguarding stability of the exchanges. Another important change was that while in earlier centuries the aim was to safeguard the supply of specie in circulation, in the 19th century Foreign Exchange policy came to concern itself increasingly with safeguarding the volume of metallic reserves in the vaults of Central Banks or Treasuries. Towards the close of the century, metallic reserves came to be supplemented in many countries by Foreign Exchange reserves, and the object of their Foreign Exchange policy was to safeguard or replenish also these reserves.

(2) MEANS OF FOREIGN EXCHANGE POLICY

The following were the means of Foreign Exchange policy applied to the above ends:

1. Influencing the volume of the note issue and the volume of bank credit.
2. Changing interest rates or maintaining them at the relatively high or low level.
3. Devaluations or revaluations.
4. Changes in the gold-silver ratio.
5. Changes in the monetary status of gold or silver.
6. Technical devices to encourage the influx of gold or to discourage its efflux.
7. Official Foreign Exchange operations.
8. Restrictions on the export of precious metals.
9. Restrictions on speculative Foreign Exchange transactions.

The last two devices were employed mainly during the wars at the end of the 18th century and the beginning of the 19th century, though some Governments with inconvertible paper currencies resorted to them also during periods of trouble in more recent times.

(3) POLICY OF DELIBERATE DEPRECIATION ABANDONED

In contrast to policies pursued in innumerable instances during the 17th century and earlier centuries and again during the 1930s, when from time to time various Governments embarked on a deliberate depreciation of the exchange, the basic aim of Foreign Exchange policy during the 18th century was to maintain the stability of exchanges. This policy was continued also during the 19th century. Whenever exchanges were allowed to depreciate, this was done under pressure, through sheer necessity, and not in pursuit of a deliberate policy. As far as is known in every instance in which it occurred the Governments concerned viewed the depreciation of their exchanges with dismay, even though their dislike for it had not been sufficiently strong to induce them to abstain from pursuing the economic or political policies which had led to the depreciation.

During the French Revolution, the growing realisation that the inevitable consequence of advanced inflation was a depreciation of the currency both internally and externally failed to induce the revolutionary régime to make an effective stand against inflation. Likewise, the belligerent countries in the Napoleonic Wars – with the notable exception of Napoleon's France – were unable or unwilling to finance their military expenditure in such a way as to avoid a depreciation of their exchanges. We saw in the last chapter that in 1810 the British authorities rejected the theory that blamed the high note issue for the low exchange value for sterling. This attitude was probably due to their dislike for the adoption of a deflationary policy that would have been the logical consequence of accepting the bullionist theory.

(4) ENDEAVOURS TO RESTORE OLD PARITIES

Throughout the period of suspensions and depreciations during the Napoleonic Wars all Governments concerned looked upon a return to the old parity as the ultimate end of their Foreign Exchange policies. With the return of peace, resistence to currency depreciations in a number of former belligerent countries on the Continent became stronger, and some of them embarked on policies aiming at causing a recovery of their exchanges. In Britain, however, it was not until 1819 that the need for stiffening resistance to inflation came to be adequately realised.

The United States, having readjusted the dollar slightly in 1837, was determined after the Civil War to withstand pressure in favour of a devaluation of the dollar and restored it to its parity. We saw in Chapter 16 that the French *franc* remained firm after the defeat of 1815. Its maintenance at the parity of 1803 was part of the sound financial policy of Baron Louis, Finance Minister of the Restoration. In spite of its slight depreciation during and after the War of 1870–71, its restoration to parity was regarded as axiomatic. It was largely owing to the ease with which depreciated exchanges were restored after the wars and revolutions of the 19th century that the policy aiming at the recovery of exchanges to their old parities came to be taken for granted after the first World War.

(5) INSTANCES OF DEVALUATION

There were, however, instances even during and after the Napoleonic War, of abandoning the efforts to restore the exchanges to their old parities. Austria devalued the *gulden* on two occasions, in 1811 and again in 1817. Russia, too, after embarking on deflation in order to improve the *rouble*, ended by accepting part of its depreciation as final and in 1839 it was devalued.

Policies aiming at a return to the old parity were often abandoned in Latin-America. In a large number of instances – some of which were quoted in Chapter 16 – depreciations caused by wars, civil wars or by maladministration came to be finalised eventually through repeated devaluations. The need for allowing exchanges to depreciate and for devaluing them eventually was sought to be averted by means of heavy borrowing abroad, which pursued the threefold object of covering Government and municipal deficits, speeding up capital investment and bolstering up the exchange against consequences of unsound finance.[1]

On the other hand, although Greece had to suspend the convertibility of the *drachma* on four occasions during the 19th century, and in 1895 its discount widened to as much as 80 per cent, nevertheless, in 1910 it was restored to its parity. Likewise, Italy succeeded in avoiding a devaluation of the *lira* before the first World War, even though it became repeatedly inconvertible and on various occasions it went to an appreciable discount. Japan, too, managed to reverse the depreciation of the *yen* that occurred during the last quarter of the 19th century and its convertibility was restored at its old parity.

(6) MONETARY AUTHORITIES' DILEMMA

It is safe to assume that between 1815 and 1914 in none of the instances when the exchange was allowed to depreciate, or when the currency was devalued, was this done as a matter of deliberate policy for the sake of such advantages as the economy would be expected to derive from a depreciation of the exchanges. Throughout the period, stability was regarded as the ideal state of affairs, even if in many instances those in power were unable or unwilling to make the sacrifices necessary for achieving it. Even staunch opponents of inflation and of exchange depreciation admitted at times that beyond a certain stage the deflationary gaem was not worth the candle. Thus Thornton admitted that in given situations it was advisable for the Bank of England to allow a depreciation of the exchange rather than create panic by unduly restrictive policies.[2]

The policy aiming at exchange stability very often confronted the monetary authorities with the choice between safeguarding the stability of the exchange and safeguarding their metallic reserves. The dilemma was largely special to the modern period. During earlier centuries the main problem of Foreign Exchange policy was to retain enough coins in domestic circulation, and to that end it appeared at times expedient to engage in a depreciation race, while at other times it was deemed essential to defend the exchange from depreciating below specie point. But as a general rule, throughout the Middle Ages and for a long time after, whenever the choice was between exchange depreciation and a depletion of the domestic circulation the former solution was chosen.

(7) EFFECT OF PAPER CURRENCY ON MONETARY POLICY

This was mainly because acute scarcity of circulating media was rightly looked upon as the worst of all known economic evils. It blocked progress, paralysed business, caused an epidemic of bankruptcies, led to general poverty and reduced the Government's revenue. Another and yet another depreciation of the currency was understandably regarded as an acceptable price to pay in order to avoid such a calamity. Even the replacement of good coins by debased coins was considered preferable to a scarcity of coins. The invention of paper money greatly mitigated the evil effects of an efflux of precious metals, because it became possible to replace by notes the coins withdrawn for export, without necessarily causing a rise in prices. So long as the additional note issue did not exceed the reduction in the volume of coins – a situation analysed by Adam Smith with great care – there was no need for the change to cause an inflationary rise in prices or a depreciation of the exchanges. In the new circumstances the arguments in favour of deliberately depreciating the exchange, or of allowing it to depreciate, an as alternative to losing bullion and specie, lost much of their force.

Nevertheless, during the Napoleonic Wars, too, the desire to retain the metallic reserve at the cost of allowing the exchange to depreciate prevailed in Britain, Austria, Russia and other countries. But attempts were made at eating the cake and keeping it. In many instances suspension of convertibility was followed by various degrees of restrictions on bullion exports and, in some instances, by some forms of exchange control, in the hope that it would mitigate the outflow of metals and/or the depreciation of the exchange. Confronted with the same problem later during the century, most Governments with inflated inconvertible currencies resorted to the same policy.

(8) SUSPENSION OF CASH PAYMENTS

For instance, on a number of occasions during the 19th century Latin-American governments, in face of persistent pressure on their exchanges, chose to close down their conversion offices and allow their exchanges to depreciate rather than accept the alternative of a further depletion of their metallic reserves. At the same time they also adopted some mild and largely ineffective forms of control. Although defence of exchange stability by means of control measures was contrary to the spirit of the times, the reluctance was overcome on many occasions even during the century of *laisser-faire*.

We saw in Chapter 13 that in Britain the export of bullion and foreign coins was freed in the 17th century but the ban on the export of British coins was upheld. This discrimination remained in force during the restriction period. The ban was applied also to bullion obtained through melting down British coins, and exporters of bullion had to affirm under oath that they had not obtained it through melting down guineas or sovereigns. Cynical contemporary writers repeatedly endeavoured to assess the extent of the profit which made it worth while to risk the consequences of perjury. A favourite device of evasion was that the gold obtained through melting down British coins was passed on to someone who was technically not acquainted with the facts of its origin.

While the suspension protected the Bank of England's own reserve against a drain through private withdrawals, it failed to prevent the export of many millions of coins withdrawn from circulation by dealers to take advantage of the higher prices obtainable in Hamburg or Paris. The Government was often criticised for trying to cover its Foreign Exchange requirements in the market, thereby causing a depreciation of sterling and stimulating the export of specie through private transactions.

In France the Revolutionary Government relaxed in 1795 the ban on the export of coins to finance essential imports.[3] No doubt it came to realise by then that the ban was hopelessly ineffective and that, in so far as it was effective, it only accentuated the weakness of the exchange.

(9) EXCHANGE RESTRICTIONS

The extent to which exchange restrictions proper, as distinct from restrictions on bullion or specie exports, were resorted to as a means of solving the dilemma was remarkably limited so far as the leading countries were concerned. While during earlier centuries it was a frequently applied if unpopular device, economic liberalism that arose during the 18th century was established sufficiently firmly in Britain and some other countries by the 19th century to prevent most Governments from adopting exchange control.

There were, however, exceptions. In France severe preventive and punitive measures were adopted during the Revolution against speculating in the form of forward buying of foreign bills – a pathetically futile limited effort to bolster up the exchange in face of the landslide-like *assignats* inflation. Apart from this, dealings in bills were free, and so were dealings in coins at an ever-increasing premium. *Émigrés* in England were able to withdraw some of their funds by means of Foreign Exchange transactions, thanks to the connections between London and Paris banking houses.[4]

Russia resorted to partial exchange restrictions on repeated occasions during the second half of the 19th century and in the early years of our century. Thus in 1894 the export of *rouble* notes was prohibited as a means of facilitating Count Witte's bear squeeze in the Berlin market for forward *roubles*.[5] Again during the Russo-Japanese War and the ensuing revolutionary unrest, there was a limited degree of exchange control to discourage speculative buying of Forward Exchanges.[6] The State Bank refused to sell exchanges unless buyers produced evidence that they needed it for imports. This meant that for speculation, arbitrage and export of capital the exchanges had to be bought in the open market at higher rates.

In the United States there was informal rationing of sales of Foreign Exchange in 1895, to discourage a too heavy outflow of gold.[7] Various European Central Banks discriminated occasionally against American finance bills.[8]

(10) DEFENDING EXCHANGES BY DEFLATION

The method of safeguarding or increasing the metallic reserve that was applied most universally in the 19th century was to prevent a depreciation of the exchange to gold export point, or to cause its appreciation to gold import point, by means of a deflationary monetary policy. It came to be looked upon as the classical system of defending exchange stability with the aid of devices affecting interest rates and the supply of money and credit. This had been by far the most important innovation in the sphere of Foreign Exchange policy. Although there may have been isolated instances of such official action before the 19th century, the origins of its systematic pursuit cannot be traced back beyond the bullionist controversy. The penetrating analysis of the Foreign Exchange system resulting from it, and the investigation of its rôle in the general economy, enabled the monetary authorities to shape their policies more efficiently than before. Moreover, the development of the Central Banking system made it easier to control the volume of credit and the level of interest rates.

(11) RELUCTANCE TO ADOPT DEFLATIONARY POLICY

It took a little time before the major conclusion resulting from the bullionist controversy – that an excessive note issue tends to depreciate the exchange, and that, therefore, the way to achieve recovery was to reduce the volume of notes and of credit – came to be adequately realised and applied. Viewed in retrospect, the delay was understandable and indeed necessary. Even if the bullionists had succeeded in converting official opinion immediately in favour of their conclusion in 1810 its application would have been prevented by the overriding necessity of financing the war against Napoleon. As Silberling, one of the most thorough students of British monetary problems during the Napoleonic Wars, observed in 1924, had the Bullion Report's recommendation been rigidly followed 'under the circumstances to which its authors believed they peculiarly applied there would probably be no British Empire today'.[9]

There was considerably less excuse for the reluctance of British official opinion to accept the bullionists' policy proposals even after the end of the Napoleonic Wars. In 1817 the note issue was expanded considerably, simply because no discipline was imposed on the economy so long as inconvertibility continued. The resulting depreciation of sterling went, however, a long way towards making the authorities and public opinion realise the need for restraining the note issue for the sake of defending sterling. This experience taught the lesson that inflation tended to produce deferred corrective, not through its effect on domestic prices, but through the effect of the resulting depreciation of the exchange on the official policy.

On the Continent, too, the existence of a casual relationship between deflation of the note issue and an appreciation of the exchange came to be realised after the Napoleonic Wars. When the Russian Government announced its intention to reduce its note issue the *rouble* appreciated by 10 per cent within a few weeks.[10]

(12) EFFECT OF MODERN BANKING AND CREDIT SYSTEM

In the course of the early decades of the 19th century it came to be regarded as a basic principle of Foreign Exchange policy that exchange stability must be defended by means of deflation. But with the realisation of the growing importance of bank deposits and credits, the accent gradually shifted to deflation of credit rather than deflation of the note issue. At the same time the accent shifted from the effect of deflationary policies on price levels and balances of payments to their effect on interest rates and the international movements of funds. The importance of the Bank rate as a device for changing the volume of credit and the level of interest rates was increasingly realised.

The development of the modern central banking system made it possible, for the first time in history, to regulate the exchanges by means of deliberately influencing the volume of credit and the level of interest rates. But on the whole in normal conditions the British policy relied largely on the self-regulating character of the system. The conception became firmly established that even in the absence of any deliberate policy the operation of the automatic gold standard tended to uphold exchange stability. An outflow of gold resulted in tighter money conditions and higher market rates of discount which again forced the Bank to raise its official rediscount rate. This in turn tended to reverse the flow of gold, not only by its effect on prices and costs, but also through attracting short-term funds to London and reducing short-term lending abroad. From time to time the Bank rate had to be changed not as a result of discount market influences but in order to forestall or reinforce such influences.

(13) THE AUTOMATIC GOLD STANDARD

The defence of sterling's stability between 1821 and 1914 was achieved by the classical policy of allowing free play to the automatic gold standard and reinforcing it as and when required by means of a Bank rate policy. Other countries endeavoured to ensure stability by maintaining the largest possible metallic reserve. Britain never aimed at holding idle gold reserves beyond the amount immediately required for the purpose of drawing upon it in times of adverse pressure on the exchange, replenishing it in times of favourable pressure. The Bank of England's gold reserve was remarkably small throughout the pre-1914 period of the gold standard, compared with the gold reserves of some other leading countries.

The main device with which the stability of sterling was assured in the absence of a large reserve arose from the wide use of sterling bills for financing commercial and financial operations throughout the world. A change in the Bank rate, and even a tightening of conditions in the Discount market reduced the extent to which such credit facilities in London were actually used, or to which sterling bills were discounted in London in preference to other centres. This alone went a very long way towards maintaining the stability of sterling. Only on very rare occasions, such as the Baring crisis, did it become necessary to supplement the Bank rate device by finacial support from abroad.

No other country was in a position to rely to a comparable extent on the automatic working of the gold standard. For one thing, as was pointed out in Chapter 15, during the years that preceded the first World War there were only two other countries besides Great Britain where the export of gold was absolutely free in fact as well as in law – the United States and Holland. The gold standard on which the stability of exchanges depended had rather narrow foundations, though the tendency was towards its broadening.

(14) CHANGES OF PARITIES

Although changes in mint parities and in gold-silver ratios as a deliberate device of Foreign Exchange policy had long ceased to be fashionable by the beginning of the period covered in this section, they were resorted to occasionally when the use of other devices came to be looked upon as ineffective or inexpedient. From time to time devaluations confirmed previous actual depreciation of the exchange.

A great deal has been published about the complicated Foreign Exchange problems arising in connection with the working and gradual abandonment of bimetallism during the 19th century and the Foreign Exchange policies adopted by various Governments to ensure the functioning of the system or the transition to the gold standard.

(15) INTERFERENCE WITH FREE GOLD MOVEMENTS

During the last few decades before the first World War it became the official policy of several monetary authorities to adopt technical devices to discourage the outflow of gold, in spite of the slight depreciation of the exchanges that often resulted from their application. Both the Bank of France and the Reichsbank pursued such policies. The former availed itself of its statutory right to pay out badly worn 10 *franc* gold coins, or 5 *franc* silver coins which had remained legal tender even after the adoption of the gold standard. It also charged a small premium on the sale of bar gold. The Reichsbank often unofficially but effectively dissuaded German banks from taking advantage of a depreciation of the *mark* beyond gold export point.

Several Central Banks resorted to artificial devices, such as the paying of a small premium on gold, or the granting of advances free of interest to finance gold imports. Even the Bank of England adopted the latter device during the Boer War. The Reichsbank accepted the delivery of gold at its Hamburg and Cologne branches, in order to reduce the cost of its import, while it only paid out gold at its Berlin head office. In 1899 it exerted unofficial but none the less effective moral pressure on German banks to induce them to refrain from withdrawing gold, when it would have been profitable to do so. The result was a depreciation of the *mark*, one half per cent beyond its gold export point.[11]

(16) OFFICIAL BUYING AND SELLING OF EXCHANGES

Active intervention by monetary authorities to support the exchange against a selling pressure was a rare exception. One of the known instances occurred during the American Civil War. The U.S. Treasury sold sterling bills on May 19, 1864, at lower rates than those prevailing in the market, in order to force down the premium on gold. The decline was negligible, however, and on May 21 premium resumed its rise. Three days later the Treasury was forced to raise its selling rate for sterling, thus acknowledging the failure of its attempt.[12]

During the last few decades before the first World War, the Austro-Hungarian Bank resorted to a systematic policy of maintaining the stability of the exchanges by buying foreign currencies during periods of export surplus or capital influx and reselling them in periods of import surplus or capital efflux. With the aid of such policy the Austro-Hungarian Bank was able to maintain the stability of the *krone* even though it was not convertible. Other monetary authorities which are known to have operated in a similar way in exchanges during the same period included those of Russia, Holland, Belgium, Sweden, Finland, Italy and Japan. They believed in influencing the fluctuation of exchanges between gold points,[13] instead of allowing the specie points mechanism to function automatically.

Of outstanding interest was the highly successful bear squeeze, referred to above, in the forward market for *rouble* notes in Berlin, carried out by Count Witte in 1894 and repeated on a smaller scale in 1895.

The operation of the gold exchange standard in India before the first World War provided an instance of pegging the exchange rate by means of systematic official operations over a prolonged period.

(17) FORWARD EXCHANGE TACTICS

The development of the Forward Exchange system provided additional scope for official intervention in the Foreign Exchange market. By pursuing tactics aiming at influencing the margin between spot and forward rates, the Austro-Hungarian Bank was able, during the years immediately preceding the first World War, to influence the movements of arbitrage funds. By such means it was able to obviate the necessity of having to raise or lower the Bank rate for the sake of preventing an unwanted influx or efflux of exchanges, at times when such Bank rate changes would had been disadvantageous from the point of view of the domestic economic situation.[14]

(18) WEAPONS OF ECONOMIC WARFARE

Before concluding this chapter we must refer to the use of Foreign Exchange policy in the service of political and economic warfare, Pitt's rôle in accentuating the depreciation of the *assignats* were, and still are, widely publicised in French text-books on history, while Napoleon's endeavours to weaken Britain through causing sterling to depreciate are familiar to British schoolboys. There was no doubt a certain degree of truth in such allegations, though its extent is difficult to ascertain. The charge of putting forged notes into circulation as one of the means to the desired end was made on both sides. When Napoleon invaded Russia in 1812 his armies put into circulation large quantities of forged *rouble* notes. Although this was mainly aimed at discrediting the currency within Russia, Napoleon was sufficiently Foreign Exchange-conscious to bear that aspect of the operation in mind.

Beyond doubt one of the main objects of the continental blockade was to increase the drain on the British gold reserve. To that end exports to Britain from France and the Continent were allowed to continue, and the blockade was largely confined to imports from Britain, or through Britain from other continents. Napoleon was in the habit of studying the exchange quotations in Hamburg and Danzig and interpreted a depreciation of sterling as an indication of specie outflow from Britain.[15]

According to Austrian writers, Napoleon pursued a Machiavellian policy aiming at aggravating the depreciation of the Austrian *gulden*. A special fund of 12 million *gulden* is said to have been allocated for buying up foreign bills in Vienna, Prague, Trieste and Venice, so as to increase their scarcity, and selling *gulden* bills in London, Amsterdam, Hamburg, Frankfurt and other markets.[1]

By the outbreak of the first World War Foreign Exchange policy, like Foreign Exchange technique and theory, had reached an advanced stage. Its ends and means varied widely in time and in place. The familiarity with its principles and the experience with its use existed, however, and was available for the monetary authorities.

NOTES TO CHAPTER EIGHTEEN

1. G. Subercaseaux, *Le Papier-monnaie* (Paris, 1920).
2. Henry Thornton, *An Enquiry into the Nature of the Paper Credit of Great Britain* (London, 1802), p. 133.
3. Hermann Illig, *Das Geldwesen Frankreichs zur Zeit der Ersten Revolution* (Strassburg, 1914), p. 85.
4. Seymour E. Harris, *The Assignats* (Cambridge, Mass.), p. 239.
5. Paul Einzig, *A Dynamic Theory of Forward Exchange* (London, 1961), pp. 402–4.
6. Karl Helfferich, *Das Geld im russisch-japanischen Kriege* (Berlin, 1906), pp. 181–2.
7. Arthur I. Bloomfield, *Monetary Policy under the International Gold Standard* (New York, 1959), pp. 51–9.
8. Bloomfield, *op. cit.* p. 59.
9. N. J. Silberling, 'Financial and Monetary Policy of Great Britain during the Napoleonic Wars', *Quarterly Journal of Economics*, vol. 38, 1924, p. 439.
10. *Evidence before the Secret Committee of the House of Commons on the Expediency of the Bank resuming Cash Payments* (London, 1819), p. 77.
11. C. Rozenraad, *Foreign Exchanges*, The London Chamber of Commerce (London, 1902), p. 148.
12. Wesley Clair Mitchell, *A History of the Greenbacks* (Chicago, 1903), p. 228.
13. Bloomfield, *op. cit.* p. 55.
14. Einzig, *op. cit.* pp. 405–19.
15. N. F. Mollien, *Mémoires d'un ministre du trésor public, 1780–1815* (Paris, 1845), vol. iv, p. 237.
16. Anton v. Coverden, *Das österreichische Staatsbankrott von 1811* (Vienna, 1912), quoted by Victor Hoffmann, *Die Devaliverung des osterreichischen Papiergeldes im Jahre 1811* (Minden, 1923), p. 10.

PART FIVE

FOREIGN EXCHANGE BETWEEN 1914 AND 1960

CHAPTER NINETEEN

Modern Developments

(1) PERIODS OF INSTABILITY

DURING the half-century that elapsed from the beginning of the first World War the Foreign Exchange system underwent many important changes. Although it had already been highly developed by 1914, it achieved further considerable progress both during the inter-war period and again after the second World War, following on temporary setbacks during both World Wars.

The present section covers some periods of unprecedented feverish activity and wide fluctuations, calling for new facilities and new techniques to cope with abnormal requirements. The instability of the exchanges during such periods has greatly assisted in the evolution of the modern Foreign Exchange system as we know it today. But this section also covers long periods of relative inactivity, during which Foreign Exchange departments had to justify their existence by adopting ingenious new devices to keep themselves fully occupied. The combined effect of these contrasts in experience had been an improvement of the system – or, at any rate, a development of its facilities and practices, for better or for worse.

(2) CHANGES IN PRACTICES

The following were the main changes in Foreign Exchange practices after 1914:
1. The volume of transactions greatly expanded.
2. Forward Exchange developed considerably.
3. Most business came to be transacted by telephone, both within the markets and between markets.
4. The importance of business transacted at the remaining formal meeting-places of dealers greatly declined.
5. Many new types of transactions came to be adopted.
6. Traffic in foreign notes increased from time to time.

I

7. Discrepancies between rates quoted at a given moment in various markets narrowed.

8. During economic difficulties and wars free exchange dealing was suspended, and even after the return of normal conditions complete freedom was not fully restored.

9. The balance of power in the international markets shifted in favour of New York, whose importance as a Foreign Exchange centre increased.

10. London recovered its lead, nevertheless, following on a relaxation of exchange restrictions.

11. The importance of official operations greatly increased.

12. Speculation of the conventional type greatly increased during the inter-war period, but its relative importance declined after the second World War.

13. The relative importance of hedging operations greatly increased.

14. Profit margins on commercial business and on interest arbitrage became narrower.

15. Facilities for long commercial covering improved.

16. Dealings in foreign currency deposits assumed increased importance.

(3) CONDITIONS DURING 1914–19

The progress made during the decades before 1914 towards a more advanced Foreign Exchange system was interrupted at the outbreak of the first World War. For a short time conditions in Foreign Exchange markets became chaotic. The interruption of relations with enemy countries made it impossible to carry out the large number of Foreign Exchange contracts entered into before the war, and it became difficult to carry out a further large number of contracts whose execution depended in turn on the execution of contracts with enemy countries. The ban on trading with the enemy was made much stricter than in the Napoleonic Wars or in any previous global wars. Enemy assets were seized in most belligerent countries and a more or less complete moratorium was declared on most foreign payments.

Over and above all, the situation in respect of sterling was greatly aggravated by the increase of the Bank rate to 10 per cent in August 1914. London's foreign short-term debtors hastened to repay their credits and the resulting scramble for sterling paralysed the market almost completely. Sterling bills needed for the requirements of financing international trade became virtually unobtainable.[1] The authorities adopted various official measures to relieve this situation, but it took several months before more normal conditons gradually returned.[2]

As a result of the ban on gold exports gold arbitrage was suspended from the very beginning, so that the exchange mechanism ceased to function normally. Moreover, at a later stage the fluctuations of sterling and, to a less extent, of other allied exchange rates were prevented by systematic official 'pegging' operations. In neutral markets the exchanges of belligerent countries fluctuated freely, and there was a great deal of speculation.

(4) POST-WAR SPECULATION

The slump of the exchanges of the defeated countries, and the more moderate depreciations of the exchanges of most victorious countries after they were 'unpegged' in 1919, marked the beginning of years of extremely confused exchange conditions. The Foreign Exchange markets witnessed wild and entirely incalculable fluctuations, and speculation figured prominently both as a cause and as an effect of these fluctuations. The practice of covering exchange risk on commercial transactions, which before 1914 was confined to trade with silver-using countries and with countries having inconvertible currencies, had to be extended to virtually all currencies. It came to be regarded as a matter of elementary prudence. The resulting turnover in exchanges became the mainstay of the largely increased number of Foreign Exchange departments.

(5) TRAFFIC IN FOREIGN NOTES

A feature of the early post-war period was the spectacular increase of the traffic in foreign notes. Already during the concluding years of the war German *mark* notes and currencies of other belligerent countries found their way into neutral countries in large quantities. From 1919 a large-scale two-way traffic developed in foreign notes.[3] Increasing volumes of notes of the financially weak countries were sold abroad, not so much through a short-sighted policy of the Governments concerned, aiming at borrowing abroad by means of selling out their paper currency, as in satisfaction of demand by non-professional foreign speculators who had seriously hoped to become millionaires one day through the recovery to par of the *mark* and of various other depreciated paper currencies. For a long time each new depreciation of such currencies increased foreign speculative buying. Later the outflow greatly increased through a flight of capital.

At the other extreme, the acquisition and holding of dollar notes and other hard currencies in countries with depreciating currencies became one of the popular means of hedging against inflation. As a combined result of the two movements, the markets in foreign notes assumed unprecedented importance during the early inter-war years.

(6) TURNOVER IN BILLS DECLINE

Nevertheless, after the first World War by far the larger proportion of Foreign Exchange business came to be transacted by means of transfers. The relative importance of the turnover in foreign bills remained high in transactions between banks and customers, but it declined in the market. In December 1920 the market in foreign bills at the Royal Exchange, which had specialised in that type of operations ever since the days of Gresham, was closed down. Long before this event most business in the Foreign Exchange market came to be transacted through a network of private telephone lines between the Foreign Exchange departments of banks and Foreign Exchange brokers.[4] For one thing, business between banks was always done in large round amounts, while most commercial bills were for relatively small broken amounts.

In many continental centres anachronistic institutions corresponding to the foreign bill market at the Royal Exchange survived right to our days – for instance, in Paris, Frankfurt and other centres a section of the *bourses* continues to be set aside for that purpose – but they operate for limited purposes and only during a small part of the normal business hours.[5] Even in centres which possess such old-fashioned markets by far the larger proportion of Foreign Exchange business has come to be transacted over the telephone.

(7) BUSINESS TRANSACTED BY TELEPHONE

The practice of regular Foreign Exchange operations through long-distance telephone calls also dates from the early inter-war

years. The new facilities made it much easier to take advantage
of discrepancies in rates prevailing at the same time in different
centres, and consequently those discrepancies tended to narrow
down considerably, except on days of hectic dealing. Progress
in the direction of narrower margins was handicapped, however,
until the resumption of free dealings after the second World War,
by the inadequacy of long-distance telephone communications.
Frequently there were long delays for lines for trunk calls to
correspondents abroad, and in the meantime discrepancies were
apt to develop and to remain. It was not until the 'fifties that the
improvement of long-distance telephone service and the adoption
of the 'telex' system made it virtually impossible for such discrepancies to continue for any length of time between markets
with identical business hours. By the 'fifties it could be said with
very little exaggeration that it was almost as easy to transact business with a bank in a foreign centre as with one just across the
road.[6]

(8) DEVELOPMENT OF FORWARD EXCHANGE

Perhaps the most important change that occurred during the
period covered by this section was the development of a really
active and efficient Forward Exchange market. During the first
World War the highly involved and delicate organisation of the
Forward Exchange market that existed before 1914 had fallen
into disuse to such an extent that even in Germany — where
Forward Exchange dealing had been fairly advanced since the
'eighties – it became necessary to rediscover the system after
the war. In most other countries, too, Forward Exchange was
treated during the early inter-war period as something new and
experimental. Amsterdam, Antwerp and Paris experimented
with special clearing houses to deal with Forward Exchange
transactions. In New York an attempt was made to establish
a system of 'put and call' contracts in Forward Exchange. All
such experiments were soon abandoned, however, and the markets
reverted to the pre-1914 system under which the Forward Exchange market was an integral part of the Foreign Exchange
market, with the difference that most forward business with
foreign centres was now transacted on the telephone.

Under the influence of continental practices much of the inter-
war forward business was at first transacted for end-of-month

delivery. Since, however, in the London and New York financial markets the last working day of the month had no special significance, from about the end of 1921 the Anglo-Saxon Foreign Exchange markets emancipated themselves from this continental influence and changed over to quotations in terms of calendar months, or for odd dates determined by commercial or financial requirements. Owing to the importance of these two markets, the bulk of international exchange transactions came to be determined by the Anglo-Saxon practice, even though much of the transactions with the Continent was for end of month.

(9) EXPANSION OF FORWARD DEALING

There was at first considerable resistence in many countries by ill-informed politicians, newspapers and even by the authorities themselves to the development of Forward Exchange on the ground that it was an essentially speculative device. Some banks of the conservative type were reluctant to take it up, but gradually this prejudice broke down in face of the insistent demand by their commercial clients for facilities to cover exchange risks. The London clearing banks which had kept more or less aloof from Foreign Exchange business in the market before 1914 established Foreign Exchange departments and became the largest regular dealers in Foreign Exchange for commercial purposes. To be able to operate more easily, the banks opened *nostro* accounts with banking correspondents abroad, providing facilities for accumulating balances in a large number of foreign currencies, and also for obtaining overdrafts in them.

By about 1921 modern Forward Exchange markets were functioning in every important financial centre, even though they broke down temporarily in Germany and other continental countries during the most advanced period of their currency depreciation. During the period of inter-war stability between the middle 'twenties and the suspension of the gold standard in Britain and in many other countries in 1931 the demand for Forward Exchange facilities, whether for speculative or commercial purposes, declined considerably. Nevertheless, by then the system was well established. Various types of arbitrage operations were also practised on a large scale and this, together with the Foreign Exchange operations arising from the large volume of international loan and credit transactions, kept the Foreign Exchange market reasonably busy.

(10) WIDE VARIETY OF ARBITRAGE TRANSACTIONS

Bullion arbitrage became an important source of Foreign Exchange activity during the late 'twenties, leading to a contraction of margins between gold points. This type of operation came to an end as a result of the suspension of the gold standard by most countries in the early 'thirties. But in the late 'thirties the development of a forward market in gold provided opportunities for new types of arbitrage.[7] Other types of arbitrage developed during the inter-war period included a wide variety of interest arbitrage, time arbitrage between long and short forward rates, triangular operations and stock arbitrage. All these types already existed before 1914, but they came to be applied much more extensively once the feverish speculative turnover of the early 'twenties and of the early 'thirties subsided.

The currency chaos that followed the suspension of the gold standard in 1931 and the simultaneous large-scale bank failures and moratoria on foreign payments in various countries brought about a setback in the Foreign Exchange system. Amidst the prevailing mutual distrust it became almost impossible for a while to transact Forward Exchange.[8] By the middle 'thirties, however, more or less normal conditions gradually returned. We shall see in Chapter 22 that throughout the 'thirties the markets were strongly influenced by systematic or frequently recurrent operations by monetary authorities, to resist unwanted trends and to iron out fluctuations.

(11) LONDON'S SUPREMACY

In the period of inter-war stability, and also during the subsequent period of fluctuating exchanges, London retained its rôle as the world's chief Foreign Exchange market. London's intermediary rôle between Europe and other continents assured her a predominant share in the Foreign Exchange transactions, apart altogether from the considerable volume of business arising from Britain's own foreign trade. Even though the bulk of British exports and imports continued to be transacted in terms of sterling, so that the resulting Foreign Exchange operations were transacted abroad, it became increasingly the practice to 'undo' the resulting commitments in the London market.

Continental Foreign Exchange Markets that achieved or maintained their importance since 1914 included, in addition to Paris, the three Swiss centres – Zürich, Geneva and Basle – Amsterdam, Berlin, Frankfurt, Brussels, Stockholm and Vienna. Owing to the pre-eminence of the dollar among the hard currencies, and to the greatly increased financial resources of the United States, New York became one of the leading Foreign Exchange markets. Most of the American Foreign Exchange business was transacted by the New York banks, and other centres in the United States declined in importance.[9] It was largely because of the differences in business hours due to its geographical position that New York could not become the world's principal Foreign Exchange market.

(12) BORROWING THROUGH FOREIGN EXCHANGE

A system of extensive international borrowing through the Foreign Exchange market developed during the 'twenties. It assumed the form of swap-and-deposit transactions, which meant that when an amount of hard currency was swapped against an amount of soft currency for a limited period, through the purchase of spot against forward, the banks of the strong financial centres deposited their temporary holdings of the soft currency with their correspondents in the weaker financial centres. The latter thus had the temporary use of both hard and soft currencies. Even though such transactions were mostly for periods up to three months, their repeated renewal placed the funds at the disposal of the weak countries for fairly long periods. Such devices were practised on such a large scale that they played a decisive part in the process of filling the vacuum created through the destruction of capital resources by advanced inflation in Germany, Austria and other countries.

From the early 'thirties speculative turnover in exchanges became supplemented by the movements of 'hot money' from centre to centre, seeking security against devaluation or depreciation. Later from the middle 'thirties, movements of funds seeking security against political persecution or war risk were added to the international flow of funds.

(13) THE SECOND WORLD WAR AND AFTER

At the beginning of the second World War the exchange rates of belligerent countries were pegged once more and free dealings in exchanges were suspended. Free Foreign Exchange markets continued to function in New York and in some neutral centres, but, owing to the impossibility of 'undoing' commitments in countries with exchange restrictions, the turnover in their currencies was essentially speculative and relatively limited. The freezing of accounts, in the United States and elsewhere, of residents in enemy-occupied countries further curtailed Foreign Exchange business.

In most countries the freedom of Foreign Exchange markets was not restored for a long time after the end of the war. In some countries, such as France, important black markets or 'grey markets' – unofficial markets which were tolerated – developed in foreign exchanges. The reopening of Foreign Exchange markets was a very gradual process and even during the 'fifties Foreign Exchange dealing was not entirely free in most countries. More will be said about this in Chapter 22. But there was a sufficient degree of freedom for normal and at times feverish activities, including international arbitrage transactions.

(14) LONDON'S POST-WAR ROLE

London recovered its supremacy as the most important Foreign Exchange centre, in spite of the handicap of exchange control during a number of years when New York, Zürich and some other continental centres were either entirely free or at any rate less restricted than London. Indeed, to some extent the existence of a type of sterling with limited transferability that continued until 1959 actually helped London's international position, because 'transferable' sterling was widely used as an international currency between countries of the 'transferable area' that included Western Europe and many countries outside Europe.

Another reason for London's increased importance was that, unlike in the past, after the war British importers and exporters became more willing to transact business in terms of foreign currencies instead of insisting on quoting and being quoted in sterling. As a result a larger proportion of the Foreign Exchange business

I 2

arising from British imports and exports came to be initiated in London instead of foreign centres.

The overwhelming importance of the dollar as the strongest currency until the late 'fifties did not prevent the extensive use of sterling as an international currency. In a way it actually assisted the recovery of London's rôle as the chief international Foreign Exchange market, because of the perennial scarcity of dollars, and also because London was always the best market in dollars. It was found easier to transact large amounts in dollars in London, without unduly moving the exchange rate against the buyer or seller, than in any other market, not excluding New York itself. Whenever the sterling-dollar rate changed during the New York business hours while London was closed, after its re-opening the rate very often reverted to the level at which it closed in London the previous day.[10]

(15) INCREASED IMPORTANCE OF HEDGING

A major change compared with inter-war days was the decline of the relative importance of pure speculation and the increase in that of hedging. This latter trend was powerfully stimulated by the growing internationalisation of industry and commerce, as a result of which many foreign firms acquired an interest in the capital of firms abroad or established branches or subsidiaries abroad. In order to protect their capital against depreciation through a devaluation they resorted to hedging against the exchange risk whenever the currencies concerned came under a cloud.

From the point of view of exchange stability these operations were much more dangerous than those arising from pure speculation, precisely because sellers of the threatened currency were in a better position than speculators to deliver on maturity the currency sold. The periodically recurrent waves of attack on sterling were largely due to such hedging operations by American and other non-British investors holding assets in the United Kingdom.[11]

(16) DECLINE OF PROFIT MARGINS

Yet another post-war technical change was the narrowing of profit margins on the conventional types of space arbitrage operations between two centres. To a large degree this was due to the improvement of communications referred to above. Interest arbitrage, too, developed to such an extent that in normal conditions such operations yielded only a fraction of the half per cent per annum which arbitrageurs considered the minimum profit-margin during the inter-war period. Many banks became prepared to operate from time to time without any profit in order to attract other types of business.[12] Moreover, since business firms had become much more Foreign Exchange-minded, banks had to quote them much finer rates to secure their business. As a result of this decline in profit margins, most Foreign Exchange departments, in order to earn their keep, had to resort to various types of highly involved transactions which had been practised only to a relatively small extent, if at all, before the war.

Commercial covering facilities greatly improved during the 'fifties. It became possible to transact Forward Exchange in some currencies for periods up to four years, compared with the pre-war maximum of twelve months, though such transactions remained largely a matter of negotiation.[13] Contracts for delivery of Forward Exchange on optional dates could be 'undone' in the market. There was a great deal more time arbitrage – the purchase and sale of short against long Forward Exchange – and also complicated operations on the cross forward rate which were considered too complicated by most dealers before the war.

(17) MARKET IN FOREIGN CURRENCY DEPOSITS

Above all, in the late 'fifties an increasingly important market developed in foreign currencies deposits. It began with the development of a market in London in dollar deposits owned mostly by European holders who, while wanting to continue to hold dollars, were dissatisfied with the artificially low deposit rates allowed on their deposits in the United States where deposit rates are subject to statutory limitations. This market came to be known as the 'Euro-dollars' market. Gradually similar markets developed in continental centres, and also outside Europe, in deposits in dollars, sterling, Swiss *francs*, *D. marks* and other leading currencies. A large proportion of these transactions did not entail any Foreign Exchange operation, since takers of the deposits could use them for the financing of foreign trade transacted in the same currency. Very frequently, however, the proceeds of these deposits were swapped into the local currency or into some other currency, to take advantage of discrepancies between interest differentials and forward rates, or simply to provide the banks concerned with additional liquid funds. All transactions in such deposits were carried out by the Foreign Exchange departments, and Foreign Exchange brokers acted as intermediaries.[14] They constituted, therefore, an integral part of the Foreign Exchange market even when no Foreign Exchange was bought or sold.

The appearance of a large volume of particularly liquid funds provided increased opportunities for both arbitrage and speculation and was considered to have been one of the causes of the recurrent runs on the dollar in 1959–60. The other side of the picture was represented by the increased ease with which discrepancies between interest rates in various centres were reduced by the new system under which in leading centres it was almost as easy to lend or to borrow in terms of a leading foreign currency as in terms of the local currency.[15] The Foreign Exchange system thus became truly international in character.

NOTES TO CHAPTER NINETEEN

1. Hartley Withers, *War and Lombard Street* (London, 1915), pp. 57–9.
2. Withers, *op. cit.* p. 98.
3. Gustav Cassel, *Money and Foreign Exchanges after 1914* (London, 1922), pp. 41–2.
4. T. E. Gregory, *Foreign Exchange before, during and after the War* (London, 1922), p. 21.
5. Hugh F. R. Miller, *The Foreign Exchange Market* (London, 1925), p. 63.
6. Paul Einzig, *A Dynamic Theory of Foreign Exchange* (London, 1961), pp. 111–112.
7. Paul Einzig, 'The Forward Price of Gold', *Economic Journal*, December 1938. 'The Forward Market in Gold', *Banker*, February 1959.
8. Einzig, *Dynamic Theory*, pp. 12–13.
9. Miller, *op. cit.* p. 61.
10. Einzig, *Dynamic Theory*, pp. 31–2.
11. Einzig, *op. cit.* pp. 234–6.
12. Einzig, *op. cit.* pp. 49–50, 166–9.
13. Einzig, *op. cit.* pp. x–xi, 42–4, 58–62.
14. Einzig, *op. cit.* pp. 116–18, 329–30.
15. Paul Einzig, 'Statics and Dynamics of the Euro-Dollar Market', *Economic Journal*, 1961, pp. 592–5.

CHAPTER TWENTY

Exchange Rates after 1914

(1) UNPRECEDENTED FLUCTUATIONS

THE first World War brought to an end a century of relative stability in Foreign Exchanges. It opened an era of unprecedented exchange movements – unprecedented not only in respect of their range but also in respect of the number of important currencies that were fluctuating widely more or less simultaneously. On earlier occasions wide exchange movements, such as the extreme depreciation of the American exchange during the War of Independence or of the French exchange during the Revolution, were isolated phenomena. The simultaneous depreciations of several European currencies during the Napoleonic Wars and that of several Latin-American currencies during various periods of the 19th century were relatively moderate compared with the much more spectacular depreciations of Central and Eastern European exchanges after the first World War.

What is important is that, during the ten years or so from 1914, all exchanges – including those of neutral countries – were simultaneously subject to abnormally wide fluctuations. The currency chaos that followed the first World War was in marked contrast with the relatively smooth transition to stability after the Napoleonic Wars.

(2) PARADOXICAL EXCHANGE MOVEMENTS IN 1914

In anticipation of the outbreak of the first World War the German *mark* was slightly weak in July 1914, while the French *franc* was very firm, presumably owing to repatriations of French balances from London and from other centres. The *franc* actually appreciated above gold import point,[1] and it remained firm for a time also after the outbreak of the war. All other currencies moved strongly in favour of sterling, mainly owing to the increase of the Bank rate to 10 per cent in August 1914, causing a strong demand for sterling all over the world. In New York sterling touched $7 at one time.[2]

Strange as this may sound in the light of experience in both World Wars, sterling remained at a premium against the dollar until the end of 1914, in spite of the adverse effects of the war on the British balance of payments. This was largely because the war was generally expected to be over in a few months. Some other European exchanges, too, remained for a time at a premium against the dollar. The *mark* rose to 96 (parity 95·20). The *franc* remained at a premium until January 1915. On the other hand, distrust in the *rouble* and the *lira* revived on the outbreak of the war, and both exchanges went immediately to a substantial discount. The *rouble* slumped 27 per cent in August 1914, even though it recovered half of its loss in September. The *lira* was quoted at a discount of 5 per cent against the French *franc*.

Even when the inevitable depreciation occurred during 1915 it was relatively mild. This may be explained partly on the ground of the lack of any recent experience with economic effects of major wars, and partly because people were obsessed with the idea that the exchanges would return to their parities sooner or later.

(3) ALLIED EXCHANGES DEPRECIATE FROM 1915

From the beginning of 1915 sterling gradually depreciated until its rate in New York declined to $4·51 in September. Thereupon the authorities intervened and, following on a recovery, it was officially pegged in January 1916 around 4·76½ for the rest of the war. The French *franc* depreciated in terms of sterling and the dollar during 1915. While in January the dollar was quoted at 5·16½ (parity 5·18), by August it was at 6·04. Anglo-American financial support brought about a recovery of the *franc* and eventually it was stabilised at about *frs* 5·85 from October 1916. The peg was subsequently raised in stages, reaching *frs* 5·50 in August 1918. The official rates in France applied to approved buyers only, and free market rates were distinctly less favourable to the *franc*, even though they were supported by the Bank of France.[13]

The *lira* tended to be weak even during Italy's neutrality. It became very weak during 1916 and the early part of 1917 largely as a result of military reverses. Following on the entry of the United States into the war it received increased support, but, together with other Allied exchanges, it weakened during the military successes of the Central European Powers in the summer of 1918, reaching nearly 9 to the dollar in July.

(4) FALL OF THE *MARK*, *KRONE* AND *ROUBLE*

The German exchange in New York declined to a discount of some 3 per cent by the end of 1914. It continued to depreciate in 1915, although military victories and exchange control brought about a temporary recovery. In Switzerland the *mark* was quoted at 84·60 at the end of 1916, compared with the par of 123·46. During 1917 it touched at one time 75 but it recovered owing to the improvement of the military outlook resulting from the Russian revolution.[4] It resumed its decline in 1918, but the decisive defeats of Germany and her allies in the late summer and early autumn caused a remarkable recovery, in anticipation of an early termination of the war, on the widespread assumption that after the end of the war the *mark* would be restored to its old parity.[5] By the end of the year it relapsed, however, to 60.

The Austro-Hungarian *krone* fluctuated largely in sympathy with the *mark* most of the time during the war, but it depreciated to a larger extent than the latter currency, because the Austro-Hungarian authorities were persuaded to cede much of their gold reserve to Germany, so that they were not in such a strong position to support the *krone* in neutral markets.

The *rouble* fluctuated between 50 and 60 per cent of its par value before the revolution and underwent a further depreciation at the beginning of 1917, but held its own remarkably well in the circumstances during the spring of that year. In the summer it slumped heavily, sterling rising in St. Petersburg from 16·2 in April to 32·2 in September. At the time of the Communist victory it was 37·7.[6] The main cause of the weakness was flight of capital in anticipation of the advent of the Communist régime. By the end of 1918 sterling was worth approximately 150 *roubles*.

(5) FIRMNESS OF 'NEUTRAL' EXCHANGES

After their initial depreciation in relation to sterling and the *franc* during the early months of the war, all neutral exchanges appreciated considerably. The *guilder*, the *peseta*, the Swiss *franc*, the Scandinavian currencies and various Latin-American exchanges all appreciated and went to a substantial premium even in relation to the dollar. Shortly before the end of the war the dollar was at a discount of about 30 per cent in Amsterdam and in Zürich. The Swedish *krona* appreciated in 1916 to such an extent that, in order to prevent an unwanted influx of gold, the Riksbank was authorised to suspend its gold purchases, with the result that the *krona* rose to a premium against gold.[7] In 1917 the dollar depreciated to 2·55 *kronor* against the parity of 3·73. Sweden's example was followed by Norway and Denmark, while Spain lowered her official buying price of gold, thereby accentuating the appreciation of the *peseta* against the dollar.

Among Latin-American currencies the Chilean *peso*, after its fall from 9½d. to 7½d. in 1914, rose gradually to above 17d. by 1918.[8] The Argentine *peso*, too, rose to a premium in relation to both sterling and the dollar. The latter, though very firm in relation to the currencies of the European belligerent countries, went to a substantial discount in relation to some Latin-American exchanges as well as to the *yen* and to the European 'neutral' exchanges.

The firmness of neutral exchanges was largely due to the favourable balance of payments of the neutral countries. Inflationary financing of war expenditure, the outflow of capital from belligerent countries as a result of the inadequacy of exchange restrictions contributed towards the appreciation of neutral currencies, and more than outweighed the effects of the inflationary conditions that prevailed also in neutral countries as a result of war-time boom and shortage of goods, and the increase of Central Bank reserves.

(6) EXCHANGE DEPRECIATIONS AFTER THE WAR

With the obvious approach of the end of the war in 1918, the assumption that all would be well once the war was over resulted in a temporary improvement of all European exchanges, with the exception of the *rouble* which was by then past any hope of improvement. A reaction soon set in, however, The Allied exchanges continued to be bolstered up a little longer, but they were 'unpegged' in March 1919. There followed a period of sharp depreciation of sterling, the French and Belgian *francs*, the *lira* and other European currencies. The sharp rise in world commodity prices changed the terms of trade heavily against the European importing countries just at a time when they had to replenish their raw material and food supplies depleted during the war. Finally, there was political upheaval in the defeated countries and their administrative organisation weakened to such an extent that it would in itself have warranted a heavy depreciation of their exchanges. The disintegration of the Russian and Austro-Hungarian Empires into a number of Succession States resulted in the creating of a number of new currencies, most of which started their existence with a depreciating trend.

Inexorable pressure of domestic inflation in defeated Germany, and large-scale flight of capital resulting from the growing realisation that the burden of reparations alone was sufficient to doom the *mark*, gradually produced their inevitable effect, though not without some sharp and at times prolonged spells of recovery. The Austrian and Hungarian exchanges, too, depreciated, though to a less extreme extent. Further East, the Russian *rouble* became demonetised through its extreme depreciation resulting from the revolution, the prolonged civil war and the total disorganisation of production through wholesale nationalisation. The Polish *mark* was also among the weakest currencies. The currencies of the Balkan States were more resistant, and the Czechoslovak *koruna* actually experienced a sharp recovery as a result of a drastic deflationary drive.

(7) RECOVERY OF STERLING, WEAKNESS OF THE *FRANC*

After their depreciation in 1919–20, sterling and other Western European currencies recovered considerably, largely as a result of more favourable terms of trade brought about by the slump of world commodity prices in 1920–21. Thereafter sterling was favourably influenced by hopes of an early return to the gold standard at its pre-war parity, hopes which materialised in 1925.

The value of the French *franc* was adversely affected by the heavy cost of the reconstruction of the North Eastern regions devastated during the war, by the military expenses of the Ruhr occupation and the maintenance of a large army, and by domestic political instability. From time to time there were large-scale speculative attacks on the *franc*. On two occasions, in 1924 and again in 1926, the *franc* recovered sharply after sterling touched 120 and 240 respectively. After the second recovery stability was at last achieved at about 124, around one-fifth of pre-war parity.

During this period of fluctuating exchanges there appeared to be a psychological link between all Western European currencies in relation to the dollar and in some measure they tended to rise and fall in sympathy. A similar phenomenon was noticeable to some extent in respect of the relationship between sterling and the continental currencies. There was also a psychological link between the three Latin currencies – the French *franc*, the Belgian *franc* and the *lira*.[9] As a result the latter two depreciated at times, not through any inherent weakness of their own, but because of the weakness of the French *franc*.

The *lira* failed to benefit immediately from the political stability achieved after the confused conditions prevailing during the early post-war years. Having depreciated at one time to 150 to the pound, Mussolini's deflationary measures brought about its recovery to about 92 in 1927.

(8) LATIN-AMERICAN AND EASTERN EXCHANGES

Most Latin-American exchanges continued their war-time firmness during the early post-war period, owing to the boom in raw materials. The Argentine *peso* was on repeated occasions in 1919–1920 at a premium in relation to all currencies.[10] Following on the commodity slump of 1920 the exchanges of raw material producing countries depreciated to varying degrees, and for years they fluctuated widely. In 1925 the Argentine *peso* reached par once more, but not until 1927 was its convertibility resumed. Salvador, Venezuela and Colombia succeeded in stabilising their exchanges at their pre-war parities.

Eastern exchanges on a silver standard came under the influence of the sharp rise in silver during and immediately after the war – the fixed value of the *rupee* had to be raised in 1920 from 16d. to 20d. – and of its subsequent sharp fall in later years. The Japanese exchange went to a premium against the dollar in 1917 as a result of the favourable trade balance. At the time of the Armistice it was quoted at 54·6 cents in New York (parity 49·85 cents), but by April 1920 it was at a substantial discount at 46·25 cents. Thereafter the *yen* recovered and remained for some time around par with the dollar.

(9) INTER-WAR STABILISATIONS

From 1923 onward successful efforts were made to stabilise a number of European exchanges. The *mark* was stabilised at one-billionth of its pre-war parity, the dollar rate being fixed at 4,200,000,000,000 *reichsmarks* compared with 4·20 *marks* in 1914. This was followed by the stabilisation of the Austrian currency at a fraction of the pre-war parity of the Austro-Hungarian *krone*. The new unit, the *schilling*, was equated to 10,000 *kronen*. The new Hungarian unit, the *pengö*, was equated to 12,500 *kronen*. The Polish *mark* depreciated to such an extent that the new unit, the *zloty*, had to be equated to 1,800,000 *marks*. While the *reichsmark*, the Austrian *schilling* and the *pengö* remained stable, the *zloty* went to a discount almost immediately after its creation and had to be devalued once more in 1927 to the extent of one new *zloty* to 1·7 old *zlotys*.

After the ups and downs during the war and the immediate post-war period, Sweden stabilised the *krona* at its pre-war parity in 1924. The restoration of sterling to its old parity in 1925 was accompanied or followed by similar action by the British Dominions, Egypt, the Netherlands and the Dutch East Indies, Later the example was followed by Denmark and Norway. Japan, too, returned to pre-war parity in 1927, in spite of the setback suffered through the great earthquake.

After an unsuccessful effort to stabilise the Belgian *franc* at 107 to the pound in 1926, it was successfully stabilised at 175. The currencies of the Balkan States were devalued more extensively and were stabilised during the late 'twenties. Following on the *de facto* stabilisation of the *franc* in 1926, Italy, too, succeeded in stabilising the *lira* after a deflationary effort, in 1927.

There was a period of almost complete stability between 1927 and 1931. But owing to the overvaluation of sterling and the undervaluation of the *franc*, the equilibrium was an uneasy one, and the maintenance of sterling at its pre-war parity in face of frequently recurrent pressure was only possible at the cost of aggravating the domestic depression. From 1930 the currencies of some agricultural countries came under pressure. The Australian and the New Zealand pounds were devalued by 25 per cent in relation to sterling, and the Brazilian and some other Latin-American exchanges were allowed to depreciate.

(10) EFFECT OF WALL STREET BOOM AND SLUMP

The Wall Street boom brought new pressure on sterling and other currencies, owing to the flow of speculative funds to the United States. The ensuing Wall Street slump in 1929 and the series of economic and financial crises that followed it brought the period of exchange stability to an end. There were heavy withdrawals of American and other credits from Germany and other Central European countries. Notwithstanding this and the resulting bank insolvencies, the *reichsmark* and other Central European exchanges were maintained at their new parities, by means of imposing a moratorium on external payments, which was followed by enforced 'standstill agreements' with foreign creditors and by permanent exchange restrictions. These currencies remained stable simply because external payments were only made to the extent to which this was possible without causing their depreciation. This system was named by Sir Henry Strakosch the 'gold insolvency standard'.

(11) THE STERLING CRISIS OF 1931

Since no exchange restrictions were adopted in Britain, sterling had to face the full pressure of wholesale withdrawals of foreign funds, aggravated by speculative operations, during the summer of 1931. Notwithstanding large American and French credits granted to the Bank of England, it became inevitable to suspend the gold standard in September 1931. This was followed by similar decisions in a large number of countries. We saw above that Australia and New Zealand had already devalued their currencies before Britain went off the gold standard. All the other Commonwealth exchanges, with the exception of the Canadian dollar and the South African pound, followed sterling immediately. After a few days the Scandinavian exchanges and the Finnish *mark* followed. The Portuguese *escudo*, too, depreciated more or less in sympathy with sterling. In December 1931 Japan suspended the gold standard and the *yen* depreciated even in relation to sterling in 1932 to 1s. 2d. against its parity of 2s. ½d. In due course the South African pound, too, was allowed to depreciate. The Canadian dollar hovered somewhere half-way between sterling and the U.S. dollar.

Sterling fluctuated between $3 and $4 during the period between September 1931 and the suspension of the gold standard by the United States in 1933. It became distinctly undervalued and this resulted in a very strong adverse pressure on the dollar, which was in any case unfavourably affected by the withdrawals of foreign funds invested in Wall Street and by the unprecedented series of bank failures.

(12) THE DOLLAR CRISIS OF 1933

In October 1931 heavy speculative pressure developed on the dollar for the first time since 1914, and the scares recurred repeatedly during the next eighteen months. On each occasion heavy withdrawals of foreign funds from the United States and flight of American capital weakened the gold reserve and aggravated the American banking crisis. Roosevelt's election as President in November 1932 and the virtual 'interregnum' of four months that followed under the American constitutional system created a feeling of uncertainty about the future of the dollar and greatly aggravated its situation. In April 1933 Roosevelt felt impelled to suspend the gold standard and to allow the dollar to depreciate. There followed a period of currency depreciation race. The sterling-dollar rate rose to 5·26 in November 1933 and even after its relapse it remained above its old parity of 4·86 throughout 1934.

The rate fluctuated around $5 during the following years. From time to time minor dollar scares forced it up to above $5, in anticipation of a further devaluation to the maximum limit authorised by Congress. On the other hand, in the spring and early summer of 1937 there was a dollar revaluation scare. From 1938 the flight of European capital in anticipation of a war, together with the effects of rearmament on the balance of payments of European countries, resulted in a firm trend in dollars which continued until well into the post-war period.

(13) DEVALUATION OF DOLLAR AND FRANC

After the stabilisation of the dollar at 41 per cent under its old parity in January 1934, the pressure became diverted to the currencies of the 'gold bloc', consisting of France, the Low Countries and Switzerland, with Poland and Danzig as outside members of the group. Owing to the widespread anticipation that they would have to devalue eventually their exchanges were subject to frequently recurrent attacks during the next two years. The *lira*, too, was under pressure, owing to its gross overvaluation, and the Abyssinian War provided Mussolini with an excuse for allowing it to depreciate gradually. It was not until October 1936, after the devaluation of the *franc*, that the *lira* was devalued formally to the extent of 41 per cent. Belgium abandoned resistance in 1935 and devalued her *franc* by 28 per cent. The rest of the 'gold bloc' continued to hold out stubbornly in face of heavy odds. Although the spot rates of the French and Swiss *francs* and the *guilder* remained within gold points, the discount on their forward rates widened considerably from time to time.

In September 1936 these currencies, too, were devalued. The French *franc* and the Swiss *franc* were cut by 30 per cent and the *guilder* by 20 per cent. While the Swiss *franc* and the *guilder* remained reasonably steady at their reduced values, the French *franc* failed to command confidence even after its devaluation. For some time it remained around 105 to the pound, but during 1937 it depreciated gradually to its new legal limit of about 110. The limit itself was raised and for some time the *franc* was left to find its own level. In May 1938 it was devalued to 179 and five months later Reynaud stabilised it at 176 around which level it remained stable, thanks to Reynaud's measures to restore confidence and to the gratifying reaction of the French public to the growing war threat.[11]

(14) LATIN-AMERICAN DIFFICULTIES

On the other hand, the Spanish Civil War played havoc with the *peseta*, which had to be allowed to depreciate considerably. The Latin-American currencies, too, suffered heavily through the slump in commodities and the curtailment of British and American loans and credits, and depreciated considerably. The Argentine Conversion Office was closed down already at the end of 1929 and during the following years the *peso* fell from 96 U.S. cents in 1928 to 58 cents in 1932. It depreciated further in 1933, but from 1934 it became relatively steady, and during the last pre-war years it was maintained stable in relation to sterling. In the late 'thirties Latin-American exchanges in general became firmer as a result of the partial recovery of commodity prices.

The Japanese exchange was more or less stabilised around 17 *yen* to the pound from 1933. At that level it was at first considerably undervalued. But the rise in prices and later the war in China resulted in growing pressure on the *yen*. Nevertheless it remained stable at 1s. 2d.

Throughout the 'thirties the nominal stability of the *reichsmark* and other currencies subject to exchange restrictions did not prevent the development of fluctuating markets abroad in various sub-species of these currencies, created under the system of multiple exchange rates, to be dealt with in Chapter 22. Their value depended largely on the respective purposes for which they were allowed to be used. A number of Latin-American countries, too, adopted similar systems of fluctuating multiple exchanges.

(15) STERLING IN THE SECOND WORLD WAR

The outbreak of the second World War in September 1939 was followed by an immediate 'devaluation' of sterling from about $4·68 to $4·04, and a little later to $4·03 – the buying rate being $4·02 and the selling rate $4·04 – a depreciation of some 14 per cent. It was maintained there rigidly stable throughout the war. In New York and other free markets sterling depreciated below its official rate and fluctuated according to the prospects of an Allied victory. For instance, a fortnight after the outbreak of the war, sterling depreciated in New York to $3·75 as a result of the intervention of Soviet Russia in the German-Polish war on the side of Germany. Later there was a recovery, but the discount against the official rate remained fluctuating according to the military outlook.

The French *franc* remained linked to sterling during the first phase of the war in the vicinity of its pre-war rate, at 176, which meant of course a depreciation in terms of dollars. It was relatively steady in neutral markets, because there was not much foreign money in Paris while there was a great deal of French money abroad and part of it was repatriated, just as in the early months of the First World War. Most of the non-British members of the Sterling Area – Sweden and Norway amongst them, and later Denmark, Japan, Portugal and the Argentine – detached their currencies from sterling, not so much because of its devaluation as

owing to its fluctuation in neutral markets. The Egyptian, Iraqi
and Israeli currencies were the only non-British currencies that
remained stable in relation to sterling.

(16) 'NEUTRAL' EXCHANGES

With the German occupation or domination of most continental
Europe outside Russia in 1940, dealings in most European
currencies came to an end in New York. The free Foreign
Exchange market came virtually to a standstill with the entry of
the United States and Japan into the war, though there were some
dealings in New York and in some Latin-American markets. The
German occupation authorities forced unfavourable exchange
rates on the countries dominated by them, as a means of securing
favourable terms of trade for Germany. This example was followed
by the Allies in North Africa and Italy where the *lira* was fixed
at 100 to the dollar in 1943.

Neutral exchanges were firm, but not so firm as in the first
World War. In July 1945 the Swiss *franc* and the Brazilian *cruzeiro*
were at a premium of 3 per cent against the dollar, and the
Argentine *peso* at a premium of 7 per cent. On the other hand, the
Spanish *peseta* closed the war at a 17 per cent depreciation against
the dollar and a small depreciation even against the pre-war rate
of sterling. The Portuguese *escudo* depreciated 6 per cent in terms
of dollars, the Turkish pound 4 per cent, and even the Swedish
krona remained at a discount of 1 per cent, at 4·20, to which level
it was devalued from 4·15 in 1939.[12]

(17) POST-WAR EXCHANGES UNDER THE
BRETTON WOODS SYSTEM

After the end of the war the principal exchanges came to be maintained within their official 'support points' fixed under the Bretton
Woods system in agreement with the International Monetary
Fund. Conditions became on the whole stable once more, though
the frequently recurrent sterling scares and other currency scares
resulted in wide fluctuations in forward rates. Throughout the
post-war period the *franc* underwent a series of devaluations. From
480 *francs* to the pound, to which level it was reduced in 1945, the
official parity was changed to 864 in January 1948 and to 1,062
in October of the same year. After the devaluation of sterling in

1949 the *franc* was linked to the dollar at 350. Again in 1957 it was devalued to 420 and finally in 1958 to 493·70. Thereafter it became stable thanks to General de Gaulle's measures. During much of the 'fifties the *franc* fluctuated in relation to the dollar and other hard currencies, while remaining artificially stable in relation to soft currencies. This anomalous arrangement resulted in discrepancies between cross rates.

The post-war vicissitudes of the *lira* were somewhat similar to those of the *franc*. During the early post-war period it depreciated even more than the *franc*. From time to time an official dollar rate was fixed – 225 in 1946, 575 in 1948 – only to be abandoned or raised when necessary. There were, in addition, various unofficial rates, always at a considerable discount. In Italy as in France there were for some time anomalous discrepancies between various cross rates. Both *franc* and *lira* regained their stability and came to command confidence by the late 'fifties.

The Belgian *franc* made a good start after the second World War as a result of stern deflationary measures adopted soon after liberation. It remained strong during most of the post-war period, thanks to the independence of the National Bank from the Government. The *guilder*, too, was firm most of the time, in spite of the heavy losses suffered by the Netherlands through the loss of her Indonesian colonies. Sweden carried out a revaluation in 1946, changing the dollar parity of the *krona* from 4·2 to 3·6 *krona* per dollar. In 1949, following on the devaluation of sterling it was devalued, however, to 5·2 *kroner*. Denmark and Norway, too, followed the British example in 1949.

(18) DEVALUATION OF STERLING

Throughout the post-war period attacks on sterling constituted a regularly recurrent feature. In 1949 it was devalued from $4·02 to $2·80. The result was an undervaluation of sterling which did not prevent, however, another exchange crisis in 1951. After the reopening of the Foreign Exchange market at the end of that year, sterling was weak for some months, but it gradually became firmer. It was subject to sweeping attacks on the occasion of the Suez crisis in 1956, and again in 1957. On each occasion the forward rate depreciated considerably but the spot rate was maintained within its support points.[13]

Some of the Central and Eastern European currencies underwent extreme depreciation comparable to that experienced after the first World War. In particular the Hungarian and Greek exchanges became virtually demonetised through extreme inflation. The depreciation of the *pengö* far exceeded even that of the *mark* in 1923 and quotations of Foreign Exchanges rose to truly astronomical figures.[14] The *drachma* depreciated considerably during the German occupation of Greece, and after the liberation in 1944 it was devalued to one new *drachma* for 50 billion old *drachmae*.[15] The depreciation continued and the *drachma* was repeatedly devalued during the early post-war years.

(19) FIRMNESS OF THE GERMAN CURRENCY

Thanks largely to the policy pursued by the Western occupation authorities, and the isolation of the currency of Western Germany from that of Eastern Germany, the runaway inflation of 1919–23 was not repeated. The military *mark* notes issued by the Allied occupation authorities were fixed at 40 for £1 and 10 for $1. After the establishment of the *D. mark* there was for a long time a separate quotation for foreign-owned blocked *Sperrmarks* which gradually rose to the vicinity of par with the official *D. marks*. Par was reached in 1954. The new *D. mark* was fixed in 1949 at the original pre-war parity of 4·20 to the dollar.

The German 'miracle' of economic recovery during the late 'forties and early 'fifties was achieved with the aid of a stable currency. The *D. mark* gradually came to command confidence and by the late 'fifties it came to be looked upon as the hardest of all currencies. From time to time revaluation rumours resulted in a heavy flow of funds to West Germany notwithstanding measures taken by the authorities to discourage it. As will be seen in Chapter 24, the *D. mark* had to be revalued twice during the 'sixties.

(20) THE U.S. AND CANADIAN DOLLARS

For something like twelve years after the end of the war the dollar commanded implicit confidence. During 1959, however, a series of dollar scares were experienced, leading to a temporary weakening of forward dollars.[16] The spot rate was firmly maintained and confidence was restored, though a vague feeling of uncertainty remained in the background.

The Canadian dollar was very firm during the early post-war period, and the International Monetary Fund authorised the Government to revalue it by 10 per cent in 1946. From October 1950 the dollar was allowed to float. For a long time it was at a premium against the U.S. dollar but this did not obviate the necessity for a high Bank rate.

The Swiss *franc* was at a premium against the dollar during the early post-war period and remained strong throughout, assisted by the relatively moderate extent of inflation in the country and by the persistent influx of foreign funds. From time to time the Swiss authorities had to adopt measures to discourage the unwanted demand for *francs*.

(21) INFLATION IN LATIN-AMERICA

Most Latin-American exchanges failed to derive any lasting benefit from their war-time favourable balances of payments during the two World Wars, and their Governments and peoples failed to heed the lessons of the 'twenties. Once more domestic political troubles and excessive Government expenditure were responsible for peace-time inflation and a series of devaluations or depreciations. This time the situation was further complicated by the continued maintenance of highly involved multiple currency systems with widely fluctuating rates which, together with various trade and exchange restrictions and bilateral trading, did not save most Latin-American currencies from coming under irresistible pressure from time to time. Thus the Brazilian *cruzeiro*, which was very firm at the end of the war, underwent a persistent depreciation during the 'fifties. The Mexican dollar was devalued in 1954 in connection with an attempt to unify the multiple currency system.

(22) INFLATION IN THE FAR EAST

Japan's early post-war monetary history, too, was characterised by a heavy depreciation of the *yen*. It began with the introduction of military *yen* notes by the American occupation authorities at an exchange rate of 15 *yen* per dollar compared with the pre-war rate of 4·34 *yen*. The *yen* remained very weak during the early post-war years, but in the 'fifties it became stable and came to command confidence.

During the war the Chungking dollar depreciated considerably and by 1945 it was only worth a negligible fraction of its original value. It continued to depreciate during the struggle with the Communists.

The currencies of the Communist countries, too, had their share of post-war depreciations. The *rouble* was repeatedly devalued, and so were the exchanges of the Satellite States.

Generally speaking, the Foreign Exchange situation was less chaotic after the second World War than after the first World War. None of the major currencies suffered extreme depreciation, and fluctuations were kept under control most of the time. The absence of a currency chaos comparable with those of the early 'twenties and the early 'thirties was due in part to the steadying influence of exchange control and in part to the application of the Bretton Woods system. About these more will be said in Chapter 22.

NOTES TO CHAPTER TWENTY

1. Hartley Withers, *War and Lombard Street* (London, 1915), p. 46.
2. Withers, *op. cit.* p. 57.
3. Lucien Petit, *Histoire des finances extérieures de la France pendant la guerre 1914–1919* (Paris, 1929), p. 67.
4. Karl Helfferich, *Money* (transl. L. Infield) (London, 1928), vol. i, p. 271.
5. Gustav Cassel, *Money and Foreign Exchanges after 1914* (London, 1922), p. 45.
6. S. S. Katznellenbaum, *Russian Currency and Banking, 1914–1924* (London, 1921), pp. 78–9.
7. Cassel, *op. cit.* pp. 79 *et seq.*
8. G. Subercaseaux, *Monetary and Banking Policy of Chile* (Oxford, 1922), pp. 157–64.
9. Paul Einzig, *A Dynamic Theory of Forward Exchange* (London, 1961), pp. 361, 375.
10. H. E. Peters, *The Foreign Debt of the Argentine Republic* (Baltimore, 1934), p. 55.
11. René Sédillot, *Du franc Bonaparte au franc de Gaulle* (Paris, 1959), p. 89.
12. Bank for International Settlements, *Annual Report, 1944–5* (Basle, 1945), p. 89.
13. Paul Einzig, *op. ci'.* pp. 307 *et seq.*
14. Bertrand Nogaro, *A Short Treatise on Money and Monetary Systems* (London, 1949), pp. 118 *et seq.*
15. Bank for International Settlements, *op. cit.* p. 88.
16. Einzig, *op. cit.* pp. 327–30.

CHAPTER TWENTY-ONE

Modern Foreign Exchange Theory

(1) PROGRESS FROM 1916

THE origin of modern Foreign Exchange theory, as we know it today, dates from the latter part of the first World War. Before 1914 no attempt was made to analyse the influences behind the balance of payments theory, while the purchasing power parity theory faded virtually into oblivion during a century of relative stability. Although it would be incorrect to say that Foreign Exchange theory stagnated between the publication of Goschen's *Theory of the Foreign Exchanges* in 1861 and the revival of the purchasing power parity theory by Cassel in 1916, its progress was certainly very slow in comparison with its truly spectacular development during the ten years or so after 1916. While in the decades before the first World War most leading economists paid relatively little attention to Foreign Exchange theory, in the second half of that war, and even more in the early post-war period, most prominent monetary economists and even some general economists took a very active interest in it.

(2) RECENT ACHIEVEMENTS

The following is a summary of the main achievement of Foreign Exchange theory after 1914:

1. The purchasing power parity theory was revived and was developed very thoroughly.
2. The theory that prices are determined by exchange rates was further developed.
3. A synthesis between the two theories was produced in the form of the equilibrium theory.
4. The balance of payments theory was further developed.
5. Attempts were made to reconcile the purchasing power parity theory with the balance of payments theory.
6. The psychological theory was further developed.
7. Elasticities in the Foreign Exchange market and in the factors

determining the supply and demand of exchanges received attention.

8. Differentiation between static and dynamic theory made some slight progress.
9. Relationship between business cycles and exchange rates was analysed.
10. A Forward Exchange theory was created and developed.

(3) PROFESSOR CASSEL'S RÔLE

It has often been pointed out that, in putting forward the doctrine that between two countries with inflated inconvertible paper currencies the exchange rate is determined by their relative degree of inflation, Cassel was merely following in Ricardo's footsteps. To be quite correct, it must be added that Ricardo himself was forestalled by Thornton, Wheatley and others writing before he intervened in the bullionist controversy, and that these pioneers were themselves forestalled by the Salamanca School in the 16th century.

What matters is that neither Ricardo nor any of the earlier economists had succeeded in developing the purchasing power parity theory sufficiently, or in making a strong enough impression with their exposition of that theory, to ensure its adoption by textbook-writers before the first World War. Cassel succeeded in doing so to a remarkable degree, partly by his more penetrating analysis based on more plentiful factual material, but largely through the flagrantly one-sided and aggressively dogmatic character of his exposition of the theory. Exaggeration and over-simplification are sometimes useful for hammering in a substantially valid point which would receive scant attention if presented in a scholarly spirit of philosophical detachment. Cassel provoked a controversy which produced some highly valuable contributions for and against his theory. A masterly summing up of the arguments is found in Howard Ellis's book on *German Monetary Theory*.[1]

In articles in the *Economic Journal*[2] in 1916 and in his book published in the same year,[3] Cassel delivered an attack on the balance of payments theory which was looked upon during the early war years as axiomatic by those trying to explain the abnormal war-time exchange movements. From 1916 onwards he was very active in propagating his theory in various articles and books, culminating in the publication of his standard work on the subject in 1922.[4]

(4) THE PURCHASING POWER PARITY THEORY

The purchasing power parity theory, as formulated by Cassel, may best be summed up by quoting the following passage from *Money and Foreign Exchanges after 1914*:

'Our willingness to pay a certain price for foreign money must ultimately and essentially be due to the fact that this money possesses purchasing power as against commodities and services in that foreign country. . . . Our valuation of a foreign currency in terms of our own, therefore, mainly depends on the relative purchasing power of the two currencies in their respective countries. . . . When the two currencies have undergone inflation, the normal rate of exchange will be equal to the old rate multiplied by the quotient of the degree of inflation in the one country and in the other. . . . The rate that has been calculated by the above method must be regarded as the new parity between the currencies, the point of balance towards which, in spite of all temporary fluctuations, the exchange rates will always tend. This parity I call purchasing power parity.'[5]

(5) SUPPORT FOR CASSEL'S THEORY

Initial support to Cassel's theory came mainly from Germany and Central Europe. Ellis quoted a pamphlet, published in Vienna by Schlesinger almost simultaneously with Cassel's articles, which argued that the true parity was the ratio between domestic and foreign prices.[6] He also quoted Lansburgh, a monetary economist with practical experience in banking, who sharply criticised the Reichsbank for denying that the depreciation of the *mark* exchange was due to inflation, and for trying to explain it entirely on the basis of the balance of payments theory.[7] Hahn drew distinction between the 'static' rate of exchange represented by mint parities or purchasing power parities, and the 'dynamic' rate which deviates from either parity; thereby he revived under another name the familiar differentiation applied in past centuries.[8]

In the United States the purchasing power parity theory found an early supporter in Noyes, who, writing in 1916, remarked:

'It is impossible to escape the conclusion that the depreciation in the German rate measured largely, and in fact primarily, the depreciation of the German currency.'[9] After the war Cassel's theory received strong support in Britain, in particular from Keynes, Gregory and Pigou. Keynes later claimed that he never endorsed the purchasing power parity theory entirely without reservations and, in subsequent years, came to lay increasing stress on the reservations. Pigou and Gregory, on the other hand, wholeheartedly endorsed the theory in its original form.

(6) SOME CONTROVERSIAL POINTS

There was an interesting controversy during the 'twenties between the various schools of thought into which the two main camps came to be split in the course of the controversy. Differences of opinion amongst those who accepted Cassel's basic principle were mainly on the following questions:

1. Is the fact that exchange movements are broadly parallel with changes in purchasing power parities due entirely to the unilateral effect of prices on exchanges, or is there some degree of reciprocity?
2. Do prices affect exchanges directly or through their influence on the balance of payments?
3. Are exchanges determined by the ratio between the average of all prices or only of prices of goods which are subject to foreign trade transactions?
4. Does the theory explain day-to-day fluctuations or basic trends?

(7) RELATIONSHIP BETWEEN PRICES AND EXCHANGES

The tables and charts published by Keynes in his *Tract on Monetary Reform* show a remarkable degree of sympathy between movements of exchanges and their purchasing power parities based on wholesale indexes. This led Keynes to the conclusion that 'purchasing power parity theory, even in its crude form, has worked passably well'.[10] The figures and charts gave, however, no indication whatsoever about the nature of the causal relationship between the two curves. They simply supported the so-called 'equilibrium theory' under which there could be no lasting major discrepancies between price levels of various countries if trade between them was reasonably free and if exchanges were allowed to fluctuate freely.

In its original form Cassel's theory assumed unilateral effect of prices on exchanges without any reciprocity. During and immediately after the war Cassel expressed the view that even if exchanges deviated from their purchasing power parities sooner or later they were bound to return to them, implying that it was always exchange rates that adjusted themselves to price differentials. At the opposite extreme, a number of continental economists maintained, on the basis of the practical experience of their countries, that any substantial movement of exchange rates – whatever may be its cause – strongly influenced price levels and therefore it affected purchasing power parities. Both extreme views were put forward with vigorous dogmatism and it took some time before a synthesis, in the form of the equilibrium theory according to which prices and exchanges tend to adjust themselves to each other and affect each other reciprocally, emerged from the controversy. Even when it did it attracted but little attention, because it was not nearly as striking as the extreme theories.

(8) A MISLEADING ONE-SIDED THEORY

One of the compromise formulae that emerged from the controversy was that while, during relatively moderate stages of inflation, prices tended to influence exchanges rather than conversely, during advanced stages of inflation it was exchanges that largely determined prices.[11] This conclusion was based on practical experience in Austria, Germany and other countries where during the runaway inflation of the early post-war period manufacturers and merchants acquired the habit of adjusting their prices every day, and indeed several times a day, to the latest exchange rates.

Another compromise formula put forward by a number of writers was that amidst conditions of advanced inflation prices and exchanges moved together simply because they were both influenced in the same sense by the material and psychological effects of inflation. In other words, prices and exchanges did not affect one another but were both affected by the excessive note issue.

Even though Cassel did refer casually to the possibility of prices being affected by exchanges in given circumstances[12] his emphasis

K

was so overwhelmingly on the side of the unilateral effect of prices
on exchanges that his influence, and that of his school, on current
opinion was entirely in that sense. The policy implications of this
static theory, which disregarded the self-aggravating dynamism
of the effect of exchanges on prices, will be discussed in detail in
the next chapter, but it must be pointed out here that this one-
sided theory misled a great many individuals between 1919 and
1922 into buying *marks*. The domestic purchasing power of the
mark was obviously above its exchange value and it was, therefore,
assumed that sooner or later its exchange value would adjust itself to its purchasing power parities by appreciating. Even after
speculators ceased to believe that the *mark* would recover eventually to its pre-war parity, their new creed in purchasing power
parities kept up their demand for *mark* notes.

(9) DO PRICES AFFECT EXCHANGES DIRECTLY?

There was a fratricidal conflict amongst adherents of the purchasing power parity theory on the question whether purchasing
power parities affected exchange rates directly or through their
effect on the balance of payments. It was widely realised that if
prices rose as a result of inflation this should tend to encourage
imports and discourage exports. According to the extreme version
of the purchasing power parity theory, however, the effect on
exchanges was produced independently of the balance of payments. The exchange rate should depreciate to its new purchasing
power parities even though exports and imports remained perfectly
balanced, simply because those parities now constituted its new
equilibrium level.

Cassel's formula implied that prices affected exchanges directly.
His view that import and export restrictions were liable to affect
the working of his theory, appeared to suggest, however, that
purchasing power parities were only able to produce their effect
on exchanges if they were allowed to produce their effect on the
balance of payments.[13] For this departure from the more dogmatic
form of the doctrine he was taken severely to task by one of his
extremist disciples, Miss van Dorp, who, writing in the *Economic
Journal*, pointed out the contradiction that appeared to exist
between Cassel's various writings on the subject.[14] In face of this
challenge Cassel reaffirmed his faith in the direct effect of purchasing power parities on exchanges, while upholding his admission

about the possibility of their lasting deviations from those parities through trade restrictions.[15]

(10) HOW BALANCE OF PAYMENTS AFFECTS EXCHANGES

In his effort to discredit the balance of payments theory Cassel and his school went so far as to maintain that any surplus or deficit on the balance of payments could not affect the exchanges because it had to be paid somehow, even if it be through exporting securities or through raising credits. His conclusion was that the balance of payments must always balance by and large automatically and cannot therefore cause lasting changes in exchange rates.[16] This argument was accepted uncritically during the early 'twenties by a remarkably large number of economists who appeared to be oblivious that it amounted to a repudiation of the entire classical theory of market mechanism.

In reality, while it is true that in all good markets supply and demand are always bound to balance each other automatically, what matters is that they balance each other largely through the effect of an imbalance on market prices. Any discrepancy between supply and demand of Foreign Exchange resulting from a surplus of imports or of exports is always balanced on a free market automatically, precisely through an adjustment of the exchange rate to a figure at which the required counterpart is forthcoming, through speculative or arbitrage operations or capital transfers. It was, therefore, utterly fallacious to argue that, because the balance of payments was always bound to balance, it could not affect exchange rates.

(11) DEVIATIONS FROM PURCHASING POWER PARITIES

All supporters of the purchasing power parity theory did not share Cassel's view about the self-balancing character of the balance of payments and regarded an import surplus or an export surplus as the medium through which purchasing power parities worked, or alternatively as one of the influences making for lasting deviations of exchanges from purchasing power parities.

Other factors that were admitted to have affected exchanges in a disequilibriating sense included international non-commercial transfers such as debt payments, capital movements or reparations. Among others, Keynes realised that there could be lasting deviations through the influence of perennial pressure on the exchanges resulting from such non-commercial payments. This aspect of Foreign Exchange theory received a great deal of attention in connection with the endless discussion of Germany's capacity to transfer reparations payments. We propose to return to this aspect of the subject later in this chapter.

Another explanation of substantial discrepancies between exchanges and their purchasing power parities was put forward by Flux, according to whom it was due to the higher degree of flexibility of exchanges compared with that of the domestic price level.[17] According to Angell's explanation, during certain phases of the German inflation the *mark* exchange was undervalued because confidence in it was higher in Germany than in foreign countries.[18]

(12) THE TERMS OF TRADE

There was a great deal of disagreement within Cassel's school – as there was among Salamanca economists some centuries earlier – on the question whether purchasing power parity should be reckoned on the basis of the general average of the price level or on that of traded goods only. Cassel himself admitted that any discrepancy between the two sets of index figures would justify a deviation of exchanges from their purchasing power parities based on general average.[19] Keynes pointed out, however, that if the divergence between the two parities was mainly due to monetary causes – such as the different degree of inflation in two countries – then it would be purely temporary.[20] Moreover, even general indexes in those days were based mainly on prices of goods figuring prominently in import and export trade.[21] Keynes contended that Cassel had overlooked the possibility of the all-important fluctuations in the terms of trade.[22] He himself went out of his way to stress their importance as a factor influencing exchange rates. There was relatively little response to his effort to draw attention to this factor before the second World War, because during the 'thirties the universal desire to export unemployment made it appear as a matter of relatively small importance if this end was achieved at a cost of a deterioration of the terms of trade. What was wanted was an increasing physical volume of exports even if this was achieved through a depreciation of the exchange which reduced the volume of imports obtained in exchange for the same amount of exports.

The situation changed fundamentally after the second World War. Owing to the prevailing shortage of goods and to the high degree of employment in most countries, Governments no longer aimed at exporting merely for the sake of creating employment. The terms of trade came to be watched more closely by theoretical economists and were made subject to closer analysis. In particular Kindleberger analysed with care its relationship with exchanges on the basis of European experience before the war.[23] More interest was taken, however, in the effect of exchanges on the terms of trade than in the effect of the terms of trade on the exchanges.

A further subject for argument was the question whether the purchasing power parity theory could explain day-to-day fluctuations or whether it only applies to basic trends. Keynes and others repeatedly warned against using the theory as a guide for predicting or explaining short-term fluctuations. They claimed that the principle laid down by Cassel was only valid very broadly and in the long run. Later Keynes lost faith in the theory even as an indicator of future basic trends. As for deviations in the short-run, they had come to be generally regarded as part of the system.

(13) NO AUTOMATIC READJUSTMENT

The sweeping attacks delivered on the balance of payments theory by Casselites provoked a reaction by supporters of that theory. Under the pressure of adverse criticism they re-examined with much care the relationship between balances of payments and exchanges. Some opponents of the purchasing power parity theory went so far as to contest that general price levels had anything to do with exchange movements; or at any rate they contended that changes in purchasing power parities or deviations of exchanges from purchasing power parities need not necessarily affect the balance of payments and through it the exchanges.

Among others, Bonn pointed out that in a wide variety of conceivable situations a depreciation or undervaluation of the *mark* would be unable to correct an adverse trade balance. Controls of imports or exports may prevent an adjustment and so could world depression which would reduce the demand for German goods in spite of the stimulus of the low exchange. According to

him, dependence on imported food and raw materials also tended
to prevent an adjustment through a curtailment of imports caused
by exchange depreciation.[24] Others went even further, contending
that a strong and persistent depreciation of the exchange tended to
stimulate demand for imported goods rather than to discourage it,
in anticipation of a further rise in their prices in consequence of
a further depreciation of the exchange. So far from being self-
balancing, the effect of a depreciation on the balance of payments
can in such circumstances become self-aggravating.

(14) THE THEORY OF 'COMMODITY POINTS'

An attempt to reconcile the purchasing power parity theory with
the balance of payments theory applied the specie points mechanism to all goods subject to foreign trade. According to Rueff,
exchanges had 'commodity points' as well as specie points. Whenever a discrepancy developed – whether through an exchange
movement or through a change in the commodity points caused
by changes in the prices in either or both of the two countries
concerned – it becomes profitable to ship goods, in the same way
as under the gold standard it became profitable to ship specie
or bullion whenever the exchange rates went beyond their gold
points.[25]

Rueff realised that, owing to the great difficulty of selling goods
compared with selling gold, commodity points may be as wide as
20 per cent or more on each side of the exchange rate. Moreover,
they were different for each commodity and varied also according
to the location of the regions from which the commodities were
exported, and to which they were imported. For instance, a slight
discrepancy was sufficient to induce movements of goods from
Northern France across the Belgian frontier. The wider apart
the districts were from each other the wider the deviation of the
exchange had to become before it induces goods movements.[26]

(15) PSYCHOLOGICAL THEORIES

The progress of the psychological theory of exchanges is another
important French contribution to Foreign Exchange theory. But
as a reaction to the rigid dogmatism of the two rival Foreign
Exchange theories, some adherents of the psychological theory
went so far as to contend that amidst chaotic conditions such as

prevailed in the early 'twenties, exchange rates did not conform to any rules whatsoever but were determined by the incalculable psychological factor of confidence. In this extreme form the theory had nothing constructive to contribute, even though it was nevertheless a useful corrective to the exaggerated doctrinaire views of the two rival schools.

A form of psychological theory had appeared in Germany during and immediately after the first World War, aiming at explaining exchange movements on the basis of changes in prospect of an eventual return to convertibility of notes into gold.[27] This theory is based on a dogmatic metallistic conception of exchanges. Its application was greatly broadened by a number of French economists headed by Aftalion,[28] who allowed for other expectations in addition to covertibility prospects. In the experience of France during the 'twenties it was mainly the appearance, or even the anticipation, of an increase in Budgetary deficits that resulted in speculative exchange operations and a flight of capital, causing a depreciation of the *franc*, followed in turn by a rise in prices. The psychological school rejected the idea of any definite or even approximate relationship between the size of an adverse balance or the extent of price increases on the one hand and the depreciation of the exchange on the other. According to Aftalion the effect of the same adverse balance on exchange rates depends entirely on the view of the market taken of future prospects.[29] During a period of depreciating paper moneys there is no such thing as a normal level of exchange. Their depreciation follows laws that cannot be reduced to formulae of economic statics, because interdependence of various influences is of an essentially dynamic character.[30]

(16) ANTICIPATION OF MATERIAL EFFECTS

Some writers, without endorsing this theory, readily admitted that both balance of payments and purchasing power parity produced their effects largely through psychological factors. The anticipation of an import surplus or of large payments to be made abroad or of a rise in domestic prices was liable to affect exchanges long before the changes actually materialised. Indeed, the extreme form of purchasing power parity theory, according to which even in the complete absence of any effect on supply-demand relationship in the Foreign Exchange market – a mere change in purchasing power parities is sufficient to affect exchange rates, is overwhelmingly psychological.

Among others, Pigou took the line that if as a result of inflation the British prices level should double 'then importers and exporters will both know that, if American stuff is to exchange on the same real terms as before against English stuff . . . a dollar must buy twice as much sterling as before. In these circumstances both sides may be ready *at once* to accept these new terms *without any mediating movement of trade*'.[31] (My italics.)

Cassel himself accepted the psychological theory in a limited sense by stating that the undervaluation of exchanges can often be explained on the ground of anticipation of future changes in purchasing power parities.[32] The difference between such theories and the French psychological theory was the French contention that exchange rates of inflated currencies did not follow any definite rules but were entirely at the mercy of capricious incalculable influences that defy attempts to define them. What the extreme psychological theory overlooked was that such psychological influences merely anticipated the effect of material influences. On the other hand, supporters of materialistic theories overlooked that, even if the assumption on which such anticipation rested was originally mistaken, it was liable to create subsequently its own justification by the effect of the resulting exchange movement on prices and on domestic economic conditions.

(17) REPARATIONS AND EXCHANGES

An aspect of Foreign Exchange theory which received a great deal of attention from the end of the first World War till the cancellation of reparations in the early 'thirties related to the effect of international transfers on exchanges. The static doctrine, born amidst the stable conditions and free-trade atmosphere of the 19th century, that a country which had external payments to make was bound to have a favourable trade balance to provide the exchanges required so long as it kept its domestic finances in good order, came to be applied too light-heartedly amidst totally different dynamic conditions in the 20th century. In many quarters the main objection to the size of German reparations was not that Germany would not be able to raise the necessary amount of exchange but that it would compel Germany to increase her exports to such an extent that it would inflict heavy losses on her competitors.

It soon became evident that in the early 'twenties Germany had no export surplus out of which to pay reparations, nor was she in a position to deflate to the extent of her transfer requirements. The demand for Foreign Exchanges for that purpose simply caused a depreciation of the *mark* to a level at which speculative counterpart to the demand was forthcoming. Yet even years after the stabilisation Keynes envisaged the policy of payment through exchange dumping. 'The easiest method [of enabling Germany to transfer reparation payments] would be to allow the exchange value of the German *mark* to fall by the amount required to give the necessary bounty to exports and then to resist any agitation to raise money-wages.' He rejected that solution because under the Dawes scheme it was expressly forbidden.[33] He had also misgivings about the degree of deflation that would be required in order to produce a big enough export surplus.

(18) KEYNES'S FORWARD EXCHANGE THEORY

An important development during the early 'twenties was the elaboration of a Forward Exchange theory. It was pointed out in Chapter 17 that rudiments of this theory existed already in the 'nineties. But Keynes was the first to present the Interest Parity theory in a systematic form, in his articles in the *Manchester Guardian Reconstruction Supplement* and in his *Tract on Monetary Reform*. According to his theory, forward margins, expressed in percentage per annum, tend to be equal to the difference between interest rates in the two centres and tend to fluctuate around these 'interest parities' in accordance with supply and demand. Keynes laid down the rule that whenever they departed from their interest parities to an extent of at least half per cent *per annum*, interest arbitrage set into motion transactions which tended to readjust them. Deviations of a lasting nature were liable to arise, however, among other reasons, because the liquid capital available for arbitrage was not unlimited and at times it was not large enough to bring about readjustment.[34]

Keynes believed that between inconvertible currencies changes of interest parities through Bank rate changes produced an immediate automatic adjustment of the forward rates without any previous change in supply-demand relationship.[35] We may conveniently call this theory a psychological theory of interest parities,

K 2

because the changes are supposed to take place in anticipation of material influences on the assumption that the latter are bound to operate. It is an essentially static theory, since it makes no attempt at analysing the process by which the new equilibrium comes to be established.

(19) DYNAMIC v. STATIC THEORY

For a long time Forward Exchange theory made very little further advance. Keynes himself paid scant attention to it after the publication of his *Tract on Monetary Reform*, though in subsequent writings he enlarged on his Forward Exchange policy proposals. In my *Theory of Forward Exchange*, published in 1937, I tried to carry the theory a little further by laying stress on the reciprocal character of relationship between forward rates and their interest parities,[36] and I made a rudimentary attempt to elaborate a dynamic theory of Forward Exchange. Among the pre-war writers Kindleberger, while admitting some aspects of Forward Exchange dynamism, came out on the side of an extreme static theory according to which the existence of Forward Exchange facilities made no essential difference to the economic impact of Foreign Exchange, and the only thing that mattered was the grand total of spot and forward transactions, regardless of whether they consisted of spot or forward transactions.[37]

There was a revival of interest in Forward Exchange theory after the second World War. Bloomfield, making good use of the official American statistics on forward transactions and short-term balances, issued between 1936 and 1949, contributed some interesting observations on the difference between stabilising and unstabilising speculation in Forward Exchange.[38] The main contribution of most post-war writers on Forward Exchange theory – especially Spraos, Jasay and Tsiang – consisted of their penetrating analysis of leads and lags and a thorough examination of the inter-relationship between speculation, arbitrage and commercial covering.

In my post-war writings on Forward Exchange I tried to stress the dynamic aspects of the Forward Exchange system far beyond the extent to which I had in my pre-war book. I sought to stress the self-aggravating dynamism of Forward Exchange and to examine the various ways in which forward rates affected spot rates and, through them, gold reserves and national economies as a whole. More will be said about this aspect of the subject in the next section in Chapter 25.

(20) INFLUENCE OF ELASTICITIES

A new tool of analysis made its appearance shortly before the second World War in the form of investigating the elasticities of supply and demand in Foreign Exchanges and in the factors lying behind them. Mrs. Joan Robinson laid the foundations of this trend of thought in 1937.[40] Machlup adopted the same line in 1939–40.[41] Both authors explained the way in which discrepancies between supply and demand, due to the balance of payments, were liable to affect the exchanges, according to the relative extent of various elasticities. Mrs. Robinson attributes exchange movements to discrepancies between the balance of trade and balance of lending. Machlup differentiated between 'spontaneous' and 'induced' international payments, the latter being either the result of changes in the exchange rate or indirectly of other items of the balance of payments.

A publication of the League of Nations on *International Currency Experience* revived one of the earliest Foreign Exchange theories attributing exchange movements not to the total volume of money in the country but to the volume of money available in the Foreign Exchange market. 'The greater the public's liquidity, the greater the danger of disruptive capital movements. . . . In fact liquidity has enormously increased by the anti-depression policies of monetary expansion in the 'thirties and by the need of war finance since then.'[42]

(21) LEADS AND LAGS IN POST-WAR THEORY

During the period following the second World War when speculation and the movement of funds were handicapped by restrictions, leads and lags came into prominence as the main causes of pressure on exchanges. The ways in which merchants and others delayed or put forward foreign trade transactions or the settlement of payments arising from them, in the hope of benefiting by a devaluation or revaluation of the exchange, became a factor of first-rate importance, and greatly influenced the degree of pressure on exchanges. Leads and lags continued to play a prominent part also after the restoration of free dealings in exchanges, but it was not until the 'sixties that their importance came to be realised by economists.

Another new line of inquiry was initiated by Morgenstern who, on the basis of a wealth of statistics, examined the connection between exchange movements and business cycles.[43] This inquiry is in keeping with the trend of integrating Foreign Exchange theory into general economic theory instead of treating it as a specialised technical study.

The bulk of the literature on Foreign Exchange after the second World War dealt with matters of policy rather than pure theory. Policy proposals must rest, of course, on theoretical assumptions, but, generally speaking, the way in which they related to those assumptions was not analysed adequately. As Weiller aptly observed, the tragedy of contemporary economic thought was its inability to find the connecting link between the statics of pure economics and the dynamics of applied economics.[44]

NOTES TO CHAPTER TWENTY-ONE

1. Howard S. Ellis, *German Monetary Theory, 1905–1933* (Cambridge, Mass., 1934), Part III.
2. Gustav Cassel, 'The Present Situation of the Foreign Exchanges', *Economic Journal*, 1916, pp. 62 *et seq.* and pp. 319 *et seq.*
3. Gustav Cassel, *Germany's Power of Resistance* (New York, 1916).
4. Gustav Cassel, *Money and Foreign Exchange after 1914* (London, 1922).
5. *Op. cit.* pp. 138–40.
6. Karl Schlesinger, *Dir Veränderung des Geldwertes im Kriege* (Vienna, 1916).
7. Alfred Lansburgh, 'Die Politik der Reichsbank und die Reichschatzanweisungen nach dem Kriege', *Veröffentlichungen des Vereines für Sozialpolitik*, vol. 166, p. 47, quoted by Ellis, *op. cit.* p. 218.
8. Ellis, *op. cit.* p. 222.
9. A. D. Noyes, *Financial Chapters of the War* (New York, 1916), p. 180.
10. J. M. Keynes, *A Tract on Monetary Reform* (London, 1923), p. 106.
11. J. van Walré de Bordes, *The Austrian Crown* (London, 1924), p. 197.
12. Cassel, *op. cit.* p. 168.
13. Cassel, *op. cit.* p. 148.
14. E. C. van Dorp, 'The Deviation of Exchanges', *Economic Journal*, December 1919, 'Abnormal Deviations in International Exchanges', *Economic Journal*, September 1920.
15. Gustav Cassel, 'Further Observations on the World's Monetary Problem', *Economic Journal*, March 1920.
16. Gustav Cassel, *Das Geldproblem der Welt* (Munich, 1921), p. 41.
17. A. W. Flux, *The Foreign Exchanges* (London, 1924), p. 94.

18. James W. Angell, *The Theory of International Prices* (Cambridge, Mass., 1926), p. 440.
19. Cassell, *Money and Foreign Exchanges*, p. 154.
20. J. M. Keynes, *A Tract on Monetary Reform*, p. 95.
21. Keynes, *op. cit.* p. 99, also *A Treatise on Money* (London, 1930), vol. i, p. 73 and p. 336.
22. Keynes, *A Treatise on Money*, vol. i, p. 74.
23. C. P. Kindleberger, *The Terms of Trade* (New York, 1956), pp. 25–34.
24. M. J. Bonn, *The Stabilisation of the Mark* (Chicago, 1922), quoted by Ellis, *op. cit.* pp. 249–50.
25. Jacques Rueff, *Théorie des phénomènes monétaires* (Paris, 1927), p. 204.
26. Rueff, *op. cit.* pp. 192–4.
27. Karl Diehl, *Über Fragen des Geldwesens und der Valuta während des Krieges und nach dem Kriege* (Jena, 1918), p. 29, quoted by Angell, *op. cit.* p. 331.
28. Albert Aftalion, 'La Circulation, les changes et les prix', *Revue Économique International*, 1924, quoted by Angell, *op. cit.* pp. 293–4.
29. Aftalion, *op. cit.* pp. 320 *et seq.*
30. Jean Weiller, *L'Œuvre scientifique d'Albert Aftalion* (Montchrestien, 1955), p. 176.
31. A. C. Pigou, *Essays in Applied Economics* (London, 1923), p. 170.
32. Cassel, *Money and Foreign Exchanges*, pp. 149–50.
33. J. M. Keynes, 'The German Transfer Problem', *Economic Journal*, March 1929, pp. 6–7.
34. Keynes, *A Tract on Monetary Reform*, pp. 715 *et seq.*
35. Keynes, *op. cit.* p. 137.
36. Paul Einzig, *The Theory of Forward Exchange* (London, 1937), chapter xxi.
37. C. P. Kindleberger, 'Speculation and Forward Exchange', *Journal of Political Economy*, April 1933, p. 163.
38. Arthur I. Bloomfield, *Capital Imports and the International Balance of Payments, 1934–39* (Chicago, 1950).
39. Paul Einzig, *A Dynamic Theory of Forward Exchange* (London, 1961).
40. Fritz Machlup, 'The Theory of Foreign Exchange', *Economica*, November 1939 and February 1940.
41. Joan Robinson, 'The Foreign Exchanges' in *Essays in the Theory of Employment*, 2nd ed. (Oxford, 1947).
42. League of Nations, *International Currency Experience* (Princeton, 1944), p. 122.
43. Oscar Morgenstern, *International Financial Transactions and Business Cycles* (Princeton, 1960).
44. Jean Weiller, *op. cit.* p. 163.

CHAPTER TWENTY-TWO

Modern Foreign Exchange Policy

(1) END OF *LAISSER-FAIRE*

THE first World War marked the end of a century of *laisser-faire* in the sphere of Foreign Exchange. We saw in Chapter 18 that between 1815 and 1914 Government interference with the Foreign Exchange markets, whether in the form of restrictions or intervention, was quite exceptional in the financially advanced countries. Bank rate changes were the only 'respectable' form of official action to influence the exchanges. From 1914 right to the time of writing official intervention in some other form has been the rule most of the time in most countries. Although there was a period between the two World Wars when exchanges were, to a high degree, free of official interference, even then the system was not one of pure *laisser-faire* in the pre-1914 sense. Progress towards freedom was again appreciable during the 'fifties, but some degree of restriction or some form of official intervention continued to limit the freedom of Foreign Exchange operations or the natural fluctuation of exchange rates in practically every country.

(2) OBJECTS AND MEANS OF POLICY

The following were the ends pursued by Foreign Exchange policy after 1914:

1. To secure and safeguard the Foreign Exchanges necessary for vital requirements in time of war and peace.
2. To maintain the stability of the exchange if that is possible without excessive sacrifices.
3. To lower the value of the national exchange for the sake of improving the balance of payments.
4. To raise the value of the national exchange for the sake of improving the terms of trade.
5. To raise or lower the exchange in order to maintain a stable price level.
6. To restore or maintain the freedom of the Foreign Exchange

market in so far as this was compatible with the above ends.

7. To borrow short-term funds abroad.
8. To lend short-term funds abroad.
9. To influence the level of interest rates.
10. To pursue economic warfare.

The following were the principal means of modern Foreign Exchange policy applied after 1914:

1. Bank rate changes and other means of regulating the volume of credit or interest rates.
2. Exchange restrictions, official or unofficial.
3. Restrictions on bullion and specie movements.
4. Tariffs or physical controls on imports and exports.
5. Bilateral exchange arrangements or trading methods.
6. Technical devices to encourage the influx of gold or to discourage the efflux.
7. Official intervention in the Foreign Exchange market.

(3) ORTHODOX POLICY IN 1914

The orthodox device of Bank rate increase came to be applied very drastically in Britain in August 1914, on the assumption that, if applied on a sufficient scale, it would meet the prevailing abnormal requirements. In addition, some temporary restrictions were applied on payments in general both in Britain and in other belligerent countries, to provide a breathing space for straightening out the confused situation. But, generally speaking, a high degree of freedom from exchange restrictions was maintained during the early part of the war.

For a long time after the outbreak of the war, Russia was the only country which applied drastic exchange restrictions, apart from those introduced also in other countries for the limited purpose of preventing their nationals from trading with the enemy. It was only from the beginning of 1916 that the British authorities came to require banks to obtain from their customers declarations that transfers of funds abroad were not undertaken for speculative purposes. And it was not until nearly two years later that a statutory ban was imposed on speculative transactions and on unauthorised export of capital. Rather than interfere with the freedom of the Foreign Exchange market, the British Government introduced in 1915 the McKenna duties of 33 per cent on a limited range of goods, to protect sterling against pressure through an import surplus. The same end was attained more effectively through the incidental effect of the control imposed over the use of shipping facilities as a result of the submarine warfare.

Nothing was done for a long time to prevent the export of Bank of England notes which commanded a premium over the exchange rate of sterling in Switzerland. When it was discovered, however, that the premium was due to German purchases for the purpose of financing their military expenditure in the Middle East, it was decided to stop the traffic.[1]

In France the question whether to adopt exchange restrictions was considered during the summer of 1915 by an expert committee consisting mostly of bankers. Its report rejected the idea on the ground that it would damage the chances of the Paris market to resume its pre-war rôle of the leading Foreign Exchange centre after the war.[2] The banks gave an undertaking that they would confine their sales of Foreign Exchange to their customers to legitimate transactions. In July 1917 the *Commission des Changes* was appointed to supervise the market, which continued to remain free.[3] It was not until April 1918 that opposition to official exchange control was overcome.

(4) ALL COUNTRIES ADOPTED RESTRICTIONS

In Germany the quotation of exchange rates was prohibited at the outbreak of the war, but dealing remained free – subject to instructions from the Reichsbank to which the German banks voluntarily submitted – until the beginning of 1916. The quotation of exchanges was then resumed, but dealing was confined to authorised banks which gave an undertaking to confine sales of exchanges to importers of goods authorised by the Reichsbank and to other authorised buyers. Official buying and selling rates were fixed.[4] The German example was followed by Austria-Hungary.

In Russia a ban on the export of capital was imposed at a very early stage, and Foreign Exchange transactions became largely concentrated in the hands of the Imperial Bank. It was not until the beginning of 1917, however, that a major loophole was stopped by imposing a ban on paying roubles into non-resident accounts.

In Italy a ban was imposed on transfers abroad in November 1917 and only transfers for commercial requirements were authorised. From March 1918 all Foreign Exchange transactions were placed under the control of the newly formed National Institute of Exchange.

Even in the United States official regulations of exchange operations were enacted in January 1918. Banks had to submit to the authorities weekly returns of the Foreign Exchange transactions. The object of this measure was mainly to prevent trading with the enemy.

(5) BANS ON GOLD EXPORT

From the very outset the export of specie and bullion was banned in belligerent countries. In Britain sterling remained convertible in theory, but Bank of England officials did their utmost to discourage anyone from insisting on his right firmly. If he could not be dissuaded, his notes would be exchanged for sovereigns, but his name was put on a 'black list' and he was subjected to special search at the ports of embarkation if he ever left the country, because the export of gold was unlawful. Even in the United States the export of gold was banned from 1917 until 1919.

In outward form free Foreign Exchange markets continued to function in London, Paris and other centres. Forward Exchange operations were suspended, but in practice there was nothing to prevent speculative buying and selling of foreign notes, and even transactions in transfers for unauthorised purposes remained possible.

(6) OFFICIAL SUPPORT OF EXCHANGES

Most Governments adopted a policy of supporting their exchanges to prevent their depreciation. In France the Bank of France began to buy and sell Foreign Exchanges over the counter from October 1914, and from March 1915 it assumed the initiative by selling Foreign Exchanges in the open market. Three months later, however, it decided to confine its sales of foreign currencies to meet commercial requirements. Consequently a discrepancy developed between official and free rates, and there were from time to time also marked discrepancies between the official and free sterling-dollar cross rates in Paris. The Bank of France intervened from time to time on the account of Allied Governments to reduce such discrepancies.[5]

From 1915 sterling was systematically supported in New York

by J. P. Morgan and Co., acting as agents for the British Treasury. They never took the initiative to intervene in the market, but they were buyers of sterling, if offered to them for sale, at the official rate of $4·7640. As a result of this policy of pegging, sterling came to be linked with the dollar also in neutral Foreign Exchange markets, even though discrepancies were apt to develop between official and unofficial sterling-dollar cross rates. The cost of supporting sterling, apart altogether from the amounts raised for paying for supplies purchased abroad by the Government, was estimated at £800 million.[6]

The Reichsbank, in addition to selling exchanges to authorised buyers at a fixed rate, intervened from time to time in neutral markets to support the *mark* exchange on a small scale. The total cost of supporting the *mark* did not exceed 450 million *marks*.

The *rouble* was supported by the Russian authorities during the early years of the war at an artificially high rate, out of the proceeds of inter-Allied loans. Its official exchange rate lost touch completely with its unofficial rate in foreign markets.

Soon after the Armistice official support of the exchanges of the European belligerent countries came to an end. Germany was no longer in a position to support her exchange and in March 1919 the pegging of Allied exchanges was also terminated. Exchange restrictions were removed or relaxed in the victorious countries, while in the defeated countries the disorganisation of the administrative machinery made their enforcement impossible. In any case even when these restrictions were at their highest they were far from effective anywhere by comparison with the much more drastic systems adopted during the second World War.

(7) POLICIES OF NEUTRAL COUNTRIES

Throughout the first World War, Latin-American countries and neutral countries in Europe allowed their exchanges to appreciate. Their reserves increased considerably, and the resulting expansion of their note issues stimulated the rise in prices. We saw in Chapter 20 that in 1916 Sweden suspended the purchase of gold at the official price, preferring an additional appreciation of the exchange to further accumulation of gold, owing to the resulting expansion of currency and credit, and that for similar considerations Spain lowered the official buying price of gold. Lack of familiarity with the technique of neutralising a gold and Foreign Exchange influx was mainly responsible for this policy. If its object was to cause a fall of domestic prices as a result of an appreciation of the exchange it certainly failed to attain that end. The rising trend caused by inflation and shortage of supplies was too strong to be offset by exchange appreciation.

As a reaction from wartime intervention to bolster up exchanges, most Governments left the markets to their own devices during the first post-war years. It was not until towards the middle 'twenties that France, Italy and other countries reverted to the policy of intervention, mainly for the purpose of discouraging and penalising speculation.

(8) INTER-WAR EXCHANGE REVALUATION

The declared policy of most Governments during the early post-war years was to restore the national exchange rate to its pre-war parity. Even in countries with fairly advanced inflation – such as France or Italy – for considerations of prestige the Governments were not prepared to admit the impossibility of that task. Countries whose exchange obviously depreciated beyond the 'point of no return' were the first to face realities and to stabilise their exchanges at drastically devalued levels. So long as their exchanges remained exposed to wide fluctuations it was impossible to deal effectively with problems of budgetary equilibrium and deflation of credit that was a necessary condition for a stabilisation of the domestic price level. In every instance, therefore, it was decided to make a start with stabilising the exchanges at a level at which there appeared to be a fair chance for holding them during the transition period. In some instances the correct parities at which it was feasible to defend the exchange had to be discovered through trial and error and the devaluation had to be repeated.

(9) INTER-WAR INTERVENTIONS

In France the authorities frequently intervened in the Foreign Exchange market on a large scale and in two instances their intervention was highly successful. In 1924, when speculative pressure appeared to have got out of control, Poincaré intervened with the aid of external credits, and his 'bear squeeze' brought about a sharp recovery. Again, in 1926, in a similar situation he repeated the manœuvre, this time without any external support, by restoring confidence with the aid of deflationary measures. Thanks to these and to more stable domestic political conditions, a heavy buying pressure developed and continued for some two years, so that it became necessary for the French authorities to defend the *franc* against an unwanted appreciation. In order to avoid inflation resulting from an excessive increase of the gold and Foreign Exchange reserve through repatriations of French capital from abroad, the Bank of France engaged systematically in swap transactions with the French banks, at rates at which it was profitable for the latter to keep large liquid funds in London. Such transactions were undertaken on a very large scale, until the legal stabilisation of the *franc* in June 1928 brought the buying pressure to an end. Thereupon the Bank of France discontinued its intervention and liquidated its accumulated commitments.

The Italian authorities adopted during the middle 'twenties a more sophisticated form of active intervention. In 1926–7 they operated systematically in both ways in Forward Exchanges, in an effort to control the movement of short-term funds to and from Italy. In later years, however, Italian intervention was confined mainly to the spot market.

In Austria and other Central European countries, Central Banks encouraged the influx of foreign funds by means of swap transactions with the local banks at rates at which it was profitable for foreign banks to invest short-term funds. This was a device of borrowing from abroad in order to replenish the financial resources depleted by advanced inflation. This method met with strong criticism on the part of the League of Nations Finance Committee and was eventually discontinued.

(10) DEPARTURES FROM ORTHODOX POLICY

Even during the period of inter-war stability there was, generally speaking, much more official activity in Foreign Exchanges than before 1914. Apart from other reasons, this was due to the operation of the gold exchange standard in a large number of countries. Central Banks which pursued a policy of active intervention developed advanced techniques of squeezing speculators.

Britain and a few other countries, on the other hand, reverted more or less to the pre-war method of confining official action to influencing exchanges by means of Bank rate changes. This orthodox policy came to be supplemented by devices of restrictions.

For instance, in Britain there was from 1924 onwards, from time to time, an unofficial embargo on the public issue of foreign loans and the private placing of foreign securities was discouraged in order to protect sterling against undue strain. The effect of the influx and efflux of gold on the volume of credit was neutralised in order to prevent it from producing its automatic effect.

In France various exchange restriction measures were adopted during the 'twenties, but for the most part they existed on paper only, judging by the gigantic scale of the flight of French capital to London, Switzerland, New York, etc. In Germany exchange restrictions were greatly reinforced from 1921. Exporters had to surrender the proceeds of their sales abroad and the purchase of Foreign Exchange was subject to licence. The restrictions failed, however, to prevent the flight of capital, partly because they were not enforced in Western districts under Allied occupation. After the stabilisation in 1924 most of the restrictions were removed.

In Austria a system of differentiation between *Inlandkrone* and *Auslandkrone* was adopted, according to whether the currency was transferable abroad. There was a wide discrepancy between the quotations of the two currencies.[7] A similar system was adopted by other Central and South-eastern European countries.

(11) EXCHANGE CONTROLS AFTER 1931

The crisis of 1931 constitutes a landmark in the history of Foreign Exchange policy, fully as important as 1914. The banking difficulties in Central Europe led to the adoption of drastic exchange control in many countries in order to prevent a large-scale withdrawal of foreign credits and the outflow of national capital, and in order to reduce the adverse balance of payments. Germany and other countries which had experienced extreme inflation preferred exchange control to the risk of a repetition of that experience. A system of exchange restrictions, far more efficient than the one applied during the first World War, came to be adopted in Germany even before the advent of Hitler's totalitarian political and economic system. Italy and several other countries also placed a ban on external payments.

(12) BRITISH OFFICIAL OPERATIONS

When following on the crisis in Central Europe a sweeping attack on sterling developed during August 1931 the authorities hoped to cope with the situation by the time-honoured method of raising the Bank rate. At the same time, however, they deemed it necessary to supplement that device by intervening actively in the Foreign Exchange market. They supported both spot and forward sterling with the aid of funds borrowed from the United States and France, preferring to use up these credits rather than allow sterling to decline below gold export point and having to announce a gold outflow day after day. When the sales of Foreign Exchange approached the amount of the gold reserve the Government decided to suspend the gold standard. At the same time, while the withdrawal of foreign capital continued to remain free, some restrictions were imposed on the export of British capital until March 1932. The embargo on foreign issues was reinforced and its enforcement was placed later in the hands of the Capital Issues Committee.

After the suspension of the gold standard sterling was allowed to find its own level for a while. But in February 1932 the Government embarked on systematic intervention in the Foreign Exchange market. The Exchange Equalisation Account was created for that purpose with an initial capital of £175 million. Right to the outbreak of the second World War it operated very actively and systematically. It was not the official policy to peg sterling at any fixed rate, even though this was also done from time to time. Generally speaking, buying or selling pressure was not resisted rigidly, but its effect on the exchange rate was sought to be mitigated by official operations. The officially declared policy was to 'iron out' fluctuations, and to safeguard the British economy against the effects of 'imported' deflation. Whenever as a result of deflation abroad there was a danger of sterling becoming once more overvalued, it was allowed to depreciate to obviate the necessity for a deflationary reduction of prices in Britain. This Foreign Exchange policy was based on the purchasing power parity theory.

The British authorities also endeavoured from time to time to stimulate exports by means of a deliberate undervaluation of sterling, and to accumulate a large gold and Foreign Exchange reserve partly through achieving export surpluses and partly through keeping sterling at a level at which it attracted foreign funds. Their intervention often aimed at squeezing speculators. In that respect it achieved such a degree of technical efficiency that in the course of time speculators came to deem it expedient to abstain for a while from attacking sterling.

(13) INTERNATIONAL DEPRECIATION RACE

The depreciation of sterling in 1931 confronted the Governments of most countries with a dilemma. They had to decide whether to allow their currencies to follow sterling or whether to maintain them stable in relation to gold and the dollar. A large number of exchanges, especially those of the Commonwealth countries and the rest of the subsequently created Sterling Area, followed sterling, but we saw in Chapter 20 that some of them detached their currencies later and linked them to the dollar, while other Governments repeatedly changed their Foreign Exchange policy, linking their currency alternately to sterling and to the dollar.

As a result of the American banking crisis and of heavy withdrawals of foreign funds from the United States, the dollar too was allowed to depreciate in 1933. Indeed, the Government declared itself in favour of a deliberate depreciation of the dollar although, inconsistently enough, exchange restrictions were adopted to prevent export of capital and speculation. This marked the beginning of an international exchange depreciation race which threatened to create chaotic conditions. An attempt to avert this by means of an agreed stabilisation of the exchanges was made at the World Economic Conference in London during the summer of 1933, but it failed to achieve any results. The dollar continued to fluctuate and the American Exchange Stabilisation Fund, founded on the pattern of the British Exchange Equalisation Account, intervened actively in the Foreign Exchange market. Even before this arrangement, the United States Treasury operated in the London and Paris markets on various occasions from 1931 through the intermediary of the leading New York banks.[8] In January 1934 the dollar was re-stabilised at 59 per cent of its old parity. Although the Administration was authorised to change the new parity in either direction within the limits of 60 and 50 per cent, it never availed itself of this power.

(14) RESISTANCE BY THE 'GOLD BLOC'

Pressure on the small number of currencies, which were sought to be maintained stable without resorting to watertight exchange restrictions, increased during the middle 'thirties. The countries of the 'gold bloc' endeavoured to resist pressure on their overvalued exchanges by means of various forms of unofficial restrictions to discourage speculation, arbitrage and the flight of capital.

They also resorted to various forms of intervention, but in the long run these proved to be incapable of preventing devaluation. Belgium, after having tried to defend the *franc* with the aid of a technical device affecting the forward rate,[9] gave up resistance in 1935. The rest of the 'gold bloc' followed in September 1936.

After the devaluation of their currencies, Belgium, Holland and Switzerland defended their exchanges at the new level, but the French authorities deemed it advisable to adopt a policy of more or less flexible exchanges, with the degree of flexibility varying according to circumstances and according to the personal policies of the Finance Ministers of the day. Although they repeatedly devalued the *franc*, and for some time it was allowed to find its level, on the whole they yielded to pressure with the utmost reluctance. M. Reynaud's verdict that successive devaluations were 'too late and too little', was fully justified.

(15) PRE-WAR DEFENCES OF EXCHANGES

In 1936, in connection with the devaluation of the 'gold bloc' currencies, an agreement was concluded between the United States, Britain and France, known under the name of the Tripartite Agreement, even though several other countries joined it later. The main object was to prevent a recurrence of the exchange depreciation race. The participating Governments undertook to abstain from a deliberate excessive depreciation of their exchanges and to consult each other if, as a result of irresistible pressure, they should find it impossible to continue to resist such pressure.[10]

During the late 'thirties Britain as well as other Western European countries was inclined to reinforce the defence of the exchange by adopting various unofficial embargoes in order to prevent speculation, withdrawals of funds through arbitrage, and a flight of national capital. These embargoes served partly the purpose of assisting other countries in the defence of their exchanges. Governments realised that it was to their interest to help other Governments to defend their exchanges.

(16) RESTRICTIONS DURING THE 'THIRTIES

The object of the German Foreign Exchange policy under the Nazi régime was the isolation of the domestic economy from international trends, not merely to the extent of safeguarding it against 'importing' deflation from abroad but to the extent of being able to inflate with impunity. As a result of expansionary measures, aiming first at a reduction of unemployment and later at financing rearmament, prices in Germany rose above the world level and the *reichsmark* became distinctly overvalued. Exchange restrictions, standstill agreements with foreign creditors, various bilateralist currency and trade arrangements and multiple currency practices prevented this disequilibrium from producing its natural effect on the German balance of payments and from affecting the stability of the *reichsmark*. An additional advantage was that Germany secured the full benefit of favourable terms of trade through a deliberate overvaluation of the *reichsmark*, in sharp contrast with the policy of deliberate undervaluation pursued by other countries. Germany was able to maintain her exports largely with the aid of a system of various types of *marks*, especially *aski marks*, which were quoted at different rates for various countries and even for various goods.[11] There was an almost infinite variety of such *marks*.

A somewhat similar system of multiple exchange rates was in operation also in Latin-America. Many Latin-American countries also adopted the system of 'retention quotas' under which exporters were allowed to retain a certain percentage of the Foreign Exchange proceeds and sell such exchanges in the free market at a considerable premium. In this respect, too, the quotas that exporters were allowed to retain were different for various currencies and for various commodities, according to whether the Government concerned was anxious to encourage or discourage exports to particular countries and of particular commodities.[12] The exchanges offered by exporters in the free market were available for financing luxury imports for which no exchange was allotted by the authorities, for debt payments, and in some instances even for capital transfers.[13]

Actually the so-called free markets were not really free, because it was the authorities who determined the categories of requirements that could be satisfied there. It was often referred to as the 'grey market' in contradistinction to the 'black market' in which illicit requirements could be met at a price.

(17) CHANGES IN CONTROLS

In Germany, Italy and all other Central and Southern European countries, with the notable exception of Austria, the severity of the exchange restrictions increased throughout the 'thirties. In Latin-America the degree of control varied according to trade conditions. Between 1931 and 1933 they were tightened considerably, but with the improvement in the world demand for commodities in the middle 'thirties they were relaxed, only to be tightened again as a result of the moderate recession of 1937. For instance, in the Argentine importers wanting to buy 'free' exchanges had to obtain a permit. Austria was able to dispense with exchange restrictions some years before she was absorbed by Germany, thanks to her satisfactory recovery and her sound economic policies.

During the 'thirties a system of exchange clearing was adopted in trade relations between financially weak countries of Central and South-eastern Europe, also between them and some Western European countries – Switzerland figuring prominently among them – and between the latter and various Latin-American countries. This system meant a complete elimination of free Foreign Exchange markets. The exchange rates for the purposes of such clearing agreements were fixed officially and were often fixed at a figure entirely unrelated to purchasing power parities, or to black market rates.

(18) SLOW ADOPTION OF CONTROLS AFTER 1939

The outbreak of the second World War found the Governments of the belligerent countries better prepared for the defence of their currencies with the aid of controls than they had been in 1914. We saw above that in a number of countries exchange restrictions had already been in force in time of peace, while others, such as Britain and France, operated unofficial embargoes. They also had an opportunity of studying the application of restrictions in Germany and other countries before 1939. Allowing for this, the adoption of reasonably watertight exchange control, though not so slow as in the first World War, was indeed remarkably slow and, for a long time, inefficient.

(19) MANY LOOPHOLES IN BRITISH MEASURES

In Britain, it is true, some measures were adopted immediately on the outbreak of the war. Holders of certain foreign currencies and securities had to surrender their holdings. Dealings in exchanges, both spot and forward, at officially fixed rates, became the monopoly of the Bank of England, acting through the intermediary of the other banks, and the main object was to prevent the flight of British capital and speculation. Authorised dealers acted as agents of the authorities in allotting exchanges to importers and other legitimate purchasers. But for a long time exporters were free to sell their goods against payment in sterling and foreign importers were able to acquire sterling in the free market in New York or in other markets where non-resident holders of sterling balances were also able to dispose of their holdings. It was not until June 1940 that all British exports were made payable in foreign currencies which had to be surrendered to the authorities.[14] Later the old sterling balances of non-residents were blocked, as a result of which measure the turnover in the New York 'free' market declined to negligible proportions.

There were many other loopholes in the exchange restrictions, and the British authorities were most reluctant to close them, official spokesmen using the same argument as the committee of French bankers did in 1915, namely that a tightening of the exchange control would be detrimental to the prospects of resuming international banking activity after the war.[15] Nevertheless, by the middle of 1940 exchange restrictions became reasonably watertight.

(20) NEUTRALS ALSO ADOPT CONTROLS

The countries of the Sterling Area adopted restrictions similar to those of the United Kingdom. There were in theory no restrictions on movements of British funds between countries of the Sterling Area. Likewise Germany formed the *Reichsmark* Area consisting of the countries under her domination, and Japan formed the *Yen* Area consisting of the countries under Japanese occupation. A 'dollar area' also came into being, but it simply consisted of countries with hard currencies and there was no formal association between them.

The measures adopted by France at the beginning of the war to prevent the export of capital went in some respects further than the British measures. Even neutral countries felt impelled this time to resort to exchange control. In Switzerland, for instance, exchanges were allotted for approved purchases at official rates, but there were also free exchange rates which moved considerably in favour of the Swiss *franc* as the war was proceeding. There were similar differential quotations also in Sweden, though the discrepancies were not so wide. Latin-American neutral countries continued to apply exchange control after the outbreak of the war, though it was relaxed as and when they succeeded in accumulating large dollar balances during the latter part of the war.

In China shortly before the second World War an Anglo-American-Chinese stabilisation board was set up in Hong Kong, Shanghai and Chungking, mainly with the object of resisting Japanese efforts to undermine the stability of the Chinese currency. After Pearl Harbour the activities of this board came to be confined to Chungking, but in face of the rapidly accelerating inflation it was quite helpless.

(21) POLICIES UNDER THE BRETTON WOODS SYSTEM

The end of the war found most belligerent countries with exchanges stabilised more or less at rates at which they stood, or to which they were reduced, at the beginning of the war, having been defended by more or less watertight exchange control. Learning from the lessons of the early post-war period after the first World War, most rates were not unpegged. Indeed, their stability was in 1946 reaffirmed – though in many instances after more or less substantial adjustments of parities – under the rules of the International Monetary Fund. It became the duty of member Governments to intervene systematically in the Foreign Exchange markets when necessary in order to maintain the stability of their exchanges. Occasional intervention was no longer sufficient. It was necessary for the authorities to be in the market all the time when the rates were approaching the 'support points' that took the place of specie points under the Bretton Woods system, and to sell or buy Foreign Exchanges to the full extent to which this was necessary in order to prevent exchange movements beyond support points.

The Governments associated with the International Monetary Fund promised also to remove exchange restrictions and multiple currency practices after a transitional period. The implementation of this undertaking proceeded very slowly, however, and even at the time of writing it is not quite completed in most member countries. And it was easier for member Governments undertaking to restore the convertibility of their currencies at the earliest possible moment than to implement it. Britain's ill-advised premature attempt to that end in 1947, which collapsed after a few weeks, made the Government realise the inexpediency of the 'dash to freedom' policy urged upon it by dogmatic enthusiasts of that policy, and pressed upon it by the short-sighted insistence of the United States Treasury on carrying out the letter of the Loan Agreement regardless of consequences.

(22) RESTORATION OF CONVERTIBILITY IN STAGES

Convertibility of sterling was restored for the second time in slow stages between 1951 and 1959. It was confined largely to non-residents. Likewise in most other European countries there remained a discrimination between resident and non-resident accounts, also between current and capital transactions. The rules of the International Monetary Fund regarding the maintenance of stability were not enforced too rigidly in every instance. Canada, Ecuador, Chile and Mexico were allowed to pursue a policy of flexible exchanges, and so were France and Italy for some time during the 'forties. In 1949 Britain's decision to devalue sterling encountered no resistance on the part of the I.M.F., and no objection was raised to devaluation by a large number of other countries.

During the early 'fifties there was strong pressure in Britain and other countries in favour of adopting a flexible sterling, or alternatively widening considerably the margin between support points. But the Government decided in favour of maintaining stability within narrow support points and continuing to decontrol the exchanges. Sterling came to be defended once more largely by means of the orthodox devices of Bank rate increases and credit restrictions, but these measures continued to be supplemented by systematic intervention and by a high if declining degree of exchange control. The multiple exchange system remained in force, though after the abolition in 1959 of transferable sterling, whose use of which had been limited to a number of countries, and of the security sterling representing the proceeds of the sale of British securities held by non-residents, the only remaining special currencies were the investment currencies representing the proceeds of foreign securities sold by United Kingdom residents.

In the late 'forties and the greater part of the 'fifties the European Payments Union provided a system of international clearing facilities for Western European currencies, and also facilities for deferring the settlement of their adverse balances. This went a long way towards assisting in the maintenance of the stability of their exchanges.

(23) POST-WAR INTERVENTIONS

A feature of post-war Foreign Exchange policy was the growing extent of official intervention not only in spot exchanges but also in Forward Exchanges. The Exchange Equalisation Account unsuccessfully attempted in 1957 to check the run on the pound by supporting forward sterling on a large scale at an artificially high rate. Although the failure of the attempt made the authorities realise the futility of employing this device in face of a major speculative trend, it was applied both by the Bank of England and by other Central Banks for less ambitious purposes. In particular the Deutsche Bundesbank used it with good effect during the late 'fifties and early 'sixties to discourage an unwanted influx of foreign funds. It adopted the same device as was applied with success by the Bank of France in 1927-8. By 1962 even the Federal Reserve authorities and the Swiss National Bank abandoned their negative attitude towards official Forward Exchange operations.

(24) WIDE VARIETY OF CONTROLS

Considerations of space prevent us from examining the almost infinite variety of frequently changing exchange restriction measures in countries of the five continents during the 'forties and 'fifties. Volumes could be written – and have in fact been written – about them. Here we have to confine ourselves to indicating the broad outlines of trends and to give a few examples.

In Britain the exchange restrictions adopted during the war under emergency legislation were consolidated under the Exchange Control Act, 1947. During the early post-war years trade with most countries outside the Sterling Area and the Dollar Area was financed through a system of bilateral sterling accounts under which the sterling earned by each country could only be used for payments by the country concerned. Later, gradually a transferable area was created within which 'transferable' sterling could be used multilaterally.

In France the system of a controlled 'free' market in which hard currencies were transacted operated during the 'forties. Later, arbitrage was developed in currencies of E.P.U. countries. Restrictions were prematurely relaxed in 1949 and had to be partially restored two years later. During the late 'fifties and early 'sixties good progress was made towards liberalisation.

Holland and some other Western European countries resorted for some time to the system of retention quotas described above. Among the Scandinavian countries Sweden was able to liberalise her exchanges at an early stage, first in relation to the other Scandinavian countries and the Sterling Area, and later to a less extent to other countries. In Italy retention quotas remained in operation for a long time and there was a fluctuating discrepancy between official and free rates. In the late 'fifties and early 'sixties a high degree of freedom was restored.

In Latin America exchanges were virtually free in Mexico and several other Central American countries and became free in Venezuela at an early stage. On the other hand, in the Argentine, Brazil and Chile drastic restrictions with multiple currency practice remained in force throughout the post-war period.

In the Far East there were restrictions after the war in Hong Kong and Thailand and much stricter controls in Japan and the Sterling Area countries – India, Pakistan, Burma and Ceylon. The Philippines adopted a system of tax on the sales of exchanges with exemption for the imports of goods which the Government wanted to encourage.

(25) PROGRESS TOWARDS LIBERALISATION

Even after the liberalisations of the 'fifties in Europe exchanges in general were not nearly as free as before 1914 or during the brief period of inter-war stability. Above all, intervention in the market remained very much in evidence. In fact, with the improvement of its technique it has come to be regarded as part of the normal activities of the monetary authorities, in sharp contrast with the basic pre-1914 policy of *laisser-faire*. Monetary policies and economic policies in general pursued largely the end of upholding the stability of the exchanges. It was with much reluctance that various Governments decided on rare occasions to alter their exchange parities, whether in an upward or downward direction. Indeed most monetary authorities adopted the practice of systematically intervening even before the exchanges actually reached support points.

This subject will be discussed in greater detail in Chapter 26, dealing with the 'sixties.

NOTES TO CHAPTER TWENTY-TWO

1. Paul Einzig, *Exchange Control* (London, 1934), p. 28.
2. Lucien Petit, *Histoire des finances extérieures de la France pendant la guerre 1914–1919* (Paris, 1929), p. 68.
3. Karl Helfferich, *Money* (trsl. L. Infield) (London, 1927), p. 260.
4. Petit, *op. cit.* p. 103.
5. Einzig, *op. cit.* p. 25.
6. J. van Walré de Bordes, *The Austrian Crown* (London, 1924), pp. 111–12.
7. Einzig, *op. cit.* pp. 53–4.
8. Paul Einzig, *A Dynamic Theory of Forward Exchange* (London, 1961), pp. 480–483.
9. Paul Einzig, *World Finance, 1935–37* (London, 1937), pp. 222–3.
10. Frank C. Child, *The Theory and Practice of Exchange Control in Germany* (The Hague, 1958), pp. 139–45.
11. Herbert M. Bratter, *Foreign Exchange Control in Latin-America* (New York, 1939).
12. League of Nations, *International Currency Experience* (Princeton, 1944), p. 164.
13. Paul Einzig, *The Exchange Clearing System* (London, 1935).
14. Paul Einzig, *In the Centre of Things* (London, 1960), pp. 201–4.
15. Paul Einzig, *Dynamic Theory*, pp. 471–2.

CHAPTER TWENTY-THREE

Recent Developments

(1) FAR-REACHING CHANGES

ALTHOUGH the annals of Foreign Exchange were seldom uneventful for any length of time since 1914, the 'sixties are certain to be long remembered as a decade that witnessed many important and interesting developments. The present chapter is concerned with institutional and technical changes in the Foreign Exchange system that occurred during that decade. Chapter 24 will give an account of trends in exchange rates, of resistance to pressures and of changes in parities when such resistance had to be abandoned. Chapter 25 summarises briefly developments in the sphere of Foreign Exchange theory, developments that arose largely from controversies over Foreign Exchange policy proposals. Chapter 26 describes the new policies actually adopted during the 'sixties, mainly for the sake of resisting persistent buying or selling pressures.

The mechanism of the Foreign Exchange system underwent some very far-reaching changes in the 'sixties, even though basically it continued to rest on the Bretton Woods agreement and on the rules of the International Monetary Fund arising from it. Indeed it was not until the closing years of the previous decade that the mechanism set up by the International Monetary Fund came to be applied effectively, as a result of the establishment of convertibility, at any rate for the benefit of non-residents, by a number of countries. The 'sixties were the first complete decade in which the Bretton Woods system was actually functioning, at any rate as far as the industrially and financially advanced countries of the free world were concerned.

(2) CHANGES IN PRACTICES

There were quite a number of more or less important changes in the Foreign Exchange system and in Foreign Exchange practices

and techniques during the 'sixties. The following are the most
important amongst them:

1. The system of the support points mechanism came to assume
   a distinct form as a result of prolonged practical experience
   in its operation.
2. Official intervention in both spot and forward exchanges
   became more frequent and more systematic.
3. Interest arbitrage came to be based very extensively on
   interest parities between Euro-currency rates.
4. A large number of new interest parities of secondary importance came into existence as a result of the development of
   new money markets.
5. The dollar replaced sterling as a trading currency to a large
   and increasing degree.
6. Foreign Exchange transactions came to be based increasingly on the dollar cross rate instead of the sterling cross
   rate.
7. The number of banks participating in market operations has
   increased very considerably.
9. Inter-bank sterling operations came to be transacted in the
   London market.
10. The new practice of transacting business between London
    and New York after the closing of the London market made
    limited appearance.
11. The relative importance of the New York Foreign Exchange
    market increased considerably.
12. The volume of long-term operations up to five years in-
    creased.

(3) THE SUPPORT POINT MECHANISM

Although the support point mechanism was established in theory
by the rules of the International Monetary Fund, in actual
practice it had a limited application until external non-resident
convertibility came to be applied in a number of leading countries.
The most important step in that direction was taken in 1958
through the conclusion of the European Monetary Agreement. It
took a year or two before its actual rules came to emerge and
came to be extended over other members of the International
Monetary Fund.

Until 1960 all countries which adhered to the system were

supposed to be under obligation to maintain each other's exchange rates at their respective support points which could not exceed a spread of 2 per cent. Under an I.M.F. rule adopted in 1960, however, the only official support points at which Central Banks remained under obligation to intervene were those in relation to their respective currencies, and the maintenance of exchange rates between non-dollar currencies in relation to each other at within 1 per cent from their parities was left to private arbitrage.

As a result of this arrangement, the spread between support points in respect of exchange rates other than those of the dollar has doubled. This is because it became feasible that, at the same time as one currency is at its minimum support point in relation to the dollar, another currency is at its maximum support point in relation to the dollar. In such a situation, if the support point of both currencies are at the permitted limit of 1 per cent on each side of their parities they can depreciate or appreciate in terms of each other to a maximum extent of 2 per cent on either side of their parities, making a total spread of 4 per cent.

Since most Central Banks fixed the support points of their currencies at about $\frac{3}{4}$ per cent on either side of their dollar parities this meant that the spread between maximum and minimum support points was fixed at about $1\frac{1}{2}$ per cent in relation to the dollar and about 3 per cent in relation to other currencies. Even though Central Banks are under no obligation to buy or sell currencies other than the dollar in order to maintain the rates of those currencies at within $1\frac{1}{2}$ per cent from their parities, operations by private arbitrage produce the same effect. This technical point is explained in detail in my *Textbook on Foreign Exchange*.

(4) ACTIVE INTERVENTION

Although there were many instances of active official intervention in the Foreign Exchange market during the period covered by Part V of this book, such operations by Central Banks became much more frequent and much more systematic during the 'sixties. In addition to fulfilling their obligation under the rules of the International Monetary Fund to prevent an appreciation or a depreciation of the dollar in relation to their currencies beyond support points by selling or buying dollars whenever support points were reached, most Central Banks intervened very often and on a large scale long before support points were reached.

While before the 'sixties intervention by Central Banks was confined to spot exchanges, and those intervening when rates were within support points usually operated on a small scale, during the 'sixties there was a great deal of official intervention also in Forward Exchanges, and operations in both spot and forward exchanges assumed considerable dimensions. Official operations – usually through the intermediary of some leading banks – became a prominent feature in the Foreign Exchange market. In many instances whenever there was one-sided pressure operators acting for the authorities provided practically all the counterparts required to offset excess supply or excess demand. More will be said about the strategy and tactics of official intervention in Chapter 26.

Although the increased extent of intervention compared with the previous period was a matter of degree, the increase was sufficiently extensive to constitute an institutional change. From time to time official operations assumed gigantic proportions. For instance, the large-scale operations necessitated by the defence of sterling against depreciation during 1964–69, by the defence of the French *franc* in 1968–69, and by the resistance of the Bundesbank to the appreciation trend of the *D. mark* during the early 'sixties and again during the late 'sixties, changed the character of the market to a considerable extent. The presence or absence of official buying or selling and the nature and extent of official operations became a decisive factor in determining the trend of exchange rates. It influenced the attitude of actual and potential private operators to a considerable degree.

(5) EURO-CURRENCY INTEREST PARITIES

While during the 'fifties most interest arbitrage between London and New York was done on the basis of the interest parities between United Kingdom and United States Treasury bill rates, in the 'sixties interest parities between Euro-dollar and Euro-sterling rates – and also between various other Euro-currency rates – assumed first-rate importance for the purposes of arbitrage. In normal conditions arbitrage kept down discrepancies between Euro-currency rates to a minimum, allowing of course for the premium or discount on Forward Exchanges.

Under the influence of persistent one-sided pressures affecting forward margins or Euro-currency rates from time to time, marked discrepancies developed, however, owing to the lack of adequately large funds available for interest arbitrage. Moreover, the trend of forward margins to adapt themselves to Euro-currency interest differentials created discrepancies between differentials in relation to other sets of interest parities. Owing to the development of a number of new money markets, especially in London and in New York, it became possible to take advantage of the difference between the various lending and borrowing rates. As a result it was often possible to practise inward arbitrage and outward arbitrage at the same time between two currencies. Although such anomalous situations did arise also during earlier decades, owing to the increase in the number of alternative short-term investment and borrowing facilities and to the wider difference between interest rates in the same market, they occurred much more frequently in the 'sixties.

(6) DOLLAR REPLACES STERLING

While during the 'fifties and the early 'sixties sterling was holding its own reasonably well as the leading international currency, during the second half of the 'sixties its relative importance in the sphere of international trade and finance declined considerably. Owing to the frequency of sterling crises culminating in the devaluation of 1967, the dollar came to take the place of sterling as the principal unit of account and medium of financing international trade. The extent to which foreign trade came to be invoiced in the currency of one of the trading partners instead of being invoiced in sterling also increased, and so did the extent to which foreign trade of countries of the Outside Sterling Area came to be financed in dollars instead of sterling.

Since the devaluation of sterling in 1967 the dollar replaced it almost completely as the currency employed by Foreign Exchange dealers in European and other centres for the purposes of operations on the cross rate. In the past Scandinavian currencies, for instance, were quoted in the Frankfurt or Amsterdam Foreign Exchange markets in terms of sterling, because the turnover between these currencies and sterling was much larger than between them and *D. marks* or *guilders*. Owing to the decline of confidence in sterling, however, currencies came to be quoted against each other in terms of dollars. In London Foreign Exchange business between banks was still transacted in terms of sterling, but with foreign centres it was transacted by the end of the 'sixties in terms of the dollar cross rates of the currencies concerned.

(7) INCREASED NUMBER OF DEALERS

There was a considerable increase in the number of active operators, especially in London, as a result of the opening of a large number of foreign branches and subsidiaries and the creation of many international banks under the joint control of banks in different countries. Most of these institutions were opened primarily for the purpose of establishing direct access to the Euro-dollar market in London and, to a less extent, in other financial centres. But, once established, they also became active in Foreign Exchange transactions. The development of the Euro-bond market also induced many financial houses to establish branches or subsidiaries in London and other leading financial centres.

Even though only a relatively small proportion of the banks with direct access to the Foreign Exchange market were really active operators, the increase in the number of banks – which much more than offset the reduction of their numbers as a result of amalgamations – contributed towards the increase in the turnover. It also increased the demand for experienced Foreign Exchange dealers.

(8) EXPANSION OF EURO-CURRENCY MARKETS

Perhaps the most spectacular change experienced during the 'sixties was the expansion of the markets in Euro-dollars and, to a much less extent, in other Euro-currencies. Although these markets came into being towards the end of the 'fifties, turnover in them remained relatively moderate and increased only gradually during the first half of the 'sixties. Many banks were far from certain whether the new institution had come to stay, and after each temporary setback in its turnover it was widely expected to disappear. During the second half of the 'sixties, however, and especially in 1968–69, the turnover in Euro-dollars increased very considerably, largely as a result of borrowing by American branches in London. By the end of the 'sixties it came to be universally realised that this institution must be accepted as an integral part of the Foreign Exchange system and of the credit system.

The influence of Euro-currencies as a factor in the Foreign Exchange market increased considerably towards the close of the 'sixties, not only because of the increase in the volume of turnover but also as a result of the sharp increase in Euro-dollar rates and of their wide fluctuations. Even earlier, the extensive use of Euro-dollars and other Euro-currencies for the purpose of speculating in exchanges increased their importance considerably from time to time. But the increase in the amount of Euro-dollar facilities has increased the influence of Euro-dollar rates on domestic interest rates and also on exchange rates, both spot and forward. The interest rate explosion in 1969 was largely due to the sudden rise in Euro-dollar rates.

(9) INTER-BANK MARKET

Until the spectacular expansion in the turnover in Euro-dollars the sterling-dollar forward margin usually influenced Euro-dollar rates to a very considerable extent. But in the late 'sixties, as often as not it was changes in Euro-dollar rates that affected the sterling-dollar forward margins. While in earlier years some clearing banks in London kept aloof from the Euro-currency market, in the late 'sixties they all became active participants through their wholly-owned subsidiaries.

Another institutional change that occurred during the 'sixties was the creation of the inter-bank sterling market. Even though transactions in inter-bank sterling need not necessarily be connected with Foreign Exchange transactions, in most banks it is Foreign Exchange departments that operate in that market. In the case of clearing banks it is usually the affiliates which deal in Euro-currencies that operate in it.

(10) LONGER MARKET HOURS

During the late 'sixties a number of London banks adopted the practice of keeping in touch with New York banks between 4 p.m. when the London market closes until 10 p.m. (London time) when the New York market closes. This practice was initiated by London branches of American banks, the operations of which increased in importance as a result of the increase in their number, the increased international use of dollars, and the expansion in their Euro-dollar operations. These branches kept in touch with their New York head offices until New York closing time. Several large

London banks followed their example and they even came to transact business – usually from the private residence of one of their senior dealers.

Until the late 'sixties, between 4 p.m. and 10 p.m., when the London market was closed and the sterling-dollar rate departed in New York from its London closing rate, next morning the London opening rates tended to be near the previous day's London closing rates. But owing to the increased importance of New York the opening spot dollar rate in London came to be inclined to be influenced by the New York closing rate of the previous day. This was not true of forward rates to anything like the same extent.

(11) MORE LONG-TERM TRANSACTIONS

An important development was the tendency to transact more long-term Forward Exchange business. It became relatively easy to deal in maturities up to five years, at any rate in U.S. dollars. This progress was largely the result of the development of a market in long-term Euro-dollars. Although during periods of acute crises or of growing uncertainty it is still apt to become difficult to transact business in forward exchanges or in deposits beyond two years, generally speaking it became much easier than it was during the 'fifties. The possibility of transactions in inter-bank sterling for periods up to five years also helped indirectly.

Altogether the mechanism of the Foreign Exchange market continued to improve during the 'sixties. It would have improved even more if it had not been for the tightening of exchange control that occurred from time to time in most countries when their currencies became subject to heavy pressure. The frequent crises and the accompanying fluctuations of forward rates, and fears of changes in parities reversed from time to time the narrowing trend of margins between buying and selling rates. On such occasions profit margins on interest arbitrage were apt to widen once more to their pre-war range of $\frac{1}{2}$ per cent or even beyond before arbitrage transactions were undertaken to a sufficient extent to balance supply and demand.

(12) RELATIVE IMPORTANCE OF MARKETS

London retained its lead as the biggest and best Foreign Exchange market, in spite of the decline in the importance of sterling as an international currency. Indeed, its declining use as a trading currency increased the volume of buying and selling orders banks received from their non-banking clients in the United Kingdom. London remains the best market in dollars and also in a number of other exchanges, mainly because the number of big banks in the London market which are prepared to keep open positions is larger than in other markets. But for their willingness to do so, even relatively moderate buying or selling inquiry would affect the rates disproportionately, until a counterpart was attracted by the favourable rate. Needless to say, the London market would be a great deal better if it were not for the low limit imposed by exchange control on the forward exchange commitments of each bank.

Although the strength of the *D. mark* during the 'sixties increased the importance of the German Foreign Exchange markets they bear no comparison with the market in London. The fact that Foreign Exchange business in Germany is shared by three centres – Frankfurt, Hamburg and Düsseldorf – prevented Frankfurt so far from becoming a rival to London and New York. There was, however, towards the close of the 'sixties, a trend for international operations to be transacted primarily in Frankfurt. Likewise, the division of the large volume of Foreign Exchange business of Swiss banks between Zürich, Geneva and, to a much less extent, Basle continued to handicap Zürich compared with the other leading Foreign Exchange markets. The extent of this handicap tended to become reduced with the progress in communications through teleprinters.

CHAPTER TWENTY-FOUR

Crises in the 'Sixties

(1) A TROUBLED PERIOD

THERE are few spheres in which the all-too familiar quotation about happy nations having no history applies to a higher degree than it does in respect of the history of Foreign Exchange. Although during the comparatively stable period between the end of the Napoleonic Wars and the beginning of the first World War there were occasional isolated Foreign Exchange crises, decade after decade passed without any widespread general upheavals in Foreign Exchanges. Since 1914, on the other hand, every single decade witnesses crises affecting a number of important exchanges simultaneously or in close succession. From that point of view the 'thirties showed no improvement over the 'twenties, and the 'sixties showed no improvement over the 'fifties.

While it appeared to be reasonable towards the end of the 'fifties to hope that a happier if duller decade might follow, the outlook for the 'seventies appeared to be far from promising at the end of the turbulent 'sixties. Even though the British and French devaluations and the second German revaluation had gone some way towards bringing about a more realistic alignment of parities, the wave of optimism that accompanied the improvement towards the close of 1969 was mingled with a feeling of uncertainty. For the emergence of new causes for instability was well on the cards. The history of Foreign Exchange crises in the 'sixties offered no real comfort for the prospects in the 'seventies.

(2) REVALUATION OF THE *D. MARK*

Further progress during the opening years of the 'sixties towards a more complete application of the Bretton Woods system of stability was far from being free of interruptions. To begin with, there was a strong and persistent buying pressure on the *D. mark*, due to the persistently favourable trade balance of Germany. In March 1961 the German Government decided to yield to the pressure and revalued the *D. mark* by 5 per cent. The Netherlands followed Germany's example, owing to her close economic relations with Germany. The *guilder*, too, was revalued by 5 per cent. These revaluations failed, however, to produce an immediate effect.

Quite on the contrary, the flight to the *D. mark* continued unabated for some time. Because a 10 per cent revaluation had been widely expected it was assumed that a second instalment would be forthcoming in due course. This expectation continued to cause a buying pressure on the *D. mark* and a selling pressure on the dollar and on sterling, until the international political tension over Berlin in 1961 reversed the trend. The right thing happened for the wrong reason. Later the *D. mark* resumed its appreciations and it remained basically strong most of the time during the decade, even though for a time in the mid-'sixties measures adopted by the German Government reversed the trend of German foreign trade.

(3) DOLLAR SCARES

Already in the closing years of the 'fifties the dollar was no longer as incontestably above suspicion as it had been almost all the time since 1914, apart from some temporary interruptions in the 'thirties. Most of the time during the 'sixties the *D. mark*, the Swiss *franc* and the French *franc* were at a premium against the dollar, and part of the time they were at their maximum support points in relation to the dollar. This was due in part to the inherent strength of the three currencies, but to a very large extent it was also the result of the persistently adverse balance of payments of the United States and of the resulting decline in the American gold reserve. The perennial deficit was largely due to heavy Government spending abroad and to excessive long-term capital exports.

Occasionally specific adverse factors aggravated the underlying weak trend. Thus in 1962 the dollar came under the influence of the crisis over Cuba, as a result of which the market price of gold rose on one occasion to $40. From time to time the adverse pressure on the dollar became stronger because of outward interest arbitrage on a large scale, for it was profitable to transfer

funds from New York to other financial centres. As we shall see
in Chapter 26, intervention by the United States monetary
authorities in co-operation with those of the receiving countries
sought to reduce such pressure successfully.

(4) STERLING'S DIFFICULTIES

Although Britain was by no means free of financial difficulties
during the early 'sixties, for some years the sterling situation was
kept well under control. No major sterling crises comparable with
that of 1957 developed again until 1964, even though the balance
of payments position had its ups and downs, and Britain, like the
United States, was lending and spending abroad beyond her
resources. But basically sterling was weak, owing to the abnormally
large size of foreign sterling balances which carried the possibility
of major crises whenever a wave of distrust developed.

A source of strength for sterling was the continued existence of
the Sterling Area and the willingness of non-sterling countries
with an export surplus on their trade with Britain and with the
Sterling Area to retain the surplus in the form of increased sterling
balances. So long as Conservative Governments held office, overseas holders of sterling readily assumed that in the event of new
difficulties the authorities would not hesitate to resort to effective
if painful measures to restore the balance, as they did in 1957 and
on other occasions. This explains why sterling remained relatively
steady during the greater part of 1964, in spite of the growing
adverse balance of payments. Not until the eve of the general election did the anticipation of a Labour victory cause sterling to weaken.

(5) CRISIS AND RECOVERY OF THE *LIRA*

Although the stability of the *lira* during the early 'sixties depended
largely on heavy Euro-dollar borrowing by Italian banks, the
Italian Government felt justified in 1962 to restore full convertibility for non-residents. In the following year reduction of Euro-
dollar borrowing by Italian banks resulted in heavy pressure on
the *lira*, because it coincided with a strongly adverse change in the
trade balance, largely as a result of the liberalisation of trade
within the Common Market. External assistance combined with
drastic domestic measures brought the crisis to an end in a remarkably short time.

During the second half of the 'sixties the *lira* was assisted by a perennial export surplus which more than offset the effects of the persistent flight of Italian capital caused mainly by political uncertainty and social unrest. Indeed the *lira* came to be regarded by 1968–9 as one of the strongest currencies, and there was even a certain amount of speculation about the possibility of its revaluation following on that of the *D. mark*. Towards the close of 1969, however, it came under a cloud owing to the aggravation of Italy's political and social troubles.

(6) CRISES OF STERLING

Following on the change of Government in Britain as a result of the Socialist victory in 1964, sterling remained relatively steady for a few weeks, in the hope that the new Government would adopt the necessary measures to deal with the large trade deficit. When it was found, however, that costly Socialist measures were given priority over the defence of sterling a sweeping selling pressure developed in November 1964. The authorities sought to resist it partly by high Bank rate and other domestic measures, but largely with the aid of large external credits obtained from the International Monetary Fund and from a group of leading Central Banks. In addition, the device of a systematic unlimited official support of forward sterling came to be adopted. As a result of this support, the discount on forward sterling was kept artificially low and pressure from spot sterling came to be diverted by such means.

The favourable effect of these measures proved to be short-lived. It was reinforced by a series of additional measures in April 1965. Among others, external investments of United Kingdom residents were sought to be reduced by compelling holders of investment dollars to sell 25 per cent of their holdings as ordinary dollars whenever they sold their investment dollars. This measure resulted in a sharp and persistent increase in the premium on investment dollars culminating in 1969 when it reached at one time in 1969 nearly 60 per cent.

Between 1964 and 1967 there were frequent acute attacks on sterling, two or three each year. These attacks were sought to be met by various measures of credit squeeze and by efforts to restrain the increase of wages and of other incomes. But on each occasion when sterling's position became precarious it was only saved by external assistance which was always forthcoming in generous measure. It was mainly the announcement of another and yet another billion-dollar credit that reversed the adverse trend of sterling. On each occasion such improvements were followed by a premature relaxation of the inadequate measures that had been adopted in sterling's defence while it was under pressure, and thereupon sterling came once more under suspicion.

(7) THE DEVALUATION OF 1967

In 1966 the enforcement of a strict wage freeze appeared to have produced a favourable effect, but its premature relaxation and termination was followed by a fresh wave of wage demands, many of them with retrospective effect. The war in the Middle East in June 1967 damaged sterling considerably, especially through the effect of the blocking of the Suez Canal on the balance of payments. But in spite of this, the moment the acute crisis appeared to have abated the Government felt justified in relaxing hire-purchase restrictions in August. The result was renewed adverse pressure. When in November the Chancellor of the Exchequer, Mr. Callaghan, pointedly abstained from repeating his oft-reasserted pledge not to devalue, speculation against sterling came to assume gigantic proportions. On November 17 the Government announced the devaluation of sterling by about 14 per cent from $2.80 to $2.40.

For a short time sterling kept firm at its new parity. But when it was found that no adequate measures were intended to be taken to increase its basic strength speculative pressure was resumed. The failure of the devaluation to improve the balance of payments in 1968 – largely as a result of the spending spree triggered off by the premature announcement by the new Chancellor of the Exchequer, Mr. Jenkins, of his intention to increase taxation and by evidence of the non-stop increase in public spending – gave rise to a fresh wave of pessimism.

(8) THE GOLD RUSH

Meanwhile Foreign Exchange difficulties were further compli-cated by the speculative 'gold rush' in anticipation of an increase in the official American price of gold. Although the devaluation of sterling was not followed by a major realignment of parities comparable with that of 1949 – this time only Denmark, Spain, Israel and the remaining British Colonies followed the British lead – it created a state of demoralisation amidst which even the possibility of a devaluation of the dollar came to be widely envisaged. Since the Central Banks' 'gold pool' supplied hoarders and speculators with unlimited quantities of gold by supporting the market price in the vicinity of the official American price, there was a strong wave of buying. It became increasingly obvious that the United States Government could not afford much longer to allow its gold reserve to decline at the prevailing rate. Sterling too was subject to strong selling pressure, and since the British authorities no longer supported the forward rate – having lost hundreds of millions on their supporting operations of 1964–7 – the forward discount rose to 10 per cent in March 1968.

In such circumstances it was decided in March to suspend the operation of the Central Banks' 'gold pool' and the unofficial price of gold was allowed to find its own level in the free market. The drain on the American gold reserve was halted and this relieved the pressure on the dollar. Moreover, during 1968 the United States appeared as a borrower in Europe on an increasing scale, both in the form of borrowing Euro-dollar deposits and through the issue of Euro-bonds on a large scale.

(9) THE *FRANC* CRISIS

Within two months from the solution of the gold crisis another major Foreign Exchange crisis developed. This time it was the French *franc* that became suddenly and unexpectedly the subject of heavy speculative pressure. Ever since the advent of General de Gaulle in 1968 and the devaluation of the *franc*, France had had a persistent export surplus. In addition, the solution of the crisis over Algerian independence was followed by large-scale repatriations of French capital that had sought refuge abroad. As a result the French *franc* became very firm not only in relation to the dollar but from time to time even in relation to the *D. mark*. The French gold reserve increased, especially as the Bank of France converted its dollar holdings into gold.

The grave disorders in France during May and June 1968 changed the *franc*, however, from being the strongest currency to being the weakest currency. In addition to the actual damage caused to the French economy by major strikes and riots, it came to be assumed that France would be forced henceforth to concede costly wage demands. The French balance of payments turned strongly adverse and French capital fled the country once more on a large scale. The gold reserve declined at an alarming rate in spite of the external credits obtained in support of the *franc*. The selling pressure increased when General de Gaulle relinquished his office, on the assumption that his successor would not feel bound by his pledge not to devalue. In fact, after some delay, M. Pompidou decided to devalue the *franc* by about 11 per cent in August 1969.

(10) FLIGHT INTO *D. MARKS*

Throughout the late 'sixties, the *D. mark* was very firm most of the time, not only as a result of the perennial export surplus but also because it was widely assumed that sooner or later it would be revalued once more. Foreign capital was flowing into Germany in large amounts in spite of all the measures adopted by the German Government to defend the country against imported inflation. Although since 1961 no interest was allowed on foreign deposits and non-residents were not permitted to acquire German short-term securities, it was possible nevertheless to earn interest on *D. mark* deposits in the Euro-*D. mark* market, and to invest capital in *D. mark* Euro-bonds which came to be issued in very large amounts from 1968. At a meeting of leading Central Banks at Bonn in November 1968 the German authorities refused to yield to political pressure to revalue the *D. mark*. Instead an export duty and import bonus scheme was adopted.

That measure failed to reduce the German export surplus, and after a brief interval the flight into *D. marks* was resumed on a large and increasing scale. This movement became accentuated in September 1969 in anticipation of the victory of the Social Democrats, which Party was expected to revalue the *D. mark*. On the eve of the election the Government suspended official purchases of dollars and the *D. mark* was allowed to appreciate. The extent of its appreciation remained relatively moderate, however, during the 'interregnum' of four weeks between the outgoing and incoming Governments, even though the Bundesbank was actually selling dollars to step up the movement. When the new régime assumed office it took the earliest opportunity to re-stabilise the floating *D. mark*, and revalued it by 8½ per cent.

(11) HEAVY AMERICAN EURO-DOLLAR BORROWING

Even though the dollar was firmer during most of the time in 1969 than it had been for some years, this was entirely the result of heavy American borrowing abroad and later of transfers of money into dollars after the revaluation of the *D. mark*. The American trade balance was deteriorating owing to the sharp rise in American wages and prices.

Repeated reference was made above to the increased activities in the Euro-dollar market during the 'sixties, and in particular during the concluding years of the decade. The expansion of the market in 1968–69 was largely the result of increased American borrowing in London and in other Euro-dollar markets. Owing to the efforts of the United States authorities to resist inflation, scarcity of credit developed and the American banks sought to increase their resources by borrowing Euro-dollars on a gigantic scale. The resulting increase in Euro-dollar rates attracted additional billions of dollar deposits into the market at the same time as stepping up the rising international trend of interest rates.

Even though the revaluation of the *D. mark* resulted in a setback in Euro-dollar rates, American borrowing was resumed because the Federal Reserve authorities indicated their intention to apply Regulation Q to commercial paper issued by banks, and because of end-of-year window-dressing purposes. There was a fresh increase in Euro-dollar rates and other interest rates which only became reversed at the end of 1969. The growing deficit of the trade balance and the over-valuation of the dollar came to be viewed with much concern. So, even though the 'sixties concluded in a more cheerful atmosphere, uncertainty about long-range prospects of the exchange continued to prevail.

(12) FIRMNESS OF THE *YEN*

Following on the revaluation of the *D. mark* the attention of the market came to be focused on the *yen*. Although it had its ups and downs during the first half of the decade, in the late 'sixties it became very firm as a result of Japan's large and increasing export surplus. Japan was able to afford to repay much of its short-term debts thanks to this surplus, and also with the aid of large amounts borrowed in the Euro-bond market. Although the continued

318

THE 'SIXTIES

maintenance of various trade and exchange restrictions in Japan inspired some doubts, the fact that Japanese workers in general did not catch the 'English disease' and were considered to be the least likely among industrial nations to catch it inspired confidence in the *yen*.

Among other currencies, the *rupee* was devalued by 36 per cent in 1967 and was maintained with difficulty even at that devalued level. Brazil, the Argentine and other Latin-American currencies were repeatedly devalued, especially the Brazilian *cruzeiro*. In Europe, the Dutch *guilder* and the Austrian *schilling* as well as the Norwegian and Swedish currencies were reasonably strong.

In the 'fifties the Canadian Government abandoned the system of fixed parities, allowing the dollar to float. But in 1962 it followed the example of the French and Italian Governments and re-stabilised the dollar. So during the greater part of the 'sixties all important currencies conformed to the Bretton Woods system, if we disregard the very brief period in 1969 during which the *D. mark* was allowed to float.

(13) END OF A BAD DECADE

The main reason why the 'sixties closed in a more hopeful mood was the apparent improvement of sterling towards the end of 1969. During the last quarter of the year it benefited by an improvement in the balance of payments, by the International Monetary Fund's decision to allocate Special Drawing Rights in the near future, and especially by the revaluation of the *D. mark*. At the end of December it rose to parity in relation to the dollar, and Mr Jenkins felt justified in greatly increasing Foreign Exchange allowances to United Kingdom residents travelling abroad. The outlook for sterling appeared to be favourable, but only in the short run. The increased frequency and extent of wage demands and a further weakening of resistance to them by employers and by the Government augured badly for the more distant future. However, the return of money from abroad and the closing of short positions in sterling enabled the Government to benefit by the wave of optimism.

The French *franc*, too, appeared to conclude the decade with a more favourable tendency than expected. The devaluation and the accompanying defensive measures together with the revaluation of the *D. mark* and the Brussels Agreement of the E.E.C. which was calculated to benefit France considerably all helped towards bringing about the improvement. But the long view about the prospects for the *franc* was no more favourable than the long view about the prospects of sterling.

CHAPTER TWENTY-FIVE

Contemporary Foreign Exchange Theory

(1) LIMITED PROGRESS

THE 'sixties produced no major new Foreign Exchange theories that would be comparable in importance with the achievements in this field during the inter-war period described in Chapter 21. Such progress as was made during the 'forties and the 'fifties also continued during the 'sixties. But there were no achievements that could be classed with Cassel's purchasing power parity theory, or with Keynes's Forward Exchange theory, or with Mrs Joan Robinson's theory of elasticities. All these theories, as indeed the original balance of payments theory and its successive improved versions, or the theory of interest rate differentials, had been based on the study of the Foreign Exchange system as it had operated over long periods.

Even though not much new ground was broken since the war, it is to the credit of the present generation of economists to have improved theories inherited from their forerunners. During the 'sixties some of these theories benefited by additional refinements resulting from more penetrating analyses and from lessons taught by additional experience. Contemporary theoretical specialists in Foreign Exchange deserve credit for having improved earlier theories that had been devised by more original minds, especially by toning down some of the one-sided exaggerations of which pioneers in Foreign Exchange theory had been guilty.

(2) THEORIES OF POLICY

A very high proportion of theoretical writings on Foreign Exchange during the 'sixties was concerned with theories of policy. Instead of aiming at translating practical realities into academic language, they enunciated theoretical principles in support of preconceived aims of Foreign Exchange policies. Foreign Exchange theories were put forward in order to create theoretical justification for policy proposals. Foremost among such proposals were those advocating the creation of fictitious international liquid reserves on an extensive scale; the adoption of floating exchange rates; the support of weak currencies by unlimited official operations in Forward Exchanges; and a substantial increase in the price of gold.

The subordination of Foreign Exchange theory to the advocacy of Foreign Exchange policy proposals was not the only respect in which theories emerging during the 'sixties were far removed from a study of actual practice. In the past theory progressed hand in hand with practice in the literature of Foreign Exchange. Gresham was the leading Foreign Exchange operator of his time. Goschen was a merchant-banker when he was writing his classic, *The Theory of the Foreign Exchanges*. Keynes gained some practical experience in a Foreign Exchange department before he elaborated his Forward Exchange theory. Cassel was for many years economic adviser to a leading Swedish Bank. What they contributed to theory was therefore largely in accordance with their actual experience or with their contact with Foreign Exchange dealers who had first-hand experience. Their task consisted largely of formulating into rigorous rules what Foreign Exchange dealers were practising day after day almost instinctively but were not sufficiently articulate to express in such rules. The aim of these pioneers in Foreign Exchange theory was not to crusade for some radical reform scheme – even though Keynes in particular did endeavour to persuade the monetary authorities to make better use of the existing Forward Exchange system and to abstain from obstructing its natural development – but to investigate the broader aspects of existing practices.

On the other hand, as already observed, since the war and in particular during the 'sixties Foreign Exchange theory was put increasingly in the service of crusades for various policy proposals. Most economists participating in such crusades were concerned with the system, not as it existed, but as, in their opinion, it ought to exist. Even though Milton Friedman included his essay advocating floating exchange rates in a volume entitled *Essays in Positive Economics*, that title was a misnomer as far as this particular essay was concerned. Positive economics is supposed to describe and analyse the laws of economics as they actually operate in practice and not as economists would like them to operate. In that sense a high proportion of the contributions to Foreign Exchange theory during the 'sixties was likewise outside the realm of positive economics.

(3) OBSCURANTIST PRESENTATION

This was one of the reasons why Foreign Exchange theory parted company with Foreign Exchange practice already before the 'sixties. The gap between them widened considerably during the 'sixties. Another reason for this was the increasingly obscurantist presentation of Foreign Exchange theory, in accordance with the general trend of methodology in theoretical economics. Most inter-war contributions by academic economists to Foreign Exchange theory had been perfectly understandable to any Foreign Exchange dealer or to any intelligent banker, Treasury official or business man concerned with Foreign Exchange. In more recent times, however, economists have invented a language of their own which would be largely unintelligible to those outside their own select circle even if it had not been made deliberately more unintelligible by the increasingly mathematical treatment of the subject.

It almost seemed as if theoretical economists specialising in Foreign Exchange had gone out of their way to segregate Foreign Exchange theory from Foreign Exchange practice. Their attitude may best be compared with that of the social and intellectual Upper Ten during the Middle Ages, and even during more recent times, in seeking to discourage those unfamiliar with Latin and Greek from making contributions towards the progress of learning. Most contributions to the literature on Foreign Exchange theory during the 'sixties applied a similar method of intellectual apartheid. They had little or no bearing on practical realities but were mainly intellectual parlour-games played between mathematical economists for each other's benefit. Men with practical experience in Foreign Exchange were thus deterred from trying to contribute their share to the progress of theory. They were no longer in a position to correct mistakes that are inevitable when anyone without practical experience writes on a highly technical and ever-changing subject such as Foreign Exchange. No contribution to Foreign Exchange theory expressed in terms of mathematical economics has added anything of substance to the subject that could not have been added to it without the use of mathematics.

(4) PROGRESS THROUGH CONTROVERSY

But it would be both incorrect and unfair to those who raised and pursued various controversial issues of Foreign Exchange policy during the 'sixties to deny that, as a by-product of these controversies, Foreign Exchange theory achieved some progress. In the course of their arguments for and against various policy proposals all parties to the controversies were doing their utmost to present the strongest possible case. Under the influence of that incentive they subjected all relevant aspects of Foreign Exchange theory and practice to a most penetrating analysis. Throughout the history of Foreign Exchange theory it was usually on occasions of heated controversies that the Foreign Exchange system came to be re-examined with special care, and as a result some of its hitherto overlooked aspects came to be discovered.

Thus the balance of payments theory, the purchasing power parity theory, the theory of elasticities and the interest parities theory of Forward Exchanges came to be reconsidered recently by antagonists searching for additional arguments in support of their respective cases. As a result of their exertions these theories emerged in improved versions from the 'sixties. Economists interested in Foreign Exchange were able to study with benefit the effects of devaluations (and of revaluations) on the balance of payments; the operation of currency areas; the meaning of equilibrium and of fundamental disequilibrium; and other subjects which were not dealt with adequately in the past. The use of reserve currencies and the rôle of international financial centres in the sphere of Foreign Exchange came under critical scrutiny. The multiplier effects of export surpluses and import surpluses, the terms of trade, the implications of full employment in the sphere of Foreign Exchange theory were among the subjects which came to be examined much more closely than before.

(5) FALLACY OF EQUILIBRIUM LEVEL

On the debit side of the balance sheet of Foreign Exchange theory in the 'sixties there are some fallacies which have come to be accepted as axiomatic as a result of the combined weight of the authority of many leading economists who put them forward or endorsed them for the sake of making out a stronger case in favour of floating exchanges or of some other policy proposals. Foremost amongst them is the existence of a mythical equilibrium level of exchange rates at which imports and exports should automatically balance and surpluses or deficits should disappear, thanks to the absence of any official interference with natural trends of exchange rates. The whole agitation in favour of floating exchanges rests on that utterly fallacious assumption. Such is the quasi-hypnotic effect of its frequent repetition by voices commanding respect that even opponents of floating exchanges have come to accept the myth of an equilibrium level as axiomatic.

This is not the place for a detailed discussion of this subject, which is reserved for my book *The Case Against Floating Exchanges*. The short answer, which appears to have been overlooked by most supporters and opponents of floating exchanges during the 'sixties is this: there might be some excuse for a mistaken belief that freely floating exchanges would adapt themselves to their trade equilibrium level if activity in the Foreign Exchange market were confined to transactions originating exclusively from imports and exports. Even in such a hypothetical situation the validity of the theory would be subject to important reservations, owing to time lags between changes in exchange rates and their effects on imports and exports, and owing to leads and lags in the payments for imports and exports. But Foreign Exchange operations arise not only from foreign trade but also from capital transfers, speculation and arbitrage, so that it could only be by sheer coincidence bordering on miracle if total supply and demand in the market ever happened to balance at the same rate which would ensure equilibrium between imports and exports. Literature on Foreign Exchange theory in the 'sixties overlooked almost completely the glaringly obvious fact that aggregate supply and demand in the Foreign Exchange market is capable of achieving equilibrium through the combined effect of capital transactions, speculation and arbitrage even during periods when there is a large import surplus or a large export surplus.

(6) EXPERIENCE IN FORWARD EXCHANGE SUPPORT

There was very little practical experience in floating exchanges during the 'sixties. We saw in the last chapter that the Canadian experiment in floating dollars – into which every economist reads what he chooses to read – came to an end in 1962. The four weeks of floating period of the *D. mark* in 1969 was of too short duration and its circumstances were too special to justify inferring any definite conclusion from it. In any case official intervention came to be applied in order to push the floating *D. mark* towards its equilibrium level which, according to the advocates of floating exchanges, it was supposed to reach automatically.

On the other hand, there was ample experience in unlimited official support of Forward Exchanges, a policy which was first advocated during the 'fifties without the advantage of being able to consider it on the basis of its prolonged practical application. The crusade in its favour continued with increasing vigour in the 'sixties. As from November 1964 it came to be applied extensively in Britain. The case for and against it was re-examined on the basis of the British experience in trying to maintain the parity of sterling by means of unlimited official selling of forward dollars.

The controversy ended abruptly when in November 1967 sterling was devalued in spite of three years of systematic support of forward sterling – indeed, I am convinced, largely because of it. This subject will be discussed in greater detail in the next chapter. From the point of view of Foreign Exchange theory, let it be sufficient here to point out that since the devaluation of sterling very little has been written in an attempt to explain away the disastrous results of theories which had lent to an irresponsible policy the appearance of respectability. On the credit side of the controversy, we must admit that, as was the case with theoretical discussions around the question of floating exchanges, the searching examination of Forward Exchange theory by advocates and opponents of that policy yielded much benefit. The right thing happened for the wrong reasons. Even so, the total value of all contributions to Forward Exchange theory in the 'sixties – indeed of all post-Keynesian contributions, including, of course, my own – is a bare fraction of Keynes's contribution.

(7) MORE LIQUID RESERVES?

The debates around the various proposals for increasing the volume of international liquid reserves, culminating in the agreement on the creation of Special Drawing Rights, did not directly contribute to Foreign Exchange theory. This was because it was taken for granted all but universally that the volume of international reserves was inadequate and that its artificial increase would be a Good Thing. The contestants during the 'sixties missed the opportunity of a thorough-going investigation of the difference between the nature and extent of reasonable requirements in normal conditions and in abnormal conditions. An impartial investigation might have led to the conclusion that an excessive increase of reserves for normal use – such as had occurred spontaneously as a result of the expansion of the Euro-currency market – tends to accentuate the inadequacy of the reserves for meeting abnormal requirements.

The question of the maldistribution of liquid reserves, about which so much was said during the 'twenties, was barely touched upon, even though it was obvious that agitation for more international credits was always the *cri de cœur* of countries whose currencies came under chronic adverse pressure. The effect of the gradual increase in I.M.F. drawing rights and other credit facilities on exchange rates will be dealt with in the next chapter.

(8) THE PRICE OF GOLD

The basic problem of an all-round increase in the price of gold – that is, a devaluation of the dollar and an adjustment of most other gold parities to its new parity – was very much in the forefront until the adoption of the two-tier system of gold prices in 1968, after which the threat of the dollar crisis that would lead to its devaluation ceased to be acute. The relapse of the free market price of gold at the end of 1969 brought this controversy temporarily to an end. On the other hand, the theoretical controversy on the question whether it is the value of the dollar which is supposed to determine the value of gold or vice-versa was given new lease of life.

At the time when the free market price of gold was rising to well above $40 it was suggested that this amounted to a *de facto* depreciation of the dollar and that sooner or later its parity would have to be adapted to the market price. On the other hand, the majority view was all along that for all practical purposes the world was on the dollar standard, so that the market price of gold was no more relevant from the point of view of the value of the dollar than the price of any other metal or indeed of other goods. This view appears to have been vindicated when in December 1969 the market price of gold declined to the level of its official American price. But the last word has not been said on this subject.

(9) LEADS AND LAGS

Adequate realisation of the relative importance of leads and lags

CONTEMPORARY FOREIGN EXCHANGE THEORY 327

among the factors influencing exchange rates was an important
achievement of Foreign Exchange theory during the 'sixties.
Although economists and practical experts had been familiar
with the influence of the timing of payments for imports and
exports, or the covering of these payments, on exchange trends,
it was not until the 'sixties that the full significance of this factor
came to be appreciated. Economists are now aware that changes
in the average length of leads and lags, resulting from changes in
the view taken by business firms of the prospects of their currencies
or those of their trading partners abroad, are capable of distorting
completely the effect of the trade balance on exchanges. They are
also aware that amidst prevailing conditions speculation in the
form of lengthening or shortening leads and lags – if it can be
called speculation – is much more important than pure speculation in the form of going long or short in foreign currencies by
those who have no legitimate commercial or investment interests
to protect.

It came to be realised that a change of one week in the average
leads and lags meant, in the case of Britain in the late 'sixties, a
difference of p.a. £240 million in the size of the gold and dollar
reserve. Attention is now paid to the length of trade credits
granted by exporters and those obtained by importers, and the
Board of Trade initiated an elaborate statistical service to cover
this aspect of leads and lags. But the most important form of
leading and lagging, through the timing of Forward Exchange
operations by importers and exporters, cannot be ascertained
statistically or even estimated reliably. Attention was drawn to
institutional changes affecting leads and lags, such as the change
in the currency in which foreign trade is invoiced or financed, or
the increase in the proportion of trade in capital goods and the
competition of industrial rivals in the form of offering longer
credits.

(10) BALANCE OF PAYMENTS STATISTICS

Another sphere in which some progress was made during the
'sixties was the improvement of balance of payments statistics. In
the past economists had to base their arguments on utterly undependable and often grossly inaccurate official figures concerning
imports and exports. Much progress had already been made
during the 'fifties to place balance of payments statistics in various
countries on a more uniform basis. But there were many instances

of mistaken conclusions arrived at on the basis of misleading figures. Some of these miscalculations came to be corrected in recent years and the controversies about the methods of calculations yielded some progress. What is even more important, efforts to express elusive invisible imports and exports in figures yielded appreciable results.

On the other hand, trade statistics came increasingly under the influence of the dogmatic belief in seasonal adjustment of trade figures. This method often produced misleading conclusions. The fashion of seasonally adjusting all statistics went so far that the British Treasury even produced seasonally adjusted figures of long-term capital transactions, even though the extent to which long-term borrowing, lending, investment and disinvestment across the borders follow a seasonal pattern is quite negligible. Another retrograde change was the increasing popularity of the habit of making cocksure forecasts of future balance of payments. This was done not only by politicians but even by economic research organisations and individual economists of high reputation. Yet the policies of various Governments that influence the balance of payments, and the response of those policies by importers, exporters, producers and consumers of goods traded internationally are entirely incalculable. The frequency and the extent to which such forecasts proved to be mistaken again and again failed to discourage this habit, even though it tended to bring discredit to economics and to economists.

(11) THE EURO-CURRENCY SYSTEM

Although the development of the Euro-dollar market and of other Euro-currency markets began in the 'fifties, it was not until the 'sixties that this institutional change came to assume crucial importance in the Foreign Exchange system. In this respect, as in several other respects, Foreign Exchange theory was lagging for a long time far behind Foreign Exchange practice. But during the second half of the decade an increasing number of theoretical economists came to realise the broader implications of the Euro-dollar market. It was subjected to theoretical analysis from the point of view of its impact on spot and forward exchanges, on interest rates and on economic trends in general.

But it was not until the spectacular increase in the volume of Euro-dollars through heavy American borrowing during 1968–9, and the resulting sharp increase in interest rates all over the world, that the full practical and theoretical importance of the Euro-dollar system came to be appreciated. At the time of writing this latest development was still too recent to give economists a chance to arrive at definite conclusions about its theoretical implications. Likewise, the expansion of the Euro-bond market was too recent to allow for the integration of its impact on Foreign Exchange into a comprehensive Foreign Exchange theory.

CHAPTER TWENTY-SIX

Contemporary Foreign Exchange Policy

(1) SOME RECENT CHANGES

THERE were some very important developments in the sphere of Foreign Exchange policy during the 'sixties. Although basically its aim remained the same – the maintenance of existing parities as long as possible even in face of strong and persistent pressures resulting from fundamental disequilibrium – the means by which that end was sought to be attained changed quite extensively. Some of the most important devices came to be applied in several countries to a much less extent, while other devices of Foreign Exchange strategy and tactics appeared on the scene and gained prominence.

The most recent changes in foreign exchange policy may be summarised under the following headings:

1. The extent of the application of 'stop-go' in defence of gold reserves and parities was considerably reduced in some leading countries.
2. It came to assume increasingly the form of reinforced control on the quantity of money towards the end of the 'sixties.
3. The use of high interest rates was resorted to more extensively, though less effectively, from the middle 'sixties.
4. In some countries the defence of parities assumed largely the form of incomes policies.
5. The trend towards liberalisation of exchanges continued for some time, but it became reversed during the late 'sixties.
6. The extent of official intervention in the Foreign Exchange market increased considerably.
7. Monetary authorities came to avail themselves of foreign assistance more systematically and on a much larger scale than ever before.
8. The extent to which intervention assumed the form of official operations in Forward Exchanges increased until the devaluation of sterling in 1967.
9. Co-operation between Central Banks, either directly or

through the intermediary of the I.M.F. and the B.I.S. increased considerably.

10. On the other hand, in more than one instance Foreign Exchange policies were pursued as a form of financial warfare.

11. The monetary authorities came to intervene in the Euro-currency markets.

(2) UNPOPULARITY OF 'STOP-GO'

During the earlier post-war period the stability of exchanges was defended mainly with the aid of monetary, fiscal and economic policy measures aimed at restraining expansion whenever it threatened to cause fundamental disequilibrium. A depreciating trend of the national exchange rate and the resulting loss of reserves induced the Governments concerned to adopt such defensive measures. The disinflationary effect of their adoption resulted in an improvement in the balance of payments and a return of confidence in the exchange. It then became possible to relax the restrictive measures to stimulate actively a re-expansion of the economy. This counter-cyclical policy came to be nicknamed the 'stop-go' policy.

That policy became increasingly unpopular, especially in Britain, during the 'sixties. The Labour Party, while in opposition, denounced it in no uncertain terms, but when it assumed office in 1964 the Government felt impelled to apply it, albeit to a distinctly inadequate extent. Between the change of Government in October 1964 and the devaluation of sterling three years later Britain pursued what could be called a 'mini-stop-go' policy. The Labour Government abstained most of the time from resorting to really effective disinflationary measures, and it hastened to relax such measures as it did apply as soon as acute pressure on sterling abated, even though the improvement was mainly the result of confidence created by foreign assistance rather than that of any genuine progress towards a more balanced economy. In consequence, 'stop' had to be applied much more frequently – once or twice a year instead of every other year or once in three years, as during the 'forties and the 'fifties.

(3) NON-STOP EXPANSION IN THE U.S.

The United States, too, relaxed its 'stop-go' policy towards the middle of the 'sixties, for the sake of the supreme end of maintaining

M

a non-stop business boom. Because the country did not experience any slump or prolonged depression since the war, American opinion came to assume that this state of affairs could and should be maintained forever by abstaining from applying the brake from time to time for the sake of consolidating progress. Quite on the contrary, there was actually a drastic cut in taxation in 1965 when discerning observers could not fail to realise that the economy was becoming distinctly overheated. The Johnson Administration reflated in spite of the perennial balance of payments deficit which reduced the gold reserve and increased foreign dollar holdings. But until the late 'sixties the United States could afford to lose gold, and in any case the attention of international speculation was focused mainly on sterling. Basically confidence in dollars was maintained and foreign central Banks allowed themselves to be persuaded to maintain and increase their dollar holdings.

France followed 'stop-go' faithfully until 1968, and the *franc* became consequently one of the strongest currencies. After the troubles in 1968 that policy which was be applied to an inadequate degree and the *franc* became the subject of persistent adverse pressure until its devaluation which was followed by 'stop' measures. On the other hand, Germany, Italy and Japan firmly adhered to 'stop-go' throughout the late 'sixties and prevented their economies from getting out of equilibrium. Consequently the *D. mark*, the *lira* and the *yen* remained basically strong. So were the Swiss *franc*, the *guilder* and currencies of other countries which pursued economic policies to prevent their economies from becoming overheated, and thereby they prevented their exchanges from becoming overvalued. Indeed they became undervalued as a result of the abandonment of 'stop-go' by Britain and the United States.

(4) HIGH INTEREST RATES BECOME INEFFECTIVE

In the past weak exchanges were usually supported by means of raising the Bank rate. In any case, even in the absence of deliberate action to that end, the weakness of an exchange tended to push up interest rates. This usually tended to correct the situation through deflating an overexpanding economy, in addition to its direct effect on the international movements of funds in a sense favourable to the exchange of the country applying the policy of dear money. To some extent that policy was effective even during the 'fifties and early 'sixties and it remained effective in some countries right until about 1968. It ceased to act as an effective brake on the domestic economy because of the growing realisation that the rising trend of prices drastically reduced the real burden of high interest rates. Its direct effect on exchanges was cancelled out by leap-frogging increase in interest rates in various countries, partly by means of competitive Bank rate increases and partly owing to the effect of rising Euro-dollar rates.

In Britain even a 7 per cent Bank rate and its subsequent increase to 8 per cent failed to reduce the excessive consumer demand that was the cause of the perennial adverse balance of payments and of the frequent sterling crises. Most borrowers could afford to pay the high charges on their overdrafts or loans, thanks to the persistent consumer demand that enabled producers and merchants to pass on to the consumer the burden of the high interest charges, together with the increases of their other costs. As far as the effect of high interest rates on international capital movements was concerned, competitive Bank rate increases and the effect of the increasing trend of Euro-currency rates on domestic interest rates deprived each country of such initial advantage as it might have derived from its attempt to attract foreign funds or prevent their outflow by means of a high Bank rate. The policy decided upon at a meeting of Finance Ministers early in 1967 to check and reverse leap-frogging Bank rate increases produced a very short-lived effect.

(5) ATTEMPTS TO RESIST WAGE INFLATION

In some countries – especially in Holland and in the Scandinavian States – attempts were made in the 'fifties to defend the stability of the exchange by means of restraining wage inflation. In Britain incomes policy came to be adopted for the purpose of resisting the pressure on sterling in the middle 'sixties. Instead of trying to keep down wages by conventional deflationary measures – or, to be quite correct, in addition to the grossly inadequate deflationary measures and other restrictionist measures adopted to that end – the Government made efforts to halt or slow down wage increases. At the same time it also attempted to keep down prices and dividends. At first this device assumed the form of exhortation and moral pressure, largely through the Prices and Incomes Board.

In 1966 legislation was adopted to secure a statutory wage-freeze for a limited period. From time to time these measures produced some results, at any rate during periods when the freeze was accompanied by measures of squeeze which tended to cause unemployment and reduced the bargaining power of the trade unions.

Evidence of such results produced a favourable effect on confidence in sterling. But on each occasion when the Government felt justified in relaxing the freeze and the squeeze unearned wage increases were resumed. In July 1967 when the wage restraint was relaxed there was a spate of excessive wage demands. This was one of the main causes of the wave of distrust which brought about the devaluation of sterling in November. Thereafter the accentuation of price increases was accompanied by wage increases well in excess of the maximum limits the Government sought to maintain. An attempt to reintroduce statutory wage restraint in 1969 encountered strong resistance and was abandoned for political considerations. Thereupon sterling came once more under pressure. It was only saved from another major crisis by the devaluation of the French *franc* and by the revaluation of the *D. mark*, but for which the improvement in the balance of payments might have been too late to save sterling from yet another devaluation in the autumn.

(6) LIBERALISATION REVERSED

During the early part of the decade the liberalisation of exchanges made good progress. In addition to the United States and Switzerland, which had been free of exchange restrictions, Germany also abandoned exchange control. Broadly speaking all advanced industrial countries of the free world restored for non-residents complete freedom for payments arising from current transactions and later also for capital transactions. Residents enjoyed a high and increasing degree of freedom for current transactions, but they remained subject to controls of a varying and changing extent for capital transactions. The basic trend appeared to be distinctly towards liberalisation.

This trend became reversed, however, during the second half of the decade. Under the pressure of frequent sterling crises Britain reinforced some of her remaining exchange control measures. Italy, too, retained some control measures and so did Japan, in spite of the strength of the *lira* and the *yen*. France, having restored freedom of exchanges at the beginning of 1968, hastened to revert to controls as a result of the political and industrial troubles in May and June 1968. Throughout the period Germany and Switzerland, while permitting sales of their currencies unhindered, maintained measures to resist an unwanted influx of foreign funds. The United States, having lost a large part of her gold reserve, adopted unofficial 'guidelines' to restrain the outflow of American capital. In 1968 many of these guidelines assumed statutory character.

In addition to a reinforcement of exchange control, the liberalisation of foreign trade also became reversed. In 1964 Britain adopted an import surcharge and after its removal it adopted a system of import deposits. In 1968 Germany sought to reduce her large export surplus by adopting export duties and import bonuses. Other surplus countries, especially Japan, continued to restrict imports for fear of a reversal of the favourable trend.

(7) INCREASE IN INTERVENTION

Perhaps the most important change in Foreign Exchange policy during the 'sixties was the striking increase in the degree of official intervention in the Foreign Exchange market and in co-operation between monetary authorities to that end. There was already a great deal of intervention and some co-operation even before 1960. But such was the change in their extent during the 'sixties that it might well be considered to have amounted to an institutional change. We saw in Chapter 23 that under the I.M.F. rules there had to be official intervention as a matter of routine whenever the spot exchange rates reached their maximum or minimum support points. Central Banks or the banks acting on their behalf had to supply the deficiency in dollars, or to take up the surplus of dollars, if this was necessary in order to prevent the dollar rate from moving beyond the maximum limit of 1 per cent on either side of the parity. In practice most Governments fixed the actual limits even nearer to their dollar parities, and there was often intervention to prevent exchanges from reaching even the self-imposed limits.

In order to be able to intervene more efficiently – indeed, in any instances in order to be able to intervene at all – co-operation to an unprecedented degree developed between Central

Banks and between Treasuries. Facilities required for supporting a weak exchange were forthcoming, not only from the I.M.F. and the B.I.S. controlled by the authorities of the leading countries but also from individual Central Banks. These facilities assumed various forms and enabled the Central Bank of the country with a devaluation-prone currency to support their exchange to an extent well in excess of their own reserves. Although there were many instances of such co-operation before 1960 it became more systematic and more co-ordinated and it assumed much larger dimensions during the 'sixties.

(8) OFFICIAL FORWARD EXCHANGE OPERATIONS

Although intervention in Forward Exchanges was practised from time to time long before the 'sixties, its extent increased considerably in the mid-'sixties as a result of the decision of the British authorities to support sterling by means of unlimited selling of forward dollars. Even that device was applied earlier occasionally – for instance during the sterling crisis of 1931 – but never before was it applied as a matter of deliberate strategy. It may be said without exaggeration that between 1964 and the devaluation of sterling in 1967, official Forward Exchange operations were one of the basic devices for the defence of sterling. Already during the D. mark revaluation crisis of 1961 and on subsequent occasions the Federal Reserve and various other monetary authorities resorted to intervention in Forward Exchanges as a tactical device. But in 1964 the British monetary authorities adopted that device as the permanent basis of their Foreign Exchange policy.

We saw in the last chapter that support given to that policy by economists was largely responsible for the conversion of the British authorities in its favour. Both theoretical and practical experts succeeded in persuading themselves that it was safe for the authorities to sell forward dollars they had not possessed, on the assumption that, since the buyers did not possess the sterling to pay for the dollars, the settlement of the forward contracts would entail no net loss of reserve on balance. The arguments for and against this policy are set out in detail in my *Dynamic Theory of Forward Exchange* (2nd edition). Meanwhile the collapse of the defence of sterling in 1967 conclusively proved that the policy had been hopelessly mistaken. The lesson taught by the experience made the monetary authorities realise that intervention in Forward

Exchanges has to be confined to operations of limited tactical scope.

(9) CLOSER CO-OPERATION

Technical co-operation, which took the form of arrangements to support each other's currencies on each other's behalf, was already referred to in Chapter 23. What was infinitely more important was the fundamental change in the spirit of the relationship between the monetary authorities of the leading countries. This was the result of the increasing realisation of the fact that stability of exchanges was, to a very large degree, indivisible. While before the war competitive devaluation was the rule and co-operative co-ordination of changes in parities the exception, this attitude became reversed in the 'sixties, owing to the realisation that an excessive devaluation of one major currency is liable to undermine the stability of other currencies and is liable to lead to leap-frogging devaluations. For this reason financial support was freely – sometimes too freely – forthcoming in support of any major currency that was in difficulties.

The ease with which it became possible to bolster up weak exchanges with foreign assistance instead of eliminating the basic causes of their weakness came to be exploited by the British Labour Government between 1964 and 1969. Owing to sterling's international rôle its stability was regarded as an essential condition of international financial stability. The United States in particular, with the experience of the 'thirties in mind, was worried about the possible effect of an excessive devaluation of sterling on the American economy and on the dollar. The Federal Reserve authorities contributed, therefore, the lion's share of the financial facilities granted to Britain in 1964 and on subsequent occasions, in spite of the gradual deterioration of the dollar's technical strength as a result of the perennial balance of payments deficit. Thanks to this attitude, it was much easier for the British Government to take the line of least resistance by borrowing again and again than to adopt and maintain measures that were bound to be unpopular in order to be really effective.

(10) NEGOTIATED DEVALUATIONS

Sterling was of course the principal beneficiary of this new spirit of international co-operation. But sterling was not the only currency to benefit by the increased co-operation. The *lira* was saved by it in 1965. The French *franc* received support in 1968–9. Even the dollar benefited greatly by the growing amount of reciprocal swap facilities arranged with foreign Central Banks by the Federal Reserve authorities and by other forms of external assistance, in addition to the willingness of foreign Central Banks and Governments to abstain from converting the holdings of dollars into gold. The I.M.F.'s drawing quotas were increased considerably in the 'sixties, and thanks to the General Agreement to Borrow, additional facilities were made available. In 1969 arrangements for the creation of Special Drawing Rights were completed, for implementation from 1970 onwards.

One of the most important manifestations of the new spirit of co-operation consisted of the efforts made by Governments which felt impelled to devalue to avoid causing difficulties to other currencies by a deliberate undervaluation of their exchanges. In accordance with the new spirit the aim was to confine the extent of a devaluation to the estimated extent of the overvaluation of the exchange concerned. Thus while the devaluation of sterling by 31 per cent in 1949 was grossly excessive, its devaluation in 1967 was limited to 14 per cent, which erred, if anything, on the moderate side. By such means it was possible to obviate the necessity for too many Governments to follow the British example. But this policy had two grave disadvantages. The negotiations that preceded the announcement of the devaluation resulted in a landslide-like selling pressure on sterling, and its support on the eve of the devaluation cost the British Government hundreds of millions of additional losses on the devaluation. What was perhaps even worse, sterling failed to command confidence at its devalued level, and its international position came to be sacrificed in order to be able to defend it.

(11) RELINQUISHING STERLING'S INTERNATIONAL RÔLE

By succeeding in persuading the Governments of practically all independent countries of the Sterling Area to abstain from devaluing their currencies in sympathy with the devaluation of sterling, the British Government virtually brought about the suicide of the Sterling Area. The reason why these Governments had been willing to keep their reserves in sterling had been precisely the assumption that, as in the 'thirties and in 1949, their exchanges would share the fate of sterling, so that they would therefore stand to suffer no loss on their reserves in terms of their currencies through a devaluation of sterling. The devaluation of 1967 inflicted heavy losses on them. And since sterling came under a cloud from time to time even after its devaluation, the independent Sterling Area Governments were strongly tempted to step up the diversification of their reserves by reducing their holdings of sterling. To prevent a resulting decline of Britain's reserves, an arrangement was made in 1968 providing a guarantee for official sterling reserves of these Governments.

Long before this step sterling's international rôle gradually declined. Until 1964 this decline was barely perceptible. Sterling was trusted sufficiently to be used on at least an equal footing with the dollar as the currency in which international trade was conducted and in which international financial operations were transacted. In particular Foreign Exchange business between continental countries was based on the sterling cross rate. But the frequent sterling scares, culminating in the devaluation of 1967, induced bankers and business men abroad to transact international business increasingly in dollars, or even in their own currencies, in preference to transacting them in sterling. This could not be helped. But it became the British Government's deliberate policy in the late 'sixties to aim at a reduction of sterling's international rôle, on the false assumption that, as a result, its dependence on the 'gnomes' would become reduced.

(12) FLAWS IN CO-OPERATION

In spite of the remarkable progress towards closer international co-operation in the sphere of Foreign Exchange, that progress was not without setbacks. We saw in Chapter 24 that after the settlement of the crisis over Algeria the *franc* came to benefit by large-scale repatriations of capital that had taken flight abroad, and the French balance of payments became favourable. General de Gaulle was not prepared to let the proceeds of the French surpluses accumulate in dollars but withdrew gold from the United States. His aggressive opposition to the gold exchange standard became in 1967–8 one of the main danger spots in the international monetary sphere. Following on the disturbances in France in May and June 1969, however, the *franc* became a weak

M 2

currency and France was losing gold heavily. General de Gaulle's successor, M. Pompidou, was more co-operative, and even though he devalued the *franc* in August 1969 without any preliminary discussions with the International Monetary Fund or with any other monetary authorities, he kept the extent of the devaluation down to the minimum required for correcting the overvaluation of the *franc*.

Another outstanding instance of inadequate co-operation was provided by the American attitude towards gold after the establishment of the two-tier system. The United States Government came to bring the utmost political pressure to bear on other Governments to induce them to accept the basic concept of American Foreign Exchange policy under which gold would cease to be a centre of the international monetary system and the dollar would assume that rôle. We shall try to show in the next chapter that such a change would carry grave dangers of instability and crisis.

(13) INTERVENTION IN EURO-DOLLARS

Owing to the increasing influence of the Euro-currency markets in general and of the Euro-dollar market in particular on exchange rates, on interest rates and on economic trends, the monetary authorities came to the conclusion during the 'sixties that it was to their interests to intervene in those markets. Already during the late 'fifties there was some passive intervention through applying restrictions on operations in Euro-currencies by residents, and through tightening or relaxing these restrictions in accordance with the requirements of the moment. In Britain the policy of the Bank of England was to encourage London banks to transact Euro-currency business. In other countries the Central Bank actively encouraged or discouraged such business by the local banks, with the aid of changing the terms on which they were granted official Forward Exchange facilities for the purpose.

In the late 'sixties Central Banks came to intervene in the market mainly through the intermediary of the B.I.S. to influence Euro-dollar rates. During 1968–9 the B.I.S. operated from time to time on a large scale in the Euro-dollar market. In 1969 the Federal Reserve authorities made a half-hearted attempt to discourage the large-scale borrowing of Euro-dollars by American banks through the intermediary of their London branches, by imposing

reserve requirements on additional borrowing. A similar device
was applied in earlier years by other Central Banks. But having
regard to the importance of the Euro-currency market, the
extent to which monetary authorities influence its trends is far
from adequate.

Conclusion

THE foregoing chapters described the evolution of the Foreign Exchange system from its rudimentary beginnings to its present highly advanced state. Although the progress has been remarkable, there is undoubtedly still a wide scope for further improvements from the point of view of its mechanism, from the point of view of Foreign Exchange policy and also from the point of view of our knowledge of the way in which the system operates or should operate.

There can be no two opinions about the high degree of technical efficiency the Foreign Exchange system has succeeded in achieving in the course of its long history. The verdict of expert opinion is, however, divided on the question whether the system, in its present form, fulfils adequately the purpose which it is meant to serve, and whether the cost of its operation in terms of human welfare is not excessive.

The object of the Foreign Exchange system must be twofold – to facilitate commercial and financial intercourse between nations, and to ensure that their domestic monetary and economic systems are given a chance to function in accordance with their basic economic and social requirements. In given situations the two objectives might appear to conflict with each other. But in the long run they serve basically the same purpose and it is a short-sighted policy to pursue one-sidedly either of the two ends to the detriment of the other.

It is clearly to the interest of mankind that there should be the highest possible degree of interchange between nations, each of which can contribute towards general progress according to the peculiarities of its national genius and of its resources. It would be an advantage if these various contributions to progress could be pooled. To that end it is essential that international trade and finance should be facilitated. So long as we are still far removed from a World Government and so long as sovereign states continue to possess separate monetary systems, efficient Foreign Exchange is indispensable for linking these systems to each other.

The improvement of the Foreign Exchange system through the

ages has greatly reduced the extent to which national sovereignty in the monetary sphere handicaps progress towards closer economic, technological, cultural integration across national frontiers. During the Ancient and Medieval Periods, and even in much more recent centuries, national monetary systems were largely isolated from each other by the absence of an adequate market mechanism. Thanks to the progress of Foreign Exchange this is no longer so to anything like the same extent as in the old days. Nor is isolation through exchange controls as grave an obstacle to integration as it was until recently.

The Foreign Exchange system has certainly travelled a long way since its early beginnings. Although the rudimentary methods still survive – that eternal character, the money-changer, is not an unusual sight even nowadays – the modern Foreign Exchange market is a highly developed and sophisticated institution. In the absence of major crises leading to chaotic currency conditions, or of drastic official interference with its freedom, it now comes as near to the theoretical ideal of a perfect market as any market in existence. Its prices are extremely sensitive and flexible and respond to one-sided pressure in a matter of seconds. Conversely, supply and demand in Foreign Exchanges are very elastic and readily respond to changes in exchange rates.

The inadequacy of the Foreign Exchange system in the past was partly due to difficulties and insecurity of transport and communications, and also to lack of confidence and to differences between national institutions in the sphere of commerce and law. All these made for monetary isolation. Transfer of money from one country to another was very difficult and costly. It usually took some time before wide discrepancies between the value of money in various countries came to be reduced to reasonable proportions.

In our time, however, the Foreign Exchange markets have become increasingly international in character. Today all relatively free Foreign Exchange markets form part of one large international market. Arbitrage has been brought to a fine art and increasingly refined techniques, undreamt of even a few years ago, have developed. Apart from such exchange restrictions as still survive – which are, at the time of writing, tolerable – the continued existence of separate monetary systems no longer constitutes an obstacle to international financial intercourse.

Thanks to the Bretton Woods system of stability, fluctuations of exchange rates are now confined within a narrow range, and the availability of Forward Exchange facilities provides means for safeguards against losses through major exchange movements resulting from occasional changes in parities. For a very long time the development of Forward Exchange lagged behind that of Foreign Exchange in general and has only caught up with its progress in our lifetime. But now it provides remarkably good facilities to cover and hedge against exchange risk, and such facilities are available for increasingly long periods, even if their cost is apt to be excessive at times. It has now become possible to hedge against exchange risk to an extent that until recently was considered inconceivable. This progress has greatly facilitated international investment and, for better or for worse, has encouraged the international flow of capital. It surely serves the interests of progress that the risk attached to the investment of capital in countries where it is needed has been reduced. The possibility of removing exchange risk attached to international investment, in addition to making for a more even distribution of financial resources, stimulates international division of labour and assists in the dissemination and interchange of culture and know-how. It is all the more remarkable and deplorable that investors resident in the United Kingdom are prevented by exchange control from taking advantage of the existence of facilities that would safeguard them against the exchange risk on their overseas investments.

To a large extent the progress of the Foreign Exchange system serves highly constructive purposes. Its covering and hedging facilities relieve producers, merchants and investors of exchange risk which is now assumed by those who are in a better position to cover it or, if needs be, to take it. As a result of the internationalisation of money markets, it is now easier to finance trade in the cheapest market where money is the most plentiful. The most recent step in that direction has been the use of Euro-dollars and other foreign currency deposits. Their unexpected appearance and their growing importance shows that the Foreign Exchange system is still in the course of evolution, and this conveys the feeling that there is still scope for further substantial improvement.

Beyond doubt, from the point of view of the efficient functioning of the Foreign Exchange system as a link between national currencies it is essential to maintain a high degree of stability of exchange rates. It is also important to reduce to a minimum the extent of interference with international transfers of money. It was largely because of instability of exchanges and the widespread adoption of drastic exchange controls that foreign trade and international investment contracted sharply during the 'thirties. And it was largely thanks to stability of exchanges and reductions of exchange controls that foreign trade and international investment expanded sharply during the 'sixties. From this point of view the Bretton Woods system had proved its worth. It had certainly served well one of the two major objectives of a good Foreign Exchange system.

In spite of this the continued maintenance of the Foreign Exchange system in substantially the existing form did not appear to be as firmly assured at the close of the 'sixties as it had been at the beginning of that decade. This was because widespread doubts had arisen on the question whether Bretton Woods stability served satisfactorily also the second main objective of a good Foreign Exchange system.

The question to be answered is whether or not the maintenance of international monetary stability during the 'fifties and the 'sixties was helpful from the point of view of enabling domestic monetary and economic systems to function in accordance with the basic economic and social requirements of the countries concenrned. Did Bretton Woods stability help or hinder economic growth and rising standards of living, and is its maintenance likely to help or hinder them? There was in recent years an increasingly widespread feeling that the rate of economic growth and of the rise in the standard of living was kept down for the sake of international monetary stability.

The fact that in spite of the maintenance of stable exchanges there was a higher degree of progress under the Bretton Woods system than during any comparable previous period was generally disregarded. Or it was sought to be disposed of with the aid of the argument that, had it not been for the measures adopted for the sake of maintaining the stability of exchanges, progress would have been even more satisfactory. Because of such considerations, and as a manifestation of the prevailing growth-hysteria, there was an increasing pressure on Governments to sacrifice stability for the sake of being able to step up the increase in production and in consumption.

Throughout the history of Foreign Exchange, whenever stability gave way to wide fluctuations or to sharp depreciations it was the result of disturbing political or economic influences,

which the authorities were unable to resist. Or it was the outcome
of inflationary official policies which caused unintentionally a
departure from stability. But at the close of the 'sixties there
appeared to be a strong possibility that for the first time in history
the Governments of some leading countries might decide to de-
stabilise their exchanges as a matter of deliberate policy. It is
possible that a system of floating exchanges will be adopted so as
to obviate the necessity of defending fixed parities. Under that
system exchange rates would be allowed to fluctuate freely. Or,
without going to such extremes, the Bretton Woods system might
be drastically modified so as to achieve a much higher degree of
flexibility of exchange rates.

The result would be a Foreign Exchange system which would
no longer serve the requirements of international monetary
integration to anything like the same extent as the Bretton Woods
system has been serving it for nearly quarter of a century. It may
be argued that this price would be well worth paying for the sake
of stepping up domestic economic growth, which is at present apt
to be handicapped by the need of defending stability of the
exchanges.

The answer to that argument is that even from the point of
view of sustained growth and of a sustained rise in the standard
of living the abandonment of international stability would be a
fatal mistake. In the short run it might obviate the necessity for
restricting production and consumption. But the resulting exchange fluctuations might well become self-aggravating, and a
stage might be reached at which it would become imperative to
adopt very drastic deflationary measures that would reverse the
trend of expansion. As I tried to explain in my *Decline and Fall ? –
Britain's Crisis in the 'Sixties*, the removal of the discipline of stability
would produce a demoralising effect. There would also be a
danger that, as a result of currency chaos, there might not be
enough Forward Exchange facilities available to meet the
increased requirements of foreign trade, because banks would
reduce their maximum limits for Forward Exchange facilities. In
the absence of ample Forward Exchange facilities at reasonable
cost many firms would prefer to forgo trading rather than expose
themselves to ruinous losses. Foreign trade would contract and
this might trigger off a world-wide slump.

An alternative method to step up economic growth without
sacrificing stability would be a return to advanced exchange

controls and foreign trade controls. Under their protective shield Governments and their countries might be able to inflate for some time with impunity, in spite of the increasing overvaluation of their exchanges. But the volume of foreign trade would become reduced. And sooner or later the disequilibrium would call for costly corrective measures. In any case, non-stop domestic expansion, whether with the aid of floating exchanges or under the protection of controls, could not go on forever. It would degenerate into runaway boom and accelerating inflation which would come to a climax sooner or later and would be followed by a violent reaction in the form of a disastrous slump similar to that of the 'thirties.

This is the reason why basically the two objectives of the Foreign Exchange system – to serve the requirements of international trade and finance and to ensure that domestic monetary systems serve basic economic and social requirements – are not incompatible but complementary. The moderating influence of the disinflationary policies that have to be pursued for the sake of the maintenance of stable exchanges applies a much-needed brake that prevents excessive economic expansion and accelerated inflation. If periods of rapid expansion alternate with periods of consolidation for the sake of maintaining the stability of exchanges, this serves in the long run the end of expansion itself, because it prevents the occurrence of drastic setbacks that unrestrained expansion would entail. It prevents a return to large-scale unemployment through sharp slumps and prolonged depressions.

We must bear in mind that throughout the operation of the Bretton Woods system the world has not witnessed a single major slump or any depression that exceeded the limits of passing recessions; that economic expansion and social welfare has made remarkable progress; and that in the 'sixties unemployment was in most countries lower than ever before in modern times. The post-war world has been spared major business cycles, the last of which had resulted in a particularly sharp setback all over the world in the 'thirties. They are now past history, thanks to the operation of the Foreign Exchange system that imposes some degree of much-needed discipline on the economy. Admittedly, in spite of this creeping inflation has been proceeding and tends to continue to proceed at an accelerating pace, and the difference between its extent in various countries has tended to result in overvaluations and undervaluations of currencies. But this proves not the need for a relaxation of the discipline but the need for its reinforcement. It was the relaxation of the discipline imposed on the economies by the Bretton Woods system that gave rise to a series of crises during the second half of the 'sixties.

I am firmly convinced that, should Bretton Woods stability be abandoned or greatly relaxed, the resulting developments would only constitute a temporary phase in the history of Foreign Exchange. It would not take very long for most Governments to realise the grave disadvantages of the currency chaos resulting from their ill-advised decisions to de-stabilise their exchanges. Sooner or later they would gladly return to the system of stability, as their forerunners did each time they were forced to abandon it in the past.

Stability need not be synonymous, however, with rigidity. In the course of the application of the Bretton Woods system there were many instances in which parities continued to be defended long after the development of fundamental disequilibrium would have made their adjustment justified and necessary. Over and above all, the stubborn defence of the dollar parity of $35 in circumstances in which that parity had long ceased to be realistic gave rise to conditions endangering the financial, economic and political stability of the free world. It was the mistaken interpretation of the Bretton Woods system and not the principles inherent in that system that was responsible for most of the disadvantages and dangers arising from it. It was excessive rigidity that gave rise to growing agitation in favour of excessive flexibility.

The next phase in the history of Foreign Exchange will depend on the Governments' decision whether to abandon Bretton Woods for the sake of such benefits as they would derive from that fateful decision.

A Selected Bibliography

ALTHOUGH the notes at the end of most chapters give an extensive list of my sources, an additional general summary of the literature on each period might be helpful.

ANCIENT PERIOD. – The factual material was derived, directly or indirectly, almost exclusively from classical literature and such sources as the Talmud and the New Testament. Among others the writings of Xenophon – especially his *Methods of Improving the Revenues of Athens*, the *Orations* of Demosthenes and Isocrates, Cicero's *Letters to Atticus*, Plutarch's *Lives* and Pliny's *Natural History*, contain useful occasional references to Foreign Exchange.

Most of the relevant passages are quoted in modern works, outstanding amongst which are A. R. Burns, *Money and Monetary Policy in Ancient Times* (London, 1927), and Fritz Heichelheim, *Wirtschaftsgeschichte des Altertumes* (Leyden, 1938). The latter contains very extensive bibliographical information that could hardly be improved upon. A revised English edition was published in 1958-64.

Gibbon's *Decline and Fall* contains much useful material and so do some 19th-century French and German standard works, especially François Lenormant, *La Monnaie dans l'antiquité* (Paris, 1878), J. Brandis, *Das Münz-, Mass- und Gewichtswesen in Vorderasien bis auf Allexander den Grossen* (Berlin, 1866), and Theodore Mommsen, *Histoire de la monnaie romaine* (trsl. from German by the Duc de Blacas) (Paris, 1873).

Among more recent general works, M. Rostovtzeff, *The Social and Economic History of the Roman Empire* (Oxford, 1926), and *The Social and Economic History of the Hellenistic World* (Oxford, 1941) are useful both for occasional direct reference to Foreign Exchange and for background material. Among monographs, articles by W. L. Westermann, L. C. West, A. C. Jones and A. H. M. Jones, quoted in my notes, deal very thoroughly with their respective subjects. These articles, and also Gunnar Mickwitz, *Geld und Wirtschaft im Römischen Reich des vierten Jahrhunderts n. Chr.* (Helsinki, 1931), could serve as models of painstaking research covering a limited period.

Much useful factual material relating to changes in the value of coins is found in the extensive literature on numismatics. To quote only one instance, Walther Giesecke, *Antikes Geldwesen* (Leipzig, 1938), though primarily concerned with coins from a numismatic point of view, contains a great deal that is interesting to the economic historian.

MEDIEVAL PERIOD. – Useful general works include Raymond de Roover, *L'Évolution de la lettre de change, XIVᵉ–XVIIIᵉ siècle* (Paris, 1953), which contains a very thorough bibliographical section, and Wilhelm Endemann, *Studien in der romanisch-kanonistischen Wirtschafts- und Rechtslehre bis gegen Ende des 17. Jahrhunderts* (Berlin, 1874), which is still the standard work on scholastic literature on Foreign Exchange. There is much interesting material in W. A. Shaw, *The History of Currency, 1252 to 1894* (London, 1895), and in two books by Albert Despaux, *L'Inflation dans l'histoire* (Paris, 1923), and *Les Dévaluations monétaires dans l'histoire* (Paris, 1936).

The number of monographs concerning individual exchanges or relatively brief periods is considerable. Of outstanding importance amongst them are Raymond de Roover's *Money, Banking and Credit in Medieval Bruges* (Cambridge, Mass., 1948) and *The Medici Bank* (New York, 1948), and Yves Renouard, *Les Relations des papes d'Avignon et des compagnies commerciales et bancaires de 1316 à 1378* (Paris, 1941). I derived most of my material relating to sterling from the *Rolls of Parliament* and the early *Statute Books*, and was assisted in my research by Roger Ruding, *Annals of the Coinage of Britain* (London, 1819). Sir John Craig, *The Mint* (Cambridge, 1953) and A. E. Feavearyear, *The Pound Sterling* (Oxford, 1931) were also useful.

FROM THE DISCOVERY OF AMERICA TO THE FRENCH REVOLUTION. – Several of the books mentioned above – especially those by de Roover, Shaw, Endemann, Craig and Feavearyear – covered also the period that followed the Middle Ages. Richard Ehrenberg, *Das Zeitalter der Fugger* (Jena, 1896), which has an English translation under the title *Capital and Finance in the Age of Renaissance* (London, 1928), was for a long time the standard work on the period. But de Roover's *Gresham on Foreign Exchange* (Cambridge, Mass., 1949) now takes the first place in the literature on the 16th and early 17th centuries. Like several other monographs referred to above or to be referred to below, it uses its narrow subject as a peg on which to hang a great deal of general material on contemporary Foreign Exchange practice and theory. Its account of the Malynes-Misselden-Mun controversy is very clear. Another modern monograph of outstanding merit covering the 16th and 17th centuries is Marjorie Grice-Hutchinson, *The School of Salamanca* (Oxford, 1952). Richard Gaettens, *Inflationen* (Munich, 1955), contains some useful chapters on the 17th and 18th centuries.

Works of outstanding merit, covering a broader field, that contain material on the Foreign Exchange theories of various periods, include James W. Angell, *The Theory of International Prices* (Cambridge, Mass., 1926), Jacob Viner, *Studies in the Theory of International Trade* (London, 1937), Chi-Yuen Wu, *An Outline of International Price Theories* (London, 1939), and Eli F. Heckscher, *Mercantilism*, 2nd ed. (London, 1955). Even though Foreign Exchange is not the main interest of these books, it is covered very thoroughly. Their extensive bibliographies are very useful. Arthur Eli Monroe, *Monetary Theory before Adam Smith* (Cambridge, Mass., 1923) and *Early Economic Thought* (Cambridge, Mass., 1924), published some useful extracts, some of them from little-known early works.

From the 16th century onwards we have an increasing volume of contemporary material to draw upon. *Tudor Economic Documents*, edited by R. H. Tawney and Eileen Power (London, 1924), contains a wealth of material, and so do various collections of reprints, especially McCulloch, *Early Tracts on Commerce* (London, 1856), W. A. Shaw, *Select Tracts and Documents* (London, 1896) and E. Daire, *Économistes-financiers du 18e siècle* (Paris, 1843). As far as sterling is concerned, the *Calendar of the Treasury Books* and the *State Papers* series, both *Domestic* and *Foreign*, provide a goldmine of information. There is a large selection of contemporary practical guides on Foreign Exchange. Books on commercial arithmetic contain useful chapters on the subject.

Monographs containing statistical material on exchange rates include Keith Horsefield, *British Monetary Experiments, 1650–1710* (London, 1960), T. S. Ashton, *An Economic History of England – The 18th Century* (London, 1955), W. Brulez, *De Wisselkoersen te Antwerpen in het Laatste Kwart van de 16e. Eeuw* (The Hague, 1956), Henri Lapeyre, *Une Famille de marchands, les Ruiz* (Paris, 1955) and N. W. Posthumus, *Nederlandscher Priesgeschiednis* (Leyden, 1943). Robert Ashton, *The Crown and the Money Market, 1603–1640* (Oxford, 1960), is yet another instance of useful specialised research.

FROM THE FRENCH REVOLUTION TO THE FIRST WORLD WAR. – The works of Angell, Viner and Wu, quoted above, cover also the 19th century and after. In particular they deal extensively with the bullionist controversy. But they do not obviate the necessity for studying the immense volume of contemporary literature dealing with this advanced period, quoted in my notes to Chapter 17. The writings of leading 19th-century economists, such as Ricardo, Mill and Marshall contain much material on Foreign Exchange theory. But Goschen's *Theory of the Foreign Exchange* (2nd ed., London, 1863), is of outstanding importance from a theoretical as well as a practical point of view.

The reports and evidence of the various Select Committees during and after the Napoleonic Wars and later in the 19th century contain much material on practices and techniques. There is also a great deal of information in the practical guides such as the various editions of *Tate's Cambist*, and in text-books, appearing mostly towards the close of the century and in the early years of our century. George Clare, *The A.B.C. of Foreign Exchange* (London, 1893), and *A Money Market Primer* (London, 1900), are particularly worth mentioning.

Among monographs, Seymour E. Harris, *The Assignats* (Cambridge, Mass., 1930), G. Browning, *Domestic and Financial Conditions of Great*

Britain (London, 1834), Arthur H. Cole, 'Evolution of the Foreign Exchange Market of the United States' in *Journal of Economic and Business History*, May 1929, Wesley Clair Mitchell, *A History of the Greenbacks* (Chicago, 1903), N. J. Silberling, 'Financial and Monetary Policy of Great Britain during the Napoleonic Wars' in *Quarterly Journal of Economics*, 1924 and K. E. Davis and J. R. T. Hughes, 'A Dollar-Sterling Exchange 1803–1895' in *Economic History Review*, 1960, deserve particular attention. The latter contains useful exchange-rate tables. Although G. Subercaseaux, *Le Papier-monnaie*, is primarily concerned with Latin America, it also contains much valuable material on European exchanges.

In the technical sphere there is N. E. Weill, *Die Solidarität der Geldmärkte* (Frankfurt, 1903), Oskar Morgenstern, *International Financial Transactions and Business Cycles* (Princeton, 1959), Arthur Bloomfield, *Monetary Policy under the International Gold Standard* (New York, 1959) and Paul Einzig, *The Theory of Forward Exchange* (London, 1937).

AFTER 1914. – There is an impressive choice of literature on Foreign Exchange during and after the two World Wars. The first World War and the immediate post-war period is well covered by J. M. Keynes, *A Tract on Monetary Reform* (London, 1923), Gustav Cassel, *Money and Foreign Exchanges after 1914* (London, 1922), Hartley Withers, *War and Lombard Street* (London, 1915), Karl Helfferich, *Das Geld* (in English translation, *Money*, London, 1928), T. E. Gregory, *Foreign Exchange before, during and after the War* (Oxford, 1922) and Lucien Petit, *Histoire des finances extérieures de la France pendant la guerre 1914–1918* (Paris, 1929).

Howard S. Ellis, *German Monetary Theory 1905–1933* (Cambridge, Mass., 1934), with its extensive bibliography, contains a masterly summing up of the literature on Foreign Exchange theory during the important period it covers. Seymour E. Harris, *Exchange Depreciation, its Theory and its History, 1931–35* (Cambridge, Mass., 1936), raises some interesting issues. Michael A. Heilperin, *International Monetary Economics* (London, 1939), and Gottfried von Haberler, *The Theory of International Trade* (London, 1936) are also useful.

A number of practical guides of the inter-war Foreign Exchange market were published by H. C. F. Holgate, H. E. Evitt, W. F. Spalding, etc. My own contributions on the borderline between theory and practice included *International Gold Movements* (London, 1929), *The Theory of Forward Exchange* (London, 1937) and *Exchange Control* (London, 1934). An excellent summary of the inter-war period was given by the League of Nations, *The International Currency Experience* (Princeton, 1944).

In Germany and other countries with exchange control in operation before the war, that aspect of Foreign Exchange came to monopolise the literature on our subject. Only gradually did exchange control come to receive adequate attention by writers in Britain and other

Western countries during and after the second World War, mostly in new editions of pre-war text-books on Foreign Exchange practice.

Post-war literature includes Raymond E. Mikesell, *Foreign Exchange in the Post-War World* (New York, 1954), Bertrand Nogaro, *A Short Treatise on Money and Monetary Systems* (London, 1945), Frank C. Child, *The Theory and Practice of Exchange Control in Germany* (The Hague, 1958), Helmut Lipfert, *Devisenhandel* (Frankfurt, 1958), Paul Einzig, *A Dynamic Theory of Forward Exchange* (London, 1961), Sidney A. Shepherd, *Foreign Exchange in Canada* (Toronto, 1953), René Sédillot, *Du franc Bonaparte au franc de Gaulle* (Paris, 1959) and Arthur I. Bloomfield, *Capital Imports and International Balance of Payments* (Chicago, 1950).

Monographs covering the period after 1914 are very numerous. They include J. van Walré de Bordes, *The Austrian Crown* (London, 1924), S. S. Katzenellenbaum, *Russian Currency and Banking, 1914–1924* (London, 1925), N. E. Hall, *The Exchange Equalisation Account* (London, 1935), Émile Moreau, *Souvenirs d'un gouverneur de la Banque de France* (Paris, 1954) and Philip W. Bell, *The Sterling Area in the Post-War World* (Oxford, 1956).

THE 'SIXTIES. – The past decade produced a flood of literature on Foreign Exchange practices, crises, theories and policies. The best sources for the history of exchange trends and policies are the official publications by the I.M.F., the B.I.S. and the leading Central Banks. Commercial banks and other financial institutions, too, provided valuable factual material and informed comment in their monthly or quarterly reviews. The I.M.F.'s Annual Report on Exchange Restrictions is a goldmine of information on its subject.

My own contributions to the literature on practices and techniques are contained in *A Dynamic Theory of Forward Exchange* (2nd ed., London, 1967), *The Euro-dollar System* (4th ed., London, 1970), *A Textbook on Foreign Exchange* (2nd ed., London, 1969), *The Euro-bond Market* (2nd ed., London, 1969), *Foreign Exchange Crises* (2nd ed., London, 1970), *Leads and Lags – The Main Cause of Devaluation* (London, 1968) and *The Case against Floating Exchanges* (London, 1970).

Theoretical literature during the 'sixties consisted largely of works on theories arguing in favour of the adoption of policies supported by their authors. Egon Sohmen's *Flexible Exchange Rates* (Chicago, 1961) is the standard work on its subject. The series of brochures published by the International Finance Section of Princeton University provide a wealth of controversial material which would be even more valuable if it were not for the distinctly one-sided point of view their overall trend seeks to convey through the selection of the contributors.

Leland B. Yeager's *International Monetary Relations* (New York, 1966), A. T. K. Grant's *The Machinery of Finance and the Management of Sterling* (London, 1967), Fred Hirsch, *Money International* (London, 1967), Robert Mossé, *Les Problèmes Monétaires Internationaux* (Paris, 1967),

H.-J. Dudler, *Diskont- und Terminpolitik* (Frankfurt, 1966), Herbert G. Grubel, *Forward Exchange, Speculation and the International Flow of Capital* (Stanford, 1966), and a number of collections of essays by Fritz Machlup, *International Monetary Economics* (London, 1966), R. N. Cooper (ed.), *International Finance* (Harmondsworth, 1969), E. van Lennep (ed.), *Maintaining and Restoring Balance in International Payments* (Princeton, 1966), and D. J. Robertson and L. C. Hunter (eds.), *The British Balance of Payments*, and many others besides, have all contributed something towards the progress of Foreign Exchange theory.

I am aware that this summary does not do justice to a very large number of books and articles that deserve mention. It merely aims at providing a 'sample survey' of the literature that is expanding rapidly in all its aspects.

Index of Names

Subject Index

THE END